THE AUTHENTIC WILD WEST

THE OUTLAWS

THE AUTHENTIC WILD WEST

THE
OUTLAWS

JAMES D. HORAN

GRAMERCY BOOKS
New York • Avenel

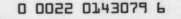

FOR

Gertrude:
Always Bob with Jingle on the Outlaw Trail

This 1995 edition is published by Gramercy Books,
distributed by Random House Value Publishing, Inc.,
40 Engelhard Avenue, Avenel, New Jersey 07001.

Random House
New York • Toronto •London • Sydney • Auckland

Printed and bound in the United States of America

Designed by Ruth Smerechniak

Library of Congress Cataloging-in-Publication Data
Horan, James David
    The authentic wild West.
    Bibliography: p.
    Includes indexes.
    CONTENTS: v. [1] The gunfighters.–v. [2] The outlaws.
    1. Outlaws–The West–Biography.
    2. The West–Biography. I. Title
F594.H79 1976 978'.02'0922 76-10758
ISBN 0-517-12373-8

8 7 6 5 4 3 2 1

ACKNOWLEDGMENTS

The Bancroft Library, University of California, Berkeley, Peter E. Hanff, Coordinator, Technical Services, Miss Estelle Rebec, Head, Manuscript Division, William M. Roberts, Reference Librarian; California Historical Society, Lee L. Burtis, Librarian, Photograph Division; California State Library, Greg Swalley; Ms. Barbara Fiester, Assistant Librarian and the Newspaper Staff of the Chicago Public Library and the Research Staff, Chicago Historical Society; The State Historical Society of Colorado, Ms. Alice L. Sharp, Reference Librarian, Documentary Resources, and Mrs. Catherine T. Engel, Reference Librarian, Documentary Resources; Denver Public Library, Western History Department, Eleanor M. Gehres; Friends of the Middle Border, William W. Anderson, Director; The Huntington Library, San Marino, California, Mrs. Valerie Franco, Assistant Curator, Western Manuscripts; Indiana Historical Society, Mrs. Leona T. Alig, Manuscripts Librarian; Indiana State Library, Ms. Jean E. Singleton, Reference Librarian, Indiana Division; Iowa Historical Society, Mrs. Joyce Giagguinta, Manuscript Librarian; Kansas State Historical Society, Eugene D. Decker, State Archivist, E. Dixon Larson, Orem, Utah; The Library of Congress, William Matheson, Chief, Reference Division, Rare Book and Special Collections Division, Bernard A. Bernier, Jr., Head, Reference Section, Serial Division; Michael Griffith and the Staff of the Little Falls, New Jersey, Library.

Los Angeles Public Library, Edith W. Johnson, Library Assistant, General Reading Services, Charles A. Lush, Senior Librarian, James E. Vale, Library Assistant; Jackson County Historical Society, Mrs. Donald B. Erlich, Director of Archives; Fred Mazzulla, Denver, Colorado; Minnesota Historical Society, Janet Moosbrugger, Reference Librarian; Minnesota State Prison, Stillwater, George L. Crust, Records Officer; The State Historical Society of Missouri, Mrs. Billie Mojonnier, Newspaper Library, Mrs. Lynn M. Roberts, Secretary, Pat Weiner, Reference Librarian, Mrs. Winfred Stufflebam, Newspaper Library, Carole Sue Warmbrod DeLaite, Newspaper Library, Debbie B. Miller, Editorial Secretary, *Missouri Historical Review*, Karen M. Duree, Reference Specialist, Ms. Lynn M. Roberts, Secretary; University of Missouri Library, Western Historical Manuscript Collection, Nancy C. Prewitt, Assistant Director, Nancy Lankford, Manuscripts Reference Head; Montana Historical Society, Mrs. Harriett C. Meloy, Librarian, Ms. Lory Morrow, Photo-Archivist; National Archives, Elaine C. Everly, Navy and Old Army Branch, Military Archives Division, C. George Younkin, Chief, Archives Branch, M. M. Johnson, Legislative, Judicial and Fiscal Branch, Civil Archives Division, Richard S. Maxwell, Civil Archives Division, William B. Fraley, Acting Assistant Director, General Archives Division, Milton O. Gustafson, Chief, Diplomatic Branch, Civil Archives Division, Michael Goldman, Natural Resources Branch, Civil Archives Division, Mark G. Eckhoff, Chief, Legislative, Judicial and Fiscal Branch, Robert Svenningsen, Chief, Archives Branch, Katherine F. Gould, Acting Head, Reference Section, Serial Division; Nebraska State Historical Society, Mrs. Ann Reinert, Librarian; Oklahoma State Historical Society, Mary Lee Ervin, Genealogist; South Dakota Department of Educational and Cultural Affairs, Historical Resource Center, Ms. Denise Ramse, Mrs. Bonnie Gardner, Photo Curator; Fort Worth, Texas, Public Library, Patricia Chadwell, Head, Southwestern Collection; Barker Texas History Center, The University of Texas at Austin, Chester V. Kielman, Librarian-Archivist; Tennessee State Library and Archives, Mrs. Fran Eads, Reference Librarian; University of Wyoming, Gene M. Gressley, Director, David Crosson, Research Historian; Ms. Annabelle McNamee, Senior Clerk; Wyoming State Archives and Historical Department, John C. Paige, Research Historian, Historical Research and Publications Department, Teresa Matthews, Curator of Photography, William H. Barton, Mrs. Vivian A. Shultz, Research Historians and Historical Research and Publications Division, Laura Hays, Curator, Photographic Section, Paula West, Photographic Section; Ruth M. Cables, Clerk of District Court, Carbon County, Rawlins, Wyoming; Stephen A. Kezerian, Director, Yale University News Bureau and Public Information.

A special note of thanks is due to the late Mrs. Zoe Tilghman for the many interviews and letters over the years about her husband, William, and his extraordinary career as a Western lawman; to the late Frank Dimaio for the many interviews and letters describing his hunt for Butch Cassidy, The Sundance Kid, and Etta Place in South America; to the late Percy Seibert for the many interviews over the years during which he gave me superb eyewitness accounts of his association with Cassidy and The Sundance Kid, along with maps and photographs; to Walter J. L. Hampton for his material on the death of Cassidy and The Kid in the San Vincente barrio, photographs and his sketch of the death scene; Moroni Gillies, for his memories of his cousin, Butch Cassidy, and many others, who at my request, took time out of their busy lives to write their reminiscences of the life and times of the outlaws of America's Wild West.

And above all to Gertrude, who accompanied me along the outlaw trail as it twisted and turned through countless libraries, historical societies, in and out of mountains of yellowing brittle newspapers, letters, and documents only she could read and then returned home to type this huge manuscript and save me from countless errors. Beloved Jinglebob.

CONTENTS

INTRODUCTION
DAY OF THE OUTLAW

MORE THAN TWENTY YEARS AGO I SET OUT TO PENETRATE the fog of mythology that for more than a century has enveloped the outlaws of our Wild West. My goal was to find out what the nation's and the world's favorite folklore figures really were: superheroes, moronic killers, cavaliers of romance.

I discovered they were fallible humans. They loved their wives and children, were courageous, imaginative, pleasant, and had a sense of humor. They bled when they were wounded, grew depressed over shattered love affairs, and grieved when a comrade fell. Some believed in a personal God and Devil, and at least one carried a much-thumbed Bible.

Curiously, many detested whiskey, and nearly all respected the Victorian trinity of mother, father, and home. While accepting violence and sudden death as part of their profession, many refused to swear in the presence of women and would not allow others to do so.

Yet they could also be ruthless and cold-blooded. They were never the figures of romance and myth who robbed the rich to feed the poor. Their lives were often empty and fearful. As Frank James said when he surrendered: "I'm tired of running. Tired of waiting for a ball in the back. Tired of looking into the faces of friends and seeing a Judas . . ."

It is impossible to defend a single crime they committed. They robbed banks

—some holding the money of their neighbors—stole horses from the stables of friends, and steers from men who had befriended them. They shot down unarmed cashiers and express messengers, killed lawmen from ambush, and derailed trains—once scalding an engineer to death.

I trailed them from the Midwest to South America through documents in government depositories, in and out of collections in state, county, and regional historical societies, and across the pages of brittle frontier newspapers. I also taped interviews with men who had ridden with them, hunted them, worked with them, shared their experiences, or were relatives; all were generous with their memories, family Bibles, papers, and rare photographs.

Some of this firm evidence helped to prove that Joaquin Murieta, one of California's folk heroes, is fictitious and had been created by John Rollin Ridge, son of the distinguished Cherokee leader. Ridge's "biography" of Murieta, now exceedingly rare, was manufactured from newspaper accounts of a manhunt and Dame Shirley's famous goldfields letters. The book was rewritten and published many times from the 1850s to the twentieth century, with stolen editions appearing in Europe and South America. I have included Murieta in this gallery of real violent men as an excellent example of how a myth of the Wild West became accepted as historic fact through repetition.

I have often been asked the trite but obvious question: which one did I find the most interesting? My choice is Jesse James. He can be viewed two ways: from one perspective, he was the resourceful victim of middle-class morality; from the other, he was a hell-for-leather desperado who made fools of the Pinkertons, a small army of sheriffs and marshals, possemen, more than one Missouri governor, bounty hunters, and informers. I endorse the latter view.

The amazing part of the saga of this strange man is that while he busily perfected the technique of robbing trains and banks—his *modus operandi* was used by generations of later outlaws—he was able to avoid capture for sixteen years. His end came in a fashion to win him national sympathy despite the enormity of his crimes.

The interesting question of how this outlaw leader was able to last for so long is answered, I believe, by a glance at the political climate of the time. To the pro-Confederate politicians who protected him he had become a romantic symbol of the South that never surrendered to the hated Yankees. Even those who hated him recognized that Jesse was a charismatic man whose fire, vigor, and courage were hard to resist; he was a born leader.

His skill at anonymity must also be considered: until he lay in the St. Joseph undertaking parlor in April 1882, he had long been a man without a face. Few of his hunters, even Clay County residents, knew what he looked like. He bared his soul to no man or woman. As Bob Ford said: "He let no one, even the old lady [his mother] know what he was doing or planning . . . Jesse was good at keeping secrets."

The factual stories of his life and the lives of his men are at times incredible, more riveting than the distorted legends. For example: his storybook romance with the girl he wed while he was the most hunted man in the nation; the chronicle of the powder-burnt Northfield Raid, when he and his men met disaster from a straight-shooting citizenry; the capture of the Youngers, the fight for their freedom, and Jim Younger's tragic suicide over a broken love affair. Finally, the death of Jesse James, the stirring surrender of his Shakespeare-quoting brother, and Frank's dramatic trial.

Jesse cannot be classified as a simple highwayman whose exploits inspired the tall tales associated with a rousing frontier. He and his band made a serious impact on the social life of the Middle Border and indirectly touched the national political scene. His deeds split the Missouri Democratic Party into pro-Confederate, pro-Union factions. The Republican Convention of 1880 charged that his bank and train robberies held back the flow of postwar capital and immigration into the Middle Border states and made Missouri the target of a contemptuous Eastern press that dubbed it "The Outlaw State."

The killing of James in St. Joseph by Bob Ford in 1882 helped to end the political careers of Governor Thomas Crittenden, who had had presidential ambitions, and the courageous Jackson County Prosecutor, William Wallace. Crittenden, who had been accused of "hiring killers" to do in Jesse, was refused nomination for a second term while Wallace, who had put Frank James on trial for murder, unsuccessfully ran for the United States Senate, the House of Representatives, and the governorship.

Another favorite of mine is Butch Cassidy, whom I helped to introduce as one of the Wild West's premier outlaws almost twenty-five years ago. In researching the life of Cassidy for this book I discovered that I had inadvertently become a legend maker. In my *Desperate Men*, published in 1949, I had depicted a scene in which Cassidy skillfully rode a bicycle before an audience of admiring whores from Fanny Porter's Sporting House in San Antonio, a favorite hideout for the Wild Bunch after they had pulled off a bank or train robbery.

The story has been lifted many times—never, of course, with credit—and down through the years has become part of the Butch Cassidy legend.

There is one thing wrong with that scene—Cassidy never rode a bicycle!

This is what happened:

Shortly after the end of World War II, I found a letter written by a Mr. Cook, whom William Pinkerton called "my male stenographer," in which Cook answered a routine query from one of the agency's superintendents who wanted background information on Cassidy, Harvey (Kid Curry) Logan, Harry (the Sundance Kid) Longbaugh, and Ben (the Tall Texan) Kilpatrick.

In his reply the secretary provided such information as physical descriptions from Bertillon charts, number of arrests, prison terms, and dates of the outlaws' deaths. He also included excerpts from an affidavit given to a detective by a young prostitute who had traveled with the deadly Harvey (Kid Curry) Logan and Bill Carver, another Wild Bunch rider, on one of their journeys to rob a train.

In her often hilarious affidavit the girl told how Kid Curry became furious because some thief had stolen his guns and part of the loot, and how "Dan" had ridden a bicycle, to the delight of Fanny Porter's girls.

The prostitutes in Fanny's place were always confused when it came to identifying their customers among the Wild Bunch riders. For example, Harvey (Kid

Curry) Logan was known to them as Tom Capeheart and Bob Nevilles. Will Carver was Will Casey, and for some reason Butch Cassidy used the name of Jim Lowe, another member of the Wild Bunch, or called himself Jim Ryan or Jim Maxwell.

However, from the physical description of the "expert bicycle rider" that the girl gave to the detective, she undoubtedly meant Ben Kilpatrick, the Tall Texan. A comparison of their Bertillon records reveals that Kilpatrick was the only one in the gang over "six foot."

In his reply to the western superintendent Mr. Cook, probably from a hasty reading of the affidavit, made Butch the rider.

I included this scene in my book on the basis of the letter. At the time I could not find the original affidavit. When I finally did I discovered Mr. Cook's error.

I hope that in the future the Tall Texan—whom Kid Curry once called the "ladies' man" of the Wild Bunch—will be given credit as the athletic, bicycle-riding outlaw of the Wild West.

Yet for all their traditional frivolity, the Wild Bunch, too, had an impact on America's fading frontier. Their crimes helped to establish a pioneering type of rogues' gallery in a period when there were no fingerprints, Federal Bureau of Investigation, teletype, or telephones to link together the rural sheriffs and marshals.

When an outlaw was killed or captured, the lawmen sent his photograph—many times the corpse of a dead outlaw was propped up against a barn wall or tied to a board—along with his Bertillon chart measurements to the Pinkertons, federal marshals in large cities, cattlemen's associations, stockmen detectives, or detectives working for public carriers such as Wells Fargo. In such a fashion the captured or dead outlaw was identified, linked to other crimes, and his associates named. This crude network helped to produce witnesses and assisted prosecutors in sending outlaws to prison.

The train robberies of the Wild Bunch forced the federal government to move to protect the utilities and railroads, vital to the expansion of a frontier. Railroads revised their archaic manhunting techniques. Posses and horses were put aboard baggage cars and transported to isolated areas where they could ride overland and cut off fleeing bandits. This replaced telegraphing ahead to a sheriff, who at times was working with the gang.

In the 1880s, imaginative lawmen introduced the technique of infiltrating the larger outlaw bands. Detectives worked as farmhands, bartenders, stagecoach drivers, riverboat gamblers—even as mysterious gunfighters. Elaborate preparations were made to give the underground agent a menacing reputation, sometimes backed up by a much-folded counterfeit wanted notice.

The main delight of historical investigation is that it is a kind of detective work, a constant adventure with peaks of satisfaction reached upon discovering important and unpublished material. During my long years of researching the lives and times of these lively frontier figures, I was fortunate to obtain the only interviews with the late Percy Seibert, Commissary General of the Bolivian

Commission for the Study of Railways and later an executive of the Bolivian Supply Company, allied to the Concordia Tin Mines in Bolivia where Butch Cassidy and the Sundance Kid were employed.

Mr. Seibert became a confidant of the outlaws, who had many Sunday dinners at the Seibert home. The first-person material and exceedingly rare photographs he supplied to me were invaluable.

Another superb source of information on Cassidy, the Sundance Kid, and Etta Place in South America was Frank Dimaio, the detective who trailed them from Buenos Aires to the interior, interviewed everyone who knew them, found out where they had banked their money and where they had filed their homesteading claim. A rainy season prevented him from recruiting a company of Bolivian soldiers at a nearby fort to storm the fortified log bunkhouse built by Cassidy and the Kid. He finally covered the coastal cities with wanted posters in Spanish which, I believe, forced Cassidy, the Kid, and Etta Place to move into Bolivia.

Two more valuable eyewitnesses to the South American scene were Victor J. Hampton, who constructed the ore smelter in San Vincente where Cassidy and Longbaugh were killed, and J. L. Rawlinson, who was connected with the Bolivian railroad and was at Eucalyptus, Bolivia, at the time the outlaws held up the train and stole a mining company's payroll. Some years ago a Cassidy relative helped me to correctly identify Cassidy as "Robert LeRoy Parker," not "George" as he was called by frontier historians for many years.

This book is not meant to be pro-outlaw or pro-lawman or pro-anything. As I said in my previous volume, *The Authentic Wild West: The Gunfighters*, I did not set out to debunk legends but rather to refer the popular imagination to verifiable facts and to emphasize the reality of those men and women who played such active roles in this wild period of our frontier history.

I have tried to reveal their faults, frailties, and humanity as influenced by their times and environments.

JAMES D. HORAN
The Notch, Winter, 1977

BOOK ONE

THE BLOOD BROTHERHOODS

THE RENOS

THE ONLY PASSENGERS WAITING FOR THE JEFFERSON, Madison & Indianapolis train at the wood and water stop of Northfield, Indiana, that Friday night of May 22, 1868, were seven armed outlaws, prepared to commit one of the most spectacular and lucrative train robberies in the history of the United States.

Two hid behind a pile of corded wood, two more blended into the shadows of a clump of trees, two were stationed on the opposite side of the tracks, and the seventh, Frank Reno, the leader, moved restlessly about the area, pausing from time to time to bend down and put his ear to the tracks.

Finally he jumped up and gave his orders; the train was coming. Several minutes later, the glow of the headlight could be seen through the trees. Then it appeared, the big wheels of the tiny locomotive gripping the rails as the engineer ordered down brakes, the diamond-shaped stack belching clouds of black smoke and showers of sparks.

As the train ground to a halt, Engineer George Fletcher swung down with his oilcan and was immediately surrounded and knocked unconscious. Two of the gang scrambled aboard the tender and overpowered David Hutchinson, the fireman. Another cut the telegraph wires. Conductor Americus Wheeler, who suspected something was wrong and had come to investigate, saw the bandits. He drew his revolver and fired. A volley hit him and he fell, badly wounded.

When the outlaws of the Wild West called out, "Throw down the box!" this is what the stagecoach drivers handed over. *Courtesy Wells Fargo History Room*

The bandit team, working with military precision, then uncoupled the engine, tender, and express car and opened the throttle. The passenger cars were soon left behind as the wood burner chugged through the night, its plume of smoke and sparks pulled back by the wind.

As the train clicked along the rails—"at a fearful rate," according to the *Chicago Tribune*—Frank Reno and two of the gang crawled across the roof of the express car, dropped to the platform, and jimmied open the car door. The messenger was quickly overpowered but refused to give up his keys to the safe.

Two of the outlaws picked him up and swung him while one shouted:

"One—two—and to hell you go!"

The messenger swung out into the darkness, tumbling heels over head down a steep embankment. Fortunately it was a sandy, marshy section and he lived to tell his story.

Reno and his men attacked the three old-fashioned safes, merely oblong iron boxes with lids that fitted into the tops; they were easily pried open with a crowbar.

Inside they discovered a treasure of ninety-seven thousand dollars in gold and government bonds with part of the shipment designated for the United States Treasurer in Washington. The gang abandoned the train just south of Farmington, below Seymour, Indiana. There, horses were waiting and they fled in the darkness.

At Marshfield the wounded conductor found a handcar, located the engineer and fireman, and caught up with the locomotive and tender and the looted express car. They backed up the engine to recouple the passenger cars and

Diamond-stack engine and train of the type held up by the early outlaws of the Wild West. *The James D. Horan Civil War and Western Americana Collection*

A Wells Fargo stagecoach, typical of those held up by the Jameses, Youngers, and other western highwaymen. *Courtesy Wells Fargo History Room*

THE ADAMS EXPRESS Cọ

THIS COMPANY HAS FACILITIES UNSURPASSED BY THOSE OF ANY OTHER EXPRESS LINE IN THE WORLD, FOR THE SAFE & EXPEDITIOUS FORWARDING & PROMPT DELIVERY OF

BANK-NOTES, GOLD & SILVER COIN, PARCELS, PACKAGES, FREIGHT, &c.

SO, FOR THE COLLECTION OF NOTES, DRAFTS & ACCOUNTS, IN ALL THE CITIES, TOWNS & VILLAGES IN THE EASTERN, WESTERN, SOUTHERN & SOUTH-WESTERN STATES.

The Adams Express Company broadside by N. Currier, 1850. The express company was the favorite target of the outlaws of the Wild West beginning with the Reno gang shortly after the Civil War. *The James D. Horan Civil War and Western Americana Collection*

finally chugged into the Union Station at Indianapolis six hours later to give the alarm.[1]

The Marshfield robbery had been the third train robbery committed by the Reno gang, an outlaw brotherhood that had looted and sacked the Middle Border states, Indiana, and Kentucky, since the end of the Civil War. In October 1866 they had "invented" train robbery when they stopped and robbed an eastbound train of the Ohio & Mississippi Railroad, a broad-gauge line that later became part of the Baltimore & Ohio system. The gang had taken thirteen thousand dollars in bills from one safe, and when the messenger insisted that he didn't have the keys to the second and larger safe, they stopped the train, removed the safe, then pulled the bell cord so the unsuspecting engineer continued down the track.

There were five brothers—John, Frank, Simeon, William, and Clinton,

Early photograph of Frank Reno, leader of the Reno gang of Indiana, the "inventors" of train robbery. *Courtesy Pinkertons, Inc.*

known as "Honest" Reno because he refused to join the others in their robberies—and a daughter, Laura.

In his rare autobiography John Reno pictures his mother, Julia Ann Reno, as a "highly educated woman." This may be exaggerated sentimental remembrance, but Jefferson County, Indiana, records show that she had a neat, legible handwriting. Wilkinson Reno, father of the outlaw breed, was born in Boyle County, Kentucky. The original name of the family is thought to have been Renault, and he was of French descent. The older Reno was so untutored that John said he could "scarcely count his own money." But the old man must have possessed a shrewd investment sense which enabled him to gather a great deal of farmland. Jefferson County records show he was one of the largest taxpayers.

Frank Reno, the leader and oldest of the brothers, was born on July 27, 1837, near Seymour, Jefferson County. He was personally courageous, completely crooked, and a natural-born leader. John Reno, his second in command, was born July 22, two years later. The birthplaces of Clinton and Laura are not known. Simeon was born on August 2, 1843; William on May 15, 1848.

In 1816 the family settled on the White River bottomland two miles northwest of the present city of Seymour, Indiana. John recalled that he had hated attending the school which had been erected on a corner of his family's property, "thinking more of sports and excitement than I did of lessons."

During the Civil War the Renos were notorious bounty jumpers. After Appomattox they bought up sections of nearby Rockford, the scene of so many mysterious fires that the *Seymour Times* called it a ghost town. The ravaged town soon became the headquarters of the gang.

One newspaper observed, "Jackson County contains more cutthroats to the square inch than Botany Bay."

The Renos controlled their community by terror and bribery. From time to time they were arrested, but they soon reappeared in Seymour, swaggering down the main street or boasting of their political power in the taverns and gambling halls.

In comparison with the long career of banditry of the Jameses and

The Adams Express Company, the nation's largest public carrier during and after the Civil War, handled not only military documents, soldiers' pay, provisions, and munitions but also the bodies of dead soldiers. When relatives could locate the body, the corpse would be shipped back home to be buried in the family plot. After a major battle there were so many coffins that the express company had to add special cars. Here are poignant receipts for delivery of the body of an officer killed at Gettysburg. *The James D. Horan Civil War and Western Americana Collection*

Youngers, the Renos were comparatively short-lived, but during their time they robbed trains and county treasury offices, and engaged in counterfeiting. Although they have been credited with "inventing" train robbery in the West, there is evidence that trains were held up in the South as early as the 1850s.

The Jameses, Youngers, and Daltons must have read of the Renos' exploits and perhaps were inspired by them, since succeeding train robberies in every part of the country usually followed their pattern.

Following a series of train robberies, the Adams Express Company, then the nation's largest public carrier, retained Allan Pinkerton, head of the detective agency, to protect its shipments of gold. Pinkerton's favorite theory—that any criminal enterprise could be broken by infiltration—was used.[2]

Unfortunately, we know little of Dick Winscott, who opened the saloon in Seymour, or the handsome man with the cold eyes, luxuriant sideburns, and

The picture secretly taken by an undercover detective who had infiltrated the Reno gang. *Courtesy Pinkertons, Inc.*

JOHN RENO and FRANK SPARKS

A United States Express Company receipt for government money carried during the Civil War. The "States," as it was known in the West, yielded an estimated fifteen thousand dollars to the James-Younger gang during the Missouri Pacific train robbery in July 1876. *The James D. Horan Civil War and Western Americana Collection*

the embroidered waistcoat of a river gambler who made the saloon his headquarters and announced he was ready for action. Both were Pinkerton agents "laying pipe with the outlaws."

The saloon was a dingy, smoky place filled with shadows cast by the oil lamp. The Renos and their raiders sat at tables or stood at the bar, drinking and making plans for their next strike while the impassive gambler flipped his cards and cashed in the chips. When "loose women" appeared, liquor flowed and the newspapers of the time solemnly reported that the saloon became "wild and boisterous." During one of these parties, Winscott persuaded John Reno and Franklin Sparks, one of the Marshfield train robbers, to sit on a stool and pose for a photographer, possibly another detective.

Reno and Sparks stared drunkenly into the lens. Within a short time the first photograph of any member of the gang had been smuggled out of Seymour to Chicago, where it was carefully studied by Pinkerton and his staff.

The next target of the gang was the Daviess County, Missouri, Treasury. In his autobiography John Reno described how he and Vallery Elliott, the member of his gang Reno identified as "E" in the narrative, staged the raid. He also revealed how—after his capture—his brother Frank frantically gathered their gang to board the train and release him, but as Frank sadly explained in a letter, he and the other train robbers "missed connections."[3]

How I Raided the Daviess County Treasury Office

On getting into the treasurer's office I found two safes, and did not know which one contained the money. One was larger than the other and comparatively new, and by far the best safe, if there was any best. So we tackled the new one at once, and spent two hours in the opening of it and going through it, for it

15

took as long to overhaul all the papers and records and trash hunting for the money, as it did to jimmy it open. We were somewhat discouraged and very badly disappointed to find nothing in it of any value to us. It was now about three o'clock in the morning. The other safe was a small one and it bore many marks of everyday use. We had a short conference and decided to try the other one too, which we opened in less than an hour of jimmying.

On opening the outer door, I saw that the drawers were so swollen with money that they would not even fit in their places. On pulling out the first one, I found it to contain sixty dollars in gold, some silver, and a key—this I found was the key to the iron chest in the safe, which I opened and I found it brim-full of big, fat packages. On tearing open one of these I found it contained green-backs, and marked "One hundred fifty-dollar bills"—"less two." I spread my big handkerchief on the floor in front of the safe and went to work emptying it of all its valuables, which, when counted, amounted to the sum of twenty-two thousand and sixty-five dollars, a nice haul indeed.

The amount of each package was marked on the back. The handkerchief was so full that with difficulty I could tie the corners together. We gathered up all our tools, leaving a sledge-hammer we had "borrowed" from a neighboring black-smith's shop. We carried our own tools about a half a mile from town and threw them away. It was now about four o'clock in the morning and bitter cold.

We started out on the Chillicothe road, and had not gone far when we had come to a sign-board. I climbed up the post, and striking a match, read that it was "twenty-eight miles to Chillicothe." One-half mile farther on brought us to the Grand River ferry; but the boat was frozen fast in the ice, and the ice was not strong enough to bear up our weight to go over to it. We then took poles, and wading in, broke it ahead of us as we went. The water was just about waist deep, and we waded in with all our clothes on. My boots got full of water, and I could not get them off, since they were tight, nor could I get the water out of them; so, having a light pair of shoes in my grip-sack, I cut the boots off my feet and left them by the road-side.

It was now coming daylight and we were not five miles from Gallatin. We had come to a prairie and did not know how far it was to timber. It was getting too late to travel, for fear we would be seen; so, coming to a field of cut-up corn, we crawled into a shock clear out of sight and lay there all day, with our clothes completely covered with ice. It was a nasty situation. We were but a short distance from the road, so during the day we could hear the tramp of horses' feet going in different directions.

About two o'clock a wagon was driven into the field, and the persons with it began gathering up the corn shocks. We were scared to death they would try to gather the shocks we were hiding in. Some one rode up to the fence and called out, "Boys, gather those short rows at the back side of the field."

"E" thought it was the owner of the farm telling our pursuers what to do, because he misunderstood, thinking them to say: "They," meaning us, "could not have got farther than the back side of my field." Because of this, he told me later that he thought the jig was up for us. I happened to be next to the mouth of a hole in the shock and could hear better than he what was going on outside of it.

As soon as it was dark, we came out to the road again very cold, stiff, and hungry, and a walk of twenty miles before us before we could reach the Hannibal and St. Joseph railroad. We soon became satisfied that we could not make this trip without something to eat, for we had been forty-eight hours without a mouthful of anything. About eleven o'clock in the morning we heard some one playing on a violin in a cabin near the road. Walking up to the door, I then peeped in through a hole where a string hung out with which to open it, and I saw an old darky baking his shins before a large fire. We rapped and were invited in. I told the darky we had been turky hunting—a common custom in that country after night—and had got lost, and would like to get something to eat. He said his wife was "sick" and that we could not get it. I told him we would pay him well for the trouble, and showed him a big roll of bills. He went to the bed in a hurry and talked to his wife, then he came back and told us she said she was too "sick" to get up. I gave him two one-dollar bills and told him to try her once more, for we must have something to eat, as we would have to travel all night, or our "families" would be "uneasy about us."

Back to the bed he went, and while there I told "E" to get out his "pop" [revolver], and that we would soon make them cook supper for us regardless, but we didn't have to use the pistol because the woman crawled out this time and went to work. She was not "sick" at all, but just lazy. Our two dollars soon cured her of that.

We drank three cups of coffee apiece and ate everything eatable on that table. I have no doubt that that meal saved our lives from starvation.

We reached Chillicothe about five o'clock in the morning. Our intention was to get on a freight train at that point. Knowing that the news of this robbery was at least a day ahead of us, we had to be cautious. We had not been in the depot but a short time when we heard a freight train coming. It proved to be a stock train, and the caboose was filled with drovers on their way to Chicago via Quincy. We "piled" in, and laid down on the floor among the stock men. At daylight we straightened up and at Macon we got ready for a square meal, and when seated at the table we made full hands.

In conversation with one of the drovers, I learned that he had five whole car loads of cattle on the train and no one to help him. We pretended that we had been looking for work and had failed to get any, that we were about out of money (we only had $22,000 with us), and that we would like to help him with his cattle if he would hire us. He said all right, and at Palmyra we went on top of the train, with poles in our hands, and guarded the cattle, rapping the bellering (bellowing) beasts over the heads often, to make ourselves appear as much like real drovers as possible.

When on the opposite side of the river from Quincy, we helped to get the cattle across, and when over we assisted in getting hay for them. When this was done the drover paid us two dollars and treated us to drinks. Just then a train going to Lafayette, Indiana, backed into the depot. We slipped into the sleeping car, and after paying our fare we went to bed.

When we reached Indianapolis, we set to work and divided the money, and I have never seen my partner since.

I soon called on my Mollie and found her in good health and spirits after my absence of six days. I counted my money in her presence, but she asked no questions; in fact, she never did on any occasion! She did not want to know anything but to have a good time as long as it lasted. I had been in her company for a year or more and was greatly attached to her—I fairly worshipped her. We occupied room No. 19 at the Palmer House, lived high, and had a chicken fight in our room occasionally by way of pastime.

I laid down and went to sleep, but was waked up soon after by a big gang of police coming into my room. Chief Wilson, Hi Minnick, Pryor Duvall, and two others, made up the party. They informed me that there were a couple of gentlemen from Missouri down at the Concordia House who wished to see me. I smelled trouble, but putting on my clothes I went with them, and on arriving at the hotel, I was soon convinced that I was about to get into real trouble. I feared this before I even left my room, and had given Mollie enough money to settle our bill and go home on.

I found John Ballinger, the sheriff and collector of Daviess county, Mo., with Major Woodruff, waiting to see me. I was put in a carriage and taken about twelve miles out on the railroad running to Terre Haute, where we waited for a train bound for St. Louis. When it came I was put on board, Chief Wilson accompanying us as far as Terre Haute. I was treated very kindly by all these officers, in fact, much kinder than one would expect under the circumstances under which I was arrested.

When we reached St. Louis, I was surprised when Frank Sparks was brought up and shackled to me. I asked him what it meant, and he answered, "I don't know." I knew Sparks had nothing to do with the robbery, but didn't dare say so at the time; but sooner than see him innocently deprived of his liberty and perhaps of his life—for I expected us to by tried by "Judge Lynch's Court" when I got to the country—I would have confessed all, which I did finally, as did others also, who were implicated indirectly.

We were taken on the North Missouri Railroad to Macon, where we changed cars for Hamilton. Captain Ballinger had telegraphed ahead that we were coming, and when we reached Hamilton there were crowds of natives from Gallatin ready to escort us over the prairie—which was very lonely!—and a distance of sixteen miles. We made this journey in wagons, with a part of our retinue following on horseback. There were about forty persons in the crowd and I think it is safe to say that two-thirds of them were drunk. The bottle was passed around several times on the way. Sparks would not drink, but I was never known to refuse! The night was very dark and Sparks was getting uneasy while I was drinking with the crowd, trying to keep cheerful.

"John," he said to me, "this is pretty hard on an innocent man. If this crowd gets much drunker we will never see Gallatin alive." He had a good idea that I knew something about the robbery, although I always protested that I was as innocent as he was, but it was sure hard to make him believe it.

We reached Gallatin about twelve o'clock, and were taken to the treasurer's office, where I had torn the safes to pieces. The room looked as it did on the night I had left it five weeks previous. There had been no repairing done to the safes; the room had not even been swept up or straightened at all. Everything showed the exact disorder I had made on that night. I glanced at the safes, and all eyes in the room were turned on me to see if they could detect any change in my countenance. I never heard that they discovered any.

Joseph McGee, at that time Judge of the Probate Court, jumped up suddenly in the middle of the floor, and addressing me, cried:

"You are the man that did this work! We will hang you to the tallest tree in Grand River bottoms if this money is not returned!"

I had played draw-poker in my time, and considered that a "bluff," although I did not, of course, ask him to show his hand! We were well guarded in the Court House that night. The jail having been condemned as unsafe, we were kept under guard all the time, lest we escape—or be lynched.

I soon found that the natives were coming in from all directions with their shot-guns and coon-skin caps and panther-skin coats, and with their hair hanging clear down to their shoulders. Some of them had not yet taken off the moss from their backs that had grown there while they had lain in the woods, hiding during the war!

John Ballinger had some stray stock to sell on the public square one day, and after selling each mule or other animal, he would make a short speech on "behalf of the little children who were behind in their schooling." As the money I had stolen had been a school fund, he would go over the years of the schooling they had lost by the war; and now, when they had accumulated a small fund, it had been stolen. All this had been done to excite a mob to get me.

This was our third day in Gallatin, and we had not said anything, nor had I confessed yet. But things were really getting hot. It was costing this county over fifty dollars a day for guards. They were kept on day and night, fifteen or twenty at a time, at two dollars and fifty cents each per day. I was frightened by this worse than by the firing of pistols at the jail which was always going on, or by the threats shouted in at us, for I knew that they would not stand to pay all these guards for five months. The court had just adjourned, and would not convene again within that time.

On the morning after we reached Gallatin, I learned by what means they had got the clue that led to my arrest. Clay Abel, the young man that wrote me from Gallatin tipping me off to come there, as there was an easy chance of "getting a raise" by burglary, had been arrested, along with his brother-in-law by the name of Clifton. They had been seized on suspicion of knowing something about the robbery. He had been caught in the act of trying to pass some counterfeit gold coins that I had found in the safe, and had left on the floor, and that he had picked up on the morning after the robbery—no doubt thinking they were genuine. This led to suspicions he had done the deed. After being questioned very closely, however, without disclosing anything, the two men were released and had returned to their work, though not entirely exonerated by the authorities. But Clifton's conscience, if that criminal had any, must have hurt him, for soon he left his work and sought out Ballinger, the sheriff, and revealed the whole secret voluntarily to him, acknowledging writing the letter to me urging me to come and rob the county treasury, knowing I would do it. As he got none of the booty, except the counterfeits, I think his contribution of tattle-taling was prompted by revenge. There were several families in Daviess county, Mo., at that time, whom I was acquainted with, and among them my old friend, Dan Smith, from Rockford, Indiana, where I was born.

Dan was in jail there when I arrived, on suspicion of being implicated in the robbery too. I had often heard of Dan praying in church while I was home, for I never attended church but my Methodist friends had told me, but I never heard so fervent a prayer as the one he offered on the night we both expected to be lynched. I never had much faith in prayer myself, but truly do believe that Dan prayed himself out of that little difficulty. He was entirely innocent of even any knowledge of the crime until committed to his cell, but of course that would make no difference at all to a mob from Missouri, or from any other state either for that matter. As there was no one there who knew of my partner "E," he and the others went free; but here I was being kept and punished as an atonement for the sins of them all.

After five or six days' siege by the angry citizens around about, I concluded I had better plead guilty and get a sentence to the penitentiary and so get out the best way I could, for as long as there was life there was hope. I would have neither life or hope if this mob had gotten hold of me.

On my pleading guilty, Sparks was released and went home. There was soon a called term of court to sit on the 16th of January, 1868. I wrote to my folks of what I had done, and when my trial would come off . . . or rather when I would get sentenced. My sister answered my letter and said that the 16th of January was her birthday, which I had almost forgotten. The angry feeling among the people died down when they heard my plea of guilty, and all was quiet then until the day of the trial.

I forgot to mention in its place that the day after I was brought back to Gallatin the negro from whom we got our supper on the night after the robbery, was brought in to identify us. I was placed in a line along with Sparks and about a dozen other men; the negro came in and was told to point out the men who were at his house on that night. He walked up and down before the line three times and finally began to look at me, showing his large white ivories. He stopped, and pointing at me said, "That one is one of them!"

A few days before my trial I had a private interview with my brother, Frank. This was obtained from the officers of the county, with a view to overhearing us talk about where I put the cash so they could get a portion of the money back. This did not succeed for them. During the interview arrangements were made for my release from the officers while on the way to Jefferson City; we whispered these arrangements quickly. As I had made a full confession of the robbery, and was sure of being sent to prison, the next thing for us to do was to plan some way of escape, which we were doing, there being but a few days until I would receive my sentence. Frank left Gallatin about twelve o'clock in the night for home to get a party (the Reno Gang) to rescue me, and I was in good spirits when he left, feeling that I could depend on him and that if it were possible for him to do it, this work of freeing me would be done regardless of the hazards.

On the day of the trial a heavy guard escorted me to the court-room, and there were a great many people in from the country. J. J. Clark was Circuit Judge at that time. S. A. Richardson was employed by the county to assist in the prosecution, although they knew I was going to plead guilty. The indictment was found and read to me, and before the words got cold I pleaded guilty. Judge Clark then made a few remarks that I don't now remember, but I do remember that he sentenced me to hard labor in the Missouri Penitentiary for the term of forty years. This seemed a cruel sentence.

There was a dead silence in the court-room for a few minutes, when Mr. Richardson rose up and said that if the court would allow him to make a suggestion, he thought that a term of twenty-five years would be long enough to end John Reno's career. He being hardly thirty years old now, he would hardly survive that time at hard labor. The judge then said that he felt the force of Mr. Richardson's remarks, and would therefore reduce my sentence to twenty-five years, and it was so recorded. This seemed to satisfy the natives, although the sheriff was still uneasy and thought there would be trouble on the way to the railroad and that I might be lynched.

On returning from the court-room to the room where I was confined, I sent for a dentist and had a tooth pulled that had been aching for some time.

On Monday morning, January 18th, we started for Cameron in a two-horse wagon to take the train for Jefferson City. We were very heavily "manned" with armed guards, to keep off the angry mobs, but if I had not had both money and friends, I know that I never would have seen the inner side of those stone walls. I placed too much reliance on my money, not counting on my friends, but I found them true to the last anyway. At the very worst, I had no idea of remaining a year in the prison; but bad luck usually comes all together.

It was now five days since I had seen Frank, in which time he would have to travel over a thousand miles, not mentioning the other delays in getting ready to meet us at Hamilton, where my guards intended taking the train with me. I was a little uneasy on the morning we left Gallatin to see the guard so strong—there were six or eight armed soldiers, well weaponed, but I knew they were not all going on the train and hoped they would leave us before my brother might make his attack. As I did not know where the attack was to be made, however, I was very restless, watching for them at every station, and even thinking they might be in the hind part of the train in another car, or in the car in front. I dreaded to see the time come, for I feared there would really be some hard fighting. The guard were all provided with long "navies" [Navy Colt revolvers] and had the reputation of being men of steel nerves.

I was very restless and fidgety in my seat. Whenever the door at either end of the coach opened, I would look to see who came in. I had not heard from Frank since that night, but I knew that between Cameron and Kansas City would be the most suitable place for the rescue, as the road was recently built, and the country was very thinly settled along the tracks. I could have felt better, and I have felt worse, than I did on that trip. Every moment I expected "the ball to open," and as I was heavily ironed I could not take any part, but would be compelled to stay and see it out. But time and the train rolled on without anything occurring until we passed Kansas City, when I began to give up all hope of any rescue. Three days after my arrival, at the prison in Jefferson City, I received a letter from Frank, saying that he had had a little trouble "getting the material ready," and also that the gang members helping him had missed train connections at Quincy, Illinois, or that he would have been as good as his word to make the rescue.

When we arrived at the prison gate I looked up and read in large letters over the entrance: "THE WAY OF THE TRANSGRESSOR IS HARD. Admission, twenty-five cents" but I was on the dead-head list and went in free.

John Reno's version of his capture is in conflict with the facts. After the raid on the Daviess treasury office the Renos were soon identified as the suspects. Pinkerton contacted his secret agents in Seymour and it was decided that any attempt to arrest the gang in Seymour would only result in bloodshed.

Pinkerton decided the only way to get John was by kidnapping him. William Pinkerton once justified this act by explaining: "It was kidnapping but the ends justified the means," a typical nineteenth-century law-bending philosophy which ruled the nation's private detective agencies for years.

Pinkerton wired the sheriff of Daviess County to meet him in Cincinnati with a writ for the outlaw's arrest. A wood-burning train with Pinkerton and "six muscular men stood at the ready" for two days while Pinkerton and Winscott synchronized their timing.

Finally the signal was given. The special train chugged into the station. The engine's big wheels were still turning when Pinkerton and his posse rushed out and swept up John, who was waiting to greet a friend arriving on the express. Within a few minutes, while the crowd gaped, Reno was carried, cursing and shouting, into the car where detectives roped and ironed him.

In defiance, Frank Reno led the gang across the Midwest, robbing banks, post offices, and county treasuries. In February 1868, they looted the Harrison County Treasury Office at Magnolia, Iowa, of fourteen thousand dollars. It was a stunning loss to the tiny frontier community—"a public calamity," as one newspaper described the crime.

Shortly after the robbery, William Pinkerton discovered that Michael Rogers, a leading citizen of Council Bluffs, Iowa, was a member of the gang and had selected the county treasury offices to be raided.

The Pinkertons raided Rogers's house and found the "pillar of the Methodist Church" drinking with the other members of the gang. The loot of the Magnolia train robbery was discovered in the kitchen stove.

The outlaws were confined in a small country jail to wait extradition to Indiana. A short time later the Pinkertons were notified they had escaped, leaving a message for the detectives chalked on the cell wall: "April Fool!" It was April 1, 1868.

The Pinkertons trailed the train robbers, who had scattered across nearby states. It was dogged, exhausting police legwork with operatives visiting boardinghouses, farmhouses, taverns, and stores, displaying what descriptions and photographs they had. In Mattoon, then the county seat of Coles County, Illinois, one detective found Frank Sparks working on a farm. Allan Pinkerton, a group of his men, and the local sheriff raided the farm and arrested Sparks. He undoubtedly informed on John J. Moore, whom Pinkerton clas-

Miles Ogle, who rode with the Renos. *Courtesy Pinkertons, Inc.*

A tintype of Pete McCartney, member of the Reno gang. *Courtesy Pinkertons, Inc.*

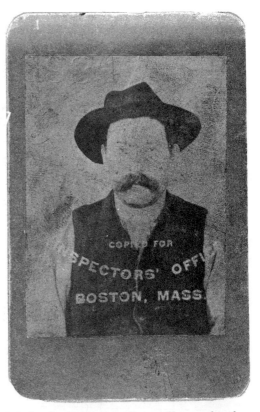

William Ogle, alias M. Odell, member of the Reno gang. *Courtesy Pinkertons, Inc.*

Michael Rogers, "a pillar of the church," who designated county treasury offices and banks to be robbed by the Renos. *Courtesy Pinkertons, Inc.*

sified as a "desperate outlaw," and Henry Jerrell, who, the agency head said, "had been led astray"; the pair was arrested in an Aetna saloon.

Earlier, Moore had been the central figure in one of the most unusual train robbery cases in frontier history. While being chased by a posse he had stolen a locomotive but jumped from the cab as it roared into a small town. The runaway engine plowed up a long length of track before it ground to a halt. Railroad officials, who realized they could not claim anything from the train robber who pleaded he was penniless, charged him with the theft of the engine. Moore's attorney shrewdly argued that under ancient English law a man could enter another man's house, move his goods from one side to another, and be charged with damage but not theft. Therefore, he triumphantly told the jury, as long as the locomotive had not been removed from the tracks, Moore had not stolen the engine. It took the jury two minutes to acquit the "desperate" train robber.

A vigilante movement was growing in some sections of the state when the Pinkertons finally won their extradition writ and brought the trio of train robbers back to Indiana in the same bullet-marked express car they had robbed. At one point the gang was transferred to wagons for the final stage of the journey to Seymour. On a lonely road vigilantes wearing crimson masks took the prisoners at gunpoint and ordered the Pinkerton guards to "trot for Seymour."

The mob lynched the three outlaws a few miles from Seymour; a coroner's jury verdict found they had been "hanged by persons unknown."

To escape the vigilantes, Frank and Simeon Reno and Charles Anderson fled to Windsor, Canada. Langdon Moore, a noted bank robber of the 1870s, described Windsor in his memoirs as a sort of Canadian Dodge City, with the town's Turf Club a headquarters of international train robbers, safecrackers, thugs, and sneak thieves who were wanted in the States for every crime from forgery to murder.

Detectives picked up the trail of the fugitives hiding out in Canada by trailing another outlaw named Jack Friday, who was known to have been hired by the Renos to drive their buggy.

Allan Pinkerton, fearful that the outlaws would be freed, rushed a copy of the arrest warrants and a description of the crimes to Secretary of State Seward, accompanied by a formal request that the robbers be returned to the United States for trial.[4]

Acting Secretary of State William Hunter turned the request over to Edward Thornton, British Minister to the United States, who in turn notified London and the Governor-General of Canada, Viscount Monck. While Washington and Downing Street exchanged polite notes, the gang voted to murder Pinkerton; Dick Barry, a noted desperado, was elected as the assassin. But Pinkerton foiled two attempts. When word of the attempted murder reached Washington, Seward, an old friend of Pinkerton from the Civil War days, sent a gunboat to Windsor. It stayed ten days and departed only after a vigorous protest from the Canadian government.

While his attorneys continued to delay the hearings, Frank Reno tried a

The house in Canada where the Reno gang hid out. *Courtesy Pinkertons, Inc.*

William H. Seward, who signed the extradition papers to return the Renos from Canada to the United States. This is a Brady photograph. *The James D. Horan Civil War and Western Americana Collection*

more direct method; the magistrate who was holding the extradition hearings announced that Reno had tried to bribe his teen-age son with six thousand dollars in gold "to influence his father in their [the Renos'] behalf."

The attempted assassination of Pinkerton, the crude bribery effort, and the international publicity finally persuaded Governor-General Monck to agree that the Renos should be returned to the United States for trial.

Before the outlaws could be turned over to Pinkerton, London notified Canada that new rules had been established by the Queen's Council in London governing the extradition of prisoners, and a delay followed. The fuming Pinkerton was finally advised by Monck's office that he would have to get written authority from the State Department signed by the President.

Secretary of State Seward received Pinkerton's angry message while he was on his way to a funeral in upstate New York. He ordered Hunter in Washington to prepare the final papers and bring them immediately to President Johnson for signing.[5]

Pinkerton was finally given custody of the prisoners, but his troubles continued. He hired a special tug to take the outlaw trio to Detroit. It was a calm, beautiful Indian summer day when the tug departed from Windsor. However, after traveling only a short distance the tug was sliced in half by a steamer. Pinkerton and his detectives clung to the leg-ironed and handcuffed outlaws until the steamer swung about and rescued them.

Pinkerton and his heavily armed men escorted their prisoners by wagon and buggy to the New Albany, Indiana, jail, where the Renos and Anderson were turned over to Sheriff Thomas Fullenlove. Pinkerton inspected the jail and urged the sheriff to remove his prisoners to the stronger jail at Indianapolis, but Fullenlove refused.

Then, on the night of December 12, 1868, an army of hooded vigilantes stormed the jail and lynched the outlaws in what a Chicago newspaper called "one of the most violent nights in the history of our country."

Years after the lynching of the Renos in the New Albany jail, the *Louisville* (Kentucky) *Courier* assigned Dan Walsh, Jr., a staff writer, to interview surviving members of the vigilante committee and reconstruct the events of the "night of blood." The names of the leader or members of the Southern Indiana Vigilante Committee have never been revealed; those who talked to Walsh insisted on anonymity. Walsh's step-by-step account is regarded as one of the most accurate accounts of what happened that winter's night in 1868.[6]

The Lynching of the Renos

At about 11 o'clock on the night of December 12, 1868, a train of mystery started south from somewhere near Seymour, Indiana. It had a clear track and an engineer who knew every inch of the way. A mob crowded into the single coach and there they sat in darkness, speaking only in whispers.

No whistle blew for a crossing, no bell uttered a warning as the train passed through the sleeping towns. At about 3:30 o'clock it pulled into Pearl Street, New Albany, and came to a stop. The mob detrained, all ready for their work. They wore red flannel hoods and every man was equipped with one or more trusty revolvers, a heavy club or sling shot. There were fifty-six in the party.

And literally did these lawless avengers take the sleeping town as completely as a victorious invading army. The morning was bitter cold and few people were on the streets, and these few who met the mob were made captive and taken along.

Patrols were stationed along the route through State Street from the jail to the train, a distance of three squares. Luther (Chuck) Whitten, the jailer, still living in New Albany, was found on guard in front of the jail, warming himself beside a fire in the gutter. They made short shift of him, disarmed and overpowered him, tied his hands and feet and carried him into the office where they deposited him in the sheriff's chair.

The mob was led by a large, portly man well dressed and of commanding presence. As he passed through the cell block issuing orders, finding positions and superintending the whole bloody business, there flashed and shimmered in the murky light a great diamond of wonderful brilliancy. Who wore that ring? Who wears it now?

"Ask something easy" most of those questioned will now reply. The leader and a few chosen assistants went to the room where Sheriff Thomas Fullenlove and his wife were sleeping. Fullenlove had heard the commotion below and met the invaders at the bedroom door. They demanded the keys and the brave officer refused.

Though "covered" by their guns he ran downstairs and climbed out a window, shouting:

"I am the sheriff, the highest peace officer in the county and if you respect the law you will not dare shoot me."

Luther "Chuck" Whitten, the Reno jailer on the night of the lynchings. *The James D. Horan Civil War and Western Americana Collection*

Travis Carter, head of the Seymour, Indiana, vigilantes, 1866-1868. *Courtesy Pinkertons, Inc.*

He attempted to rush through the gates and give the alarm. As he did a dozen revolvers belched at him and he fell, severely wounded in his right arm. The bullets he carried to his grave.

Immediately Fullenlove was dazed by the blow from the butt of a revolver.

"Don't kill him—take him into the house," the leader ordered.

In the meantime the mob had directed its guns on the sheriff's plucky little wife but despite their demands and their threats she refused to disclose the hiding place of the keys. The mob then spent their time searching for the keys while Fullenlove, his wife, children and guard Whitten were locked in the sleeping apartment.

The mob then found the keys. When they approached the cell door, Guard Tom Matthews from the inside, drew his revolver and declared he would shoot any man who tried to unlock the door that stood between the Renos and death.

The leader calmly held up five ropes already prepared with a hangman's noose and said four were for the outlaws and the fifth would be for himself if he didn't "behave himself."

The leader then tried the key they had found but it did not open the door. Not wishing to lose such time on a minor detail, he gave Matthews the choice of unlocking the door or having them batter it down and hanging him along with the Renos.

Realizing the hopelessness of the situation the guard swung open the gate.

The mob rushed in, forced Matthews to point out the cells of the Renos and Anderson, then tied him up; and placed him in the room with the other captives.

Frank, the leader, was first hanged and as he gasped he prayed,

"Lord, have mercy on my soul."

Simeon was second, William third and Anderson last. William, the younger brother, still a lad in years but of giant build and strength, fought like a tiger seriously wounding more than one of his lynchers.

All the while, he protested and swore, with God as his judge, that he was innocent of any part of the crimes of his brothers. The other outlaws confirmed his pleas, and begged that at least the "kid" be spared.

But the mob was thirsting for the blood of every Reno, and every Reno friend and gave no quarters to doubt, or to youth or to sentiment.

After Anderson had been strung up, the rope broke and he fell to the floor begging forgiveness for his sins.

"It's too late now for prayers, Charlie," the leader shouted and they hoisted him up for a second time.

To do the work as quickly as possible and to make sure it would be well done, members of the mob swung on to the dangling bodies of their victims, breaking the necks and all but severing the bodies from the heads.

Several prisoners were in jail at the same time awaiting trial for murder. Like beasts of prey, maddened at the sight of blood and lusting for more, some one in the mob proposed, "let's hang every murderer in here!"

Trembling beneath the bunks in their cells, those referred to, heard the awful words and died a thousand deaths of terror.

But as the leader commented: "We've done the work we've come to do."

So they filed out of the jail, taking with them Floyd County Commissioner Henry Perrette, who had been spending the night with Sheriff Fullenlove. When they had boarded the train, they released Perrette with instructions to get a doctor for the wounded sheriff and to release the others.

Now all was ready for the return journey. The engine was switched around and headed northward, its expectant cylinders panting with full steam. The only signal to start was the verbal command of the leader and the engine sped into the darkness and was lost.

There was a token investigation of the lynching but nothing came of it. Secretly state and local officials congratulated themselves that the power of the outlaw gang had finally been shattered. No one pointed out that the vigilante action only underscored the total breakdown of law and justice in their state.

The bodies were cut down and placed on planks in the Floyd County Jail. Laura Reno was summoned from St. Ursula's Academy in Louisville to identify formally the bodies of her brothers. A mob surrounded the jailhouse when she arrived. The jeering and shouting died down as she hurried up the steps, her face white and drawn, her eyes red from weeping. When a deputy removed the handkerchiefs from the blue, swollen faces, Laura screamed, then rushed to the window, shaking her fist in a frenzy at the sea of upturned faces, as she shrieked over and over that the blood of her brothers was on all of them.[7]

Later that day the doors were opened and thousands streamed into the jail to pass the pine coffins. The roads leading into Seymour were jammed with buggies, horsemen, wagons, and men and women on foot. Special "excursion trains" chugged into the Seymour Station, engine bells clanging, as passengers fought among themselves to be the first to get off and run for the county jail.

John Reno recalled how he heard the news in prison: "The awful news came near dethroning my reason but I was kept at hard work which may have saved me. . . ."[8]

NOTHING IN IT

NO RENO TREASURE BURIED IN WINDSOR.

TALE IS A PIPE STORY

PAT O'NEILL TELLS THE HISTORY OF RENO GANG.

REMARKABLE ADVENTURES

But Justice Overtakes Them in Indiana, Where They Are Hanged by a Mob.

Pat O'Neill, head of the widely-known detective agency here, says the story of the burial of the Reno treasure in Windsor, published by an afternoon paper recently, is a pipe story.

"I remember the Renos and their remarkable adventures very well, although I was little more than a boy at the time. I was serving my apprenticeship as a detective in those days, under Allan Pinkerton, and was known in the business and by the crooks as 'The Pinkerton Kid.' In the Reno affair I acted as a shadow and general lookout under direction of Mr. Sullivan of Detroit. When the alleged Reno story was printed lately I had forgotten some of the points, but a talk with Will Pinkerton since then has brought the whole thing back to my mind. The Renos were almost as great a gang of crooks as ever landed 'swag,' and their career made a lasting impression on my mind.

BEGINNING OF THE GANG.

"It was in 1866 the gang began to get in its fine work. They were known as the 'Reno Brothers'—Sim, Bill and Frank—who lived in the vicinity of Brownstown, Ind., on a farm. The Reno family consisted of five brothers, the other two being called John and Clinton. The latter was known by the name of 'Honest Reno,' as he had never been mixed up in any of the troubles or scrapes his brothers had. In 1867 John Reno had been arrested for the robbery of the Davis county safe in Missouri and convicted and sentenced to the penitentiary for 20 years. His arrest was brought about by Allan Pinkerton, the head of Pinkerton's National Detective agency at that time, and he was acting for the Adams Express Co. under directions of Alfred Gaither and his assistant, L. C. Weir, the present president of the Adams Express Co. Mr. Gaither at that time was manager with headquarters at Cincinnati, O. The depredations of the Renos on the trains running through Indiana became so strong that the express and railroad companies combined to run the gang to earth.

"Reno and the rest of the gang got back to Indiana, where a fresh start was taken, and the next heard of them was the robbery of a train at Marshfield, Ind., on the Ohio and Mississippi road. This robbery was afterwards found to have been perpetrated by Frank Sim and Bill Reno, aided by Mike Rogers, Miles Ogle and Charles Anderson. Anderson was a professional burglar and made his headquarters in and around Detroit and Windsor. He lived in Windsor and Frank Reno had become acquainted with him during one of his raids through the country and had no trouble in inducing Anderson to go into an express robbery with him. They entered the car near Marshfield, seized the messenger and while the train was running at 30 miles an hour opened the express door and hurled the messenger from the train. Luckily he struck on a sand bank and was not badly hurt. This same messenger, only a short time ago in Portland, Ore., learning that Wm. A. Pinkerton was there, called and made him a visit to chat over old times with him.

"The investigation was put into the hands of Allan Pinkerton by Mr. Gaither, manager of the Adams Express Co., who detailed his assistant, L. C. Weir, to accompany the detectives and render them every assistance. Sim and Bill Reno had started from Seymour, but the detectives found them in Indianapolis, Ind., and placed them in custody. It was not deemed advisable to keep them at Seymour and they were accordingly taken to New Albany, where they were placed in jail.

"In the meantime Frank Reno and Anderson had been located at Windsor, as was also old Mike Rogers. As soon as the other brothers were placed in custody, these men were arrested on a warrant sworn out by Mr. Weir for assault with attempt to kill the messenger and highway robbery. Previous to this, they had been arrested by John Stanley, then connected with the Detroit police, but the Adams Express Co. did not believe in Stanley's sincerity and thought the arrest was made at Reno's instigation, for the purpose of bringing out what testimony could be shown against them. The men were, therefore, discharged, but rearrested again at the instigation of Allan Pinkerton and were taken before Judge Caron, of Windsor, who also discharged them, but they were immediately rearrested and taken before Magistrate McMickum of Windsor. The trial was postponed from day to day, witnesses were brought up for the defense, an alibi was attempted by them and they were ordered extradited.

"The prisoners were ably defended by John O'Connor, a noted lawyer of Windsor, who afterwards became attorney-general, and the prosecution was in the hands of Albert Prince, one of the ablest attorneys in western Canada. Thugs and thieves from all over the country had gathered in and around Windsor and did everything they could to break jail, not only in the interest of Reno and Anderson but of Morton and Thompson, who had robbed a New York Central train of over $30,000, and were being held at Windsor before McMickum for extradition."

ALLAN PINKERTON ASSAULTED.

"While the trials were going on Dick Barry, a noted burglar, made a desperate assault on Allan Pinkerton just as he was leaving a ferryboat at Detroit. Mr. Pinkerton grabbed the pistol in Barry's hand and got his finger over the trigger in such a way that Barry could not shoot. Mr. Jennings, captain of the boat, came to Mr. Pinkerton's help and succeeded in taking the gun away from Barry. Barry was afterwards allowed to escape from the Detroit prison, but was afterwards captured by William A. Pinkerton at Cincinnati and returned to Detroit for prosecution. The prisoner at last broke down, took the witness stand and stated that he was instigated in the attack on Pinkerton by William P. Wood and others who were acting for Reno.

"In the meantime an attempt was made to get Reno and Anderson out of Detroit in such a manner that the

"Early in the spring of 1868 Frank Reno associated himself with a desperate gang of safe burglars and made a tour through the west. This gang consisted of Frank Reno, Albert Perkins, Miles Ogle and old Mike Rogers. Mike Rogers was a prominent citizen of Council Bluffs, Ia., a pillar of the methodist church and a large property owner all over Iowa. Rogers' work consisted of going out and paying his taxes, when the taxes were due, and in doing so looking at the make of the safe, finding out whether there was any watchman and other particulars necessary for the gang to operate on. Then he would send to Seymour and bring on Frank Reno and the gang and rob the safe. In that way they robbed nearly all of the county treasurers' safes, which were a little better than the fire-proof safes of these days and it was very easy work for the burglars to get into them.

"In the spring of 1868 another one of the places visited by Frank Reno and his gang was Magnolia, Harrison county, Ia., where the safe was robbed of about $12,000; and Glenwood, Mills county, Ia., where the safe was robbed of about $9,000. After the time of the Harrison county robbery the matter was placed in the hands of Allan Pinkerton, who detailed Wm. A. Pinkerton and another operative to go to the scene of the burglary and investigate it. Magnolia is situated about 35 miles from Council Bluffs. The two detectives soon found that the safe had been torn open by burglars, and they got a trace of the men stealing a handcar on the Northwestern railroad, going in the direction of Council Bluffs. They abandoned the handcar about six or seven miles out on account of some machinery breaking and threw it in a ditch and started to walk to Council Bluffs. Wm. A. Pinkerton, then quite a young man, decided to follow the trail up by inquiries among people who had seen the men after they left the handcar. On arriving in Council Bluffs all track was lost of them, and although it was known that detectives were in town, it was kept out of the papers and everything went quietly.

"A saloonkeeper at Council Bluffs was kept under watch, the object being to connect him with old Mike Rogers, and this led to the watching of his house. On the morning of the Glenwood, Mills county, robbery, his house was raided, three strange men having been seen to approach the house. The men were arrested and turned out to be Mike Rogers, Frank Reno, Albert Perkins and Miles Ogle. The latter later became a very notorious counterfeiter, said to be the cleverest in the United States. At the present time he is serving a long term in the penitentiary for counterfeiting treasury notes. After getting into the house Mr. Pinkerton noticed in the kitchen a sudden flash of fire from the stove. On lifting a lid the stove was found to be full of money, which had been put on a smouldering fire when the house was raided. The notes would have been burned up had not the detective's quick eye discovered the fire. The money was pulled out. only a small amount being destroyed by the fire. Among the money was some torn bills which had been pasted together by the cashier the day before.

THEY BREAK JAIL.

"The men were taken to Glenwood and confined in jail. They were positively identified by parties who had seen them in the vicinity the day before and they were also identified for the robbery of the Harrison county safe at Magnolia, Ia., about a week previous. Frank Reno was identified by Wm. A. Pinkerton, as was also Ogle and Perkins. Rogers had always stood well in the vicinity of Council Bluffs and this was the beginning of his downfall. They were all held for trial on the charge of burglarizing the two safes, but on the first day of April the jailer at Glenwood discovered a hole in the wall of the jail through which his prisoners had escaped, after taking a piece of chalk and writing 'April fool' on every available place in the jail.

For years after the Renos had vanished into folklore treasure hunters searched for their legendary buried loot. A Detroit paper in the 1890s quoted a lawman as describing the treasure as "a pipe dream." *The James D. Horan Civil War and Western Americana Collection*

That Christmas week the vigilantes voted to complete their work. Posters appeared in and around Seymour listing all members of the gang and ordering them to leave town or be strung up. Hysteria gripped the community; officials known to have been friendly to the gang were warned they were being watched while highwaymen, posing as vigilantes, killed, robbed, and looted.

Then England, through the Governor-General of Canada, demanded an apology "for the shocking and indefensible lynching" of the Renos. Diplomatic relations were strained while legal experts predicted Great Britain would eliminate the extradition clause in its treaty with the United States, "thus providing in Canada a haven for American outlaws and desperadoes."

A bill which would give federal protection for extradited criminals was hurriedly introduced by an Illinois senator. Secretary of State Seward enclosed a copy of the bill with his official apology, which soothed Downing Street.[9]

Gradually the Renos passed into outlaw history. From time to time in the 1870s and 1880s, there were rumors of buried Reno gold. Men with shovels, picks, and lanterns dug in the forests along the railroad tracks outside of Seymour but admitted "all they got were blisters."

THE JAMES-YOUNGER GANG

Jesse Woodson James

As Theodore Roosevelt wrote, "Jesse W. James is America's Robin Hood." He will always be the boy eternal, the merry-eyed outlaw who rides across the western plains on a magnificent bay, the bag of gold stolen from the hated railroads slung across his saddle horn while behind him, helplessly outclassed, comes the lumbering posse. He steals only from the rich to help the poor. Minutes after the sneering landlord takes the last dollar from the weeping widow, he is robbed by Jesse, who gallantly returns the precious dollars to the grateful woman as her children look on, their shining faces filled with love and admiration.

It is an image that has lasted for more than a century. Countless such stories have been sworn to by old men; pioneers have testified to Jesse's humility, his skill with horse and Navy Colt, his tenderness, and his love of his fellow man.

It is the stuff of a nation's myth and legend, and while attractive, it is distorted and without foundation. In reality Jesse was a thief and a callous killer. His unarmed victims included bank cashiers, citizens caught on the street during a robbery, a train conductor, a young stone cutter shot in the back. It should be pointed out that in one train robbery Jesse ordered the tracks removed to derail the train. The engineer's alertness and skill saved the train, but he was scalded to death when the engine toppled over.

As for James's Robin Hood qualities, there is no evidence he ever robbed a

BASIL DUKE'S STORY.

Basil Duke, of St. Louis, attended college with Robert James, the father of the notorious Jesse and Frank. " I see by some of the papers," said the Colonel, "that the James boys came of bad parents. That is all wrong. It was in 1840 that I attended college at Georgetown, Scott county, Ky., and Robert James, the father of the boys, was then one of my classmates. The institution was presided over by Howard Malcolm, and was then the only Baptist College in the State. At this time Robert James was 21 years of age, one of the oldest boys in the college, and he gave out that he had been sent there by the trustees of a church at Russellville, Ky. The boys at school looked upon James as a high-minded, honest fellow. He was a general favorite and much esteemed. The boys at first called him Bob James but after a while this was abbreviated until he became universally known as Bob Jim. He had been sent there to finish his education. It was the custom in those days for congregations who could not afford to hire a minister to call upon the college students. James was a good speaker, and was often favored with a call. It was while he was preaching in one of the neighboring churches that he met Miss Cole, a bright and pretty orphan girl of 16. Her parents had left her a neat property valued at $10,000, a big sum in those days, and she was looked upon as a good catch for any one. James proved the lucky suitor, married her quietly, and a little later announced the fact to his classmates. They were married in the fall of 1841, and a year later Frank was born. His mother's parents were in life looked upon as very respectable people, and she was always considered a good girl. In 1843 I left the college at Russellville and went to Yale. Upon my return from the latter institution I heard that Robert James and wife had gone to Missouri to live. She is the woman they now call Mrs. Samuels."

As for Mrs. Samuels, he said she had never shown herself to be a bad woman until incited by officers throwing a lighted hand-grenade into her house, which exploded, killed her little boy and mutilated her.

An interview with the famous Confederate cavalry officer Basil Duke, who recalled his college classmate Robert James, father of the outlaws, and their mother, Zerelda Cole, who James married in the fall of 1841. *The James D. Horan Civil War and Western Americana Collection*

landlord to save a widow's home; Jesse firmly believed charity began at home.

He was a strange man with a dark streak of violence running through his makeup. He was a born leader but psychically lonely. As the old ballad goes:

"He was born one day in the County of Clay and came from a solitary race."

He was poised—even when relieving his victims of their rings, stickpins, and watches—and at times showed a wry sense of humor.

He called outlawry "the business," and as one of his former riders recalled, he was a leader who shared his secrets with no man:

"He told me, 'It is better for only one man to know my business—even my wife doesn't know any of my business. It is not good to let too many know the details. . . .' "

It was also apparent that he gloried in his deeds. Shortly after Bob Ford had killed Jesse James in St. Jo that April day in 1882, the Ford brothers gave a series of marvelous interviews in which they described the legendary outlaw chief as eagerly reading the newspapers for details of what he called "my exploits." Jesse was killed on the eve of what he predicted to the Fords "will be one of my greatest exploits," the robbery of the Platte City Bank.

"It's a fine scheme and will be published all over the country as another daring robbery," Charlie Ford quoted Jesse as telling him.

Zerelda Samuel, mother of Frank and Jesse James, on the porch of her farmhouse. Note the missing arm blown off by the "bomb" thrown into the farmhouse by the posse. *Courtesy Collection of Fred and Jo Mazzulla, owners of the original negative*

Very rare photograph of a teen-age Jesse James. *Courtesy Jackson County Historical Society. Photo copyrighted by the Jackson County Historical Society*

An early photograph of the Samuel homestead near Kearney, Clay County, Missouri. *The James D. Horan Civil War and Western Americana Collection*

Jesse James, a seventeen-year-old Civil War guerilla under William "Bloody Bill" Anderson. *The James D. Horan Civil War and Western Americana Collection*

Fletcher Taylor, a lieutenant of "Bloody Bill" Anderson and Frank and Jesse James. Taken in 1864. *The James D. Horan Civil War and Western Americana Collection*

When Charlie asked what would happen if someone gave the alarm, as had happened at the disastrous Northfield raid, Jesse casually told him:

"We will shoot down anyone who interferes and if necessary clean the entire town out. . . ."[1]

For all his cold-bloodedness, no man questioned Jesse's courage.

"He feared nothing," his uncle, Wood Hite, told an interviewer, "nothing at all."

And of Jesse's philosophy, Hite quoted the outlaw:

"He has said to me often, 'If you hear they have captured me alive, say it's not true. They can kill me but they will never get me otherwise.'"[2]

Jesse sincerely loved his wife, Zerelda, Zee, or Josie, as she was variously called, whom he had married after a storybook romance.

Jesse had been severely wounded by Union soldiers when he attempted to surrender, probably at Lexington, Missouri. He fled into the woods and survived the night by dragging himself to a creek where he constantly bathed the wound in his chest. In the morning he made his way to where a farmer was plowing and the man took him in and passed him on to friends. When he got

A youthful Jesse James. *Courtesy State Historical Society of Missouri*

left: Arch Clement, who rode under "Bloody Bill" Anderson, was with Frank and Jesse James at the killings of the Union soldiers at Centralia, Boone County, in September 1864. Clement is credited with having killed the first of the twenty-five unarmed Union soldiers on furlough. Clement is on the left, Frank James on the right. *The James D. Horan Civil War and Western Americana Collection*

stronger he was put in a wagon and taken to Rulo, Nebraska, where his mother and stepfather had settled.

Weeks passed, and when the wound did not get better, Jesse begged his mother to take him back to Missouri. She finally consented and Jesse was put aboard a riverboat and taken down the Missouri to what is now North Kansas City. They stopped at a boardinghouse of his uncle, John Mimms. His special nurse was his cousin, Zee, pretty and dark-haired. Before Jesse and his mother left for Clay County, Jesse and Zee were engaged to be married. Following a hazardous nine-year courtship between stagecoach and train robberies, they were finally married when he was the most wanted man in the West. They had two children.

After he was killed by Bob Ford one newspaper story described him as a "cruel, lustful man" who had fathered more than one child in a series of backwoods romances, but that is doubtful; adultery was not one of his sins.

Jesse and Zee remained together for all the time he was "on the dodge," Zee gathering up the children in the night after Jesse hurried home with news that a stranger had been seen in the town where he was hiding out. She would help him pack their few belongings and hitch up the horses to move down some lonely back road to seek another hideout.

Evidently Zee never had much to pack; when a reporter visited a home Jesse had rented under his favorite alias, "Tom Howard," the landlord told him the outlaw and his family had moved in with only a few chairs and some clothes.

"The woman [Zee] told me she was going to fix the place up after they settled," he said. "But they never had much as far as I could see."

Thief, killer, or the innocent boy who had been warped by the savage Civil War which had split his state into two ruthless camps, Jesse was a natural leader. Men followed him gladly, eagerly, into the small-town banks or lonely railroad cuts where the gang stopped the trains in the classic manner: using rocks piled on the tracks and having the telegraph operator, a cocked pistol to his head, wave a red lantern in the darkness.

The courage of this ruthless, handsome man called Dingus by his friends was never doubted by his men. Nor was his skill with horses. His marksmanship, however, never came up to the reputation. In his confession Dick Liddil, one of Jesse's favorite riders, described how Jesse fired six unsuccessful shots at a man who apparently didn't care to be robbed, missed a point-blank shot at a cashier, and during the Gallatin train robbery fired three times at a conductor and missed.[3] At Northfield, farmers and townspeople—one a young medical student using an ancient musket—easily emptied the saddles of Jesse's gang until the outlaw raiders fled, leaving behind two dead riders and an unarmed citizen.

Tales which have become fact by repeated telling depict strangers and friends gladly yielding their best horses when they heard Jesse needed fast transportation. But according to Liddil, Jesse was an excellent horse thief, stealing many horses "while the owner was sleeping," some from the stables of his Clay County neighbors.

There is little doubt that Jesse was very close to his mother. He always fled back to her protection when the manhunters were on his trail. Liddil tells an amusing story of how Jesse called off a train robbery because he had a toothache. The bandit chieftain, whose name was so feared that his exploits held back immigration into the Middle Border states, rode back to the Samuel farmhouse so his mother could treat his aching molar.[4]

Aside from the romantic pageantry there is an important aspect to the saga of Jesse James and his gang. For years their crimes were campaign issues which split Missouri's Democratic Party, composed of pro-Confederate and pro-Union men. Indirectly the Jameses and Youngers also influenced national elections. In the 1870s the Republicans—ironically then called the Radicals—had a fragile hold on important political posts; it was important that as many states as possible be won. In an attempt to drive a wedge between the northern and southern Democrats, the Republicans gleefully used every state convention to blast the Democratic administration for its incompetency in ridding the state of banditry.

The nation's press took up the cry and Missouri was soon known to the eastern press as "The Outlaw State," "Poor Old Missouri," "The Outlaw's Paradise," or "Haven for Outlaws."

John Newman Edwards, the Missouri newspaperman who created the Robin Hood legend for Jesse James. After the robbery of the Kansas State Fair, Edwards compared Jesse and his men to the knights of King Arthur's Round Table. *The James D. Horan Civil War and Western Americana Collection*

The careers of two important Middle Border politicians, Governor Thomas T. Crittenden and William Wallace, were severely damaged by the roles they played in the life and times of Jesse James. After Bob Ford, "that dirty little coward," killed Jesse to collect the ten-thousand-dollar reward put up by the railroads, Crittenden, a Democrat, was severely censured even by his own party. He lost the nomination for reelection and any presidential ambitions he had vanished. In 1885 Crittenden, a member of an old and distinguished Missouri family, was also refused a diplomatic post by President Cleveland. The incredible explanation given by the White House was that "he had bargained with the Fords for the killing of Jesse James."[5]

Wallace, the courageous backwoods prosecutor who broke up the Jameses and Youngers by skillfully using one, then another member of the band as state's witnesses, was refused his party's nomination for a congressional seat.

Jesse's principal and perennial defender was John Newman Edwards, a Missouri newspaperman who more than anyone helped to mold Jesse's Robin Hood image. In the 1850s Edwards, a Virginian, was editor of the *Lexington Expositor*. In 1862 he joined General Joe Shelby's command and became his adjutant. Edwards was also historian of the guerilla movement; his *Noted Guerillas or the Warfare of the Border*, published in 1877, was reverently read and reread by generations of Missourians; the florid prose, however, contains a number of errors. Edwards has Jesse James riding into Lawrence with Quantrill's guerillas and sparing the life of a Union soldier on the plea of a blushing and trembling young girl.

It makes a fine story but historians have proven Jesse was never at the terrifying sack of Lawrence.[6]

Edwards also developed the "they-drove-us-to-it" theme, picturing the former guerillas-turned-outlaws as helpless men forced into a life of crime by a relentless, unforgiving enemy. He neglected to include the many former guerillas who became law-abiding citizens, businessmen, and even law enforcement officials.

So protective was Edwards of Jesse and Frank James and the Youngers that he once sent a telegram to his city editor from Jefferson City, the state's capital, ordering him not to carry any more stories of how the James gang had robbed the Iron Mountain Railroad train at Gads Hill, a hundred miles south of St. Louis. The report that the James boys had committed the robbery, he wired, "was remarkable for two things—utter stupidity and total untruth."[7]

When Edwards took over the *Kansas City Times*, the newspaper became virtually a house organ for the Jameses and Youngers.

Edwards released a flood of print after Jesse was killed by Bob Ford and lashed out editorially at any of the state's newspaper editors who praised Governor Crittenden's successful if unorthodox method of getting rid of a menace.

Along with his maudlin editorials praising the dead outlaw leader as a courageous patriot struck down by a Judas, Edwards started a public fund for the James widow and her children. He was outraged when another newspaper started a fund for the widow of William Westfall, the unarmed conductor shot in the back by Jesse.

In the end, Edwards was triumphant. He canonized Jesse James, firmly entrenched him as America's Robin Hood, and defeated his political enemies.

Jesse's bank and train robberies are part of our folklore, woven into ballad and poems. They began in 1866 and ended in 1882 when he was killed. Most of the details of the early frontier bank robberies are obscure, but we know what happened on that cold afternoon of February 13, 1866, when Jesse led his howling bravos into the small town of Liberty, Missouri, to rob his first bank.

In 1936 WPA workers found an original account written by Greenup Bird, the bank's cashier, shortly after the event happened.[8] There have been many estimates of the amount taken from the vault but Bird claimed a total of $57,072.64.

It was the first peacetime daylight robbery of an American bank; Confederates had staged a daylight raid on the St. Albans, Vermont, banks as an act of war.

As Jesse led his gang out of the town, one of his riders shot and killed a college student walking down the street. The gang soon outdistanced the posse; no one ever attempted to collect the ten-thousand-dollar reward offered for the outlaws and killers.

Three years after the robbery Mrs. Zerelda Samuel, mother of the James brothers, came into the bank and attempted to pay off a loan with revenue stamps taken in the robbery. It was reported that she became "indignant" when she was forced to pay cash.

Statement of Greenup Bird, Cashier of the Liberty, Missouri, National Bank, February 13, 1866:

About 2 o'clock of the afternoon of Tuesday 13th instant whilst I was writing at this desk and William Bird, my son, was writing at the desk on my left, two men entered the Bank dressed in soldier's blue overcoats—They both came up to the stove, one of them turned and went up to the place at which we receive and pay out money, and said he wanted a bill changed. William Bird left his desk and went to the counter to change it. On his arrival at the counter, the man on the opposite side drew a revolver and presented it at William Bird and demanded the money of the bank. The man jumped on and over the counter as also the other man, drawing his revolver followed over the counter, one presenting his revolver at Wm. Bird and the other man presenting his revolver at me, told us if we made any noise they would shoot us down, demanded all the money in the bank and that they wanted it quick. Wm. Bird not moving, one of the robbers struck him on the back with his pistol, said to him, "D——you be quick" and shoved him to the open vault door and followed him in—drew out a cotton sack and made Wm. Bird put the coin on the lower shelf of the safe in the sack (this coin was special deposits of gold and silver in rolls, bundles and bags).

The other robber had me in tow outside of the vault, and demanded the greenbacks, 7-30's [post-Civil War bills] and N. M. bonds, and told the robber in the vault to put them in the sack and to be in a hurry. The robber in the vault told Wm. Bird to remain in there, the robber at my side then told me to go in also—I hesitated and began to parley. He told me if I did not go in instantly he would shoot me down. I went in. They asked for the keys to the vault door. We told them they were in the door. They shut the door on us—This is the last we saw of them until we got out of the vault. After they left the vault door, I found it was not locked—I opened the door a short distance to see if the robbers were out of the house—Found they were out. We then opened the door, rushed to the front window, hoisted it and gave the alarm. As we were going from the vault door to the window, I saw several men on horse back pass the window, going east, shooting off pistols.

The Liberty bank robbery was the beginning; there would be many more banks, trains, and stagecoaches held up by Jesse James and his gang during the sixteen years they reigned as America's legendary outlaws.

Curiously, during this period when he was the most wanted man in the West, Jesse was also an indefatigable writer of letters to the editor. His literary efforts usually appeared in John Newman Edwards's *Kansas City Times*, but his letters were also published in other Missouri and Tennessee newspapers. It makes a dramatic picture to visualize this dangerous man laboring over words and phrases with the stub of a pencil in the glow of a lantern or a campfire.

The original letters have long since vanished, but when they were published an editor's note usually attested to their authenticity. After Jesse was killed by Bob Ford, his brother Charlie told an interviewer he was present when the bandit chief wrote his longest letter in Deer Lodge, Montana Territory, where they were hiding out. It was published in the *St. Louis Dispatch* and picked up by other newspapers around the state and in the Eastern press. Ford also claimed that Jesse liked to admire his published work and bought at least three papers every day: "the St. Louis papers and the *Police News.*"

The letters are surprisingly well written; curiously, the smaller words are misspelled, the larger ones are not. They contained a great deal of self-righteousness and much hell and brimstone. Crimes are indignantly denied, detectives are denounced, and names of witnesses who could offer alibis are supplied—usually kin and well-known sympathizers of the gang.

The Jameses and Youngers rode hard during 1868-69. In March of 1868 they robbed the banking house of Nimrod & Co., in Russellville, Kentucky, wounding the owner of the bank during the holdup. The following year they

Frank and Jesse James. The Denver Public Library reports that this rare tintype came from the archives of the *Record-Stockman*, a livestock publication in Denver. *Courtesy Denver Public Library, Western History Department*

raided the Richmond, Missouri, bank, leaving behind three dead, including the mayor of the town and his son. The next winter the gang held up the Daviess Savings Bank. During the robbery one man, said to be Jesse, shot and killed the unarmed cashier, John W. Sheets.

The murders and robberies aroused the frontier. Two men identified as members of the band were taken from their cells and lynched. Posses searched the borders and all signs pointed to Clay County and the James-Younger band as suspects.

Jesse's first two efforts, both open letters to Missouri's Governor Joseph W. McClurg denying that he or his brother, Frank, had taken any part in the robberies or killings, were published in the *Liberty Tribune* in the summer of 1870.[9]

The Letters of Jesse James

(Liberty Tribune, June 24, 1870)

June, 1870

GOVERNOR McCLURG:

DEAR SIR: I and my brother Frank are charged with the crime of killing the cashier and robbing the bank at Gallatin, Mo., Dec. 7, 1869. I can prove by some of the best men in Missouri, where I was the day of the robbery and the day previous to it, but I well know if I want to submit to an arrest I would be

Dated *Jefferson City Mo Dec 24th 1869*

Received at *Independence Mo Dec*

To *Sheriff of Jackson Co*
                                        Independence

You will at once organize arm and equip as Militia thirty (30) or more men and aid Tomilson Deputy Sheriff of Clay County if called on in capturing or killing Frank James and Jesse James or hold such force in readyness to aid you in such capture or Killing if they be found in your county, the State will pay expense of force for actual service. And five hundred (500) Dollars for the capture of or Killing of each. I write by mail

50 Paid, 4.25   *J. W. McClurg*

The Nimrod Long and Company Bank, Russellville, Kentucky, held up by the Jameses and Youngers on March 20, 1868. Long, who fought with the bandits, received a scalp wound when one of the outlaws fired at him point-blank. *The James D. Horan Civil War and Western Americana Collection*

Telegram from Missouri's Governor Joseph W. McClurg on Christmas Eve, 1869, ordering the sheriff of Jackson County to organize and equip a band of thirty men "or more" to assist the Clay County Deputy Sheriff John S. Thomason in arresting Jesse and Frank James. The governor also offered a state reward of five hundred dollars for the pair. *Courtesy State Historical Society of Missouri*

mobbed and hanged without a trial. The past is sufficient to show that bushwackers have been arrested in Missouri since the war, charged with bank robbery, and they most all have been mobbed without trials. I will cite you to the case of Thomas Little, of Lafayette County, Mo. A few days after the bank was robbed at Richmond, in 1867, Mr. Little was arrested in St. Louis, charged with being one of the party who perpetrated the deed. He was sent from St. Louis to Warrensburg under heavy guard. As soon as the parties arrived there, they found out that he, (Mr. Little) could prove, by the citizens of Dover, that he was innocent of the charge—as soon as these scoundrels found out he was innocent a mob was raised, broke in the jail, took him out and hanged him.

Governor, when I can get a fair trial, I will surrender myself to the civil authorities of Missouri. But I will never surrender to be mobbed by a set of blood-thirsty poltroons. It is true that during the war I was a Confederate soldier and fought under the Black Flag, but since then I have lived a respectable citizen and obeyed the laws of the United States to the best of my knowledge. The

Frank James in about 1871. *Courtesy State Historical Society of Missouri*

authorities of Gallatin say the reason that led them to suspect me, was that the mare left at Gallatin by the robbers was identified as belonging to me. That is false. I can prove that I sold the mare previous to the robbery. It is true that I fought Deputy Sheriff Thomason of Clay County but was not my brother with me when we had the fight. I do not think that it violated the law when I fought Thomason as his posse refused to tell me who they were.

Three different statements have been published in reference to the fight I had with Thomason.

They are all a pack of falsehoods. Deputy Sheriff Thomason has never yet given any report of the fight that I have seen. I am personally acquainted with Oscar Thomason the deputy's son, but when the shooting began his face was so muffled up with fur that I did not recognize him. But if I did violate the law when I fought Thomason, I am perfectly willing to abide by it.*

But as to them mobbing me for a crime that I am innocent of, that is played out. As soon as I think I can get a fair trial I will surrender myself to the civil authorities of Missouri, and prove to the world that I am innocent of the crime charged against me.

Respectfully,
Jesse W. James.

(Liberty Tribune, July 15, 1870)

July, 1870

GOVERNOR McCLURG—

Dear Sir: Since my letter to you of June, I have been influenced by my friends to prove an alibi and to let those men know who accused me of the Gallatin robbery, and who tried to swear away the life of an innocent man.

---

*After the Gallatin robbery, a posse led by Deputy Sheriff John S. Thomason and his son, Oscar, raided the Samuel farmhouse. Frank and Jesse, mounted on fine horses, burst out of the barn. Only the deputy's horse could clear the fence and he pursued the pair alone. When he dismounted to aim and fire at Frank and Jesse, his horse bolted. Jesse killed the horse and Thomason was forced to walk back to the Samuel place and borrow a horse to ride back to town.

Governor, the testimony of my witnesses will be published in the column of the Kansas City *Times* in two or three weeks and it will be such as you and all men can believe.

> Respectfully,
> *Jesse W. James*

On April 29, 1872, five men robbed the Deposit Bank in Columbia, Kentucky. The cashier who tried to give the alarm was shot dead. Five months later three mounted men stole the gate receipts of the Kansas City fair in view of thousands of spectators. Jesse and Frank James and Cole Younger were identified as the leaders of the robber band. In the fall of 1872, the *Kansas City Times* published Jesse's third letter.[10]

(Kansas City Times, Oct. 20, 1872)

Jackson County, Mo., Oct. 15, 1872.

TO THE EDITOR OF THE KANSAS CITY TIMES:

I have just read an article in the Independence *Herald* charging Frank and myself with robbing the ticket office at the Kansas City Fair Exposition Grounds. This charge is baseless and without foundation, and as you have always published all the articles I have sent you for publication, I will now write a few lines on this subject, and here is what I have got to say to the public.

I can prove where I was at the very hour the gate was robbed, and fortunately for me there were several persons close by with whom I am very well acquainted and who will testify that I was miles away from Kansas City. I will meet Marshal Page and any two men who say they knew the robbers and convince them that I am innocent.

The *Herald* further says that Frank and myself have been in Fort Osage Township very frequently during the spring and summer. As for myself I have been in Jackson County for all of the summer and have been hiding from no one. I have been in Independence frequently, attending to legitimate business and have harmed no man and taken nothing from no man.

As the matter now stands, however, I cannot be arrested. A man charged with robbery these days [is] most invariably set upon by a mob after he is captured and hung or murdered without judge or jury. If I could have a fair trial I could prove myself innocent before any jury in the state.

It is also generally talked about in Liberty, Clay County, that Mr. James Chiles of Independence said that it was me and Cole and John Younger who robbed the gate for he saw us and talked to us on the road to Kansas City, the day of September 26th. I know very well that Mr. Chiles did not say so for he has not seen me for three months and I will be under many obligations to him if he will drop a few lines to the public and let it know he never said any such thing. If the civil authorities have anything to say in reply to this, let them answer through the TIMES.*

> Very Respectfully,
> *Jesse W. James.*

*A few days after the robbery of the Fair's receipts of $978, Edwards wrote an editorial, "The Chivalry of Crime," comparing the outlaws to the Knights of the Round Table: "It was as though three bandits had come to us with the halo of medieval chivalry upon their garments and shown us how the things were done that poets sing of." Newman forgot to remind his readers that a small child had been severely wounded by one of the bandits.

J. J. Chiles, mentioned in Jesse's letter as having identified Jesse and Cole Younger as the Fair's robbers, promptly wrote to the same editor vigorously denying he was an eyewitness to the crime or had seen Jesse or Cole. One can detect Mr. Chiles's nervousness.[11]

(Kansas City Times, Oct. 25, 1872)

A STATEMENT FROM J. J. CHILES

Independence, Oct. 23, 1872.

TO THE KANSAS CITY *TIMES*:

A letter from Jesse W. James, published in your newspaper, makes the statement that it is reported in Liberty, Clay County country, that I saw Jesse James, Cole and John Younger, on Sept. 26, last, and as Mr. James requests a communication on this subject, I will now state I had not seen either of said parties on that date or at any time during the Exposition at Kansas City. I should not have appeared in print had not the request been made and my name used, as I am engaged in attending to my own business, and hope the good people of Clay County and elsewhere will also report the truth concerning me, as I hold myself responsible at all times for my acts and statements.

Respectfully,

J. J. Chiles.

In the fall of 1874, Cole Younger also picked up the pen to defend himself in the public press. On November 30 he wrote "a short history of the notorious Cole Younger" to a friend, L. ("Clurg") Jones, who delivered it to the *St. Louis Republican.*

While containing the usual alibis, the letter reveals for the first time the rivalry and enmity existing between Jesse and Cole. They were a study in contrasts: Jesse, secretive, a man of suppressed violence; while Cole was the happy-go-lucky extrovert, even in the serious business of outlawry. More important, there could be only one leader, and that spot Jesse was determined to fill.

In his letter Cole talks of his brother, "poor John," killed a few months before in the gun battle with Pinkerton operative Captain Louis Lull. However, he neglected to add that John had been wanted in Texas for the murder of a deputy sheriff whom he had killed in a jailbreak. He had originally been arrested while drunk for shooting too close to the head of an old man.

One can visualize the harassed and very worried Mr. Chiles reading Cole's letter.[12]

Cole Younger's Letter

(St. Louis Republican, Monday, Nov. 30, 1874)

[From the Pleasant Hill (Mo.) Review]

MR. EDITOR: Supposing that your readers might be interested in a short history of the notorious Cole Younger, one written by himself and sent to me to exonerate himself from the many crimes laid to his charge, I herewith send it for publication, knowing it to be truth, so far as it goes. This is a verbatim copy of the original which I have in my possession.

E.JONES

DEAR CLURG: You may use this letter in your way. I will give you this outline and sketch of my whereabouts and actions at the time of certain robberies with which I am charged.

At the time of certain robberies I was gathering cattle in Ellis County, Texas—cattle that I bought from Pleas. Taylor and Rector. This can be proven by both of them; also by Sheriff Barkley and sixty other respectable men of that county. I brought the cattle to Kansas that fall and remained in St. Clair County until February. I then went to Arkansas and returned to St. Clair County about the first of May. I went to Kansas where our cattle were, in Woodson County, at Colonel Ridge's—or Rayes—I can't make out the name—during the summer I was either in St. Clair, Jackson or Kansas, but as there was no robbery committed that summer it makes no difference where I was.

The fair grounds at Kansas City were robbed that fall. I was in Jackson County at the time. I left R. R. Rose's that morning, went down the Independence Road, stopped at Dr. Noland's and got some pills. Brother John was with me. I went through Independence and then to Ace Webb's. There I took dinner and then went to Dr. L. W. Twiman's. Staid there until after supper then went on to Silas Hudspeth's and staid all night; this was the day the gate was robbed at Kansas City.

We crossed the river at Blue Mills and went down the other side; our business was to see E. P. West. He was not at home but the family will remember that we were there. We crossed on the bridge, staid in the city all night, and the next morning we rode through the city. I met several of my friends there; among them was Bob Hudspeth. We then returned to the Six-Mile country by way of Independence. At Big Blue we met James Chiles and had a long talk with him. I saw several friends standing at or near the gate and they all said they didn't know any of the party that did the robbing. John nor I were accused of the crime for several days.

My name would never have been used in connection with the affair had not Jesse W. James, for some cause, best known to himself, published in the Kansas City *Times*, a letter stating that John, myself and he were accused of the robbery. Where he got his authority I do not know, but one thing I do know, he had none from me. We were not on good terms at the time, nor haven't been for several years. From that time on, mine and John's name have been connected with the James Brothers. John hadn't seen either of them for eighteen months before his death. And as for A. C. McCoy, John had never seen him in his life. I know A. C. McCoy during the war but haven't seen him since, not withstanding the Appleton City papers say he has been with us in the county for two years.

Now, if any respectable man in the county will say he ever saw A. C. McCoy with me or John, I will say no more; or if any respectable man will say he ever saw anyone with us that fitted the description of A. C. McCoy, than I will be silent and never more plead innocent.

McCoy is 48 or 49 years old, 6 feet and over high, dark hair and blue eyes and low forehead.

Poor John, he has been hunted down and shot like a wild beast and never was a boy more innocent. But there is a day coming when the secrets of all hearts will be laid open before that All-seeing eye and every one of our lives will be scrutinized, then will his skirts be as white as the driven snow while those of his accusers will be dark, dark, doubly dark.

I will come to the St. Geneveve robbery. At that time I was in St. Clair County. I don't remember dates but Mr. Murphy, one of our neighbors, was sick about that time and I was with him regularly, where I met with some of the neighbors every day. Doctor Lewis was his physician.

As to the Iowa train robbery—I have forgotten the date—I was in St. Clair at the time and I had the pleasure of attending preaching the evening previous to the robbery at Monegaw Springs. There were fifty or a hundred persons there who will testify in any court that John and I were there. I will give you the names of some of them: Samuel Bruce, John Wilson, Jas. Van Allen, Parson Smith and lady; Helvin Fickle and lady of Greenton Valley were attending the springs at that time and either of them will testify to the above, for John and I sat in front of Smith while he was preaching and had the pleasure of his company for a few minutes, together with his lady, and Mr. and Mrs. Fickle, after services. They live at Greenton Valley, Lafayette Co. and their evidence would be taken in the court of heaven.

As there was no other robbery committed until January, I will come to the time. About the first of December, 1873, I arrived in Carroll Parish, Louisiana. I staid there until the 8th of February, 1874. I and Brother staid at Wm. Dickerson's, near Floyd. Dickerson was master of a Masonic lodge, and during the time the Shrevesport stage and the Hot Springs stage were robbed; also the Gad's Hill robbery. Now, if the governor, or anyone else wants to satisfy himself, in regard to the above, he can write to the Masonic Fraternity, Floyd, Carroll Parish Louisiana. I hope the leading journals will investigate the matter, and then if they find that I have misrepresented anything, they can show me up to the world as being guilty but if they find it as I have stated they will surely have no objection to state the facts as they are.

Now Clurg, you can appeal to the governor in your own language, and if he will send respectable men to investigate the above, and is not satisfied of my innocence, then he can offer the reward for Thos. Coleman Younger, and if he finds me to be innocent, he can make a statement to that effect.

I write this hurriedly and I suppose I have given outline enough. I want you to take pains and write a long letter for me and sign my name in full.

THOS. COLEMAN YOUNGER

The first train robbery committed by the James-Younger gang took place near Council Bluffs, Iowa, on the evening of July 21, 1873.

As the Chicago, Rock Island & Pacific Railroad train approached, Jesse's riders used a hawser to pull the track away from its bed. When the engine's headlight illuminated the scene the engineer slammed his brakes in reverse, but the momentum of the heavy engine pulled it across the open section and it toppled over, scalding the engineer to death.

The hooded outlaws swept out of the darkness, yelling and firing their Navy Colts. The disappointed gang discovered only two thousand dollars in the express safe; they had just missed a hundred-thousand-dollar gold shipment. Jesse led his men through the cars, cursing the passengers, who gladly dropped watches, rings, and cash into the wheat sack. The band left with a volley of shots and shouted farewells.

Posses trailed the gang to Clay County and once again the outlaws were identified as the James and Younger gang; the man in command was Jesse.

In January 1874 Jesse sent the *St. Louis Dispatch* a letter written from Deer

Blank No. 1.

THE WESTERN UNION TELEGRAPH COMPANY.

The rules of this Company require that all messages received for transmission, shall be written on the message blanks of the Company, under and subject to the conditions printed thereon, which conditions have been agreed to by the sender of the following message.

ANSON STAGER, Gen'l Sup't, } Chicago, Ill.   WILLIAM ORTON, Pres't, GEO. H. MUMFORD, Sec'y. } New York.

No. of Message,

Dated _Jefferson City Mo._ 187__

Received at _North East cor. Third and Olive Sts._

St. Louis, _Feby 11_

To _Stephens Despatch of_

Put nothing more in about Gads Hill the report of Yesterday was remarkable for two things utter stupidly & total untruth

J. N. Edwards

A telegram from John Newman Edwards to Walter B. Stevens, his city editor, ordering him not to publish any more stories about the Jameses and Youngers. They had been accused by the newspaper of staging the train robbery on January 31, 1874, at Gad's Hill, a small station on the Iron Mountain about one hundred miles south of St. Louis. *Courtesy State Historical Society of Missouri*

Lodge, Montana Territory, which was picked up by the Liberty *Tribune.* For the first time he talked of surrendering with Frank if Governor Silas Woodson would promise them "a fair trial."[13]

(Liberty Tribune, Jan. 9, 1874)

TO THE EDITOR: Perhaps nothing that I might say in the way of denial would change any man's opinion of me, either one way or the other, but this I do say, that neither Frank or myself have been in Missouri since the 3rd day of October, 1873, nor nearer Missouri than Denver City. Neither one of us was in Cass County at the time mentioned, nor at any time within the past year. I am guiltless of this Cass county store robbery as a child unborn, and know nothing whatever of it until I saw it in a newspaper.

We have been charged with robbing the Gallatin bank and killing the cashier; with robbing the gate at the Fair Grounds at Kansas City, with robbing a bank at St. Genevieve; with robbing a train in Iowa, and killing an engineer, with two or three banks in Kentucky and killing two or three men there but for every charge we are willing to be tried if Governor Woodson will promise us protection until we can prove before any fair jury in the State that we have been accused falsely and unjustly. If we do not prove this than let the law do its worst.

We are willing to abide the verdict. I do not see how we could well offer anything fairer.

JESSE W. JAMES

Public opinion swung toward the Jameses and Youngers after the aborted raid on the Samuel farmhouse by the Pinkertons and local law enforcement officers the night of January 26, 1875. In the raid a "bomb," actually an iron illuminating flare filled with kerosene, was kicked into the fireplace by Dr. Samuel and exploded. The mangled right arm of Jesse's mother was amputated, while his younger brother died from stomach wounds.

But the territory was shocked on April 12, 1875, when Daniel Askew, a neighbor of the Samuels, was shot and killed while standing on the porch of his home. It had been reported that Askew had aided the raiders.

According to Wood Hite, Jesse's uncle, Jesse had stalked William Pinkerton in Chicago, hoping that he would lead him to his father, Allan, founder of the Agency. Jesse's plan was to kill Allan Pinkerton on the street. But Hite revealed that Jesse abandoned the scheme because he couldn't find "the old man" and had decided shooting "was too easy." Hite quoted James as saying, "When I do it, I want him to know it's me who's doing it."

The struggle between the Pinkertons, Jesse, Frank, and the Youngers intensified that winter. Allan Pinkerton, writing to one of his superintendents, called it "war to the hilt." But the outlaws continued to win the battles.

Pinkerton decided to use his favorite technique—infiltrating the enemy's ranks—but this time his outrageously haphazard planning was fatal to two of his best men.

John W. Whicher, a twenty-six-year-old operative, courageous and incredibly naïve, arrived in Liberty on March 10, 1874. He sought out the president of the local bank and a former sheriff; both tried to dissuade him from attempting to pose as a farmhand looking for work. The sheriff told him, "The old woman will kill you if the boys don't."

No.

Record

St. Louis, *September 3d 1874*

Hon Chas. P. Johnson
Jeff. City, Mo.
   Governor

     The bearer Off.
Yancy has been ordered to report to
You for special duty. He is an
excellent Officer, an experienced soldier
and a brave and determined man.

     I am satisfied
that a Detective could accomplish
nothing, acting in that capacity.

    In my judgment the only way to
capture these outlaws will be to call on
the Sheriff of Ray or Clay Cos to organize
a posse of say 25 men and let them
accompany and assist the Officer in through
ly scouring the country and ferreting these men
out. They can be found and either killed
or captured if they are in the country.
     Yours truly,
     C. C. Rainwater
     Vice Prest Board

During their terms the governors of Missouri tried desperately to break up the James-Younger gang, which had many political supporters among pro-Confederate politicians. Here Acting Governor Charles P. Johnson is being introduced in 1874 by letter to Flourney Yancy, "an excellent officer, an experienced soldier and a brave determined man." Yancy, a member of the St. Louis Police Department, was assigned by Johnson to capture or kill the Jameses and Youngers. He later flushed out the outlaws in a gunfight but reported that he had had great difficulty because Jesse and his men were mounted on "the fleetest horses in the country" and the citizens either protected them out of loyalty or fear. *Courtesy State Historical Society of Missouri*

Forty-Four of the St. Clair County Rioters Indicted by the Grand Jury.

A St. Louis Wife-Murderer Convicted on the Testimony of His Little Son.

Miscellaneous Criminal Matters.

ATTEMPT TO CAPTURE THE MISSOURI TRAIN ROBBERS.

[*Special Telegram.*]

KANSAS CITY, Mo, Jan. 26.—This morning, about half-past 1 o'clock, an attempt was made to capture the celebrated James boys, at their homes three miles from Kearney, a small station 24 miles east of this city, on the Hannibal and St. Joseph railroad. A reporter of THE TIMES visited Kearney this evening and obtained the particulars from Sheriff John S. Groam. The parents of the James boys are named Samuels, the mother, a widow, having married since her first husband's death. Their house is in a thick wood, no houses within a half a mile either way, a most dreary spot. The family was first awakened by some noise, when Samuels arose and went outside to ascertain the cause. He found the house on fire, and after putting it out he returned inside, where he discovered a hand grenade or small bomb-shell lying on the floor, and Mrs. Samuels attempting to throw it into the fire. Not knowing what it was, he, ignorant, picked it up and threw it in a large fireplace. The whole family then came in the room, and almost immediately it exploded, wounding four of the family. Mrs. Samuels lost an arm, a child, eight years old, was killed, and two others were injured. This hand grenade had been thrown in through a window. Firing then commenced outside, and from the tracks of horses and men, it is evident that a terrible battle ensued. The James boys were either in the house or barn, and, going out, the battle commenced. It is impossible to tell who or how many were wounded. Blood was found about the fences and the back of the house. The wounded were carried off into the woods, as was shown by bloody tracks. No further particulars could be gathered. The whole vicinity is in great excitement. It is feared that the town will be burned, and anything may be hourly expected. It is supposed that Pinkerton's detectives, assisted by men in this neighborhood, are the ones who made the attack. Some suppose that the James boys are captured.

The Chicago Tribune.

Tuesday Morning, February 2, 1875.

MORAL RUINS.

A "Tribune" Correspondent Among the Missouri Outlaws.

Pinkerton's Detectives Seeking for Revenge.

Murder of Henry L. Reed, of Sheffield, Ill., by His Brother.

Sarah Jane Mann's Breach-of-Promise Suit in Danville, Ill.

Robbery of an Express Messenger in Memphis, Tenn.

The Criminal Record.

THE JAMES BROTHERS.

THE RECENT ATTACK UPON THEIR HOME.

Special Dispatch to The Chicago Tribune.

KEARNEY, Clay County, Mo., Feb. 1.—The excitement over the early morning attack upon the James boys last Tuesday seems rather increasing than subsiding. The whole State has jumped at the conclusion that the assault was the work of Pinkerton's men, and done partly with the hope of capturing one or both of the famous "James boys," as everybody here knows them, and partly with the intention of taking revenge for the murder of poor Whicher last summer.

Your correspondent has been here right IN THE HOME OF THE SO-CALLED BANDITS for two days, has been received kindly, has been furnished a vast amount of information from which only such as is beyond question reliable has been received. The wildest rumors have been accepted by the superficial and not over-courageous newspaper men of Kansas City and sent abroad as news. Had the facts been told, the sensation would have been no less, and the ends of truth better subserved.

There is not the shadow of a doubt but that these men who made the attack were part of "Pinkerton's Grand Guard." After the Iowa train-robbery, Pinkerton undertook what the Louisville and St. Louis detective forces and the Secret-Service of this and other States had attempted and failed,—the capture of these out...... Detective Whicher disguise........ harvest-

Whicher foolishly ignored their warnings. Assuming his transparent disguise—he had neither the appearance nor the calloused hands of a farmhand—he set out for Kearney. The next day his riddled body was found in Jackson County. From the description of the men who took him aboard a ferry and told the ferrymen he was a "horse thief," Deputy Sheriff Thomason named Jesse and two of his riders as the killers.

Following Whicher's murder, Captain Louis J. Lull and James Wright of Pinkerton's Chicago office invaded the gang's territory. Lull, a twenty-seven-year-old Union Army officer and former captain on the Chicago police force, and Wright were considered two of the best men in the private detective agency.

Lull and Wright had been part of a posse that chased the bandits after they robbed the Iron Mountain Railroad train at Gad's Hill in Wayne County, Missouri, on January 31, 1874. After several days of trailing the outlaws across the bitter winter countryside, the posse broke up but Lull and Wright continued until March, when they arrived at the Commercial Hotel in Osceola.

Posing as cattle buyers, they stayed in Osceola until Lull obtained information that the Youngers were hiding out at the home of Theodore Snuffer, who had fought with Cole in the guerillas. Lull then hired Edwin B. Daniels, who had served occasionally as a deputy sheriff, as a guide and the trio set out for the Snuffer farm.

On the evening of March 16, 1874, they stayed at the Roscoe Hotel, about twelve miles from Osceola, and in the morning crossed the Osage River and rode up the Old Chalk Road. For some reason Captain Lull stopped at the Snuffer place and asked directions for the home of "Colonel Sims who had some cattle to sell."

Above them in an attic, John and Jim Younger listened as Snuffer gave Lull directions. The brothers debated between themselves, then agreed they should question the well-dressed and heavily armed strangers.

John Younger carried a double-barreled shotgun; Jim had two pistols, one cocked and ready to fire.

When they neared the lawmen Jim shouted an order to halt and fired a shot that sent Wright's hat sailing through the air. Wright put the spurs to his horse and soon disappeared, but Daniels and Lull pulled up and waited.

The Youngers ordered them to drop their weapons, which they did; Jim dismounted and collected the guns.

"These are damn fine guns," the outlaw said, examining Lull's English-made .43-caliber revolver. "Where are you fellows from?"

"Osceola," Lull replied. "We're buying cattle."

When John Younger accused them of being detectives, Daniels insisted he could "prove who I am and where I'm from."

As they were talking, Lull slipped his hand inside his coat, pulled out a small No. 2 Smith and Wesson pistol, and shot John Younger in the neck. The outlaw fired, the shotgun load hitting Lull in the left shoulder and arm. As Lull, one arm shattered, tried to steady his rearing horse, Jim Younger shot and killed Ed Daniels, who fell out of his saddle.

By this time Lull had calmed his horse and ridden off, but a low-hanging

The Monegaw Springs (Missouri) Hotel, the log building where John and Jim Younger attended a dance on Tuesday evening, March 16, 1874, the night before the savage gun battle in which Captain Louis Lull, a Pinkerton agent; Ed Daniels, a local lawman; and John Younger were killed. *Courtesy State Historical Society of Missouri*

The cabin near Monegaw Springs where the dying Captain Lull was carried after his gun battle with John and Jim Younger. *The James D. Horan Civil War and Western Americana Collection*

Ed Daniels, a lawman of Osceola, hired by Captain Lull as a guide, who was killed by the Youngers in the gun battle at Roscoe, Missouri, March 17, 1874 *Courtesy State Historical Society of Missouri*

The Roscoe House, where Captain Lull died in the second-story room with the window at the far left. Lull, Daniels, and another Pinkerton agent, John H. Boyle, stayed here on the night before the gun battle. *Courtesy State Historical Society of Missouri.*

John Younger about the time he was killed in the Roscoe gun battle. *The James D. Horan Civil War and Western Americana Collection*

Chicago July 8 '74

Dan O'Conner Esq
Chief Detective
St Louis

Dear Sir:

Your letter to Captain Hickey in regard to John H Boyle, was shown to me by the Captain, and requested any information which I might have. In reply I would say: that Boyle was at one time a member of this force. but he was found to be cowardly, deceitful, and utterly unreliable therefore discharged. Had he been half a man, Captain Lull would now have been living.

If he is applying for a situation, I would tell you simply: have nothing to do with him, he is a dirty dog; but for reason that he knows some of the business transacted at

William Pinkerton's bitter letter to Daniel O'Connor, Chief Detective of the St. Louis Police Department, in which he described O'Connor's former detective, John H. Boyle, as a coward. Boyle fled from the Roscoe gun battle when the first shot was fired. *Courtesy State Historical Society of Missouri*

51
o

limb knocked him to the ground. John Younger, covered with blood and swaying in the saddle, rode after him. As Lull tried to get to his feet, John Younger shot him in the chest. Turning his horse around, the dying outlaw reached his brother before he slid to the ground.

A farmer who had heard the shooting found Lull, bleeding badly and sitting against a tree trunk. He was first taken to a nearby cabin and later to the Roscoe House, where he died.

That summer a bitter and frustrated Jesse James wrote two long letters to the Nashville *Banner* denouncing the Pinkertons and his Northern enemies who had driven him into a life of outlawry.[14]

(Nashville Banner, Aug, 4, 1875)
(Clay County, Missouri, Aug. 4, 1875)
(Confidential to the Editor)

I will be under many obligation to you to publish the enclosed article. Publish it just as I have written it, though I wrote in great haste. Please correct all bad spelling in the article. Have gave you nothing but the truth.

There is no doubt about the Pinkerton force committing the crime & it is the duty of the press to denounce him, the St. Louis *Times & Dispatch* and many other Democratic papers in Missouri have stood up faithfully for us [The Jameses and Youngers] and last winter when the Amnesty Bill was before the Legislature, every Ex-Confederate in the Legislature voted for our pardon, among the number were, Gen. Shields, Gen. Jones, who forwarded the bill, & Col. Stichan Hutchens, Editor of the St. Louis *Times*, and is against reason to suppose we are guilty of murder and robbery, the best men in Mo. are our friends, and it is only a question of time about us being granted a full amnesty, our friends will forward the Amnesty Bill again this winter in the 29th Assembly of the Mo. Legislature. As soon as I get time I will write you a sketch of the James & Youngers, Major Jn. Edwards of the St. Louis *Dispatch* is at the present time writing the history of Quantrell and his men, which gives the history of the lives of the James & Youngers.

Pinkerton has gained great notariety as a Detective but we have so easily baffled him & he has got his best men killed by him sending them after us, & he is fast losing his laurels & he wants to poison the minds of all Democrats against us. He would rejoice at our extermination. Pleas. send one copy of the *Banner* to Mrs. Dr. Samuel, Kearney, Clay co. Mo. so I will get the article, I wish to publish. If Pinkerton has any cards published, also send them to my mother, burn this note. Yours,

J.W. James.

(Nashville Banner, Aug. 4, 1875.)
Kansas City, Mo. Aug. 4, 1875.
(Special to the Nashville Banner.)

My attention has been called to an article published in the Banner of July 28th, in which W. A. Pinkerton denounces my statement to the *Banner* as a pack of falsehoods. It does not become me to reply to an article written by Pinkerton but as the present opportunity gives me the opportunity to reply to the true character of Pinkerton & his force I will reply, alto I consider it the greatest stain ever thrown on my charcater to notice an article written by him.

Pinkerton sed my statement to the *Banner* was false. If any honest man will investigate my statement to the *Banner* and say I misrepresented anthing, I will acknolledge my guilt to the world. If Mr. Tom Marshall, proprietor of the hotel at Chaplin Nelson Co. Kentucky, will say I was not at home March the 20th, 1868 the day the Russelville Ky. Bank Robbery I will acknolledge I was in the Russelville Bank Robbery, and if D. B. Blackburn, Ex-Sheriff of San Louis Obispo co Cal. will not say Frank James was not at work on Mr. Thompson Ranch on that day in Cal. I will say Frank James is guilty, and if the officers in Mo. that I sed I had been corresponding with, will say my statement is false I will say Pinkerton has told the truth. As for Pinkerton proveing he was in Chicago at the time he committed the outrage at mothers I do not doubt as far as that is concerned.

Pinkerton can prove he was in Chicago that Black is White and white is Black so can Gen. W. T. Sherman prove in Chicago that Jeff Davis had Lincoln assassinated & that the brave and gallant Gen. Wade Hampton burnt Columbia, N.C. all this can be proven in Chicago, if people in the south didn't know that Chicago was the home of Phil Sherdin and filled with Sherman Bummers.

It might have some efect for Pinkerton to say he can prove in Chicago, there is hardy a child in Mo. but knows it was Pinkertons force that committed the crime at mothers & to day Gov. C. H. Hardin has a Remington Navy pistol in his possession that was found at mothers the morning after the Tragedy, branded P.G.G. which stands for Pinkerton Government Guards & it is a well-known fact that Pinkertons force and no other force has pistols branded in that manner. Pinkertons men did commit the crime and it is absurd for them to deny it.

Pinkerton's force charted a special train on the H&St. Joe R.R. and came in to Clay Co. at night & crept three miles through the woods to mothers residence and fiered it in seven places and hurled incendiary ball in to the house to kil and criple the entire family & then gives them over to the mercy of the flames. But Providence saved the house from being burnt altho it was saturated with Turpentine & fiered with combustible materials and the shell did not do fatal work and they fled away to the special train that was waiting to carry them be on the reach of outraged justice. this is the work of Pinkerton, the man that sed in his card he just wished to set himself right in the eyes of the world. he may vindicate himself with some, but he never dare show his Scottish face again in Western Mo. and let him know he is here or he will meet the fate his comrades, Capt. Lull & Witcher meet & I would advise him to stay in New York but let him go where he may, his sins will find him out. He can cross the Atlantic but every wave and white cap he sees at sea will remind him of the innocent boy murdered and the one armed mother robbed of her child (and Idol). Justice is slow but sure and there is a just God that will bring all to Justice. Pinkerton, I hope and pray our Heavenly Father may deliver you into my hands & I believe he will for his merciful and protecting arm has always been with me and Shielded me, and during all my persecution he has watched over me and protected me from workers of blood money who are trying to seek my life, and I have hope and faith in Him & believe he will ever protect me as long as I serve Him.

Oh, Pinkerton (if you have a heart of conscience), I know the spirit of my poor, innocent brother hovers around your pillow, and that you never close your eyes, that you don't see his poor delicated & childish form about you & him holding his shattered arm over you and you looking at the great wound in his side and seeing his life blood eb away.

You may vindicate yourself with some people but God knows, if you did not do the deed it was done by your force. The public press of Missouri has time and again charged this to you and you have never denied it until your card to the *Banner.* Joe Witchers came to Clay Co, Mo. March 9, 1874 and went to the honorable sheriff of Clay County with ten thousand lies, and that night he was kidnapped and got his just deserts; and it was in revenge for him that the Pinkerton force tried to destroy an innocent helpless family.

And a man by the name of Angle came after Witcher's remains to carry them back to Chicago. Angle went to Chicago and filled the Northern Press with his stories, charging the Missouri officials with being with the outlaws and that said Sheriff Patton of Clay County, betrayed Witchers into the outlaws' hands.

George E. Patton, sheriff of Clay County, is a relative of Gen. Frank Cheatham, of Tennessee, and a one-armed Confederate, and one of the noblest and bravest officers that ever was in Missouri. It was this honorable sheriff that Pinkerton's force denounced to the world as being in with the outlaws, and Pinkerton's force also tried to injure John S. Graham, the present sheriff of Clay County, a more conscientius, braver and honorable officer never lived than Captain Graham.

I have made these statements because they can't be disputed. I defy man to prove any word of my statement to be false. Pinkerton's force—Blythe of Kentucky and Jim Tracy of St. Louis, are the men who have filled the world with stories about the James and Youngers. I could fill pages with Detective Tracy's doings but from the papers it is not necessary for me to tell the people of Nashville anything about Tracy. Pinkerton, let me hear from you again.

Respectfully,   J. W. James.

The following year, in July of 1876, Jesse led his riders to Rocky Cut near Otterville, Cooper County, Missouri, to rob the Missouri Pacific Railroad train; the Adams Express Company safe gave up an estimated fifteen thousand dollars. The newspaper reporters and lawmen who interviewed the passengers declared the robbery was "the work of men who were well versed in their business." Again the posses trailed the gang to Clay County and the robbery was declared the work of those professionals, Jesse and Frank James and the Youngers.

Governor Charles A. Hardin now offered a reward of three hundred dollars for the capture of each member of the gang.

The first break in not only solving the crime but actually penetrating the secrets of the Jameses and Youngers came when St. Louis Chief of Police James McDonough arrested Hobbs Kerry, a member of Jesse's gang. Kerry was captured after he had boasted how much money he had and proved it by waving a thick wad of bills.

McDonough, a precise and conscientious police officer, located witnesses who identified Kerry as having stopped at their farmhouse shortly before the robbery. Kerry broke down and confessed that he was one of the train robbers. He named Jesse as his leader, along with Frank James, Cole Younger, Bob Younger, Clem Miller, Charlie Pitts, and Bill Chadwell.

One day a rider delivered a letter from Jesse to the *Kansas City Times* and vouched for its authenticity in an accompanying statement. The paper denounced the professional "thief catchers," obviously the Pinkertons, who invaded Missouri with their mercenary armies "to kill the twelve-year-old boys and blow off the arms of old women."[15]

(Kansas City Times, Aug. 18, 1876.)

Oak Grove, Kansas, Aug. 14, 1876.

TO THE KANSAS CITY TIMES:
    You have published Hobbs Kerry's confession which makes it appear the James and the Youngers were the Rocky Cut robbers.
    If there was only one side to be told, it would probably be believed by a good many people that Kerry has told the truth. But this so-called confession is a well-built pack of falsehoods from beginning to end. I never heard of Hobbs Kerry, Charles Pitts and Wm. Chadwell until Kerry's arrest. I can prove my innocence by eight good and well-known men of Jackson County, and show conclusively that I was not at the train robbery. But at present I will only give the names of two of those men to whom I will refer for proof. Early on the morning of the train robbery, east of Sedalia, I saw the Honorable D. Gregg of Jackson County and talked with him for thirty or forty minutes. I also seen and talked with Mr. Thomas Pitcher of Jackson County, the morning after the robbery. These two men's oath cannot be impeached. I refer the Grand Jury of Cooper County, Missouri and Gov. Hardin to these facts before they act rashly.
    A LIAR, THIEF AND ROBBER
    Kerry knows the James and Youngers can't be taken alive so that is why he has put it on us. I have referred to Messrs. Pitcher and Gregg because they are prominent men and they know I am innocent and their word cannot be disputed. I will write a long article for you for the Times and send it to you in a few days, showing fully how Hobbs Kerry has lied. Hoping the Times will give me a chance for a fair hearing and vindicate myself through your columns, I will close.

                    Respectfully,   J. W. James

    Shortly after Jesse sent the letter to the Kansas City Times denying he had taken part in the train robbery at Otterville, he wrote another to the same paper. In this long letter he denied he had ever met Kerry, charged the son of a railroad official with trying to stage a phony payroll robbery so he could collect half of the money, denounced the Pinkertons, and named Bacon Montgomery, a prominent citizen of Sedalia who had headed the posse which chased the train robbers, as the bandit chief who had planned and executed the crime.[16]
    In an accompanying editorial, the paper revealed that the letter had "reached us by mail yesterday, with a Kansas City postmark. Persons who know assure us the handwriting is his. Of course everybody will read with several grains of allowance what he has to say against those whom he regards as his personal enemies. . . ."
    Jesse was shrewdly appealing to his pro-Confederate supporters. As he pointed out, Montgomery, the law and order man, had been leader of the state militia under Governor Thomas Fletcher during the bitter postwar years.
    Arch Clement, that "noble boy," had helped Jesse and the other guerillas under Bloody Bill Anderson kill twenty-five unarmed Union soldiers during the Centralia massacre in the summer of 1864.

SAFE RETREAT, Aug. 18, 1876

TO THE KANSAS CITY TIMES:

I have written a great many articles vindicating myself of the false charges which have been brought against me. But last fall after I proved to the world that the James and Youngers had nothing to do with the robbery in West Virginia and branded old Detective Blythe as one of the biggest liars and poltroons that ever lived, I thought I would let the public press say what it would and I would treat it with silent contempt. Detectives have been trying to get proof against me for years for certain criminal offences so they could get a large reward offered for me dead or alive and the same on Frank James and the Younger boys but they have been foiled at every turn and they are fully convinced that we will never be taken alive and now they have fell on the deep laid scheme to get Hobbs Kerry to tell a pack of base lies. But I thank God I am a free man and have the power to defend myself against the charges brought against me by Kerry, a notorious liar and poltroon. I will give a full statement and prove his confession to be false.

Lie No. 1. He said a plot was laid by the James and Youngers to rob the Grandy bank. I am reliably informed there was never a bank in Grandy.

Lie No. 2. He said he got with Cole Younger and I at Mr. Tyler's. If there is a man in Jackson County by the name I am sure I am not acquainted with him.

Lie No. 3. He said Frank James was at Mr. Butler's in Cass County. I and Frank don't know any man in Cass County by that name. I can prove my innocence by eight good citizens of Jackson County, Missouri, but I do not propose to give all their names at present. If I did the cut-throat detectives would find out some of my friends they think are my enemies. I think the names I gave in my article of the 4th are sufficient for the present.

Will the Times please correct a statement they made in my other statement? I saw Mr. Gregg and talked to him and only met Mr. Pitcher in the road and we passed the compliments of the day and rode on.

My opinion is that Bacon Montgomery, the scoundrel that murdered Capt. Al J. Clement, Dec. 13, 1866, is the instigator of this Missouri Pacific affair. I believe he planned the robbery and got his share of the money and when he went out after the robbers he led the persuers off the robbers' trail. But one thing I know he did do when he was in command of Tom Fletcher's cut-throat militia. He had Arch Clements, one of the noblest boys and one of the most promising military boys of his age, murdered in cold blood and if Arch was living today he would be worth more than old Tom Fletcher and all the militia outfits that ever were in Missouri. I would like the Times to send a reporter to Lexington and Dover and ask the good citizens about Montgomery and his thieves that were there in 1866. If half the truth was told about Montgomery, it would make the world believe that Montgomery had no equal, only the Bender family and the midnight assassins who murdered my poor helpless and innocent eight-year-old brother and shot my mother's arm off, and I am of the opinion he had a hand in that dirty, cowardly work. Montgomery, roll in your special trains and break down doors and arrest quiet citizens. Everywhere you turn you make friends for me.

Now a word to Mr. Garrison: Ain't you afraid those special trains will injure the Missouri Pacific? You are liable to have trouble if you don't stop such weak brain work. I don't believe that Gov. Hardin has any hand in this special train work. I give him too much credit for that. Gov. Hardin is a man of too much brains to act in a manner like that to kill him in the eyes of the people who elected him. I think he is the best Governor Missouri has had since the war.

If we [the Jameses and Youngers] had been granted full amnesty I am sure we would of been at work, trying to be good, law-biding citizens. If we have a wise Congress this winter, which I believe we will have, I am sure they will grant us a full pardon. I will not say pardon for we have done nothing to be pardoned for. But they can pass a law that will destroy all those bogus warrants sent out for us and let us live in peace. What sense is there in spending so much money to have us arrested? I am sure we have thousands of friends that cant be bought although the detectives think they are playing things very fine. Poor fools they are.

If the Express companies want to do a good act they can take all the money they are letting those thieving detectives beat them out of and give it to the poor. The Detectives are a brave lot of boys, break down doors and make the gray hair stand up on the heads of their unarmed victims. Why don't President Grant have the soldiers called in and send the Detectives out on special trains after the hostile Indians? A Pinkerton's force with hand greanades will kill all the Indian women and children and with the women killed it will stop the breed and the warriors will all die out in a few years. But if Montgomery gets in with the Indians as he is with the Otterville boys, he would be a bad man on the trail.

If Montgomery gets offended at this and comes out on the scout, I hope he and his party won't get drunk as he did on a previous ocassion, and shoot and yell and scare women and children as they did.

A few words to Mr. Oil Garrison, son of Mr. Garrison, Missouri Pacific Railroad officer—have you forgot the time when you was paymaster of the Sedalia & Lexington Railroad? Yes, well you do remember when you proposed to get someone to rob you and then give you half; and you failed to get your job put up? I got this from a friend of yours who gets drunk—but he wasn't drunk when he told me this—but probably the old man doesn't know what kind of a rascal you are or he would send special trains after you. I believe the railroad robbers will yet be sifted down on someone at St. Louis or Sedalia, putting the job up and then trying to put it down on honest men as Kerry has done.

Hoping the *Times* will publish just as I have written, I will close,

Jesse James

The next day Bacon Montgomery, in an indignant reply to the *Times*, scoffed at Jesse's charges and offered to appear and be questioned by any law enforcement body if Jesse would do the same.

There were no more letters from Jesse James. He was now struggling for survival; the manhunters were everywhere and physically he was fading. The wartime wound in the right side of his chest had reopened and was discharging. He had lost weight and was constantly tired. The horns of the hunters were loud in his ears when he and Frank said good-bye to their mother and left the primitive security of Clay County to ride south. They made several stops, finally fleeing to the backwoods "mansion" of their uncle, "Major" George Hite, two miles from Adairville.

Hite owned six hundred acres "of the best land in Logan County" and as the *Courier-Journal* estimated, "he was worth $100,000," which included a prosperous dry-goods store in Adairville.

Friends and supporters later described Hite as "a man put on" by his Missouri relatives; a kind man who refused to turn away anyone who sought help.

Hite was described as over six feet tall, spare and angular, with a full beard and graying dark hair.

Jesse Tries Suicide

A private road branched off from the Adairville Pike through the woods to a narrow lane. Towering oaks screened the house, flanked by tilled fields and forests. The two-story "mansion," built on a knoll in a clump of cedar trees, was painted white with green shutters. There was a spacious veranda, rolling lawns, and an orchard whose blossoms perfumed the spring night air.

Four hundred yards from the house was a large barn, the site of a later duel fought on horseback between Dick Liddil, Jesse's rider, and Wood Hite, the major's wild young son who sometimes joined the gang on raids. Less than half a mile away was the Tennessee line and a bend in the north fork of the Red River where Jesse would kill Ed Miller, who had ridden with him on the Winston train robbery.

Jesse and Frank arrived on a bitter January morning. They were surprised to be greeted by their sister, Susan Lavinia, who was waiting to tell them the glorious news that she was getting married to Allen Parmer, who had served with Jesse under the Black Flag of Missouri's guerillas.

Susan, two years younger than Jesse, was the bandit's favorite. An attractive, light-haired, vivacious girl, her personality was in vivid contrast to Jesse's dark and violent moods. The news shattered Jesse, who despised Parmer, probably from some unknown incident during the war years.

Jesse grimly told his sister there would be no wedding.

From the extant evidence one can conjure up the scene in the farmhouse: an angry, unreasonable Jesse denouncing Parmer; Susan torn between the love of her brother and the handsome ex-guerilla fighter she had promised to wed; Frank, anxious, troubled, trying to placate his raging brother and weeping sister; Hite and his wife, the older members of the family, desperately seeking to restore peace to their home and to calm their dangerous, explosive nephew.

Late that night the incident ended with the weeping Susan running to her bedroom. Frank and Hite retired for a session of bourbon and talk. Jesse remained in the room to brood over Susan's defiance, his illness, and the manhunters which had left few places for him to hide.

Jesse sat in the room all night, probably staring into the dying fire as better men have done in their troubled hours. At dawn he had come to his decision; life wasn't worth the candle—he would commit suicide.

He saddled his horse and rode into Adairville, where he purchased sixteen grains of morphine; there is evidence that he had been using the narcotic to dull the constant pain of his chest wound.

On his return Jesse went to his room and swallowed a lethal dose. However, when he felt the drug taking hold Jesse undoubtedly changed his mind—life had suddenly become precious—and he staggered out into the hall and called for Frank, who came on the run with Susie and Hite.

Barely conscious and aware he was dying, the outlaw chief whispered to them what he had done and "gave direction in regard to messages."

His shocked brother sent Hite for the nearest doctor. It was about 7 P.M. when the Adairville physician arrived to find Jesse on the brink of death. What took place in that farmhouse remained a secret for years; it was only after Bob

terday afternoon. The Judge's wife is with him, and they are at the Southern.

JESSE JAMES AS A SUICIDE.

A Graphic Sketch of How Jesse Tried to Suicide on Morphine, but Failed to Die —His Brother Frank and Sister Susie Assist in Restoring Him.

From the Louisville Courier-Journal.

ADAIRVILLE, KY., April 30.—While so much is being said and written about Frank and Jesse James, I am forcibly reminded of an incident in connection with them, in which I was a party. It may prove not uninteresting to your readers, and serves to illustrate some of the characteristics which their notable career has rendered so prominent since.

At the time of which I write Jesse was suffering from the effects of a gun shot wound in his right breast, and from the long continued discharge was rather thin and in feeble health, and was spending some time with his uncle, Maj. Geo. B. Hite, who lived within two or three miles of Adairville.

In a fit of despondency, produced party by his low state of health, and partly, as I afterward learned, by his bitter opposition to the prospective marriage of his sister Susie to Allen Parmer, whom she afterward married, Jesse determined to commit suicide, and, impelled by his impetuous nature, lost no time in his efforts at executing his desire.

For this purpose he rode to town and procured sixteen grains of morphine, which he took at one dose immediately on his arrival at his uncle's, which was late in the afternoon of an early January day.

When he felt the drug beginning to produce its Lethean effects, and he deemed it too late for any remedial efforts to prove effective, he called his brother Frank and sister Susie to him, advised them of what he had done, and gave such directions in regard to messages and trusts as he wished.

Frank, in order, if possible, to frustrate the design, immediately posted a messenger after a physician. It was 7 o'clock p. m., when I arrived, and found him apparently in the embrace of death, in a profound stupor, insensible to his surroundings, except under the influence of the strongest excitement; pulse slow, full and very forcible, and respiration of that heavy, slow and stertorous nature characteristic of opium poisoning. There had been some degree of tolerance to the drug acquired by a resort to it some weeks previously, to mitigate the violence of the sufferings incident to the wound above referred to.

I found willing and very capable assistants in Frank and Susie, whose attentions and ministrations were unremitting throughout the night. In addition to the usual evacuant and antidotal remedies, it was imperatively necessary to combat the narcotic influence of the poison by all sources of mental and physical excitement that could be brought to bear. When appeals and circumambulatory stimulants had been used for some hours, till finally he failed to respond to them, then I appealed to Frank to know if there was anything or any subject that would, more than anything else, be likely to excite him, suggesting that unless he could be kept aroused for some time longer, till the drug had been partially eliminated from the system, he would necessarily die.

Then the force of habit manifested itself in a striking degree. I shall never forget the powerful excitement he evinced, and the ⸻use he continued to make when ⸻isper to him certain warning ⸻rsons who were very ob⸻ ⸻ and it was neces⸻ ⸻never

"WELCO

ABSOLUTELY

An original copy of the extraordinary account of Jesse James's attempted suicide after his sister announced that she was planning to marry Allen Parmer, who had fought with Jesse under "Bloody Bill" Anderson. In the same issue there is a story of how the Missouri state legislature "amid wild excitement" defeated a resolution praising the "vigilance and success" of the Clay and Jackson County lawmen in breaking up the James-Younger gang. *The James D. Horan Civil War and Western Americana Collection*

Ford had killed Jesse that the Kentucky physician revealed to the *Kansas City Journal* the dramatic story of how he and Frank had struggled through the night to save the outlaw's life.

Near dawn there was barely a "thread" of life remaining. At the suggestion of the physician, Frank whispered a "warning" in his brother's ear. The instinct of the hunted was so strong that Jesse struggled to his feet, reached for his guns, and staggered around the room waving his weapons at the ghosts of the posses pounding across his brain. Whenever he sagged, Frank would catch him and urge him on. . . .

The backwoods physician who signed his letter to the *Journal* as "D. G. S." arrived with Hite as the winter darkness closed in on the countryside.

"JESSE JAMES AS A SUICIDE—

A GRAPHIC SKETCH OF HOW JESSE TRIED TO SUICIDE ON MORPHINE BUT FAILED TO DIE—HIS BROTHER FRANK AND SISTER SUSIE ASSIST IN RESTORING HIM."*

It was seven o'clock when I arrived and found him [James] apparently in the embrace of death, in a profound stupor, insensible to his surroundings, except under the influence of the strongest excitement; pulse slow, full and very forcible, and respiration of that heavy, slow and stertorous nature, characteristic of opium poisoning. There had been some degree of tolerance to the drug acquired by a resort to it some weeks previously, to mitigate the violence of the sufferings incident to the wound [Jesse's chest wound].

I found willing and very capable assistants in Frank and Susie, whose attentions and ministrations were unremitting throughout the night. In addition to the usual evacuant and antidotal remedies, it was imperatively necessary to combat the narcotic influence of the poison by all sorts of mental and physical excitement that could be brought to bear.

When appeals and circumambulatory stimulants had been used for some hours, till finally he failed to respond to them, then I appealed to Frank to know if there was anything or any subject that would, more than anything else be likely to excite him, suggesting that unless he kept aroused, for some time longer till the drug had been partially eliminated from his system, he would necessary die.

Then the force of habit manifested itself in a striking degree. I shall never forget the powerful excitement he evinced, and the prompt response he continued to make when Frank would whisper certain warning words to him, as if certain persons who were very obnoxious to him were coming and it was very necessary to escape or defend to the death.

Whenever he seemed to sink in the fatal narcotism Frank's cabalistics would for hours bring him to his feet, and he would call for his pistols and flourish them while carried around the room between two assistants, every few seconds relapsing into profound slumber, even while walking, but instantly aroused again by the same talisman.

His eyelids seem to have millstones suspended from them, and it was impossible for him to keep them open for two seconds at a time. About 4 o'clock A.M. all efforts to keep him awake proved futile; his pulse had reduced in volume to a mere thread, his breathing was feeble and very slow and it seemed the death angel was hovering over him, ready in a few minutes to seize his prey. I suggested to Frank that we leave him alone awhile and let him rest; that he in all probability would die; but possibly just now rest might be an advantage to him.

*Kansas City Journal, May 6, 1882.

While his sister and friends were hovering over him, mourning as for one dead, Frank sat in mute and stern despair at the foot of the bed, with his eyes fixed upon the floor, still as a statue. If I were an artist I could paint a picture as he thus sat, so indelibly was his appearance impressed upon my memory. His arms folded on his breast, his ordinary penetrating eye vacant, his massive jaw and beautifully outlined lips sternly and firmly compressed, his oval face and features well exposed from being clean shaven—I thought I had never seen a handsomer man, and at the same time one exhibiting more sternness and firmness of character.

I sat with my finger on the pulse for perhaps a half hour, when it began to show evidence of improvement with greater regularity and with more frequent and natural breathing. When this improvement had continued till there could be no longer any doubt of its existence, the fact was communicated to the relatives and friends. Within an hour he was sleeping a natural and refreshing sleep, which he really very much needed, from the exhaustion induced by his long continued efforts to keep awake and moving.

By 6 o'clock he aroused and recognized his friends, and by the time breakfast was announced he was ready for a hearty meal. When consciousness was thoroughly aroused he expressed considerable emotion of joy that he had failed in his efforts at self destruction, and was profuse in his thanks to Mrs. Hite and all parties for their strenuous efforts through the night to restore him. He evinced both shame and contrition for his act. There was but little resemblance between the brothers. Jesse was taller and more slender with dark hair and eyebrows and rather hazel eyes; while Frank had light hair and blue eyes, a symmetrical and beautiful form, in perfect and vigorous health, and exhibiting evidence of great physical endurance. Both were eminently handsome, and of easy, polished, pleasant and agreeable bearings, as different in appearance from the caricatures with which some of their biographers illustrate their pages, as their manners differed from the ordinary conception of a western rough and bully.

D. G. S.

The Marriages of Jesse and Frank James

There were two dominant women in the life of Jesse James—his mother: stern, domineering, aggressive, protective, and possessive; and his sweetheart, Zee or Josie, as he called her: loving, gentle, fiercely loyal, and always trustworthy. Ironically, both women were named Zerelda.

In the dark days of 1874, plagued by posses, depression, and his unhealed wound, and shaken by his brush with death in his suicide attempt, Jesse turned to Zee, who had loved the blue-eyed bandit from the days after the end of the Civil War when he was recovering in her home from the Yankee-inflicted bullet wound.

After her mother had died, Zee went to live with a married sister in Kansas City. Even when the manhunters were close, Jesse continued his courtship. It makes a wonderful picture: the most wanted man in the United States and his sweetheart sitting in the prim parlor, a fire on the grate and Jesse, his sandy beard trimmed, boots glistening, and a Winchester nearby, entertaining Zee with the story of how Deputy Sheriff Thomason had to walk back to the Samuel farmhouse and borrow a horse to get back to town.

From what she later revealed, Zee was a realist, never a starry-eyed young

SATURDAY, MARCH 28, 1874.

THE WESTERN LOWRYS.

A STORY OF BLOOD, PUNCTUATED WITH PISTOL SHOTS.

THE CAREER OF THE JAMES AND YOUNGER DESPERADOES—COUNTIES TERRIFIED INTO SUBMISSION—INCIDENTS OF THEIR LAW-LESS LIFE—DYING WITH THEIR BOOTS ON.

[FROM OUR OWN CORRESPONDENT.]

APPLETON CITY, Mo., March 22.—It is a quiet Sabbath, and the land is fair with early spring. Beautiful prairies stretch away to belts of forest, and on the southwest the country swells and breaks into little hills. The land is a goodly land, and the railroad runs through it, bringing civilization and commerce to the doors of its dwellers. But there is from almost immemorial time a curse upon the country, and on either hand of the two shining lines of iron that vanish in the distance into shining needles there is hardly a section of land that has not been wetted with the blood of a murdered man, and the graves of the dead are more numerous than the houses of the living. The Southwest has been settled by outlaws, who bequeathed their names, feuds, and weapons to younger outlaws. Civilization to them has had no humanizing mission; all that it has meant was more deadly instruments of offence. Coffins, guns, and buckshot seem to be all that the railroad has brought into the country. Men go armed to the teeth up and down the roads, and acquire respect and repute from their ruffianism. This is especially true, of course, of the country lying back of the railroads. The hands that laid waste ...

am not sure which, but the published history states one or the other—murders.

Even this tiger in human shape has not inspired more awe than the Younger and James brothers. There are—or were—four of the Youngers, who came of good Kentucky stock. Coleman and James Younger were educated in Kentucky before the war broke out, the others in Missouri. All are good-looking, manly, to a certain degree, accomplished gentlemen. They would pass muster at any hotel or on any Mississippi steamer and hardly be taken for what they are—desperadoes without pity or fear. Their father was killed by a gang of bushwhackers in the war at Harrisonville; their uncle is Judge Younger, of St. Clair County, and they have a brother who, I am informed, is a wealthy and respectable farmer living only a few miles from here.

John Younger, who was killed last week, was about twenty-four years old, and, as the coolest and most intellectual of the four, had of late come to be their real if not their nominal leader. He was a handsome, dashing fellow, affected the beau, and was quite a ladies' man. At fifteen he killed a man, but was acquitted. In 1869, or thereabouts, temporarily sojourning in Texas, he shot the ... of Dallas County, who attempted to blow a hole through ...

THE VERY LATEST.
4.80 P.M.

CAPTURED.

The Celebrated Jesse W. James Taken at Last.

His Captor a Woman, Young, Accomplished, and Beautiful.

(Special Correspondence to the St. Louis Dispatch.)

SHERMAN, Tex., June 5, 1874.

Not many days ago I saw the celebrated Jesse W. James in the city of Galveston, talked with him, was introduced to his wife, and recognized in her an old acquaintance of Jackson county—a lady whom I had known both before and since the war, and one who had been of immense service to the Southern guerrillas when they were operating upon the border in 1862 and 1863.

I had a long talk with Jesse. He was waiting for a vessel bound for Mexico, when it was his intention to go with his wife to Vera Cruz, and from there into the interior and take him a farm. Frank was with him and they appeared to have many friends and acquaintances in Galveston.

Jesse gave me some interesting items concerning his marriage, and told me that it was his intention to keep the matter a secret as long as he could, but that before he left home the event had been talked of much, both in Kansas City and Clay county, and so now that as he was going to leave the country in a few days, he would give all the particulars concerning it. Jesse's statements to me were about these:

"On the 23d of April, 1874, I was married to Miss Zee Mimms, of Kansas City, and at the house of a friend there. About fifty of our mutual friends were present on the occasion, and quite a noted Methodist minister performed the ceremonies. We had been engaged for nine years, and through good and evil report, and notwithstanding the lies that have been told upon me, and the crimes laid at my door, her devotion to me has never wavered for a moment. You can say that both of us married for love, and that there cannot be any sort of doubt about our marriage being a happy one."

This is about the substance of the talk I had with Jesse. His wife is a young lady of about twenty-two, with an elegant form, beautiful eyes, and a face that would be attractive in any assembly. When Jesse James was so badly wounded in 1864, in a fight with some Wisconsin cavalrymen, she nursed him uninterruptedly in the brush for nine weeks, and until he could be removed to a house. She is also a true and consistent Christian, and a member of the M. E. Church, South. She is a sister of the Hon. Judge Mimms, of Helena, Montana Territory, and a niece of Mr. J. H. West, a most respectable and prosperous merchant of Kansas City. The whole courtship, engagement and final marriage has been a most romantic series of events, and some day I may write them up for you. By this time the parties have left the country. Jesse, however, declared it to be his full intention to return and take his trial when he thought he could get a trial other than at the hands of a mob.

RANGER.

In the 1870s the fame of the James-Younger gang was nationwide. Large Eastern city newspapers published stories of a terrorized Missouri they dubbed "The Outlaw State." *The James D. Horan Civil War and Western Americana Collection*

romantic who viewed her lover as a plumed cavalier who robbed the rich to help the poor. She believed that, as the grave diggers many years later would say: "He was driven to it." Until that fatal day in St. Joseph when Bob Ford would pull the trigger, Zee was always loving, never complaining, never questioning the man she loved so blindly.

During the nine years of their courtship many a beau had spoken for Zee's hand but she refused all their pleas. Finally she had her wish: on April 24, 1874, she and Jesse were married by a clergyman in the parlor of her sister's home.

"Fifty mutual friends" attended the ceremony and reception. Because of the intense, almost fanatical loyalty this strange man inspired, not one guest leaked the news. It was only when the honeymooning Jesse and Zee met a correspondent of the St. Louis *Dispatch* that the country learned that its most wanted fugitive was so anonymous and well protected that he had been courting his sweetheart for nine years and had been married in a well-attended ceremony in Kansas City under the eyes of Missouri's governor, the state's police chiefs and detectives, and the Pinkertons, who were triumphantly announcing that the outlaw band had been broken up and Jesse had left the Border States for California, South America, the Northwest, or Canada.

In Texas, Jesse dictated the public announcement of his wedding to the newspaperman, including a poignant line:

"Both of us married for love . . ."

"CAPTURED . . . THE CELEBRATED JESSE W. JAMES . . . TAKEN AT LAST!"

Not many days ago I saw the celebrated Jesse W. James in the city of Galveston, Texas, talked to him, was introduced to his wife and recognized in her an old acquaintance of Jackson County—a lady I had known both before and after the war, and one who had been of immense service to the Southern guerillas when they were operating upon the border in 1862 and 1863.

I had a long talk with Jesse. He was waiting for a vessel bound for Mexico, where it was his intention to go with his wife to Vera Cruz, and from there into the interior to take him a farm. Frank was with him and they appeared to have many friends in Galveston.

Jesse gave me some interesting items concerning his marriage, and told me it was his intention to keep the marriage a secret as long as he could, but before he left home the event had been talked of so much both in Kansas City and Clay County, and so now that he was going to leave the country in a few days, he would give all the particulars concerning it.

Jesse's statement to me:

"On the 22nd of April, 1874, I was married to Miss Zee Mimms of Kansas City at the home of a friend there. About fifty of our mutal friends were present for the occassion and quite a celebrated Methodist minister performed the ceremony. We have been engaged for nine years and through good and evil report, and not withstanding the lies told about me, and the crimes laid at my door, her devotion to me has never wavered for a moment. You can say that both of us married for love, and there cannot be any sort of a doubt about our marriage being a happy one."

This is the substance of the talk I had with Jesse. His wife is a young lady of about twenty-two, with an elegant form, beautiful eyes, and a face that would be attractive in an assembly. When Jesse was badly wounded in a fight with some Wisconsin cavalrymen in 1864, she nursed him uninterruptedly in the brush for nine weeks, and until he could be removed to a house. She is also a true and insistent Christian, and a member of the M. E. Church South. She is the sister of the honorable Judge Mimms, Montana Territory, and the niece of Mr. J. H. West, a most respectable and prosperous merchant of Kansas City. The courtship, engagement and final marriage has been a most romantic series of events.

By this time the parties have left the country. Jesse, however, declared it to be his full intention to return and take his trial when he thought he could get a trial other than at the hands of a mob.

Frank James was also married about the same time in what the *St. Louis Dispatch* correspondent would call "a romantic series of events . . ."

His bride was Annie Ralston, daughter of a wealthy Jackson County farmer; they eloped with the father of the bride not knowing for some months that his son-in-law was one of the most notorious and wanted outlaws in the West.

The *Kansas City Times*, which broke the story of "the mysterious and romantic flight of a young girl with one of the James Brothers," revealed that Annie, on the pretext of visiting her brother-in-law in Kansas City, met Frank and they eloped. A few days later she wrote her parents a brief note that she was "married and going West."[18]

The story came out when a posse raided the Ralston home after the gang had robbed the Missouri Pacific train at Otterville in July 1876; the lawmen told Ralston they were looking for his son-in-law.

Some months before the raid Frank had visited the Ralstons, "riding up on a handsome chesnut colored horse," and spoke to Ralston, who was reading in his yard.

When Ralston demanded to know what had become of his daughter, Frank told him, "We were married in Omaha and Annie has the certificate."

There were bitter words between Frank and Ralston "and Frank James mounted his horse and galloped away, to be seen no more at the Ralston house afterwards . . . and the parents can rest in uncertainty of ever seeing their daughter again. . . ."

Frank and Annie joined Jesse and Zee in Texas for a honeymoon. Then romance was put aside as Jesse gathered his riders together for his disastrous strike at the bank of Northfield, Minnesota.

The Northfield Raid

The raid on the Northfield, Minnesota, bank by the James and Younger gang in the fall of 1876 is one of the most exciting and colorful incidents in frontier history. For the first time citizens refused to be intimidated or awed by "the greatest revolver fighters in the world" and struck back, shattering the gang of outlaws with rocks and bullets.

There were numerous theories as to why Jesse had led his gang to make a strike at a bank so far from home. Some said it was an act of vengeance, that Jesse had vowed to bankrupt the town because some of its citizens had played a part in the raid on the Samuels' farmhouse. An uncle of the Youngers claimed that "the boys" were on their way to Canada when Jesse and Frank lost their money gambling and persuaded the others to recoup their losses in a bank robbery.[19]

Years later Cole Younger in an interview claimed that the Youngers, along with Frank and Jesse, had decided to move out of the state and settle down. They selected the Northfield bank to finance this plan because they had heard

Bridge Square, Northfield, Minnesota, at the time of the bank raid by the James-Younger gang on Monday, September 4, 1876. *The James D. Horan Civil War and Western Americana Collection*

The First National Bank of Northfield. The bank was the heart of the tiny shopping center known as the "Scriver Block," named after Northfield's pioneering merchant. Off to the right is one of the two hardware stores owned by J. S. Allen and Anselm R. Manning, who played leading roles in the bloody drama. *The James D. Horan Civil War and Western Americana Collection*

General Ben Butler, the squint-eyed former Union general, and his son-in-law had money invested in the institution. Because of Butler's treatment of Southerners during the war, Cole concluded, they "felt little compunction" in robbing the bank.[20]

A more logical explanation is that William Chadwell alias William Stiles, a Minnesotan, convinced Jesse that the Northfield bank had large deposits of farming money and that he knew the territory so intimately the gang could make an easy escape.

The robbery began to misfire when Joseph Heywood, the cashier, resisted all threats to force him to open the vault. In addition, the alarm was given and the people in the streets began to fight back, with a sharpshooting young medical student picking off the outlaws riding up and down the street. Stiles/Chadwell was the first to fall; with his death Jesse and the gang were in an alien, hostile territory. After the robbery had taken place, George Huntington, a Northfield newspaperman, interviewed eyewitnesses to the battle and the subsequent manhunt and wrote what is probably the most accurate account of what took place on that quiet morning of September 7, 1876.[21]

Northfield Invaded

The center of operations was the corner of Bridge Square and Division Street. On this corner stood a two-story stone building known as the Scriver Block. Its upper story was used for offices, and was reached by an outside stairway on Division Street. The larger part of the lower story was occupied by two stores, ranging north and south, and having their front entrances on the northern or Bridge Square side. At the extreme southern end of the building, and having its entrance on the eastern or Division Street side, was the object of attack—the First National Bank. On the western side of the block ran a narrow alley, affording rear entrances to the stores and the bank. West of the alley, and fronting on the square, were two hardware stores whose respective proprietors were leading actors in the scene that followed,—J. S. Allen and A. R. Manning. On the eastern side of Division Street, opposite the Scriver Block, were a hotel and a number of stores, in front of one of which stood a young man who was also to have a prominent part in the coming affray,—Mr. H. M. Wheeler, then at home on a vacation from his medical studies in Michigan University.

A floor plan of the Northfield bank showing where Heywood, the cashier, was shot and killed. (Prepared for George Huntington's history of the raid.) *The James D. Horan Civil War and Western Americana Collection*

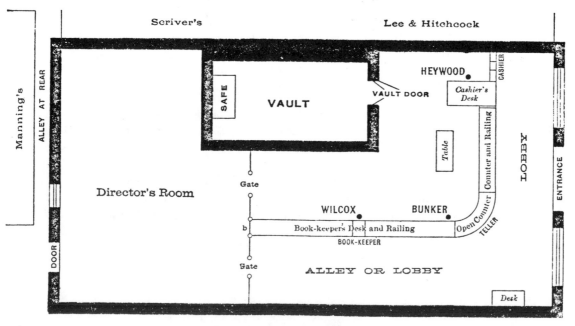

Miller's

The robber band comprised three subdivisions,—the two James brothers, the three Younger brothers, and three odd ones,—Miller, Pitts and Stiles. In their active operations another threefold division was adopted, each of the squads containing one of the Younger brothers and one of the odd ones, and two of them containing one of the James brothers. That is there were two trios and one couple. Of these, one trio was detailed to commit the robbery, while the couple cooperated with them on Division Street, and the other trio acted as a rear guard on Bridge Square, the direction in which the band intended to retreat.

It was about 2 o'clock in the afternoon that the first trio, consisting of Pitts, Bob Younger and, it is believed, one of the James brothers, came over the bridge, and crossing the Square from Northwest to southeast, dismounted in front of the bank, throwing their bridle reins over some hitching-posts beside the street. They then sauntered to the corner and lounged upon some dry-goods boxes in front of the store (Lee and Hitchcock's) assuming an air of indifference, and whittling the boxes, like the most commonplace loafers. Presently the two horsemen constituting the second detail entered Division Street from the south, and rode toward the bank. They were Cole Younger and Clel Miller. Upon their approach the three men at the corner walked back to the door of the bank and went in. Miller, dismounting in front of the door, left his horse unhitched, went to the door and looked in, and then, closing it, walked back and forth before it. Younger dismounted in the middle of the street, where he made a pretense of tightening his saddle-girth.

By this time the attention of several citizens had been attracted to the maneuvers of the robbers.

Among those whose suspicions had been especially aroused were Dr. Henry M. Wheeler and Mr. J. S. Allen. Dr. Wheeler was sitting under an awning in front of his father's store on the east side of Division Street when the men entered the street; and as their actions seemed to him to indicate some mischievous intent, he rose and moved along the sidewalk till he was opposite them. Mr. Allen was on the other side of the street; and when he saw the three men enter the bank, he attempted to follow them in. He was instantly seized by Miller, who had been placed there for that purpose, and who, drawing his revolver, and pouring forth a volley of oaths, ordered Allen to stand back, and warned him on peril of his life not to utter a word. Allen jerked away from the ruffian's grasp, and ran back to and around the corner toward his store, shouting in a voice that resounded blocks away, "Get your guns, boys! They're robbing the bank!" At the same time Dr. Wheeler had stepped into the street, and was shouting, "Robbery! Robbery!" his alarm being at once justified and intensified by the sound of pistol shots within the bank.

Upon this, Miller and Younger sprang into their saddles, ordering Wheeler back, with oaths and threats, and firing one or two shots over his head, to intimidate him and to give notice to their confederates that their game was discovered. Then the two robbers began riding up and down Division Street, at their utmost speed, shooting right and left, and with horrible oaths calling upon every one they saw to "get in"—an order that was obeyed with pretty general promptness and unanimity. At the same time the three men near the bridge took up the same tactics, and came dashing across the Square, shooting and shouting like their comrades, whom they joined on Division Street. Wherever they saw a head, out of doors or at a window, they sent a shower of balls. The air was filled with the sounds of the fray,—the incessant bang bang of the heavy revolvers, the whistling of bullets, the crashing of glass and the chorus of wild yells and impreca-

For many years this photograph has been identified as that of Oscar Seeborn, a young Scandinavian who could not understand English and was killed by the outlaws as they drove citizens off the streets. News accounts of his death in Minnesota newspapers, however, reported his name as Nicholas Gustavson. *The James D. Horan Civil War and Western Americana Collection*

Joseph Lee Heywood, cashier of the bank, killed by one of the gang when he refused to open the safe. *The James D. Horan Civil War and Western Americana Collection*

tions. The first intention of the robbers was not to kill any one, but to strike terror into the minds of the people, and, by driving everybody from the streets, to give the men in the bank time to work, to prevent any attempt at interference, and to secure themselves an unobstructed line of retreat. Strange to say, during this part of the affray, though the robbers kept up a constant fusilade from their revolvers, but one person was shot,—a Scandinavian who could not understand English, and who was fatally wounded while persistently remaining on the street.

Meantime, a very different scene was enacted within the bank, where the first trio of robbers were dealing with a trio of bank employes as resolute as themselves. These were Mr. A. E. Bunker, teller, Mr. J. L. Heywood, book-keeper and Mr. F. J. Wilcox, assistant book-keeper. The cashier, Mr. G. M. Phillips, being out of the state, Mr. Heywood was acting cashier. The bank was at the time occupying temporary quarters, not arranged with reference to emergencies of this kind. A counter, constructed somewhat like an ordinary office or store counter, extended across two sides, between the lobby and the interior of the room. This was surmounted for nearly its entire length by a high railing containing glass panels; but in the angle between the two sections of the counter there was an open space, entirely unprotected, wide enough for a man to pass through.

When the three robbers entered the bank the employes were busy at their tasks, and had no suspicion of approaching danger. Mr. Bunker, the teller, hearing footsteps in the lobby, and supposing that some customer had entered, turned from his work to wait upon him, coming to the open space before referred to. There three revolvers were pointing at him, and he was peremptorily ordered to throw up his hands. His first impression was that some of his friends were playing a practical joke upon him. Before he had time to comprehend the situation, the three robbers had climbed over the counter, and covering him and his associates with their revolvers, commanded them to hold up their hands.

Alonzo E. Bunker, the bank teller and also a teacher at nearby Carleton College, who was wounded by the gang when he escaped from the rear door. Bunker later became a frontier newspaper correspondent and an executive of the Western Newspaper Union. *The James D. Horan Civil War and Western Americana Collection*

Frank J. Wilcox, the bank's bookkeeper, who refused to open the vault but was not wounded. Son of a Baptist minister, Wilcox had joined the bank a short time before the raid, after graduating from Chicago University. *The James D. Horan Civil War and Western Americana Collection*

"We're going to rob this bank," said one of the men. "Don't any of you holler. We've got forty men outside." Then, with a flourish of his revolver, he pointed to Heywood and said, "Are you the cashier?"

"No," replied Heywood.

The same question was put to Bunker and to Wilcox, each of whom made the same reply.

"You are the cashier," said the robber, turning upon Heywood, who was sitting at the cashier's desk, and who appeared to be the oldest of the employes. "Open that safe—quick, or I'll blow your head off."

A second robber—Pitts—then ran to the vault and stepped inside, whereupon Heywood, who had risen to his feet, followed him and attempted to close the door. He was instantly dragged back, and the two robbers, thrusting their revolvers in his face, said, "Open that safe, now, or you haven't but a minute to live," accompanying their threats with oaths.

"There is a time lock on," Heywood replied, "and it cannot be opened now."

"That's a lie!" retorted the robbers, again repeatedly demanding, with threats and profanity, that the safe be opened, and dragging Heywood roughly about the room.

Finally, seeming to realize what desperate men he was dealing with, Heywood shouted, "Murder! Murder! Murder!" Whereupon one of the robbers struck him a terrible blow on the head with a revolver, felling him to the floor. Pitts then drew a knife from his pocket, and opening it, said, "Let's cut his —— throat," and made a feint of doing so, inflicting a slight wound on Heywood's neck as he lay helpless upon the floor. The two men then dragged him from where he lay, at the rear of his desk, back to the door of the vault, still demanding that he open the safe. Occasionally also they turned from him to Bunker and Wilcox, pointing their revolvers at them and calling on them to "Unlock that safe." To this demand the young men answered that they could not unlock the safe. The statement was true, though in a sense quite different from that in which the robbers understood it. The reason that they could not unlock it was that it was unlocked already. The door was closed and the bolts were shot into place, but the combination dial was not turned. This was one of the humors of the situation, but one which those in the secret were not in a position to enjoy. As a last resort for coercing Heywood, who was still lying on the floor, in but a partially conscious condition, Pitts placed his revolver close to Heywood's head and fired. The bullet passed into the vault and through a tin box containing jewelry and papers left by some customer for safe keeping. This was the first shot fired in the bank, and its futility well foretokened the failure of the whole effort.

While Bunker and Wilcox received occasional attention from Heywood's assailants, their special custodian was Bob Younger. As Bunker had his pen in his hand when first ordered to hold up his hands, it remained for a time poised in the air, when he made an effort to lay it down. Younger, noticing the movement, and thinking it an attempt to reach a weapon, sprang at Bunker, and thrusting his revolver into his face, said, "Here, put up your hands and keep 'em up, or I'll kill you!" Then, to hold his prisoners more completely under his control, he compelled them both to get down on their knees under the counter. All the robbers were very much excited, and increasingly so as they found themselves baffled and resisted. Younger would point his pistol first at one of the young men and then at the other, turning from time to time to search among the papers on the desk, or to open a drawer in quest of valuables.

While still on his knees, Bunker remembered a revolver kept on a shelf under the teller's window, and edged toward the place in hope of reaching it. Turning his head that way while Younger's back was toward him, his movement was instantly detected by Pitts, who leaped before him, and seizing the pistol, put it in his own pocket, remarking, "You needn't try to get hold of that. You couldn't do any thing with that little derringer, anyway." It is no doubt fortunate that Bunker did not succeed in reaching the weapon, as he would almost certainly have been shot down by the robbers before he could use it. The pistol was found upon Pitts at the time of his capture and death.

Bunker now rose to his feet, intending to make some effort to escape or to give an alarm. As he did so, Younger turned to him and said, "Where's the money outside the safe? Where's the cashier's till?" Bunker showed him a partitioned box on the counter, containing some small change and fractional currency; but did not call his attention to a drawer beneath the counter, containing $3,000 in bills. Again ordering Bunker to get down on his knees and keep his hands up, Younger drew from under his coat a grain-sack, which he began to fill from the box. Presently he turned again to Bunker, and finding him on his feet, he said, with a wicked look and with an outburst of horrible profanity, "There's more money than that out here. Where's that cashier's till? And what in —— are you standing up for? I told you to keep down." Seizing Bunker, and forcing him to the floor, Younger pressed the muzzle of his revolver against Bunker's temple and said, "Show me where that money is, you —— —— —— or I'll kill you!" Receiving no answer, he left Bunker and renewed his search for the money.

Bunker once more regained his feet, and taking advantage of a moment when the robber's face was turned, he dashed past Wilcox, into and through the directors' room, to the rear door, then closed with blinds fastened on the inside. His intention was to enter the rear of Manning's hardware store, on the other side of the alley, and give the alarm. He knew nothing yet of what was going on in the street, and he believed Heywood to be dead from the effect of the pistol shot apparently aimed at his head.

The first of the robbers to notice the escape was Pitts, whose eyes seemed to be everywhere at once, and who was then with Heywood in front of the vault. Before he had time to shoot, however, Bunker was out of his range around the corner of the vault, and making for the door. With a mad yell Pitts bounded after the fugitive, and coming in sight of him, fired as he ran, the ball whizzing past Bunker's ear and through the blind in front of him. Bunker threw his weight against the blinds, bursting them open, plunged down a flight of outside steps, and had nearly reached the rear entrance of the next building when he was again fired upon by Pitts. This time the ball hit its mark, passing through the right shoulder, near the joint, barely missing the sub-clavian artery, and coming out just below the collar-bone. As he felt the sting and shock of the wound, he stumbled; but keeping his feet, and not knowing how badly he might be wounded, he ran on across a vacant lot and around to a surgeon's office in the next block. Pitts gave up the chase and returned to his companions in the bank, but only to hear one of their confederates on the outside shout, "The game is up! Better get out, boys. They're killing all our men." Hearing this, the three robbers sprang through the teller's window and rushed into the street. As the last one climbed over the counter, he turned toward poor Heywood, who had gotten upon his feet and was staggering toward his desk, and deliberately shot him through the head.

The battle in the street was now at its height, and the spirit in which it was waged on the part of the citizens showed how grossly the robbers had mistaken the mettle of the people with whom they had to deal. The community was taken by surprise and at a great disadvantage. It was at the height of the prairie-chicken season, and a majority of the men who had guns were away in the field. The excellent hunting in the neighborhood had drawn many sportsmen from the larger cities, accustoming the people to the presence of strangers, while they had no reason to expect a hostile invasion. When the mounted bandits on Bridge Square and Division Street began riding and shooting, the first impression was that of surprise. Some thought it the reckless fun of drunken scapegraces. Some took the riders to be the attaches of a traveling show, advertising their performance. When the bullets began to fly about people's ears, and the character of the invaders became evident, every body was stunned and dazed, and there was a general scramble for shelter. But the next moment there was an equally prompt rally of brave men to repel the attack.

Dr. Wheeler, who had been one of the first to give the alarm, and who had been driven from the street by the imprecations and bullets of the robbers, hastened to the drug-store where he usually kept his gun. Remembering as he went that he had left it at the house, he did not slacken his pace, but kept on through the store, heading first for the house of a neighbor, where he hoped a weapon might be found, but on second thought turning into the Dampier Hotel, close at hand, where he remembered to have seen one. There, instead of the fowling-piece he looked for, he found an old army carbine, for which, with the help of Mr. Dampier the clerk, three cartridges were discovered in another part of the house. All this was so quickly done, that he was at a second-story chamber window, with his gun loaded, in time for the beginning of the fight.

Meantime Mr. Allen, who had also sounded so prompt and vigorous an alarm, ran to his store where he had a number of guns, and loading them with such ammunition as came to his hand, gave them to anybody who would take them. One

Henry M. Wheeler, a medical student at the University of Michigan, who was home on vacation at the time of the raid. Armed with an old army carbine and three shells, he ran to the second floor of the Dampier Hotel, overlooking the battle in the street. He killed Clel Miller with one shot, then shattered Bob Younger's elbow with another. Wheeler sent the bodies of Miller and Stiles to his medical school for dissecting. He kept Miller's skeleton in his Grand Forks, North Dakota, office for more than half a century. *The James D. Horan Civil War and Western Americana Collection*

Anselm R. Manning, owner of one of Northfield's two hardware stores, was described by his neighbors after the Northfield raid as "quiet, good natured and peaceful." Armed with a breech-lever rifle, he ran into the street at the first cry that the bank was being held up to kill Bob Younger's horse and wound Cole Younger. When his weapon jammed he found a ramrod, dislodged an empty shell, and returned to the gun battle. While bullets whistled about him and his neighbors pleaded with him to fire, Manning coolly waited until he found a target, then with one shot killed William Stiles alias Bill Chadwell. *The James D. Horan Civil War and Western Americana Collection*

of them was taken by Mr. Elias Stacy, who used it to good purpose in the battle that followed.

As Mr. Allen went to his own store, he had passed that of Mr. Manning, to whom he shouted his warning concerning the robbers. Up to this time Manning had no suspicion of what was going on. One of the robbers had been in the store in the forenoon, looking about and pretending he wanted to buy a gun. He was a genteel, well-dressed fellow, and Manning supposed him to be some stranger who had come to Northfield to hunt; though he did not believe that he wanted any gun, and thought there was something wrong about him. Even when the three horsemen dashed through the Square so noisily and belligerently, he thought little of it. But when he heard Allen's shout, and made out the words "Robbing the Bank," he recalled what he had seen and the meaning of it all flashed upon his mind. Abruptly leaving the customer he was serving, he rushed for a weapon, thinking hard and fast. Pistols? No, they would be of little account. His shotgun? Yes—No; he had left all his loaded cartridges at home. His breach-loading rifle! That was the thing; and here it was in the window; and there in a pigeon-hole of his desk were the cartridges, where they had been carelessly thrown months before. All this came to him without an instant's loss of time. He forgot nothing and he made no mistakes. Stripping the rifle of its cover, and seizing a handful of cartridges, he hurried to the scene of battle, loading as he ran.

The scene on the street is indescribable. People had not only made haste to get out of the way of the leaden hail-storm that had burst forth, but had also taken

o

measures to protect themselves and their property against the raiders, whose intention was believed to be not only to rob the bank but to pillage the entire town. Stores and offices were hastily closed. The postmaster, Capt. H. S. French, who chanced to have an exceptionally heavy registered mail on hand that day, hastened to lock it in the safe and close the Office. Jewelers and others who had valuable and portable stock pursued a similar course. The news of the invasion, emphasized by the sound of the shooting, spread swiftly through the town. Warning was sent to the public school and to Carleton College to keep the students off the streets. The general impression was that the town was in possession of a horde of robbers, numbering nobody knew how many, and coming nobody knew whence, and bent on ruthless plunder, nobody knew to what extent.

The scene of the actual conflict was that part of Division Street on which the bank faced, and scarcely a full block in length. Here the five mounted robbers were riding back and forth, up one side of the street and down the other, doing their utmost with voice and arms to keep up the reign of terror which they had begun. The citizens whom they had driven in were looking for weapons, and the bolder ones were coming back, some armed and some unarmed, around the margin of the field. Capt. French, having made Uncle Sam's property as secure as possible, stood in front of the locked door, wondering where he could soonest find a gun. Justice Streater and ex policeman Elias Hobbs stepped out into the Square determined to do something by way of resistance to the invasion.

Mr. Hobbs, who had no weapon at all, fell back upon more primitive methods, and at the height of the fray came on shouting, "Stone 'em! Stone 'em!" and suiting the action to the word, and choosing not "smooth stones from the brook," but big and formidable missiles, more fit for the hand of Goliath than for the sling of David, hurled rocks and curses at the enemy, and not without effect. Col. Streater also joined in this mode of warfare, which, if not the most effective, certainly evinced as high a degree of courage as they could have shown in the use of the most approved weapons. Other citizens, too, took a hand in the affair, as opportunity offered, and some of them had narrow escapes from the bullets with which the robbers responded to their attentions.

But while there was no lack of good intentions on the part of others, it was the two men with rifles, Manning and Wheeler, who were able to do real execution upon the enemy, and finally to put them to rout. We go back, therefore, to the moment when Manning came running from his store with the rifle in his hand. Taking in the situation at a glance, and intent only upon getting at the robbers, he stepped out into the open street, and amid a shower of bullets, coolly looked for his game. Before him stood the horses of the men who were still in the bank, and over the backs of the horses he saw the heads of two men, upon whom he instantly drew a bead. The men ducked behind the horses, whereupon Manning, without lowering his gun, changed his aim and shot the nearest horse, rightly judging that this would cripple the band almost as effectually as shooting the men. He then dropped back around the corner to reload; but finding to his chagrin that the breach-lever would not throw out the empty shell, he was obliged to go back to the store and get a ramrod with which to dislodge it, thus losing valuable time. The interruption proved a good thing for him, however, moderating his excitement and rashness, and preparing him to do better execution. Soon he was at the corner again. Peering around the corner, he saw one of the robbers between the horses and the bank door, and fired at him. The ball grazed the edge of a post, deflecting it slightly; but it found Cole Younger, wounding him in a vulnerable though not vital place. Again Manning dropped back to reload. The shell gave him no trouble this time, and he was quickly at his post once more. As he looked cautiously around the corner, he saw Stiles sitting on his horse, some seventy-five or eighty yards away, apparently doing sentry duty in that part of the street. Manning took deliberate aim at him—so deliberate as to excite the impatience and call forth the protests of some who were near him—and fired, shooting the man through the heart. Manning, as before, stepped back to reload, the robber fell from his saddle, dead, and the horse ran to a livery-stable around the corner.

While these things were going on, Dr. Wheeler was not idle. His first shot was at the head of Jim Younger, who was riding by. The gun carried high, and the ball struck the ground beyond him. Younger looked first at the spot where it struck, and then turned to see where it came from, but did not discover the sharp-shooter at the window above him. Wheeler's next shot was at Clel Miller, whom Stacy had already peppered with bird-shot. The bullet passed through his body almost precisely as Pitts' bullet had passed through Bunker's; but in this case the great artery was severed and almost instant death ensued. Wheeler's third and last cartridge had fallen upon the floor, bursting the paper of which it was made, and spilling the powder. Hurrying in search of more, he met his friend Dampier coming with a fresh supply.

The robbers were now badly demoralized. Their shooting had been wild and fruitless. They had lost two men and a horse killed; a third man was wounded; two riderless horses had escaped from them, and an armed force had cut off their proposed line of retreat. It was at this juncture that Cole Younger rode to the door of the bank and shouted to the men inside to come out, which they made all haste to do. Two of the men mounted their horses, which still stood before the door. There was no horse for Bob Younger, and he was compelled to fight on foot.

By this time Manning and Wheeler had both reloaded, and returned to their places. As Manning showed himself, ready to renew the battle, Bob Younger came running toward him down the sidewalk. Manning raised his rifle to shoot at the approaching robber, and at the same instant Younger drew his revolver to shoot Manning. In the effort to get out of each other's range, Younger dodged under the outside stairway of the Scriver Block, while Manning stood at the corner beyond it. The stairs were thus between them, and neither of them could get a shot at the other without exposing himself to the fire of his adversary. For a time they kept up a game of hide and seek, each trying in vain to catch the other off his guard and get the first shot. At this point Wheeler, though he could but imperfectly see Younger's body beneath the stair, took a shot at him. The ball struck the robber's elbow, shattering the bone. He then coolly changed his pistol to his left hand and continued his efforts to shoot Manning.

It then occurred to Manning that by running around through the store he might reach the street on the other side of the robber, and so drive him from his hiding-place. This plan he instantly put in execution. At the same moment Wheeler was engaged in reloading his gun. But the robbers had their plans, too, and took advantage of this momentary lull to make their escape. Bob Younger sprang from his hiding-place and ran up Division street, where he mounted behind his brother Cole; and the entire band,—or at least what was left of it,— turned and fled. Wheeler returned to his window and Manning emerged upon the sidewalk only to find that their game had flown. Even then there was an excellent chance for long-range shooting; but the intervening space was immediately filled with people, making it impossible to shoot without endangering innocent lives.

This battle between desperados and peaceful citizens has well been cited as proof that the prowess, courage and dead-shot skill at arms commonly ascribed to the border ruffian are largely imaginary. On the one side was a band of heavily armed and thoroughly trained and organized banditti, carrying out a carefully made plan, in their own line of business, after weeks of preparation. On the other side was a quiet, law-abiding community, unused to scenes of violence, taken utterly by surprise and at a fearful disadvantage, with no adequate means of defence except two long-disused rifles in out-of-the-way places, and one of them on the retired army list. Yet the banditti were beaten at their own game, and their courage lasted only while the odds were in their favor. As to marksmanship, they were vastly outdone by their citizen opponents.

"Goodbye Jesse"*

After Jesse led his shattered band out of Northfield, the telegraph hummed with news of the raid. Farmers and townspeople volunteered by the hundreds and large posses began scouring the territory.

The gang was in desperate straits. Bill Chadwell, who knew the trails and back roads, was dead. Cole Younger and his brother, Jim, were riding double, while the severely wounded Bob Younger was barely able to cling to his reins.

They left in a cloud of dust, the church bells clanging wildly. Their luck still held. At Dundas, three miles away, the telegraph operator was at lunch, his key clattering in an empty office. Townspeople looked puzzled as the horsemen galloped down their main street and minutes later disappeared.

They pushed on steadily, riding five abreast guerilla-style, forcing horsemen and wagons off the road. At Millersburg they stole a farmer's horse but the saddle-girth snapped, spilling Bob Younger into the road. While Jesse watched impatiently, Cole and Jim pulled him back into the saddle.

The weather turned cold and drizzly as they continued to dodge posses. There were brief encounters: at Shieldville they surrounded a posse who had left their rifles leaning against a barn, and held them under guard while they watered their horses. They had no food and finally, in desperation, they bought supplies in Mankato. Again the alarm was given and the manhunters began moving in. It was about this time that Jesse, haggard and savage, demanded that Bob Younger be left behind. Cole stood up to him and it was decided they would split into two parties.

Fourteen days after the raid, the gang was surrounded in the small village of Medalia. In the gunfight Charlie Pitts was killed and Cole, Jim, and Bob Younger were seriously wounded. They were taken to jail at Faribault, Minnesota, where they were fed and their wounds treated. Rather than risk hanging, they all pleaded guilty and were sentenced to life imprisonment in the state penitentiary at Stillwater.

But Jesse and Frank successfully slipped through the lines, made their way to Dakota Territory, and finally back home to Clay County. While the Republican and Democratic newspapers engaged in an editorial war over the issue of

*Headline in the *Kansas City Journal*, April 4, 1882.

A story in the *St. Paul Pioneer Press* and *Minneapolis Tribune*, September 12, 1876, of the intense manhunt for the James-Younger gang. *Courtesy State Historical Society of Missouri*

THE CHASE.

Latest Details of the Pursuit of the Brigands.

Probability that the Robbers Have Left the Woods.

Officers and Citizens Everywhere Warned to be on the Qui Vive.

Conflicting Statements and Rumors from the Pursuing Detachments.

Nothing Reliable that the Villians Have Been Seen Since Friday.

Full Details of Sunday's Operations in the Lake Elysian Country.

Reinforcements Sents from St. Paul Sunday to Assist in the Capture.

Major Strait at the Council of War —A Sensible View of the Case.

Romantic and Thrilling Episode, by an Occasional Correspondent.

The Latest.
Special to The Pioneer-Press and Tribune.

WATERVILLE, Sept. 11.—There is a chance that the Northfield robbers have left the woods. Advise all over the state that all suspicious characters be watched. We have organized a thorough search of these woods. SHERIFF BARTON.

DEATH OF THE WOUNDED SWEDE.
Special to The Pioneer-Press and Tribune.

NORTHFIELD, Sept. 11—6 p. m.— Nicholas Gustavson, who was shot by the robbers last Thursday by the robbers while walking near the bank, died this afternoon. He was a Swede, a single man, and could not talk English. He had been living out at Morristown.

IN A NEW PLACE.
Special to The Pioneer-Press and Tribune.

ST. PETER, MINN., Sept. 11.—Deputy Sheriff Moll brings the intelligence that at 3 o'clock this afternoon, about one mile north of Marysburg, they found where the robbers had camped this morning, the ashes of their camp-fire still being warm. Mayor Sackett is sending out men, and all the guards at this city will be doubled.

BACK AT THE OLD PLACE.
Special to The Pioneer-Press and Tribune.

OWATONNA, Sept. 10.—Latest report by citizens just in from Waterville says the report is false that robbers have been seen to-day. Traces have been found where they stayed last night, and there is no doubt the robbers are still secreted in the woods near Elysian.

GONE EAST.
Special to The Pioneer-Press and Tribune.

OWATONNA, Minn., Sept. 11.— Captain C. L. Smith, with a force from Faribault, is patrolling the roads near Elysian. He reports driving the robbers out of the woods near Waterville this morning, about 7 o'clock. The robbers then took an easterly direction, and were afterwards seen near Morristown, going southeast. They are evidently striking to cross the Winona & St. Peter railroad between here and Waseca. A special train from Winona with 125 armed men passed here at 5 o'clock this evening, and the men are now at Waseca. A train has gone to Eagle Lake to bring the men from St. Paul, Minneapolis, Northfield and Faribault, who are now at that place, back to Waseca. A force of twenty horsemen have just left here to patrol the bridges between here and Meriden, which the robbers must cross if they attempt to go south. The information herewith is fully confirmed, and is reliable.

DISAPPEARED NEAR MARYSBURG.
Special to The Pioneer-Press and Tribune.

JANESVILLE, Minn., Sept. 11, 1 p. m.—Drs. Sickett and Cummings, of this place, have come in, and report having seen and followed the trail yesterday of six horsemen until lost near Marysburg. The horsemen avoided the road and even the cowpaths, and everywhere made across sodded ground where it was possible. The tracks correspond to the descriptions of those made by the gang. The reporters that several reliable parties have already gone to the front, and Sheriff Dill, of Winona, Brisette and party and the twenty men from St. Paul, who have just arrived, are now arranging for a concentrated plan of action. Sheriff Barton, of Faribault, has not communicated with this point to-day.

The posse that captured the Youngers after the Northfield raid. L. to R., top row: Captain W. W. Murphy, Ben M. Rice, C. A. Pomeroy. Bottom row: Sheriff James Glispin, G. A. Bradford, and Colonel T. L. Vought. Murphy, wounded three times in the Civil War and made a captain on the field for bravery under fire during the Battle of Piedmont, Virginia, led the posse in an attack on the hiding place of the outlaws. *The James D. Horan Civil War and Western Americana Collection*

The dead, wounded, and captured outlaws after the Northfield raid. *The James D. Horan Civil War and Western Americana Collection*

PITTS

BOB YOUNGER

JIM YOUNGER

COLE YOUNGER

STILES

MILLER

FRANKLIN CO. ENG CHI

THE ROBBERS—KILLED AND CAPTURED.

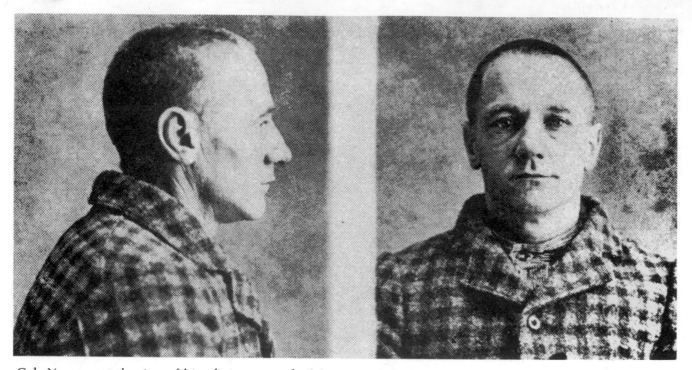

Cole Younger at the time of his admittance to the Minnesota State Penitentiary, Stillwater. *Courtesy Minnesota Historical Society*

the James gang, lawmen advanced on the Samuel farmhouse but the outlaws successfully made their getaway, again skimming the fences and vanishing into the woods.

Jesse James and Billy the Kid

The trail of Jesse and Frank abruptly faded out. There were many legends: Jesse was in South America; Frank worked with a Texas cow outfit; then both were miners in or around Leadville, robbing stages when the veins of gold were exhausted. One excited newspaper report had Frank leading a band of army deserters in Wyoming's Wind River country.

For a time they may have hidden out in the Hite farmhouse near Adairville, Kentucky, with Frank moving across the border into Tennessee, where he later lived very happily as a farmer, while Jesse, as "Mr. Howard," rejoined his family in various cities.

However, in the summer of 1879 Jesse rode into New Mexico, where, according to two reputable eyewitnesses, he met Billy the Kid, who like Jesse was becoming an American legend.

When Jesse arrived the famous "Lincoln County War," the most savage social and political range war in the West, was nearing its bloody crest. The lines had been drawn: on one side were the riders of Alexander McSween, a Lincoln lawyer, and John Tunstall, a quiet, cultured Englishman who had settled in the Rio Feliz country; on the other a ring of corrupt officials. Tunstall was murdered by hired gunmen with Billy the Kid as an eyewitness.

During the summer before Jesse arrived, the county sheriff had been gunned

PERIODICALS

The Furniture Journal
SEMI-MONTHLY

The Embalmers' Monthly

•BOOKS

ART AND SCIENCE OF EMBALMING, BARNES
CONTAGIOUS AND INFECTIOUS DISEASES,
DISINFECTION AND DISINFECTANTS, BARNES
MODERN FUNERAL, HOHENSCHUH
DISINFECTION AND DISINFECTANTS, BRACKEN
VEST POCKET QUIZ COMPENDS, BARNES
CHEMISTRY FOR EMBALMERS, M'CULLY
CONFESSIONS OF AN UNDERTAKER, ROGERS

WHITTAKER'S ANATOMICAL MODEL

P. D. FRANCIS,
PRESIDENT & MANAGER

L. M. ALBERTSON,
SECRETARY

J. NEWTON NIND,
VICE-PRES'T & EDITOR

79
0

Trade Periodical Company

PUBLISHERS OF

The Furniture Journal
The Embalmers' Monthly

355-357 DEARBORN ST., CHICAGO

MINNEAPOLIS   LONG DISTANCE TELEPHONE   ROCKFORD
                        HARRISON 2036

Chicago, June 30th, 1905

My Dear Mr. Curtis:

I have just read your letter about the James and Younger Brothers in the issue of the Record Herald of Sunday last. Was out of town and missed it at the time. You are mistaken about Bob Younger being still alive. He died in the prison at Stillwater, about ten years after his incarceration. The only survivor of the family is Cole, who was out last year with

Rare and unpublished letter from J. Newton Lind, a member of the Northfield posse, who gives an eyewitness account of the capture of the Youngers. *The James D. Horan Civil War and Western Americana Collection*

The Youngers were all captured at Madelia, Minn., which is less than 150 miles west of Northfield. They were captured after a chase lasting over three weeks. It has never been positively established that the James Brothers were in the Northfield raid with them, although there is every reason to beleive that such was the case. The men who entered the bank answer the discription of the James Brothers. But the Younger Brothers never disclosed the identity of their companions, other than the three who were killed at Northfield, or at Madelia. I have a vivid recollection of all this for I joined in the chase of the robbers while I was connected with the Pioneer Press

Excerpt from Lind's letter in which he reveals how he unsuccessfully tried to get the Youngers to name Jesse and Frank James as their companions on the Northfield raid. *The James D. Horan Civil War and Western Americana Collection*

down and Lincoln became the scene of a week-long battle with Billy the Kid, McSween, and their supporters under siege in the McSween house. When it was set afire, Billy led the others through the billowing smoke; McSween and a young law clerk were killed in the flurry of shots, but the Kid got away to the Benito River and vanished into the hills.

On July 26, 1879, Jesse rode into Hot Springs, six miles from Las Vegas, and checked into W. Scott Moore's Old Adobe Hotel. By the time he had settled down in his room Jesse had been contacted by—or had contacted—Billy the Kid.

A meeting took place the next day, a Sunday, July 27, surely the most intriguing date in the history of western outlawry.

There were two reputable witnesses in the dining room: Henry Hoyt, once Chief Surgeon on the staffs of Major General McArthur and the former governor of New Mexico, Miguel Antonio Otero. In his highly regarded autobiography, *A Frontier Doctor*, published in 1929, Hoyt tells how he walked into the dining room and was surprised to see Billy the Kid, whom he knew, sitting with two men at a corner table. Gesturing to the man on his left, the Kid said:

"Hoyt, meet my friend, Mr. Howard from Tennessee."

The physician joined the two most wanted men in the nation and they had dinner. Before Hoyt left, Billy pledged him to secrecy and identified "Mr. Howard" as Jesse James, who, Hoyt later insisted, fitted the description of the Missouri bandit leader.

In his memoirs, *My Life on the Frontier, 1864-1882*, published in 1935, Otero tells the same story. Moore's place was widely known on the southwestern frontier for its fine Sunday meals cooked by Moore's wife, Minna, and this day Otero followed his usual practice of riding to Hot Springs and having dinner at the hotel. He also knew Billy the Kid and, like Hoyt, was introduced to Jesse, who Moore explained had been a boyhood friend in Clay County.

In addition to the versions of Hoyt and Otero, the *Las Vegas Optic* published this item on December 8, 1879: "Jesse James was guest at the Las Vegas Hot Springs from July 26 to July 29. Of course it was not generally known."

At the time, Billy was a fugitive after escaping from the Lincoln jail. He realized that he had been made a scapegoat by Governor Lew Wallace, who had broken his promise of amnesty in return for Billy's appearance before the grand jury and a statement naming the rustling gangs and hideouts for stolen beef. A year before, the Kid had given his eyewitness account of Tunstall's murder to Frank Warner Angel, who had been sent into Lincoln County on orders of President Hayes and Secretary of the Interior Carl Schurz.

Billy had returned to Fort Sumner, a favorite hideout where he had many friends, and could have easily ridden back and forth between Hot Springs and Sumner.

There is also evidence that Billy knew Moore. In a letter written in 1881, after his conviction at Las Cruces, the Kid discussed the selling of his mare to Frank Stewart, a member of the posse that had captured him at Stinking Springs, and the subsequent sale of the animal by Stewart to Moore.

Three months after the meeting, Jesse and his riders staged the daring train robbery of the Chicago Alton Road at Glendale, Jackson County. Billy may have read an account in a local newspaper of how Jesse and his men had taken over the village and marched their captives to the depot. There they wrecked the telegraph equipment and changed the signal from green to red. To make sure the train would stop, they piled rocks on the rails.

The Kid might have whistled at the initial estimates of thirty to fifty thousand dollars taken from the express car—the company later whittled it down to six thousand.

It is only speculation, of course, but what an odd couple of outlawry they

The announcement in the *Las Vegas Daily Optic*, December 8, 1879, revealing that Jesse James was a guest at the Las Vegas Hotel. Evidence shows that he could have met Billy the Kid. *Courtesy New Mexico Highlands University, Las Vegas, New Mexico*

Jesse James was a guest at the Las Vegas Hot Springs from July 26th to 29th. Of course it was not generally known.

would have made: the gay-hearted Billy and the grim Jesse. Yet it is doubtful that the Kid would have remained very long in the dark and bloody ground of Missouri—he preferred fandangoes to camp meetings . . .

Following the Glendale robbery there was another sensation when George Shepherd, the one-eyed former guerilla leader who had served time for the Russellville bank robbery, claimed to have shot and killed Jesse. There were many who believed his story, but Robert Pinkerton told the *Kansas City Times* that Shepherd would never face the bandit leader because "Jesse is completely devoid of fear and has no more compunction about cold-blooded murder than he has about eating his breakfast."[22]

The issue of the James gang was again featured in the Missouri political wars. The Republican State Convention of 1880 not only charged the Democrats with refusing to seek out and arrest the outlaws but also claimed that banditry had held back immigration into the state, along with outside capital.

Thomas H. Crittenden, a member of an old and honored Missouri family, was nominated by the Democrats and elected governor. It had been a shrewd selection; Crittenden was a fervent Union man and the Democrats knew that this would blunt the campaign of the Republicans, who could scarcely charge Crittenden with whitewashing the James gang because of pro-Confederate sympathy.

In his inaugural speech Crittenden vowed to break up the James and Younger gang and send the leaders to jail.[23] As if in defiance, Jesse led his riders to Winston in Daviess County, sixty-five miles from Kansas City, to rob the Chicago, Rock Island & Pacific Railroad train.

The dark streak of violence that ran through Jesse was becoming more apparent now; while his gang passed what Dick Liddil would call "a common meal sack" among the passengers, Jesse shot conductor William Westfall in the back. When the wounded man staggered down the aisle, Jesse followed him, firing a second shot until the dying man slipped off the platform as the train sped through the darkness. In the fusillade Frank McMillan, a young stone-mason, was also killed.

"Jesse said he shot one, he knew, and that Frank killed another," Liddil later testified.[24]

After killing the two men, the gang beat the express messenger insensible with their revolver butts, took his key, and emptied the safe. The other members of the gang forced the engineer to stop the train and they rode off into the darkness.

Lawmen charged that Jesse's riders included his brother, Frank, Jim Cummins, Ed Miller, and Dick Liddil.

After the robbery there were reports, never confirmed, that Jesse had killed Westfall because he had been a member of the train crew that brought the Pinkertons and deputies to raid the Samuel farmhouse in January 1875.

Anger was now statewide, with only the loyal John Newman Edwards protesting that Jesse and Frank James had been named as the robbers and killers by a press "that will sell its soul for a sensation."[25]

Governor Crittenden, who had only authority to offer three hundred dollars

Missouri's Governor Thomas Theodore Crittenden, who was elected on his promise to break up the James-Younger gang. After Jesse was killed by Bob Ford in April 1882, the political career of Crittenden, often accused of "hiring killers" to do in Jesse, gradually faded. This is a Brady photograph taken in Washington. *The James D. Horan Civil War and Western Americana Collection*

for the apprehension of a criminal, decided to ask the railroads to put up a large cash reward for the capture of Frank and Jesse James. He went to the railroads, he explained, "because they were the greatest sufferers the travelling public avoiding the state, especially the Eastern tourists, Missouri being known as the Robber State."

Crittenden called on Colonel Wells H. Blodgett, General Counsel for the Wabash Railroad. Blodgett, who had been a young attorney with Crittenden in their hometown of Warrensburg, Missouri, conferred with the general counsels and officials of the other railroads. They met in St. Louis on July 26 and agreed to provide funds from which Crittenden could offer a cash reward for the outlaws.

On July 28, 1881, Governor Crittenden issued his proclamation in the expectation, as he later said in his autobiography, that one of the gang would turn informer.

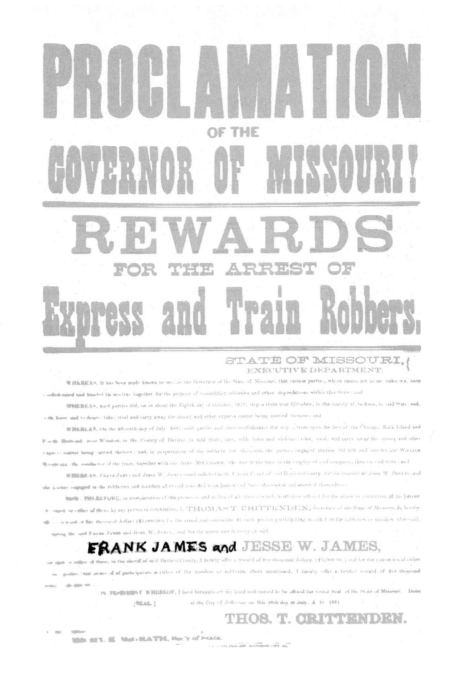

PROCLAMATION
OF THE
GOVERNOR OF MISSOURI!
REWARDS
FOR THE ARREST OF
Express and Train Robbers.

STATE OF MISSOURI,
EXECUTIVE DEPARTMENT.

FRANK JAMES and JESSE W. JAMES,

THOS. T. CRITTENDEN.

Governor Critten-
den's official procla-
mation of 1881 post-
ing rewards for
Frank and Jesse
James. Note that the
poster does not call
for the death of the
bandits. *The James D.
Horan Civil War and
Western Americana
Collection*

Then the James gang struck again. The backdrop was the same—Blue Cut in Jackson County; the Chicago, Alton Railroad; and a lantern waving in the darkness. The Adams safe yielded only $200 and the express messenger was savagely beaten.

Tucker Bassham, a member of the gang, was arrested and sent to prison by the newly elected prosecutor, William Wallace, who had campaigned in the backwoods country despite threats against his life. When another of Jesse's riders, William Ryan, was captured, Wallace persuaded Crittenden to pardon Bassham so he could use him as a People's Witness against Ryan.

The strategy worked. Although the courtroom was packed with armed thugs and Jesse James sympathizers, Wallace successfully convicted Ryan and sent him to prison. As the state's principal witness, Bassham did the unpardonable: he told in open court the secrets of the gang and how they planned and executed their robberies.[26]

Jesse and Frank James were now on the run; Frank disappeared into Tennessee to work as a farmer and Jesse took to the large cities, posing as soft-spoken Tom Howard, father of two children. In 1882 he and his family rented a small clapboard house in St. Joseph. A law officer later said it was so well situated, "the resident could withstand a siege." In March of that year the headlines told the story that Dick Liddil, one of Jesse's most trusted riders, had surrendered to Clay County Sheriff James H. Timberlake.[27] If Jesse and Frank were captured, Liddil would be the state's chief witness against them. Then on Monday morning, April 3, 1882, came the news that not only shocked the state but the nation:

JESSE JAMES IS DEAD!

The outlaw leader had been killed by Bob Ford, who with his brother Charlie had been recruited by Jesse to rob the Platte City Bank. Charlie, a former member of the gang, had introduced his younger brother, Bob, to Jesse some months before they had met with Governor Crittenden "to deliver Jesse to you."

The most dramatic and detailed eyewitness account of the shooting and the bizarre events which took place in St. Joseph was written by an anonymous reporter for the *St. Joseph Western News* who arrived at the scene along with Kansas City Police Commissioner Henry H. Craig.[28]

"JUDGMENT FOR JESSE!"

When we approached the door leading into the front room, our eyes beheld a man lying on the floor, cold in death with the blood still oozing from his wound. From the few who gathered around the door more out of curiosity than anything else, we inquired what was the cause of the shooting. None of them knew but said we could find out from the man's wife who was in the rear room.

Walking into the room and around the dead man's body, we opened the door leading into a kitchen where we found a woman with two small children, a boy and a girl.

When she discovered us with notebook in hand, she began to scream and said:

"Please do not put this in the paper!"

At first she refused to say anything about the shooting but after a time she said "the boys" who had killed her husband had been living with them for some time and their name was Johnson. Charles, she said, was a nephew, but she had never seen the other, Robert, until he came to the house with her husband a few weeks ago. When asked what her husband's name was, she said it was Howard.

"Where was your home before coming here, Mrs. Howard?"

"We came from Baltimore and intended to rent a farm and move to the country but so far we have been unsuccessful."

"Had your husband and the Johnson boys had any difficulty before?"

"Never. They have been always on friendly terms."

"Why did they do this deed?"

"That is more than I can tell. Oh, the rascals!"

At this point she began to cry and begged God to protect her.

The last photograph taken of Jesse James. It appears that he was starting to grow the beard he was wearing when he was killed in April 1882. *Courtesy State Historical Society of Missouri*

An excerpt from an unpublished letter written by Jesse James a month before he was killed. He had been hiding out in St. Joseph under the name "Thomas Howard," and posing as a horse dealer, from November 1881 to the day he was killed. Previously he and his family had lived in Kansas City using the name of Jackson. *The James D. Horan Civil War and Western Americana Collection*

Photograph taken at Sidenfaden Undertakers, St. Joseph, Missouri, shortly after Jesse had been killed by Bob Ford on April 3, 1882. James W. Graham, the photographer, recalled in a 1948 interview shortly before he died that the body was tied to a board and then stood upright for Graham's single-plate 8 x 10 studio camera. Graham said that crowds followed him to his studio and waited until the plate was developed so they could buy prints. When he died, Graham still had the original glass plate. *The James D. Horan Civil War and Western Americana Collection*

The house on Lafayette and Thirteenth Street, St. Joseph, Missouri, where Bob Ford killed Jesse James. As former Missouri governor Brockmeyer observed when he visited the house on the morning of the killing, Jesse had selected a site on a hill "so that he could defend himself to an advantage, while at the same time he could escape." *The James D. Horan Civil War and Western Americana Collection*

Bob Ford, taken shortly after he had killed Jesse James. As one newspaper reported: "The Ford boys sat for photographs today. . . . Orders for [their] likenesses are pouring in from every direction, especially from New York." *The James D. Horan Civil War and Western Americana Collection*

Charles (Charlie) Ford, who plotted with his brother to kill Jesse James. Although he was present when the outlaw was killed, he was reluctant to grant interviews. As he once said: "Bob does all the talkin' for us." Charlie had helped Jesse rob the Chicago & Alton train in September 1881. Bob had been recruited by Jesse but had never taken part in any robbery. The Fords went on a national tour, appearing in theatres in New York, Chicago, and other large cities. *The James D. Horan Civil War and Western Americana Collection*

"Where were you when the shooting was done?"

"I had been in the kitchen and Charles had been helping me all morning. He entered the front room and about three minutes later I heard the report of a pistol. Upon opening the door I discovered my husband lying in his own blood upon the floor.

"I ran to the front door as Charles was getting over the fence but Robert was standing in the front yard with a pistol in his right hand.

"I said, Oh, you have killed him! and Charles said, 'No, we didn't kill him' and then turned around and walked back into the kitchen and then left with Charles who was waiting outside the fence."

At this juncture the Johnson boys made their appearance and gave themselves up to the officer and told them the man they had killed was Jesse James and now they claimed the reward.

Those who were standing nearby drew their breath in silence at the thought of being so near Jesse James even if he was dead.

Marshal Craig said, "My God, do you mean to tell us this is Jesse James?"

"Yes," answered the boys in one breath. "This is Jesse James and we have killed him and don't deny it. We feel proud that we have killed a man who is known all over the world as the most notorious outlaw who ever lived."

"How are we to take your word?" asked the marshal.

"We don't ask you to take our word. There is plenty of proof. The confession of the wife will be enough."

The marshal then took the woman who called herself Mrs. Johnson into another room and he told her the name of her dead husband was not Johnson.* She denied it at first and after the marshal left, the News reporter entered the room with three other gentlemen and a lady who was present.

Walking up to her, the *News* man said, "Mrs. Howard, it is said your name is not Howard but James and that you are the wife of Jesse James."

"I cannot help what they say," she replied. "I have told you the truth."

"The boys who killed your husband have come back and say your husband is Jesse James."

"Oh, is it possible they have come back? I can't believe it!" she cried. Then she placed her arms around the shoulders of her little boy and girl and wept bitterly.

The *News* man and the others present then told her it would be much better for her to tell the truth, that the public would think more of her and she would not want for anything.

Then walking through the room where her dead husband lay, she caught sight of the men who had killed her husband. Screaming at the top of her voice she called them cowards and asked, "Why did you kill the one who had always befriended you?"

Then turning to the body of Jesse she prayed that soon she and her children might be in the hands of Death's cold embrace.

She then left the room followed by the reporter who told her that the boys were not mistaken that the dead man was her husband, Jesse James.

She uttered not a word but the seven-year-old son standing at her side said:

"God Almighty may strike me down if it is not my Pa."

"The boys outside say their names are Ford and not Johnson as you said," the reporter told her.

"Do they say that? And what else do they say?" she said.

"That they killed him to get the reward money."

Then holding her little children to her bosom, she said, "I cannot shield them much longer. Even after they shot my husband who has been trying to live a peaceful life, I tried to withhold his name. But it is true. My husband is Jesse James and a kinder hearted and truer man to his family never lived."

The confession from the wife of the most notorious outlaw who ever lived, created a profound sensation in the room. The thought that Jesse James had lived for six months within our city and walked our streets daily caused one to shudder with fear.

When the wife made her confession, we begged her to tell us about Jesse, Frank and the Ford brothers who had killed him and she said she would, if we would help her to keep them from dragging her husband's body all over the country.

"The deed is done," she said, "and why should I keep quiet any longer? I will tell you the truth. Charlie and Robert Ford are brothers and reside in Ray County, near Richmond. They have been here with my husband and little did I think they would kill him."

"Were either of the boys engaged in the Blue Cut Robbery?"

"Yes, Charlie was there and was the one who hit the expressman in the head."

*Apparently Jesse's wife first gave her name as "Johnson."

Mary and Jesse Edwards James, the children of Jesse James. In honor of John Newman Edwards, the man who had created his Robin Hood legend, the outlaw gave Edwards' name to his son. Both children were at home when their father was killed. *The James D. Horan Civil War and Western Americana Collection*

"Where was Robert?"

"He was not at Blue Cut but was at Winston."

"Was Jesse at Blue Cut?"

"Yes but not at Winston."

"Jesse has been accused of being engaged in nearly all the robberies committed in the United States."

"Yes that is true. But he was not half-bad a man as his enemies have reported. He has endeavored to lead an honest and peaceful life but wherever he went he was hunted down by a lot of scoundrels who were not better than himself. We lived in Kansas City and Jesse was not discovered by anyone."

"Where is Frank?"

"I don't know. I have not seen or heard of Frank in a long time."

At this point the officers began prowling about the house and Mrs. James said: "I wish they would quit. They have no business with my dead husband's outfit."

The reporter then went outside and interviewed the Ford brothers. They were both young, the oldest not more than twenty-one years of age. When we asked them why they had killed Jesse James they said they wanted the reward.

"You are young but gritty."

"We are all grit," said Charlie. "You never expected to see the body of Jesse James in St. Joseph but we thought we would create a sensation and put him out of the way."

The boys then showed us two revolvers. Charlie had a .44 caliber Colt and one .41 caliber of the same name but double action.

Then the reporter returned to speak to Mrs. James in her room. She was very calm and said her greatest trouble was knowing what would become of her and her children.

In speaking of the shooting she said:

"Dick Little [Liddil] betrayed Jesse. In fact he has been a traitor for some time. Had it not been for this, Jesse would be still alive."

[The reporter then was taken on a tour of the house by Mrs. James and described it:]

The house is situated on the corner of Thirteenth and Lafayette Streets, on the rear of a pretty steep bluff. The house is a frame, plain, unassuming frame of seven rooms, one story high and painted white. It is a most unpretentious place, one that would not attract the attention of a passerby for it has no marked or attractive features. The shooting occurred in the front room near the center of the floor. The house occupies a very large lot, being some ninety feet front and 110 wide and surrounded by a plain board fence with pickets in front.

[The reporter also pointed out that at the time of his death, Jesse was a faceless legend. He returned to the sitting room and described the dead outlaw:]

He is about five feet eight inches in height. Of a rather firm and solid, compact build, yet rather on the slender side. His hair is black, not overly long, blue eyes with dark lashes and the entire lower portion of his face is covered by a full growth of sun-browned suit [sic] of whiskers which are not long and shaggy but which are trimmed and bear evidence of care and attention. His complexion is fair he is not sun-burned as the reader is generally led to suppose. He was neatly clad in a business suit of cashmere, of a dark brown substance which fits him very neatly. He wore a shirt of spotless whiteness, with collar and cravat, and looked more the picture of a staid businessman than the outlaw and robber that he was.

The woman, his wife, is neat and rather a prepossessing lady, and bears the stamp of having been well brought up and surrounded by influences of a better and holier character than the reader would at first suppose.

She is rather slender, fair of face, light hair, strikingly apparent.

She was clad in neat fitting calico and when the shooting took place was attending to her household duties in the kitchen. When she stood face-to-face with the awful deed and had realized what had really occurred, she took the matter in a cool and philosophical manner and acted as if she was not surprised at what had occurred and that she had lived in expectation of something of the kind happening at any moment.

The city is in a state of wild excitement and crowds followed the police who took the Ford boys to jail.

More than 2,000 men were hanging around and the halls and corridors were packed with people. The men [Fords] were in the center of a corp of police, each one was well armed as they went through the streets and the police were also armed with deadly instruments of death.

[The following day the same reporter returned and had an extended interview with the widow in which she spoke as follows:]

I know Frank and Jesse have done wrong but they have not been guilty of all that has been charged. Jesse was as kind to me as he could be and for the children, he got everything they asked for. He was a reticent man and never told me where he intended to go but I had an idea of what he was doing.

The Ford boys say Jesse intended to rob the Platte City Bank the night he was killed. That is not so. I know for a certainty he never contemplated any such thing. When Jesse was home, he did what he could about the house. The day he was shot he had been in the kitchen with me all morning until he went into the sitting room with the boys. I was sick at the time and he was helping me because it wasn't safe to hire a girl.

There are some people who believe I have loads of money. That is not true. I have less than two hundred dollars. When Jesse read that Dick Liddil had surrendered he was furious and said Dick was a traitor and should be hung.

Jesse used to get the papers regularly. When he read about that robbery in Arkansas the paper connected him with it. When he read it he said he hoped the robbers were caught so the people would see that he was not connected with every robbery.

Kansas City was the safest place we had lived. The people there never suspected us. St. Joseph was also a safe place. We lived there nearly a year and Jesse would go all over the town. When we were living here no one knew it except my brother who clerks in the city. My sister didn't even know it.

[Mrs. James told the reporter her husband wasn't a "grim man" and told him an anecdote to prove Jesse had a sense of humor:]

Jesse used to often visit his mother. He told me after one trip that he had gotten on the train at the nearby depot. When the conductor came along Jesse noticed he was missing the tip of one finger. On his return trip he saw the same conductor and asked him if he wasn't really Jesse James. He told the conductor he had known Jesse as a boy and Jesse was also minus the tip of one finger. They had a good laugh about it.

Last winter Jesse said he wanted to settle down on a farm. We could never keep in one place though, the officers were always after us. We were living in Nashville, Tennessee for two years under the name of Howard but we were driven away. If the officers had let Jesse alone we would have lived all right and I am sure Jesse would have been an honor to his country.

Never a line passed between Frank and Jesse, it was not safe. But they did meet, however. The story that Frank was in town for Jesse's burial is absurd. Frank has too much sense to expose himself in a crowd.

Despite Zee's confession that the dead man was her husband, there was a great deal of doubt—it seemed impossible that this legend was a mere mortal who could die from an ordinary bullet.

The first one who raised a doubt that the dead man was Jesse James was George Shepherd, the one-eyed former guerilla leader who had served time for taking part in the Russellville bank robbery. Two years before, after his release from prison, Shepherd had created a sensation by claiming to have killed Jesse. The Kansas City Marshal, James Liggett, had recruited Shepherd to kill the outlaw leader.

Shepherd told Liggett that he had rejoined the gang and had killed Jesse after an aborted bank robbery. Liggett and a posse searched the area at the time but failed to find a body. After an investigation of Shepherd's story Liggett revealed that Jesse had been "buried in Clay County turf" and that a physician had told him he issued a death certificate when friends claimed the body of a man he had treated for gunshot wounds.

The controversy died away and Shepherd returned to his job as a Kansas

City teamster. As he told reporters, he was completely disillusioned with the public; he said that John Newman Edwards's *Kansas City Times* had not only called him a Judas Iscariot but that he had "received more abuse than Jesse ever had."[29]

The most prominent figure in the Middle Border was Joseph O. Shelby, celebrated as the only Confederate general who never surrendered. Shelby, a prosperous landowner and businessman in Lafayette County, was a friend of Frank James's and a constant defender of the bandit brothers.

When he was asked by a newspaper to write Jesse's obituary, Shelby instead sent a letter to the editor warning that it was "barely possible" that Jesse was still alive and that the "affair at St. Joseph was a prearranged affair done by parties who seek to obtain the great reward offered for the bold raider, dead or alive."

The editor added a comment to Shelby's letter, pointing out that Jesse "is as dead as any bandit that lived a thousand years ago."[30]

The initial identification of Jesse's body was done by Clay County Sheriff James Timberlake, who had known Jesse for years; two former guerillas who had ridden with the bandit during the war; Kansas City Police Commissioner Henry H. Craig, who had hunted the James gang for a long time; and Jackson County Prosecutor, William Wallace.

What made the identification exact, Wallace pointed out, were the wartime bullet scars and the missing tip of the middle finger of the bandit's left hand. Later Jesse's wife and mother formally identified the body.[31]

The Ford brothers were big news, and reporters sought them out. In a series of interviews Charlie and Bob Ford gave a fascinating and intimate picture of America's greatest outlaw at home with his wife and children, planning a robbery, or discussing his philosophy of life and death.

Bob Ford, "the boy who did the shooting," was reticent and let Charlie do most of the talking.[32]

Charlie Ford on Jesse James

JESSE JAMES THE BANDIT LEADER

When Jesse talked of robbing the Platte City Bank he called it a "fine scheme" and said it would be published all over the United States "as another daring robbery."

He called the bank and train robberies his "exploits" and used to say that he thought his style "was a damn good one."

We went to several cities because Jesse said he wanted to make a raise on a bank, finally he settled on the Platte City Bank. He said he had gone in to make change from a large bill and when the teller had turned around he had taken a good look and said we could take it.

He said I was to go in with him and Bob would stand guard outside. He told me to kill any man who stepped near us. Jesse also said he would clear out the whole damn city if necessary.

Once I asked him if he had killed Conductor Westfall and he admitted he had killed the man. He said he wanted to get the whole gang to be liable for murder so they would be too desperate to be caught and would never give him away.

A youthful Bob Ford, later to be the killer of Jesse James. *The James D. Horan Civil War and Western Americana Collection*

Captain Harrison Trow, who had ridden with Jesse James under "Bloody Bill" Anderson. At the request of Jackson County prosecutor William H. Wallace, he assisted authorities in identifying the body by wartime wounds in the right side of the chest. *The James D. Horan Civil War and Western Americana Collection*

Kansas City Police Commissioner Henry H. Craig, who for years led the hunt for the James-Younger gang. He witnessed the deathbed confession of Wood Hite, Jesse's rider, who described the details of the train robberies of Winston, Blue Cut, and Glendale, and had helped to identify the body of the outlaw leader after he had been killed by Bob Ford. *The James D. Horan Civil War and Western Americana Collection*

JESSE JAMES' SLAYER

Rigs Himself Out in a Genteel Suit for the Capture.

It may not be developed in the evidence, but it is no less a fact that Ford, the slayer of Jesse James, while under the assumed name of Jackson, only a few days ago purchased a genteel suit at the Famous Boston One Price Clothing House, 506, 508 and 510 Main street. This is not mentioned to indicate that this has anything to do with the capture, but merely to suggest that when anyone wishes to personate the gentleman or wear good clothes of any kind they are sure to buy them at the Boston.

MEN'S Spring Overcoats, elegant assortment $10 to $25, opened April 3d at 707 Main street. It will pay you to wait.
WM. H. PARET.

Millinery Opening.

Ladies, it will pay you to wait for the opening of the season at G. G. Rounds' new store, 719 Main street.

A Signal Victory.

The value of electricity as a remedial agent has gained a signal victory over prejudice. Thomas' Eclectic Oil

A few days after the killing of Jesse James this enterprising St. Joseph, Missouri, clothier advertised in a local newspaper that Bob Ford had purchased a "genteel suit" in his shop. For the first few weeks after the killing the Fords lived high, earning one hundred dollars a night for appearing at theatres in Kansas City. Governor Crittenden later revealed that he had given the brothers a share of the ten-thousand-dollar reward but never said exactly how much they got. It is believed that their share was meager. Charlie Ford gradually became depressed and committed suicide a few years later. After the collapse of his "theatrical career" Bob Ford opened a saloon in New Mexico with Dick Liddil. When that venture failed, he began drifting about the country. *The James D. Horan Civil War and Western Americana Collection*

He said he had rented the house [in St. Joe] because it was so situated that he could stand off 100 men until he got to the stable and ride away from any pursuit should it occur.

The story about Jesse having specially trained horse is all bosh. He never cared anything about them except that they be good travellers. He rode hard and soon killed his horses.

JESSE JAMES THE FATHER

Jesse was always kind to his two children but he did not pretend to have any control over them. When his wife tried to control them he would be rough with her . . . he would get mad if she corrected them . . .

I once asked him if Zee [his wife], knew what he was doing and he said:

"My wife doesn't know anything about my exploits and I never want her to."

After he robbed the Monmouth Stage in Kentucky he gave his wife the ring he had taken from Lawyer Rountree's daughter. He wore the watch he had taken from the same man in the same robbery. I was with him for five months and he didn't do much of anything in the house except sit in the sitting room and read the newspapers or curry his horses.

I think his wife knew something of what was going on when we left to visit the various cities but I don't think she knew everything.

In fact none of us knew everything until Jesse told us. As he once told me, "I give full confidence to no one . . . I will tell you only what is necessary to know and that is so with the others."

JESSE JAMES AND WOMEN

Yes, I do believe that Jesse James really loved his wife. The real "masher" in the gang was Dick Liddil. He stood well with our sister, the Widow Bolton. Mattie Collins says she is married to Dick but that is all nonsense.

Jesse was very respectful toward women. He was always ready to give them the time of day and would tip his hat. But when it came to telling anyone where he was hiding out, well, that was different, no woman could get that secret out of him.

After he left Kansas City he didn't even tell his mother. He would ride to his mother's place and see her but he would not tell her where he was living.

PREPARING THE KILLING OF JESSE JAMES

Jesse James was watchful and no man could get the drop on him. Earlier my brother and I decided to go to Kansas City when Jesse lived there with the intention of perhaps making up a party and watching the house so that if he came around we could get him. But then the weather turned bad so we gave up the idea.

He never let us out of his sight. He wanted us everywhere with him. Since he moved to St. Joe we were with him day and night. During the day we stayed in the sitting room and at night we would walk down to the town and get the newspapers. Jesse always got the Kansas City papers and the *Police News.* He read a great deal but only newspapers. He never read any books. Sometimes during the day when he got restless he would walk out east of the town.

While we were with him we got to know his arms. Jesse owned one 45 calibre Colt, one 45 calibre Smith-Wesson, one breech-loading, double-barreled shotgun and one Winchester rifle.

We knew it was nonsense to try and take him alive. Jesse once told me he would never be taken alive.

"If three men move in front of me," he said, "I will take all three before I fall."

One day I thought the ball would open when we were in the sitting room. The blinds were down but the slats were open. Suddenly Jesse jumped to the window. When I looked out I saw a policeman had stopped at the end of the yard and was looking about. Jesse opened the slats a little wider, cocked his revolver, took a dead sight on the man and said he was going to kill him in his tracks if he walked enough to reach a certain spot. The policeman came a little nearer and Jesse's finger was on the trigger but just as the officer came within a pace of the spot, some fancy made him turn around and go off into the direction of the railroad depot.

He will never know how close he came to being a dead man that day.

Jesse never suspected us. He used to pride himself on his skill in reading men. He said he could not be fooled by any man. Only a few days before we killed him, Jesse told me about the plans he was making to rob the Platte City Bank. When he looked at me, he said:

"I give you these plans because I am a good judge of men and character. I know you won't go back on the business and I never make a mistake."

I did not correct him, you bet.

The Testimony of Charles and Robert Ford and Other Witnesses in the Coroner's Inquest into the Shooting and Killing of Jesse Woodson James.[33]

When Charles Ford was called to the witness stand on Monday morning, he testified that he was about 24 years old, and had lived in Ray county near Richmond for about three years. He met and became acquainted with Jesse James soon after his residence began, and last November left the farm and went to Kansas City. While there he met Jesse James.

"Did he ask you to join him?"

"Jesse James asked me if I did not want to take a trip with him, and we would go and make a raise somewhere. He was living in Kansas City then. We left Kansas City on the 5th and arrived in St. Joe on the 8th, and went to Twenty-first and Lafayette streets where we lived until the day before Christmas, when he rented the house where he was killed and we lived there ever since. He said he wanted to take a trip out through Kansas and see how the banks were situated and said he would get the men, and wanted to know if I knew of any one we could get to help us. I told him I thought I could get my brother to help if I could go down and see him. So we went down there and we went to his mother's and stayed there until Friday night, and then went to my brother's and stayed until Saturday and started to St. Joe. On the way a storm came up and we stayed that night in a church. We stayed there until just before daylight and then we came on to within two miles east of St. Joe, where he said for us to stay until night and he went on in. He said there was going to be a murder trial in Platte City, and we would go up there and if the bank was all right we would rob it. He said when they were making the speeches everybody would be up to the court house and we would rob the bank."

"Well, now, explain how it was you came to kill him?"

JESSE JAMES' SLAYER.

The Bandit Who Subscribed for Five Newspapers.

And Read the Accounts of His Misdeeds With Pleasure.

The Ford Brothers in Town—They do Not Answer the Popular Idea— Their Quiet and Cool Behavior.

Here a discussion arose between the brothers whether Jesse James was really brave. Charles, who was with him longer, maintained that he was. Charles said:

"I think he was a brave man, for the reason that he never took any liquor when he was on one of his raids. All the rest of the men would drink to get their courage up before going into a town, until they were half drunk. Jesse James was as treacherous as he could be. He would laugh and talk with a man when he could cut his heart out, and was only waiting for a chance to kill him when he was not on the watch."

"How do the people of Missouri regard you?"

"They seem well disposed toward us, with the exception of a few roughs. Those who knew the most of Jesse James liked him the least. He made a good impression at first. He was polite, and could talk well on almost any question."

"Were not the men of his gang afraid of each other?"

"They were always on the watch and feared each other. This is the reason they made so many escapes. They were afraid to leave each other, too. If a man should talk of leaving, he would be killed instantly."

unless it is some cranks who would like to gain some notoriety."

Said Bob Ford, speaking of the bandit's habits: "Jesse James always hid in the cities. Whenever he committed one of his robberies he always made for the nearest town, and lived quietly until the search for him was over. If he had gone to the bush he would have been captured. But while they were looking in the woods for him he was in town under an assumed name, reading the papers and keeping himself informed. After a robbery he always tried to get the newspapers and read an account of it; so he always found out who the officers were who were after him, and laughed at the steps taken to capture him."

"He wasn't known in St. Joe, then?"

"No one knew him in St. Joe. He rented a house there and was living quietly with only his wife and children and Charley with him. The next morning after the Blue Cut robbery, near Independence, he was at home reading the papers. While he was sitting there at the open window, with his feet on the window sill, reading a newspaper account of the affair, a lot of officers went by, talking of what they were going to do to capture him. One of the officers said: 'We are going to get him this time.' He was not twenty-five feet away from them at the time. He laughed heartily at this."

"Would Jesse James betray his men?" asked the reporter.

Excerpts from a fascinating interview with the Ford brothers in September 1882, while they were on tour "in a drama written for them, 'The Outlaws of Missouri.'" Bob Ford revealed that Jesse James subscribed to five newspapers "to keep himself informed" after a robbery. They believed that Jesse's brother, Frank, was not the "Frank James" who had sent them threatening letters. As Charlie pointed out: "Frank James is not in the habit of sending notices, he generally carries them himself." *The James D. Horan Civil War and Western Americana Collection*

SILENT SOLONS.

After the Session's Fitful Fever They Sleep Well—Barring Uneasy Consciences.

DISTURBING THE DEMOCRATS.

The Session Adjourns at Noon, After Passing the Apportionment Bill.

JESSE JAMES' JOCULARITY.

The Old Joke Ran On to the Last—A Number of Resolutions.

ALL RULED OUT OF ORDER.

Couldn't Even Vote to Meet After Adjournment--Other Political News.

Soon after the house was called to order Mr. Allen, of Jackson, introduced the following resolutions:

Resolved, That to the civil officers of Missouri, the courts of Jackson, Cass, Clay, Platte and Saline counties, is due the honor of breaking up and bringing to justice that band of outlaws known as the James gang; therefore, be it

Resolved, By the house of representatives that said county officers and citizens are entitled to be congratulated upon the success of their efforts in that behalf.

Mr. Major raised the point of order. The resolution was the same as those heretofore ruled out of order.

Mr. Richardson, speaker pro tem., ruled the point of order well taken.

Mr. Allen

TOOK AN APPEAL,

and five Republicans, with Mr. Dale, of Cass, arose and joined him in it. The chair was sustained by a vote of 80 ayes to 36 nays.

Mr. Dale, an old and gray Democrat, of Cass, then sent to the speakers' desk the following:

Resolved, That in view of the fact that the state of Missouri has been declared by her enemies

THE ROBBER STATE,

and the citizens of Western Missouri as being in sympathy with train robbers and outlaws, the house, in refutation of such charges and in vindication of the law abiding character of the citizens of Western Missouri, commend the vigilance and success of the civil officers of Clay and Jackson counties and citizens of Western Missouri for their efforts in bringing outlaws to justice.

AMID INTENSE EXCITEMENT

Mr. Major again raised his point of order, and it was sustained by the chair. Mr. Dale attempted to speak, and the spittoons were rolled on him, mingled with cat calls and yells. The chair recognized Mr. Wade, of Green, who sent up the following:

WHEREAS, The majority of the house is determined that an expression of the opinion of the members shall not be heard touching the action of the governor in the killing of Jesse James, therefore be it

Resolved, That the use of this hall be granted, immediately after adjournment to-day, to such members as approve of the course of Gov. Crittenden in ridding the state of the cutthroat and robber Jesse James and that part of his gang which has been either killed or confined in the penitentiary, for the purpose of holding an informal session to give an expression of their approval of the action of Gov. Crittenden in the matter above referred to.

The confusion was more pronounced than ever, and it was ruled out of order when the preamble was read and a recess taken, on motion of Mr. Major, for ten minutes.

Ed. O. Kelly, the man who killed the man who killed Jesse James. When he was arrested in the silver-mining boom town of Creede, Colorado, in June 1892, Kelly gave his name as "Ed. O. Kelly" but the policeman wrote it down as "Ed O'Kelly" in what was to be the source of many errors in frontier histories. Kelly, who had bright red hair and was known as Red Kelly, was killed in January 1904 in Oklahoma City by Joseph Burnett, a policeman who had previously arrested him as "a suspicious character." *Courtesy Collection of Fred and Jo Mazzulla, Denver, Colorado*

Even in death, Jesse James was protected by a number of pro-Confederate politicians. In May 1882, "amid wild excitement," pro-Union and law-and-order factions of the state legislature tried without success to pass a resolution praising the lawmen who had broken up the James gang. The sponsor of the resolution was the target of a barrage of spittoons, "mingled with cat calls and yells." *The James D. Horan Civil War and Western Americana Collection*

"Well, we had come in from the barn where we had been feeding and currying the horses, and Jesse complained of being warm and pulled off his coat and threw it on the bed and opened the door, and said that he guessed he would pull off his belt as some person might see it. Then he went to brush off some pictures and when he turned his back I gave my brother the wink and we both pulled our pistols, but he, my brother, was the quickest and fired first. I had my finger on the trigger and was just going to fire, but I saw his shot was a death shot and did not fire. He heard us cock our pistols and turned his head. The ball struck him in the back of the head and he fell. Then I went out and got our hats, and we went and telegraphed Captain Craig and Sheriff Timberlake what we had done. Then we went to the marshal's office and asked a policeman that was there if he knew where the marshal was. He said that he did not, but that he would go with us to look him up. I asked a gentleman up town if he knew where the marshal was, he said he had just seen him get on a car going down in that direction. I said that that was probably where they were going, and that we might as well go down there, and I told them who it was in the house and who it was that killed him, and how it took place and where his pistols, gun, and jewelry could be found and from there we came up here."

"How did you know it was James when he came to you?"

"He came to my house two years ago last summer; he was a sporting man and so was I; gambled and drank a little, so did I. I was acquainted with Miller, and he came with him and introduced him as Mr. Johnston. He stayed until the next day and he left, and after that Ed Miller told me it was Jesse James. I did not see him any more for some time, and when I did see him I asked him where Miller was, and he said that Miller was in bad health, and that he did not think he could live long. Then I did not see any thing more of him until the next spring. He was there two or three times last summer. Then he came down last fall."

"He asked you to do what?"

"To help rob trains and banks. I have been with him ever since."

"Had you any intention of leaving St. Joe soon?"

"Jesse said he would like to rob a bank and look around a little beforehand and I started out with him. He went first to Hiawatha, then to Pawnee City, from there to Forrest City, then to White Cloud, Kansas, from there to Forrest City to see how the bank at that place was situated. He said that he liked the way the bank at Forrest City was situated, and said he wanted to take that bank, but I told him I did not want to go into that as I was sick then. We came up to Oregon. He said that he wanted to look at that bank, and from there we came down here, and that is the only trip I ever made with him. He would go into a bank with a large bill or several small ones to get changed and while the cashier was making the change he would take a look and see whether they were caged up, what sort of looking man it was, and whether they had a time lock or not."

"How did you get your living?"

"I was not at any expense. I did not spend any money. He had a good deal of money. He had some $1,500 or $1,600."

"Where did he keep it?"

"I don't know."

"Where did he get it?"

"I have no idea where he got it. I guess he must have got it robbing."

"Did Bob, your brother, come here to assist in robbing a bank?"

"Jesse had looked at a bank at Platte City. He said they were going to have a murder trial there this week, and while everybody would be at the court house, he would slip in and rob the bank, and if not he would come back to Forrest City and get that."

"What was your idea in that?"

"It was simply to get Bob here where one of us could kill him if once he took his pistols off. To try and do this with his pistols on would be useless, as I knew Jesse had often said he would not surrender to a hundred men, and if three men should step out in front of him and shoot him he could kill them before he fell."

Robert Ford, the young man who did the shooting, was then called, and as the individual who shot Jesse James walked forward he was the center of every eye in the room. He gave his evidence clearly, and stated that when he went to Ray County to live, he heard about the James boys, but did not meet Jesse until three years afterward. He came with Ed Miller. Witness had known Miller and he knew they were talking and planning a train robbery. Last January he went to Kansas City and had an interview with Governor Crittenden about capturing Jesse, at the St. James hotel.

"Did the governor tell you any thing about a reward?"

"He said $10,000 had been offered for Jesse or Frank dead or alive. I then entered into arrangements with Timberlake and Craig. I afterward told Charlie of the conversation I had with the officers and told him I would like to go with him. He said if I was willing to go, all right. We started that night, and went up to Mrs. Samuels and put the horses up.

"John Samuels (Jesse's half brother) was wounded, and they were expecting him to die. There were some friends of the family there whom Jesse did not wish to see him, so we stayed in the barn all night until they left, and that was pretty nearly daylight, and we stayed in the house all next day, and that night we started away. That was on Thursday night; Friday night we stayed at his brother-in-law's. We left Mrs. Samuels' and went about three miles into the woods for fear the officers would surprise us at her house. We started from the woods and came up to another of his brother-in-laws and got supper there and started from there here."

"This was last week?"

"Yes. We came at once to St. Joseph and then talked over the matter again, and how we could kill him."

"What have you been doing since you came here?"

"My brother and I go down town sometimes at night and get the papers."

"What did you tell Jesse you were with him for?"

"I told him I was going in with him."

"Had you any plans made to rob any bank?"

"He had spoken of several but had made no particular selection."

"Well, now will you give us the particulars of the killing and what time it occurred?"

"After breakfast, between 8 and 9 o'clock this morning, he, my brother and myself were in the room. He pulled off his pistols and got up on a chair to dust off some picture frames and I drew my pistol and shot him."

"How close were you to him?"

"About six feet away."

"How close was the hand to him which held the pistol?"

"About four feet I should think."

"Was Jesse James unarmed when you killed him?"

"Yes, sir."

This closed the testimony on Monday, and court adjourned to meet at 10 o'clock this morning, and at that hour an immense crowd filled the room. There was great excitement to see Little, Mrs. Samuels and Mrs. James, both of whom entered the court after the testimony was about half over.

Mr. Henry Craig, police commissioner of Kansas City, was the first witness.examined, as follows: I was not acquainted with Jesse James personally, but am positive the body of the dead man is the outlaw, as it corresponds with the descriptions I have heard. I know Robert Ford, and for two months he has assisted Sheriff Timberlake and myself in the endeavor to capture Jesse James. He was not employed regularly by us, but acted in good faith, and according to our instructions, and assisted in every way he could to aid us. Charlie Ford I had never seen until I came to St. Joe, but understand he and Robert had some understanding."

Sheriff Timberlake of Clay county was next called, and said he was sheriff and was acquainted with Jesse James during life and recognized the body as that of Jesse. Had known him since 1864, and saw him the last time in 1870. Knew his face as well as any one. He had the second joint of his third finger shot off by which I also recognize him. Ford was acting under my instructions and said if he could see Charlie Ford we could accomplish our end the sooner, and he acted squarely to all agreements.

Dick Little was then called and resumed his testimony; I have seen the body of the dead man and recognize it; I was with him a good deal last summer and know him perfectly; I also recognize him from the wounds on hand and on the right side.

Deputy Marshal Finley of St. Joseph said he resided in this city; I was not acquainted with Jesse James; went to the house where he was killed in answer to the telephone where the man was killed; found him on his back, and from Mrs. James got a description of the two men who killed the man and started out in search of them. She said one was her nephew and the other a young man, both named Johnson, but no relation. As we were going out we met the boys coming back. Bob said; I am the man who killed the person in the house. He is the notorious outlaw, Jesse James, or I am mistaken, and I can identify him. He described the wounds on Jesse James' body. He told us there were two watches and some diamonds in the house. We could not find them at first, but did find a necktie and a gold ring with the name of Jesse on the inside. Afterward we found two watches in the trunk. There was some small change in an old pocketbook, which I gave Mrs. James. On a $1 gold piece as a scarf pin were the initials J. W. J. Most of the property is now in the hands of the city marshal.

When the name of Mrs. Zerelda Samuels was called every man in the court room stood up for a good look at the mother of the dead bandit, and as she passed up the center aisle with the wife and the children of Jesse and a Mrs. Turner, the crowd parted right and left, and the party passed the reporters' table and took seats directly in front of the coroner. Her testimony was as follows: "I live in Clay county, and am the mother of Jesse James." Here she broke down and moaned several times "Oh, my poor boy. I have seen the body since my arrival and have recognized it as that of my son Jesse; the lady by my side is my daughter-in-law, and the children hers." (Mrs. Samuels again broke down at this point.) "He was a kind husband and son." Mrs. Jesse James was here asked if any valuables had been taken from the house at the time the officers arrived and she detailed the articles found by the city marshal.

This concluded the testimony, and it was announced that a recess would be taken, and the court room began to empty. Mrs. Samuels arose as did Mrs.

James, and as the former turned and faced the crowd she spied Dick Little, and a most sensational scene occurred.

The coroner's jury then retired for deliberation, and in about half an hour returned the following verdict:

State of Missouri
County of Buchanan } ss.

An inquisition taken at St. Joseph, in the county of Buchanan, on the third day of April, 1882, before me, James W. Heddens, M. D., coroner of the county aforesaid, upon their view of the body of Jesse W. James, then and there lying dead, S. H. Sommers, W. H. Chouning, J. W. Moore, Thomas Norris, William Turner, W. H. George, good and lawful householders of the township of Washington, who, being duly sworn and charged diligently to enquire and true presentment make, how and in what manner, and by whom the said Jesse W. James came to his death, upon their oaths do say:

That the body of the deceased is that of Jesse W. James and that he came to his death by a wound in the back of his head, caused by a pistol shot fired intentionally by the hand of Robert Ford, in witness whereof as well the jurors aforesaid, have to this inquisition put their names at the place and on the day aforesaid.

James W. Heddens, *Coroner*
S. H. Sommers, *Foreman*
W. H. Chouning,
J. W. Moore,
Thos. Norris,
Wm. Turner,
W. H. George.

The Surrender of Frank James

The week of April 3, 1882, was a tremulous one for the citizens of St. Joseph, Missouri. First came the shooting of Jesse James, and then the Coroner's Inquest, at which Jesse's wife made her first public appearance along with the Ford brothers. That was followed by the dramatic confrontation between Jesse's mother, Mrs. Samuel, and "the traitor," Dick Liddil, the outlaw's former rider. The one-armed old lady screamed, "Traitor . . . traitor . . . why did you kill my son?" at the impassive Liddil, while the stunned spectators looked on.

Thousands were waiting outside Sidenfaden's funeral parlor to get a glimpse of the legendary outlaw when a dispute took place between Kansas City Police Commissioner Craig and Clay County Sheriff James Timberlake over who owned Jesse's body and guns.

Timberlake finally wired Governor Crittenden:

"What must I do? The officers won't either turn over the body of Jesse to his wife or his arms to me?"

Crittenden ordered the local authorities to release the dead man to his wife "in the name of humanity" and to preserve Jesse's arms "as relics for the state."[34]

During the dispute there were reports that a gang of Jesse's sympathizers was riding toward St. Joe to take the body by force. Crittenden mustered the militia, and troops marched into the city with officers and police "sleeping under the awning across from the funeral parlor."

Finally the outlaw's body, "enclosed in an elegant galvanized iron casket with the silver name plate bearing the name 'Jesse James' and other silver ornaments" was put in the baggage car of a special train headed for Kearney, Clay County. Before the door closed Mrs. Samuel insisted on being led back to make sure that the five-hundred-dollar coffin had not been stolen.

This led the *Ralls County Herald* to observe:

"When he gets across the creek the people over there will think he's a banker."[35]

Appropriately, Jesse left St. Joe in a burst of gunfire. As the doors of the baggage car slammed shut, "a man pulled a gun on Mrs. Samuel." The Clay County neighbors escorting the body began firing from the car windows. Newspaper accounts reported that a number of shots were exchanged "but the man was thrown out into the street and no one was hurt."[36]

Crowds lined the tracks hoping to get a glimpse of either the coffin or the widow. It was a momentous journey, as the *Kansas City Times* reported, "with the *New York Herald* man sending dispatches at every stop."

In Kearney the coffin was placed in the lobby of the McCarthy House, the local hotel, and the lid was removed. Large crowds filed past. Many were local residents who knew Jesse only as a legend. More than one was heard to gasp and whisper:

"Is that Jesse James! Why, I used to see him riding down the street!"

In the quiet of the next afternoon Jesse was finally lowered into a deep grave at the foot of a coffee bean tree in the corner of the Samuel place.

Jesse James had come home.

Jesse James was dead but there was still one last legendary outlaw "on the dodge"—Frank James.

For over three years, Frank had been living as a farmer, "B. J. Woodson," in Tennessee with his wife and children. He was later described by his neighbors as a well-spoken man who liked to race horses at county fairs, quote Shakespeare, and argue about the philosophy of Robert Green Ingersoll, the American political leader and agnostic.

It was generally accepted that Frank would suddenly appear in St. Joe to claim vengeance for Jesse's killing, but in Kansas City, George Shepherd scoffed at the tales. Instead of some violent, melodramatic act he predicted: "Frank will come in . . . he's lonely, afraid and discouraged."

Revenge was *not* on Frank's mind. As Shepherd had said, the last outlaw was lonely and fearful. During the summer he contacted the gang's loyal champion, John Newman Edwards, with a proposal that he surrender to Governor Crittenden.

The complete details of the negotiations between the outlaw and the Missouri governor have never been revealed but Frank wrote a long letter to Crittenden denying that he and Jesse were guilty of all the crimes they had been

The death of Jesse James was national news. Some of the headlines which appeared are journalistic classics.

ly Times

JUDGMENT FOR JESSE.

The Notorious Bandit at Last Meets His Fate and Dies With His Boots On.

He is Killed by Charles and Robert Ford of Ray County.

The Boys Acknowledge the Deed and Give Themselves Up to the Marshal.

Jesse's Weeping Wife on the ...... compan....

known to the annals of criminal history, created a profound sensation. The th... that Jesse James has lived among us f... past six months and walked our streets ... causes one to shudder with fear. Wh... wife had made her confession we asked ... tell all about Jesse, Frank and the Fo... who had killed him, she said she wo... begged us to do all for her we could ... them from dragging her husband's b... the country. We promised to do thi... told her that she and her children ... taken care of. Well said she, "th... done and why should I keep quiet a... I will tell you the truth. Charlie a... F... and reside in R... they have been ... and little ... r kill him. of the boys en... CUT ROBBERY? e was there, an... expressman in the ...

would at first suppose, fair of face, light hair forehead, and marks of ingly apparent. S calico, a

VOL. XXIV.

THE TRAITOR'S TRI

A Day of Excitement and Turmo Joseph—Is it Jesse? the Ques on Every Tongue.

Continuation of the Coroner's Inquest ly Dramatic Scenes at Dick Little's Appearance.

Mrs. Samuels and Mrs. James Bre in Fierce Invectives—Gossip Around the City.

A Talk With Little—Cole Younger viewed—Governor Crittenden's E pressed Satisfaction.

Identification of the Remains—The Bu Kearney To-Day—The Trials at Independence.

The Day's Developments.
[Special to the Kansas City Times.]
St. Joseph, Mo., April 4—At a very ... hour this morning, hundreds of people, ... women and children began to wend their ... toward the undertaker's establishment, wh... the dead body of the outlaw had been place... a cooler, eager for a look at the noted train r... ber, and so dense was the throng at 9 o'ch... that the doors had to be closed and a spe... detail of police called in to keep the tide of l... nanity back. The morbid curiosity of all clas... was never more plainly shown than on this o... asion, and as one man said: I believe th... ou i all come in the same way to see the dev... bout the establishment, the long watches of t... ght had been to many any thing but wakef... s, and for several hours the members of th... sas City police force—Sergeant Ditsch an... iceman Nugent—were the only officers or ... rd, and the suspicion entertained late las... ing that an attempt might be made to steal ... bo...y of Jesse from the hands of the officers, ... t false one. To be sure, there were many ... ns in St. Joseph who

TALKED OPENLY
...h a move, but no sane man could have ... like idea in his head. Sheriff Timberlake ... ptain Craig, who have really had all ar... ...ents touching the future disposition of ... ...dy and of the Ford boys in their hands, ... retire to their quarters at the Pacific ... ...til a very early hour this ... ...lock w...

PRICE TWO CENTS. | Saturday's Last Editi...

ty Daily Jour

ANSAS CITY WEDNESDAY, APRIL 5, 1882.

THE DEAD OUTLAW

Fully Identified by His Mother and Others Who Have Known Him.

RESULT OF THE INQUEST.

Jesse James Came to His Death at the Hands of Robt Ford.

WHAT THE SLAYERS SAY

Interviews with the Two Fords, Dick Lidi and Gov. Crittenden.

JESSE'S HOME IN THIS CIT

Interesting Reminiscences of His Famil...

THE DAY AT ST
Special Dispatch to the Kansas C
St. Joseph, Mo., April 4.
election and the shooting of t...
excitement ran high throughou...
this morning at an early hou...
was filled to await the concl...
ner's inquest.
In the excitement of las...
sympathy of not a few was ...
James, more for the maun...
than for any feeling of re...
robber was dead. The c...
"HURRAH FOR
was several times heav...
the Fords and Dick L...
seemed impossible fo...
that the Fords were ...
the officers of the s...
could the robber ...
fatal bullet.
THE OF
seemed to thi...
some great ...
tenance Sh...
Craig havi...
the lead...
with a...
Ditsch ...

MISSED HIS MARK.

A Crank Attempts to Shoot Mrs. Samuels as She Is Leaving St. Joseph With

THE REMAINS OF HER SON.

The Body of the Dead Bandit Being Taken to the Old Home.

BEFORE THE FRONT DOOR

It Will Be Buried, that the Mother Can Watch the Grave.

EXCITEMENT AT KEARNEY.

What Was Learned Yesterday In Connection With the Life of the Desperado.

by the treasurer. The bill is gen... in similar to the several acts passed ... of duty foreign articles exhibit... ...nial and subsequent expoai... ...mittee after listening to Mr. ... ...t referred the bill to the ... ...passed unanimously.

...O TO-DAY.
...4.—The house com...
...ill probably con.
...rd to-morrow.
adopted
case of
agree-
...port
...to the

Sedalia Daily

SEDALIA, MISSOURI, TUESDA...

JESSE JAMES KILLED.

There Is no Mistake About It This Time.

HE WAS BRUTALLY MURDERED BY TWO OF HIS PALS.

Shot Down At His Own House in St. Joseph.

THE ASSASSINS CLAIM THAT THEY ARE DETECTIVES.

Killed With a Pistol He Presented a Supposed Friend.

His Wife was in a Room Adjoining that in Which He was Murdered.

STATED TWO MONTHS ... when they secured the house in 90... Lafayette street, the property of Coun... cilman Aylesbury, paying fourteen dol... lard a month for it, and giving the name ... of Thos. Howard. The house is a one ... story cottage, painted white, with green ... shutters, and is romantically situated ... on the brow of a lofty eminence in ... the East of the city,

COMMANDING A FINE VIEW ... of the principle portion of the city, the ... river and railroads, and adopted as by ... nature for the perilous and desperate ... calling of James. Just East of the home ... is a deep gulch like ravine and beyond ... that a broad expanse of open country, ... backed by a belt of timber. The house, ... except from the West side, can be seen ... for several miles. There is a large yard ... attached to the cottage, and a stable where ... ...esse had been

WEEPING TWO THINGS

The ... hous ... lies t... they ... the ... court ... the ... solve ... polic... that ... had ... resid...

FRANK LESLIE'S ILLUSTRATED NEWSPAPER

Entered according to Act of Congress, in the year 1882, by Mr. Frank Leslie, in the office of the Librarian of Congress at Washington.—Reenter at the Post-Office, New York, N.Y., as Second-class Matter.

No. 1,387—Vol. LIV.   NEW YORK—FOR THE WEEK ENDING APRIL 22, 1882.   [Price 10 Cents.

JESSE JAMES AS AN ANGEL.

A satirical cartoon in a Texas magazine ridiculing the stories picturing Jesse as a fallen Robin Hood. *Courtesy Library of Congress*

A STORY THAT JAMES IS NOT DEAD AFTER ALL.
Special to the Chicago Times.

SEDALIA, Mo., April 5.—The *Times* correspondent was told in St. Louis this morning that Jesse James was not dead, and that there were men in that city who were ready to bet money on it. In passing through Jefferson City, the capital of this State, to-day, the correspondent had the good fortune to meet Gov. Crittenden, who had just returned from Kansas City. He said there was no doubt about the dead man being Jesse James, and that Ford killed him. He said the Fords were in custody, and the law would take its course. He remarked significantly: "It will be their turn next." He was asked if there would be no immunity for them, but evaded the question. This city is the center of a confederate element of high standing in Missouri. It is the home of James Wood, one of the trusted leaders of Gen. Joe Shelby; Major John N. Edwards, editor of the *Democrat*, who was on Shelby's staff, Bacon Montgomery, who, as a brigadier general in war times, made a reputation, and fifty miles from here lives the redoubtable Shelby himself. It is the opinion of this coterie, with one exception, that Jesse James is not dead. When asked what the identification of the body by his own mother means, they shrugged their shoulders and said: "Well, you wait and see." When asked what object Ford could have in killing an innocent man, they replied: "Ford gets money and immunity, and Crittenden, the governor, thinks he has satisfied the people and made a point." When asked what the confession of the widow means, they said: "Oh, you wait and see. She is posted and plays her part well. Do you suppose if she had been Jesse James' wife she wouldn't have got away with one of the Fords?" They say that the action of Crittenden in the matter will show him up in a very reprehensible light. Bacon Montgomery says Crittenden will get more money out of it than anybody else. This is the sentiment found here on the writer's first arrival and after an hour's sojourn.

Before Jesse James was buried the legend had already arisen: "He is not dead and there are men in the city who were ready to bet money on it." From the 1880s to 1948 many "real" Jesse Jameses have appeared from time to time. *The James D. Horan Civil War and Western Americana Collection*

Jesse had been in his grave only two days when his mother sent a telegram to N. D. Thompson, head of the Thompson Publishing Company in St. Louis, offering photographs of her son for a revised edition of *Life and Adventures of Frank and Jesse James and the Younger Brothers* written by J. A. Dacus, a St. Louis newspaperman, and published in 1880. *The James D. Horan Civil War and Western Americana Collection*

Kearney, Missouri, April 8th, 1882.

Mr. N. D. Thompson:

Respected Sir:—I received your letter, and will try to respond, in regard to the pictures. I will send all the pictures you call for if you will pay the price for them. * * * Write immediately if you will take them.

yours respectfully
Zerelda Samuel.

Mrs. Jesse (Zee) James exhibiting her husband's rifles, gun belts, and pistols. Almost penniless after the killing of her husband, she had to auction off her household goods in St. Joseph before joining relatives in Kansas City. While the auction was being held, souvenir hunters cut splinters from the blood-soaked floorboards where Jesse had fallen. Little Mary's high chair was sold for seventy-five cents, while the coffee mill young Jesse was playing with when Bob Ford killed his father went for two dollars. *The James D. Horan Civil War and Western Americana Collection*

Kearney, Clay Co., Mo., April the 12th, 1882.
Mr. N. D. Thompson, St. Louis, Mo:
I received the money. I have sent the pictures by express. I want you to send me a book as soon as you finish them. Yours with respect,

Zerilda Samuel.

Mrs. Samuel apparently accepted the bid of publisher Thompson and sent him pictures of Jesse. A year later she was charging the curious twenty-five cents to tour the Samuel farmhouse and gave each visitor a fierce harangue on the evils of the Pinkertons, the lawmen who had hunted her sons, and of the cruel Yankees, who had driven them into a life of outlawry. Pebbles from "Jesse's grave" were also sold for twenty-five cents. A cynical newspaperman suggested that when the day's supply was used up, another was gathered at a nearby creek. *The James D. Horan Civil War and Western Americana Collection.*

charged with and hoping that there would be some form of amnesty or even a pardon.[37]

The governor replied that he could not grant amnesty or a pardon but promised Frank: "If you abandon the life you are charged with leading . . . you shall have a fair and impartial trial. . . ."

Frank surrendered to Governor Crittenden in his office at the state capitol, Jefferson City, on the afternoon of October 5, 1882. The outlaw, accompanied by Edwards, entered the chief executive's office, with Edwards turning to Frank and introducing him:

"Governor Crittenden, I want to introduce you to my friend, Frank James."

After Missouri's governor and the outlaw had exchanged greetings, Frank removed his pistol and cartridge belt.

"Governor Crittenden," he said, offering the belt and pistol, "I want to hand over to you that which no living man except myself has been permitted to touch since 1861, and to say I am your prisoner."

Then the many newsmen and state officials who had been invited by Crittenden to view his "Christmas box surprise" crowded around Frank to shake his hand and to interview him.

It was an incredible scene: the beaming Crittenden and the awed politicians listening to the outlaw-fugitive solemnly tell them that he now knew crime didn't pay and he was glad a new day was aborning.[38]

The officials decided that Frank would be turned over to the sheriff of Jackson County at Independence to await trial; while James and Edwards waited at their hotel, Finis C. Farr, the governor's secretary, made the arrangements.

Word quickly spread throughout the city that Frank James had given himself up to the governor, and hundreds came to the McCarty house in Jefferson City to see the outlaw.

The next morning Farr, Edwards, and Frank O'Neill, a *Missouri Republican* reporter, accompanied Frank to Independence. The trip to Independence was a triumphant one. Crowds swarmed aboard the train at every stop, with long lines of spectators eagerly waiting to shake the outlaw's hand.

Mrs. Samuel, who knew something about personal publicity, made a dramatic appearance as the train pulled into the depot. One reporter wrote:

"The crowd fell back as he emerged from the car, and hushed all its noisy muttering and whispering as the old mother fell on her son's neck and sobbed loud and pitifully. And yet by a single great effort she mastered her grief and turned to the masses behind her, a calm and impenetrable face, fixed and set as though the beginning of the end had not arrived.

"But it was when Frank took the handsome little boy in his arms, and the child began to prattle and touch his father's cheek, that the crowd broke down and stout men and sympathetic women wept. . . ."[39]

It made a vivid incident but one wonders if Mrs. Samuel was not aware that a jury could be selected from that weeping crowd . . .

Frank held a hero's reception in Independence's Merchant's Hotel, "with the wealthiest, most popular and influential men waiting to shake his hand." Bankers, who only a few years before had trembled when they heard the names of Frank and Jesse James, pledged to post $100,000 bail if necessary![40]

HE CAME IN.

Frank James, the Chief of the Missouri Robber Band,

Surrenders Unconditionally to Gov. Crittenden.

He is Tired of Being Hunted Like a Beast,

And Wants to Stand His Trial and Settle Down.

The Railroad Companies Don't Have to Pay the Big Reward.

The Bandit Tells a Republican Correspondent

Some Pleasant Tales About His Career and His Chums.

He Lived Four Years at Nashville Under the Name of Woodson.

He Says Dick Liddel is a Right Nice Fellow,

And Jim Cummings is Too Nervous and Lazy to Hurt Anyone.

Geo. Shepherd Enjoys the Distinction of Being the Only Outlaw Detective Bligh Ever Caught.

AN EVERY DAY AFFAIR

And after expressing his pleasure at meeting Mr. Winfrey, assigned the two to a room on the second floor of the south wing looking east. About 9 o'clock they were bestirring, and putting on their hats they took in the town, the major, of course, meeting numerous acquaintances in his stroll and introducing his friend Winfrey. Returning to the hotel they took dinner and devoted the afternoon to reading the St. Louis morning papers. About a quarter before 5 o'clock they again emerged and walking over to the capitol grounds climbed the hill and entered the window leading to the private office of Gov. Crittenden. The latter having a few hours notice of their coming naturally felt jubilant over this gratifying culmination of his long fight against the outlaw band and he had, without indicating what the occasion, was summoned a number of the state officials to be present at the appointed time and witness this historical event. As they arrived one by one he jokingly told them that there was

A CHRISTMAS BOX

To be opened pretty soon, and he wanted his friends to enjoy it. While waiting he entertained them just as a sort of side issue by exhibiting the Frank James letter, which was perused by all with intense interest, and the good penmanship and easy style of which was generally commented upon. While the company were so engaged Maj. Edwards and his companion walked in and right over to where the governor sat in the midst of the row. The light shone in from the west, and as the outlaw walked in that direction with his hat in his hand the most conspicuous feature about him were his eyes, which seemed unusually dark and shone like brilliants, and his face, being clean shaven, was unusually pale, but his walk and manner were as easy and natural as though this occasion, which was one of life or death, was nothing unusual for him. The assembled company halted in their laughing and joking merely out of respect to strangers, and when Maj. Edwards said: Gov. Crittenden, I want to introduce you to my friend Frank James, a death-like stillness took possession of the room, and the men sat like statues. Gov. Crittenden arose and stepping forward shook hands with the visitors. Meanwhile the spell which had come over the spectators held its sway. After shaking hands the outlaw stepped back two steps and unbottoning his coat, reached to his waist, and

UNBUCKLED A BROAD BELT

Which had become visible. Giving it a swing he held out the belt heavy with cartridges and made bright by the polished revolver, but "Gov. Crittenden," said he, "I wish to hand over

you that which no living man except myself has been permitted to touch since 1861, and to say that I am your prisoner. I have taken all the cartridges out of the weapon and you can handle it in safety." The governor reached out and took hold of the weighty gift, remarking smilingly, "Not since 1861." Frank James replied, "That remark applies to the revolvers. The cartridge belt has been mine only 17 years." Then turning, he looked with perfect composure at all who surrounded him, bowing slightly as Gov. Crittenden remarked: "Gentlemen, this is Frank James." Being invited to take a seat he did so. The governor went on to say that he had called in a few officials to witness the episode. He need hardly say that he was glad, extremely glad, to meet Mr. James.

"Not more glad than I am, Gov. Crittenden," said he.

The spectators had by this time recovered themselves to some extent, and there was a general buzz as they inspected the features and clothing of the famous man.

"When did you come to Missouri, Frank?" asked the governor.

"A week ago last Sunday," said he. "I have come in the hope that you gentlemen will let me prove to you that I am

NOT NEARLY SO BAD A MAN

As I have been represented."

Gen. Waddill, who sat only a few feet away with a pale face and an "Oh my" sort of an expression, exclaimed at this juncture, "Why, didn't you sit right opposite me at dinner to-day and wasn't I introduced to you as Mr. Somebody or other?"

"I guess you are right," said Mr. James, and Gen. Waddill remarked: "Well, I'll be blanked."

opinion of the prisoner was unanimously expressed, moved out and scattered the news over town. In 15 minutes Jefferson City was talking of nothing else, and great crowds were thronging to the McCarty house, whither Mr. Farr had accompanied Mr. James.

It may be stated as a matter of interest at this point that the revolver presented is one which Frank James captured from a man who had first shot him through the body with it. He promises when all is over to give its history.

THOSE WHO WITNESSED THE SURRENDER

Were the following: Gov. Crittenden, Secretary Farr, Judge Henry of the supreme court, State Auditor Walker, Treasurer Chappell, Gen. Waddill, Maj. Tales, W. K. Bradbury, deputy clerk of the supreme court, V. M. Hobbs of the register of land office, L. E. Davison of the treasurer's office, Geo. W. Plattenburg of the adjutant-general's office, Jno. T. Clark of the auditor's office, P. T. Miller of the treasurer's office and several newspaper correspondents.

Within five minutes of the time of the prisoner's arrival at the McCarty house after his surrender, the yard in front and office were thronged with people. The assemblage comprised ladies, doctors, lawyers, tradesmen, laborers and hoodlums. Mr. James retired to his room which was at once crowded, and such a levee has never been seen as was held there from six to nine o'clock—everybody sought an introduction, and distasteful though the notoriety was to him, he assumed a cheery air and received every one with a good-natured dignity which was the subject of much comment. Several of the callers were acquaintances of his immediate friends or relatives and with these he discussed family affairs. A lawyer happened to mention the stubborn Cass county judges who are incarcerated for their contempt of court, and he was at home on that, and discussed their case

A SKETCH OF THE SCENE

Would have been worthy of perpetuation. An outlaw the central figure, sat on a table with coat and hat off, hemmed in by a mob, which filled the entire room and extended into the hall, sitting on the stairs and bed near him were the more dignified class of his auditors. In the front row of the standups were a number of boys, including two little

Headlines and excerpts from Frank O'Neill's exclusive interview in the *St. Louis (Missouri) Republican*, October 6, 1882, with Frank James before and after his surrender to Missouri's Governor Crittenden at the statehouse in Jefferson City. *Courtesy State Historical Society of Missouri*

Frank James after his surrender to Governor Crittenden. *The James D. Horan Civil War and Western Americana Collection*

A biting comment about the adulation given to Frank James upon his surrender appeared on the front page of *Judge* in December 1882. *The James D. Horan Civil War and Western Americana Collection*

Even Governor Crittenden showed up with his wife for a brief visit. It was enough to make the *St. Louis Globe Democrat* wonder editorially if it was the state that surrendered, and not Frank James.

In October the *Missouri Republican* published an interview with the outlaw, written by Frank O'Neill, the reporter who had accompanied Frank to Independence. According to O'Neill, several days before the surrender he had been approached at a political barbecue and asked if he wanted to interview James. O'Neill, one of the best political newsmen in the state, agreed, and talked to Frank in his hideout several hundred miles from the capitol.

In this fascinating interview, Frank James told of his life as a hunted man, how he had hidden out in Tennessee, his close calls, his association with Jesse and the other members of the gang, his reaction to the news that Jesse had been killed, and his hopes for the future. Frank told O'Neill at the start of the interview he would hold nothing back but would give "name and dates so anyone interested can fully investigate my statement."

His return to Missouri, he said, "involves the most important step of my life."[41]

Interview with Frank James in His "Hideout," October 6, 1881

I have returned to Missouri to try and regain a home and a standing among her people. I have been hunted like a wild animal from state to state. I have known no home, I have slept in all sorts of places—here today—there tomorrow. I have been charged with every great crime committed in Missouri or in her neighboring states. I have been taught to suspect my nearest and dearest friends of treachery and where is the end to be?

I am tired of this life of taut nerves, of night-riding and day-hiding, of constant listening for footfalls, cracking twigs and rustling leaves and creaking doors; tired of seeing Judas on the face of every friend I know—and God knows I have none to spare—tired of the saddle, the revolver and the cartridge belt; tired of the hoofs and horns with which popular belief has equipped me. I want to see if there is not some way out of it.

I intend to work—Oh, so hard—to make amends for the past. If I am not allowed to do this, I don't know what I shall do. Of course the world is wide and I can go where my safety is absolute but I have had enough of exile. I don't want any more.

I think I can give the state substantial proof for what I ask and I think the dignity of the law will not suffer if I prove myself worthy of mercy. I have proved my ability at good citizenship and I think I can demonstrate it in Missouri.

[At this point O'Neill observed: "Frank's face lighted up, his cheeks flushed and when he had finished he was in quite a glow." The outlaw then went on to describe the years he spent in Tennessee while "on the dodge":]

In August 1877 I arrived in Nashville accompanied by my wife. I was then in very poor health and had been for some time. A great many emigrants from Ohio were arriving that time and it was easy for us to assume that character. I went by the name of B. J. Woodson. We first applied to a farmer named Ben Drake who received us kindly and strangers though we were, made us comfortable for a week.

We then moved over to a house of Mrs. Ledbetter, a widowed sister of Mr. Drake and we stayed there until I effected the rental of a piece of land from a man named Josiah Walton, on White Creek, a few miles from Nashville.

My health rapidly improved and I worked on the farm, seldom failing to put ten hours a day in the fields. At the end of the year I engaged to team for one year on for Jeff Hyde's place for the Indiana Lumber Company and I carried out this agreement to the letter, driving a four-mule team.

I took my meals in the woods with the darkies, never missing a full day's work. At the expiration of teaming I rented a farm from Felix Smith on White Creek and I remained there until the time of my departure in April of 1881.

During those four years I was never absent from my work and I maintained a reputation for good citizenship equal to any man in the county.

Among my many friends was J. B. Shute, a member of the legislature and he will undoubtedly be surprised that he was in the company of the notorious Frank James. I went with Shute to many political meetings but I never took any prominent part. In my whole experience down there I never had but one approach to trouble.

One day I was sitting in the blacksmith shop of Dood Young, brother of the constable, when Dood who had been drinking freely, came in. He had suddenly conceived I was one of those damn Yankees who had come down to run things. Being in a belligerent mood he cursed me out and said he intended to slap my face. He was a great big double-fisted fellow and I was no match for him. For a moment I was in a great dread. I knew if he started to beat me I could not restrain myself from killing him. And then it would be goodbye to this long endeavor to settle down.

I took all he said good naturedly and tried to reason with him and by this pacific course I finally quieted him down and was able to slip away. Subsequently we became good friends and I have no doubt he will read your newspaper with a great deal of interest.

That reminds me of a couple of Nashville citizens who will also take a particular interest in your newspapers if this comes out.

Among the detectives in Nashville was a man named Fletch Horn and a man named Watson. Horn is a Falstaffian sort of fellow, full of good nature and I always liked him. Watson, on the other hand, was morose, saying little and staring at everything and everybody.

One day Jim Cummins came down to visit me and we were in Warner's Restaurant and Watson was standing nearby.

You know Jim Cummins is an apprehensive, nervous sort of a chap, who always feared the worst. I jerked him by the sleeve and asked him to come over and be introduced to a detective.

He paled and grew very fidgety. As he backed away he said, "Not by a —— sight. Do you think I'm a —— fool?" He got as far back in the restaurant as he could and all I could get out of him was, "You know you don't have a bit of —— sense. Some day you'll get pulled in by your brashness."

I explained to Jim the safest course for us was "cheeking it out" and the man most liable to get pulled in was the man who sneaked. But I never converted him to that view as the results will show.

Was Cummins there with you?

No, he was there with Jess.

What! Did Jesse live there too?

I forgot to tell you about that. It was something curious. I had not seen Jesse for two years and I had no idea where he was. One day in the Spring after my arrival, I stopped in the grain store of Ray & Sons to buy some red oats. Whom should I see in the office talking to Ike Ray but Jess! Ike knew him as Joe Howard. Jess was as surprised as I was and we stepped out and had a chat. He told me he was living near Waverly, Humphreys County, West Tennessee, and had come up to sell some corn. After some talk we separated. A year and a half later he moved to North Nashville.

What was Jesse's occupation?

He was a great patron and lover of the race tracks and spent much of his time there. He had several fine horses, among them the great Jim Malone, which won a big race not long ago in St. Louis, a four-mile race in Louisville and a big cup at Atlanta, Georgia. Jesse moved with perfect freedom down there.

When did Cummins go there?

He and Dick Liddil came down in the fall of 1880. Dick came on horseback and Jim came through by the cars. Jim was a happy-go-lucky, trampish sort of a fellow, not fond of work and I'll bet that wherever he is, he doesn't have ten dollars to his name.

He is not at all dangerous and the state does not have to worry about him. I have no doubt if he reads that I am telling you, he will say (with a most comical drawl): '' 'Yass, there's that damn fool go in 'n turned state's evidence. I'll kill the —— scoundrel as soon as I lay eyes on him. By —— I will!''

But Jim won't you know, that's one of his plays of fancy. He frequently has them and he never kills anybody. It's just too much trouble. Jim stopped with Jesse and so did Jack Ryan. Dick Liddil stayed with me and was a right good industrious young chap. I never thought there was anything vicious about Dick but he was easily influenced.

Well, our residence in Nashville was cut short due to a curious circumstance and it was a strong illustration, try as we may, to break off from my bohemian life, something would always occur to drive us back. Jim Cummins had always been the fearful frightened wretch that I have described and he somehow got the idea that he wasn't safe at Jesse's place. His fidgeting and restlessness attracted Jesse's attention and he become suspicious that Jim was nerving himself up to betray us.

We both kept a close watch on Jim and made it our business to know where he was going and what he was doing. One night in April, 1881, he was at my house and was more nervous than usual. He started up and I asked him where he was going. He said he was going to Jesse's. I asked him if he was coming back that night and he said he might but then he might not.

He did go to Jesse's but after staying a short time he said he was coming back to my place. But he never showed up. When Jesse found that Jim had not taken his overcoat and overshoes he became suspicious and came to see me. Considering his abandonment of his clothing, we agreed that Jim had gone to betray us. We decided to take proper caution, we kept our accoutrments in readiness, saddled our horses, and staying away from the house, waited all night for the officers to make their appearance.

They never appeared and this satisfied us that Jim had not said anything to the Nashville police.

We then thought it possible that Jim had gone to some distant point to meet officers from Missouri whom he had sent for, so during the next week, we were constantly in the saddle and in the balance had our horses ready in the barn.

Our fears proved groundless and we became convinced, and I still am, that Jim ran away because he feared capture and not to raise any mischief. Jesse wrote to several places making inquiries about him but we never saw Jim again.

Then just as we were settling down to security again, and less than two weeks after Jim Cummins' departure, Jack Ryan, known here as Bill Ryan, got drunk one day and was arrested in White Creek for disorderly conduct by Squire Erthman, who I knew well and who lived three miles from my place.

When they arrested him they found him heavily armed and with evidence as to his real identity and character. He was removed, as you know to Missouri to answer a charge there. As soon as we heard of his arrest, we mounted our horses, rode away and have never been back since.

Jess went one way with Dick Liddil and I went another. I never saw Jess again. I need hardly tell you that since that time I have done very little business. Those four years of an upright life were the happiest I have ever spent since my boyhood, notwithstanding the hard labor attending them. My old life grew the more detestible the more I got away from it and it was with a sense of despair that I rode away from our little house on the Smith place to again become a wanderer.

Did you attend public gatherings at Nashville freely and without fear of identification?

I did. For example I took the prize for exhibiting the Poland-China hogs at the Nashville and Jackson fairs, and I entered my horse, Jewel Maxey for the gents stakes at Nashville two years in succession, winning the first prize the first time and second money, the second time.

I rode myself the second time and would have taken first money, I believe if the starter, Ben Cockrell, had not ruled me down unfairly at the start. A year ago last Christmas, I took dinner with Clint Cantwell in the home of County Clerk Eastman who is Mr. Cantwell's son-in-law.

And no one in that region knew your identity?

Nobody but those of my own household and of Jesse's. Before I leave that subject I would like to mention that my little boy was born on the Walton place near Nashville.

When did you hear of Jesse's death?

The morning after it occurred. I went out early that morning to take a walk with my son and by the way I would like to say that he is the brightest four-year-old that ever blessed a family. When I returned my wife had the *New York Herald* in her hand. She told me that Jesse had been killed.

I asked by whom. She said by Bob Ford. When she said that I knew it was true, Jesse never trusted Bob. He loved Charlie but he suspected Bob of treachery. I believe that if the whole truth were known, Charlie took no part in that assassination, no matter what he may have been drawn into saying since it occurred.

Charlie Ford was always a warm-hearted boy and Jesse always treated him as if he was a brother. You may have noticed from the statements of the police that they did not consider Charlie in their employ. Charlie never fired a shot that day and anybody knows Charlie is a quicker man with a pistol than Bob. No, I can't believe Charlie was in it.

I don't blame Governor Crittenden for the part he had in the affair. I am satisfied there was no contract for assassination. If I were governor charged with upholding the laws of a great state cursed by such a band of outlaws who terrorized the state, I would take desperate measures to meet such desperate men. They would have to go as in this case they have gone. Such is the fate of all such bands. But what must be the suffering of such a pitiful creature as Bob Ford. For a few paltry dollars he has, while on the verge of manhood, brought upon himself a blighting curse that will never leave him in all the years to come.

Did you notice how remorse seized him soon after he got his blood money? He was rushing away from his victim with all the horror of Macbeth when the poor, desolate wife called to him to come back. What did he say? "I swear to God I did not do it."

Again like Macbeth, "I'll go no more. I'm afraid to think of what I have done. Look upon it again I dare not." Watch him again in New York. He is certain he saw the face of my wife there while as a fact she was at her father's home in Missouri. His imagination has already started to begin its deadly work and he sees blood and horror wherever he looks.

They said, as they have said many idle things, that I have sworn vengeance against the assassin and that I would have a life for a life. Would that be vengeance? Would it be vengeance to shorten a life which is now an agonizing torture to him? Would it be vengeance to send a corpse to break the heart of a mother who loves him as mine does me? Would it be vengeance to come home to my wife and my mother and show the red brand of a murderer?

No. When I took the paper and read the account of Jesse's death that morning, my wife and I sat down and talked about it. I said then the air would be full of rumors of what I would do and I proposed to do nothing. I have never made a threat against the life of any man in my lifetime and I was not going to now.

It was rumored that you came to Missouri that time. Did you?

I did not. What sort of generalship would it have been to come when everyone was expecting me?

The Trial of Frank James

When Frank James surrendered there were indictments against him for the murder of Pinkerton detective J. W. Whicher in March 1874 and for the robbery of an Independence bank in 1867.

On the recommendation of Prosecutor William Wallace, the bank robbery indictment and the Whicher murder charge were dismissed; the James and Younger gang had never officially been connected to the Independence crime even in the confessions of the gang members who had pleaded guilty, and Wallace admitted that there were no witnesses or evidence to link Frank to the murder of the Pinkerton man.

However, James was indicted for the Gallatin bank robbery in 1869 that resulted in the murder of cashier John Sheets, and for the Winston train robbery in the summer of 1881 in which Jesse had killed Conductor Westfall and Frank James had killed the young stonemason, Frank McMillan, according to Dick Liddil, the state's witness. Frank was then removed from Independence to the jail at Gallatin to stand trial. He had an impressive array of defense counsel headed by Former Lieutenant Governor Charles Johnson, former Congressman John F. Phillips, and five other prominent Missouri attorneys. All were Democrats.

Jackson County Prosecutor Wallace was joined by Daviess County Prosecutor William D. Hamilton and four of Gallatin's most prominent criminal attorneys. Wallace realized that his case, now drawing national attention, was legally weak. In addition to Liddil, his principal witnesses were former gang members Bill Ryan and Clarence Hite, both in the state penitentiary. Neither wanted to testify. Then, shortly before the trial began, Hite died in prison.

Liddil was the best of the lot. A handsome, impassive man, he had demonstrated that he possessed an excellent memory for convincing detail. There was one grave problem: Liddil had been convicted in Alabama for the gang's Muscle Shoals United States mail robbery and was awaiting sentencing in federal court. Wallace decided to seek a presidential pardon for Liddil. Letters asking President Chester A. Arthur to pardon Liddil were written by Wallace; Clay County Sheriff Timberlake, Kansas City Police Commissioner Craig, the publisher of the *Kansas City Journal*, United States Senator Francis M. Cockrell, members of the jury that had convicted Liddil, the prosecutor, the United States Marshal, and his four deputies all wrote to President Chester A. Arthur asking him to pardon Liddil. However, the President turned down the request. Then the federal judge before whom Liddil had been tried released him on his own recognizance. On this legal technicality he could testify for Wallace against James.

In the pretrial skirmishing, it was evident that Frank James intended to wave

Dick Liddil, one of Jesse's favorite riders, who turned state's evidence and became the principal witness against Frank James in his trial for murder. When Liddil appeared to testify at the coroner's inquest into the killing of Jesse, Mrs. Samuel pointed a finger at Liddil and shouted: "Traitor! Traitor! Traitor! God will send vengeance on you for this; you are the cause of all this! Oh, you villain!" *The James D. Horan Civil War and Western Americana Collection*

William H. Wallace, the courageous prosecutor of Jackson County who tried Frank James for murder. As Wallace recalled, he carried "a pistol on my hip" during the trial. Because of the many threats of violence the judge ordered all weapons to be checked at the door. *The James D. Horan Civil War and Western Americana Collection*

the Confederate Stars and Bars over the courtroom. Guerillas who had fought with him rallied to his support and, as always, the Missouri newspaperman John Newman Edwards led a vigorous editorial campaign to make sure the public knew that Frank was being prosecuted as a patriot who had shed his blood for the South and not as an outlaw.

Finally on August 21, 1883, Frank James came to trial for murder. Huge crowds flocked to the city and Judge Charles H. S. Goodman finally ordered the proceedings moved to the Gallatin Opera House, where the sheriff checked each spectator for carrying arms.[42]

It is significant that the members of the jury were solid, unwavering Democrats, two of whom had actually served in the Civil War on the Confederate side.

During the trial, when Prosecutor Wallace discovered that Sheriff George Crozier had selected the jury from a panel of pro-James supporters supplied by the defense, he and Daviess County Prosecutor Hamilton were so outraged that they asked the judge to declare a mistrial. Incredible as it may seem, the judge warned them not to make any move because there would be "bloodshed" in the tense and volatile city. As Wallace later recalled in his autobiography, he was ready to return to Jackson County but was persuaded to stay by his colleagues, who pointed out that he was the only one familiar enough with the case to have a chance of convicting James.

Liddil supplied explosive details of the train robbery, which he said was planned by Jesse James, who also killed Conductor Westfall; he insisted that Frank had killed the stonemason, Frank McMillan.

Liddil's testimony as he gave it that sultry August day in the Gallatin Opera House ninety-two years ago follows.[43]

> I am thirty-one years old. Was born and raised in Jackson county. I know Frank and Jesse James. First got acquainted with them in 1870, at Robert Hudspeth's, in Jackson county, eight miles from Independence, in Sinabar Township. The Hudspeths are farmers. I was working for them, first for Robert Hudspeth. I saw the James brothers there a dozen times or more from 1870 to 1875. I saw them together sometimes and sometimes separate. I saw Frank and Jesse James, Cole and John Younger and Tom McDaniel. I have seen two or three of them there together—namely, Jesse James, John Younger and James McDaniel; never saw all five together; they were generally armed and on horseback; they would stay around there maybe a day and a night, or two nights, or maybe not more than two hours; I supposed from what I heard and saw that they went together in a band.
>
> [Objection being made to the wide range of the testimony, the court ruled that the State must confine itself to showing the preparation for a perpetration of the robbery and murder at Winston.]
>
> [Witness further testified:] There was a gang known as the James boys; I

The opera house in Gallatin, Missouri, where the trial of Frank James was held in August 1883. *Courtesy Jackson County Historical Society*

belonged to it at one time: I joined four years ago this fall, in the latter part of September, at Hudspeth's; I saw Jesse James at Ben Morrow's one day; Ben lives in Fort Osage Township; I didn't go with him at once. I did afterward. The band was Jesse James, Ed. Miller, Bill Ryan, Tucker Basham and Wood Hite. That was in the fall of 1880, in Jackson county, of this state. From there we went to six miles from Independence. I left shortly after that. The others left—that is, part went and part remained. Jesse James and Miller told me they went to Tennessee. I went to Tennessee in the summer of 1880. I went to Nashville. First I went to the High Ferry pike. I went with Jesse James. There we found Frank and Jesse James and their families. We stayed there two weeks. We remained in Nashville nearly a year after that. The others came there in the winter of 1880—that is, Bill Ryan and Jim Cummings [sic]. Bill Ryan was from Jackson county. Bill Ryan, myself and Jesse James went there together. . . . Frank and Jesse and I left March 26, 1881. Bill Ryan had been captured, and we took a scare and lit out. I had seen Bill the day he was captured. He was going to Logan county, Kentucky, to old man Hite's. I first learned about his capture when I got a paper on Saturday describing Ryan's capture on Friday. We got ready and left about dark.

We left on horseback. Frank had a horse of his own. Jesse and I captured a couple. We were twenty miles when those two horses gave out, and we got a couple more. We went to old man Hite's. We were armed. I had two pistols. Jesse and Frank had a Winchester rifle apiece. It was forty miles from Nashville to Mr. Hite's. We got there at sun-up. At the house we found Mr. Hite, wife and daughter; Mr. Norris, wife, and girl, and Wood Hite. We stayed there a week. There were some officers from Tennessee came after us. We went from there to Mr. Hite's nephew's, three miles off—Frank, and Jesse, and Wood Hite and myself. We stayed there a week, and went back to the old man's. We were all armed. We remained there only one night, leaving on Sunday night for Nelson county, Kentucky, one hundred and fifty miles off. Frank and Jesse and I went up there on horseback. There was no one I knew when I got there. We stopped at Johnny Pence's, Bud Hall's and Doc Hoskins'. An arrangement was there entered into for robbery by myself, Frank and Jesse James, and Clarence Hite. Wood Hite came afterward. We first agreed to take the express where the train crossed the river. The river was high, and they had to transfer by boat. The river went down, and we got there too late, and we arranged to take a train here somewhere. This was talked over at Bob Hall's. Wood Hite was there at his father's. This was the latter part of April or first of May, 1881. Jesse's family at Nashville was a wife and one child. Frank's consisted of a wife and two children, living at Fatherland street. Jesse's wife came to Nelson county shortly after we got there.

From there she said she was going to Missouri. I never saw her after that till Jesse was killed. Jesse told me she came to Kansas City. He told me he was renting a house in Kansas City. He told me this in the fall of 1881. I don't know about Frank's wife except that Jesse told me she came out on the train to Gen. Joe Shelby's at Saline. She brought a sewing machine with her and gave it to her mother. Jesse first told me, and Frank told me afterward about it. That sewing machine was shipped to Gen. Shelby's; so Jesse told me. Jesse made some kick about Frank's wife coming here, and Frank told me that it was all right, and that he told her to come and give the machine to her mother. This he told me on some road somewhere between here and her mother's. He objected because he said she told some things she ought not to. Her mother was Mrs. Ralston, and she lived some six miles from Independence. At Nashville Frank James went by the name of B. J. Woodson, Jesse was J. D. Howard, Ryan was Tom Hill, and I was Smith, from Nelson county. Frank and Jesse shipped two guns by Johnny Pence to John

T. Ford, at Lexington. They were a Winchester rifle and a breech-loading shot gun. Jesse and I came here together on the cars to Kearney in May, 1881. We came over the Hannibal and St. Joseph part of the way. We went from there to Mrs. Samuels'. Frank came out a week later on the following Saturday via the Louisville and Indianapolis. Mrs. Samuels is mother to Frank and Jesse James. She lived four miles from Kearney. I had been to her house before. Wood Hite came afterward. We found Clarence Hite here, he having come out with Jesse's wife to Kansas City, and then came to Mrs. Samuels'.

Wood Hite was not at Hall's when the plan for the robbery was made. The others left word where they would meet him. Clarence Hite was twenty years old. Wood was thirty-three or thirty-four years of age. When in Missouri I don't think he wore whiskers. If he did they were thin and light. His name in the gang in Missouri I could not give. We had to change names many times. I was Joe. Frank was Ben in Tennessee and Buck here, and Jesse was Dave in Tennessee. We started out in pursuance of an agreement about a week after. We four started on horseback—Frank, Jesse, Wood and myself. Clarence went on the cars to Chillicothe. We were going there to take a train. I rode the sorrel, Jesse rode a bay, and Frank and Wood Hite rode horses that Wood Hite and I took from a rack in Liberty. We got to Chillicothe about ten, stopping a mile and a half from town in the timber. Wood Hite went in after Clarence, and found him, and Clarence came out with him. The roads were so muddy that we went back, Jesse and myself to the old lady, Wood and Frank to the Fords', and Clarence to Mrs. Samuels' also. We stayed there three or four days.

Shortly after this we started out again. At that time I had short whiskers all over my face. Jesse was five feet eleven inches and a half high, round face; pug nose, dark sandy whiskers and blue eyes. He weighed 195 pounds and stood very straight. Frank James had burnsides and mustache. His whiskers were darker than his mustache. We went to Gallatin, first stopping in the timber to wait for Wood Hite. This was almost a mile from the town, on the road to Winston. I have never been to the place since.

We met Wood there. We started back. Jesse got sick with toothache, and the creosote he used swelled his jaw and his face and he had to go back. Clarence went on foot, and Frank, Jesse, Wood and myself went on and stopped with a man named Wolfenberger, some sixteen miles from there. I helped him load up a load of wood next morning. We had supper and breakfast there, and left next day. Clarence stayed somewhere else. Jesse was very sick and we had to wait on him. We started for Mrs. Samuels', and Jesse was so sick we had to stop at an old stockman's. Wood Hite took the train to the old lady's and Clarence stayed with us. [Witness described the stockman's place, as he described every other place where they stopped, with great minuteness.] Jesse got the stockman to take him in a buggy to Hamilton depot. The others then started for Mrs. Samuels', but Frank and I went to Mrs. Bolton's, in Ray county. There was a week or ten days between the first and second trip. Frank and I stayed at Mrs. Bolton's a week, and then met Jesse, Clarence, and Wood at Mrs. Samuels'. In about a week or ten days we went on another trip. I rode the same horse as before; so did Jesse. Frank was riding a mare he got close to Elkhorn.

We started at night. I assisted in robbing the Winston train on this trip. We started from Mr. Samuels' at dark, coming northeast to Gallatin. We rode till daylight, when we came into a skirt of timber, where we stayed all night till sunrise. I don't reckon we came over fifteen miles that night. Next day we scattered. Frank and Clarence went together, and I, Jesse and Wood Hite together. We three ate dinner at a white house on the road, with an old shed stable back of it. There we met Frank and Clarence late in the evening. That night we stayed in the timber where we next met Wood on the former trip. We didn't get supper that night. We left next morning. We left, Frank and Clarence together, Jesse and Wood together and I by myself, all going different routes. I got my horse shod in Gallatin on the last trip we were here. I can pick out the shop. It is off the square. It is an old frame shop. There is another shop right below. I had my horse shod all around. I also got a pair of fenders on the square to keep my horse from interfering. The saddler who sold them was a heavy man, with a dark mustache and a dark complexion. We had quite a little conversation over this trade. We were to meet about a mile from Winston. I got dinner on the way, and went on to meet the boys in a skirt of timber near where the road crosses the track. We waited till dark, hitched our horses and went up on foot to the train. Wood and I went together, and met Frank, Jesse and Clarence at the depot.

The arrangement was as follows: that I and Clarence should capture the engineer, fireman and engine and start it or stop it as we might be directed by Jesse and Frank. Jesse, Frank and Wood were to get into the passenger cars and at the proper time rob the express car. We carried out the program when the north bound C., R. I. & P. passenger train came along. After getting outside of town Clarence and I got up back of the tender, and went over on top to the engine. We had two pistols. We kept quiet till the train stopped; then we hollered to go ahead. We shot to scare those fellows, who both ran onto the pilot. The first run was about two hundred yards, then a stop. About this time one of the boys pulled the bell rope and the engineer stopped the train and firing back in the cars commenced. Don't know how many shots. Jesse got into express car through the rear door and Wood and Frank tried to get in through the side door. The baggageman was standing in this side door and Frank seized him by the leg and jerked him out of the car and left him on the ground. He, Frank, dived into the express car and he or Jesse hollowed to us to go ahead. The engineer pretended he could not move the train as the brakes were down. We then struck him with a piece of coal and told him we would kill him if he did not start the train. He then threw open the throttle and started it under a full head of steam. The engineer and fireman then got out of the cab and hid in front of the engine. We, firing a number of shots to frighten them, did not aim to hit them, as we could have easily killed them, being most of the time within a few feet. I then started back to the express car, but Clarence called to me and I returned to the engine. Frank came out and shut off steam, and as she slacked we jumped off while it was running. Frank and Clarence got off first. I went back after Jesse who was still in the express car. Jesse jumped first, and I followed. We got $700 or $800 that night in packages. It was all good money. We all got together then, except Wood, who had been knocked down as Frank pulled the baggage-man out of the car, and we never saw him. Frank talked to me about the robbery afterward. He said he thought they had killed two men. Jesse said he shot one, he knew, and that Frank killed one. He saw him peep in at the window, and thought he killed him. From there we went to our horses, taking our time. We all unhitched, except Clarence, who cut his halter-strap. From there we went to Crooked River. The money was divided in a pasture, just before daylight. Jesse divided, giving us about $130 apiece.

We were all armed with pistols at Winston. I had on a plaid suit; Frank had a bluish suit, all alike. I don't remember Jesse's suit. He had a dark striped coat and pants, and had on a big duster. Clarence had a dark suit, all alike. Wood had pants and coat of different cloth. I saw the guns that were shipped. I saw them at

Mrs. Samuels'. Frank and Jesse had them. We didn't have them at Winston. The robbery was in 1881, in July. Either Frank or Jesse designated the meeting place at Gallatin, because no one else knew anything about the country.

[At the close of Liddil's direct examination a recess was taken for fifteen minutes, when Liddil, being recalled to the stand, further testified in reply to questions put by the defense, as follows:]

[By Mr. Philips]: I went back to Jefferson City with Sheriff Timberlake in 1882, in January or February. I was there shortly after that with Mr. Craig, of Kansas City. I saw Governor Crittenden both times, first at the depot and the other time at his office. I don't remember telling the Governor at either of those times that after the Winston robbery Frank James upbraided Jesse for killing any one, or reminded him of the agreement before the robbery that no one should be hurt or killed.

[At this stage of the proceedings *Governor Thos. T. Crittenden* was, by consent of counsel, called out of time, in order to save him the trouble of staying here till his name could be reached in the usual order, and testified in behalf of the defense as follows]:

[By Mr. Philips]: Liddil did make such a statement to me as propounded just now. I think it was the second time he was at Jefferson City. It grew out of asking him why they killed an innocent man engaged in his duties. He said that it was not the intention to do it; that the understanding was there was to be no killing; that Frank had said there was to be no blood shed, and that after it was over Frank said, "Jesse, why did you shoot that man? I thought the understanding was that no one was to be killed, and I would not have gone into it if I had known or thought there was to be anything of that sort done." To which Jesse said, "By G——d, I thought that the boys were pulling from me, and I wanted to make them a common band of murderers to hold them up to me."

The climax of the trial was the outlaw's testimony. Soft-spoken and articulate, he calmly denied all of the state's charges, spoke humbly of his war exploits, and proudly described how he had lived the role of a peaceful, industrious farmer in Tennessee.

Wallace hammered at him for hours during the cross-examination but Frank was never ruffled. In the end he left the stand still a hero to the adoring crowds.

After three hours of deliberation the jury acquitted him.

The verdict sent reverberations across the country, with editorial writers in most of the big cities either defending the jury or contemptuously dismissing them as pro-James sympathizers. In Missouri the James gang was again a political issue, Pulitzer's *St. Louis Post-Dispatch* leading the attack against the "political influence" which had permeated the trial, the "bullying partisans" of Frank James who had packed the Opera House, and the "rustic jury" who had believed the myth that Jesse and Frank had been hunted down only because they had fought for the Confederacy.[44]

But Frank's troubles were not over. Wallace, who later revealed he had carried "a pistol in my hip pocket" because of threats, announced that he was going to put the outlaw on trial for the Blue Cut robbery. Then the state's high court ruled that testimony of a felon was not permissible in a criminal trial unless he was pardoned. Wallace immediately demanded that Governor Crittenden pardon Liddil.

Curiously, Crittenden, who had petitioned the President for the same thing, refused to pardon Liddil. Wallace was stunned, for now he no longer had a case against Frank. He bitterly dismissed the indictment against the outlaw but then turned him over to the Alabama authorities to stand trial for the Muscle Shoals stage robbery. The story there was the same: the jury refused to believe that the mild balding man was the notorious train and stagecoach robber. Mrs. Samuel and her family were on hand, and Frank's service to the Confederacy was brought out at every opportunity.

Missouri again claimed Frank as a defendant in the Otterville train robbery trial. But the Republicans scoffed at the idea that any prosecutor could produce witnesses for the eight-year-old robbery. Rather, they claimed, it was a plot by the Democrats to make sure that "their pet" would not be turned over to the Minnesota authorities who had sent the Youngers to prison for life.

That fall William Wallace, surely the unsung hero of the James saga, resigned and tried to win the Democratic congressional nomination. Although he carried "every ward and every precinct in Kansas City," he was refused the nomination at the convention. John Newman Edwards gleefully told Frank the news.

The shadow of the James gang also touched the political career of Governor Crittenden. He was defeated for renomination, the Democrats instead selecting former Confederate General John S. Marmaduke. Significantly, the Democrats did not mention the James-Younger gang during their convention.[45]

In turn the infuriated Republicans blasted the Democratic Party at their convention, charging that the "banditti" had been allowed to pillage Missouri for sixteen years, halting immigration and preventing the flow of new capital into the state.

In the winter of 1885 the train robbery charge against Frank James was dismissed; the one witness was long in his grave.

The election of Marmaduke was important to James, for Edwards had assured him that the newly elected governor would never honor his extradition to Minnesota. In 1889 Edwards, the perennial champion of the Jameses and Youngers, died; but his fight to prevent Frank from being turned over to Minnesota was successful.

There was one last chapter to the turbulent political wars revolving about the outlaws. Crittenden had been nominated for a foreign post, but despite the recommendation of the powerful Senator George G. Vest, President Cleveland turned the nomination down. It is hard to believe, but one presidential reason was that "Crittenden had bargained with the Fords for the killing of Jesse James."

Frank returned to the old Samuel farmhouse, where he lived for many years, a friendly old man who bounced his grandson on his knee, held court in the lobby of the local hotel, and was the principal attraction at the reunions of the Missouri guerillas.

In 1897 he visited the Centralia battlefield with Walter Williams, a young reporter for the *Missouri Herald*. Williams' eyewitness account of the paunchy, aging outlaw remembering that savage day in the fall of 1864 is a moving end to the saga of Jesse and Frank James.[46]

When the proclamation was issued it was said by cavillers that it would wholly fail in its objects and that no good would be accomplished by the offer of such large sums of money for the apprehension of those desperate men. The results which followed so closely upon its issuance furnish an ample vindication of the policy which inspired it. No tie, no faith in honorable comradeship, is stronger with an outlaw than the power of money.

On the 13th day of February, 1882, Bob Ford surrendered to Capt. H. H. Craig, of Kansas City. On the 24th day of January, 1882, Dick Liddil surrendered to J. R. Timberlake, sheriff of Clay county.

On the 13th day of February, 1882, Clarence Hite was captured in Logan county, Kentucky, by Capt. Craig and J. R. Timberlake, and was taken to Daviess county, Missouri, where two indictments—one for the murder of William Westfall and one for participation in the Winston train robbery—were pending against him. He was arraigned under the indictment and pleaded guilty to the charge of robbery, and was, on the same day, sentenced to twenty-five years' imprisonment in the penitentiary, which sentence he is now undergoing.

On the 3d day of April, 1882, Jesse W. James was killed in the city of St. Joseph by Charles and Robert Ford—his followers and associates in crime. The Fords immediately surrendered themselves to the legal authorities of Buchanan county, and were placed in jail.

An indictment charging them with murder in the first degree, was preferred against them by the grand jury, to which, at the April term, 1882, they both pleaded guilty in the Buchanan county circuit court, and were pardoned by me on the same day, upon the grounds of public policy.

Frank James voluntarily surrendered himself to me, in my office, in Jefferson City, on the 5th day of October, 1882. I immediately delivered him to the law officers of Jackson county, where he is now incarcerated in jail, awaiting trial on one or more indictments.

I paid twenty thousand dollars in rewards to various persons for the capture and overthrow of this band of desperadoes, not one dollar of which was taken from the State Treasury. It is not probable that Missouri will again be cursed and disgraced by the presence of such a band of men, confederated together for desperate purposes. It is fully redeemed and acquit of that unwarranted appellation of "robber State."

Crittenden admitted in his review that he had paid out twenty thousand dollars in rewards but failed to say who got what amount. In praising the various law enforcement officials he curiously overlooked William H. Wallace, the tough, courageous, unyielding prosecutor of Jackson County who had broken up the James gang and put Frank James on trial. *Courtesy State Historical Society of Missouri*

Excerpts from Governor Crittenden's message of 1883 in which he reviewed his battle against the James gang. *Courtesy State Historical Society of Missouri*

There could scarcely have been a contrast more striking to Frank James' eyes as he drove out to the battle-field. The weather was much the same as in September of '64. There was the same blue sky with the chill of early fall. The timber along the head of Young's Creek was much the same, green and stubby. Here and there the prairie grass, long and coarse, bent to the morning breeze. The ridge upon which Major A. U. E. Johnson's men formed and the "swag" in the prairie across which pursuit followed were unchanged. But now there were fences—then an open prairie. Now there was cornfield and meadow land and the fine farms of S. L. Garrard and Valentine Miller—then the ground was unbroken and only the prairie grass to be seen, as far as the eye could reach. Now the quietude of the Sabbath morning, the cattle standing peacefully for the milking—then the shouts of desperate men and the sharp report of gun and pistol. Now green grass, autumn leaves, rosy cheeks in the peach orchard—and peace. Then war—which Gen. Sherman said was hell and Frank James declares "a game of chess with human lives as pieces on the board." No blood stains reddened the white flowers of the prairie after this ride and no ghastly upturned faces lay upon the sun-kissed sward.

FRANK JAMES TELLS HOW IT TOOK PLACE

"There is the spot," said Frank James, two miles and more from Centralia, shortly before the main road was left for a broad lane which led to S. L. Garrard's home. "Yonder on the rise near the hayrick was the line of the Federal troops. Just this side, towards Centralia, stood the detachment which held their horses. On the edge of the woods beyond our men formed."

His memory served him well. He had not been to the field before nor since the day of the fight, thirty-three years ago next Monday. No word had been spoken to indicate the locality. But he remembered accurately the entire surroundings. "I can go," he said, "to any battle-field where I was engaged and pick out almost instantly the locations. I guess it's the closeness to death which photographs the scene on one's memory."

A few moments later he came onto the field itself. Corn was growing rank and there was a herd of cattle calmly feeding on the pasture land. Where the Federals stood was the golden yellow of a hay field. Here Mr. James wandered around for a few moments drinking in his surroundings with almost passionate eagerness. Then he told the story, quietly at first, but as he proceeded, his face lighted up, there was a ring in his voice and his whole frame seemed ready for the fray again.

"The day before we had had a small skirmish down in Goslin's Lane, between Columbia and Rocheport. I don't know what day it was. We could scarcely keep account of months and years at that time, much less days. We killed a dozen Yankee soldiers in Goslin's Lane and captured a wagon train of provisions and stuff. Out in the Perche hills that night we joined forces with Bill Anderson. I was with Capt. George Todd, one of the hardest fighters that ever lived but less desperate than Anderson."

James paused a moment—his conversation was in scraps all day and only here put in connected form—he paused a moment and continued: "But Anderson had much to make him merciless. You remember the treatment his father and sisters received at the hands of the Kansas Jayhawkers. That night we camped on one of the branches leading into Young's Creek not far from the home of Col. M. G. Singleton. There were about 225 men, all told, in our combined command. Funny, isn't it? I've met or heard of at least 10,000 men who claimed to be with Quantrill or his lieutenants during the war when the truth is there were never more than 350 or 400 from one end of the war to the other.

"In the morning Anderson took about thirty of his company and went into Centralia. I was not with him nor was any of Todd's company. In Centralia Anderson captured a train, carried off a lot of stuff, shot down some soldiers who were on the train and did other things about which I know nothing save from hearsay and which Todd condemned when the boys returned. In the afternoon Capt. Todd detailed a detachment of ten men under Dave Pool to go out and reconnoiter. We had heard there were some Yankee troops in the neighborhood. This squad was composed of Dave Pool, Wood and Tuck Hite, Jeff Emery, Bill Stuart, John Pool, Payton Long, Zach Sutherland and two others whose names I don't remember. They were to find out if the Federals were around, how many and, if possible, 'toll them down toward our camp. Pool did his duty well. He found out the location of the Federals, rode close to them and then galloped rapidly away as if surprised to see them. The Federals followed. I have never found anybody who could tell how many there were of them. Pool reported to us there were 350 and he was usually very accurate. On they came out from Centralia. Pool and his men came on and reported. Todd called out 'mount up, mount up.'"

The sharp, piercing eyes of James flashed. "I can see them now yonder on that ridge. On they come. I don't care what your histories say, they carried a black flag. It was apparently a black apron, tied to a stick. We captured it in the battle that followed. No, we had no flag. We had no time to get one and no chance to carry it if we had one. The Yankees stopped near the rise of the hill. Both sides were in full view of each other, though nearly a half mile distant. The Yankees dismounted, gave their horses into charge of a detail of men and prepared to fight.

"John Koger, a funny fellow in our ranks, watched the Yankees get down from their horses and said: 'Why the fools are going to fight us on foot!' And then added in seriousness: 'God help 'em.'

"We dismounted to tighten the belts on the horses and then at the word of command started on our charge. The ground, you will notice, rises sharply and we had to charge up hill. For a moment we moved slowly. Our line was nearly a quarter of a mile long, theirs much closer together. We were still some 600 yards away, our speed increasing and our ranks closing up when they fired their first and only time. They nearly all fired over our heads. We were laying low on our horses, a trick that Comanche Indians practice and which saved our lives many a time. Only two of our men were killed, Frank Shepherd and 'Hank' Williams. A third, Richard Kinney, was shot and died three or four days afterward from lock-jaw. Shepherd and Kinney rode next to me on either side. The blood and brains from Shepherd splashed on my pants' leg as he fell from his horse. Kinney was my closest friend. We had ridden together from Texas, fought side by side, slept together, and it hurt me when I heard him say, 'Frank, I'm shot.' He kept on riding for a time and thought his wound wasn't serious.

"But we couldn't stop in that terrible charge for anything. Up the hill we went yelling like wild Indians. Such shrieks, young man, you will never hear as broke the stillness of that September afternoon now nearly thirty-three years ago." There was the silence of hopeful assent from every listener.

"On we went up the hill. Almost in the twinkling of an eye we were on the Yankee line. They seemed terrorized. Hypnotized might be a better word though I reckon nobody knew anything about hypnotism then, though George Todd, by the way, looked like Svengali. Some of the Yankees were at 'fix bayonets,' some were biting off their cartridges, preparing to reload. Yelling, shooting our pistols upon them we went. Not a single man of the line escaped. Every one was shot through the head. The few who attempted to escape we followed into Centralia and on to Sturgeon. There a Federal blockhouse stopped further pursuit. All along the road we killed them. The last man and the first man was killed by Arch Clements. He had the best horse and got a little the start.

"That night we left this woods and this neighborhood and scattered. I re-crossed the river near Glasgow and went southward."

JESSE JAMES WAS IN THE FIGHT

"It has been reported that my brother, Jesse James, was not at the Centralia fight, that he was sick in Carroll county at the time. This is a mistake. Jesse was here. He it was who killed the commander of the Federal troops, Major Johnson. The Younger boys were not at Centralia."

AN EAR OF CORN FOR A SOUVENIR

The plowshare had taken the place of the sword on the hillside. Frank James took an ear of corn from the battle-field. "I want some sort of a relic," he said, "and this is the most peaceful-looking I saw." Later in the day Adam Rodmyre, of the Guard, gave him a bullet found on the field.

VISIT TO THE GRAVES OF THE GUERRILLAS

After two hours on the battle-field a visit was made to the Pleasant Grove burying ground on the Silver farm where Frank Shepherd and "Hank" Williams were buried. The burying ground is a typical country cemetery, lying in a secluded spot, away from the main-traveled road, some four miles from Centralia. It is reached through a half-cleared piece of timber and contains a number of newly-made graves. The graves of the two guerrillas are unmarked, not even a head board indicating their last resting place. A great pine tree stands near by and sobs their requiem as heaven's breezes blow. "I would give $100 for that tree," said a bystander who had followed the party. "That would be like robbing a grave-yard," commented James.

The living guerrilla stood with his black slouch hat in his hand at the side of the sunken graves of his dead comrades. " 'To this complexion must we come at last,' " he said, looking down at the withered grass. "Our boys are scattered everywhere. You will find their graves in the hollows and on the hills, by the gulf and on these prairies. Many have no monument. They don't need any. They made their monuments while they lived. They left a record for daring courage that the world has not surpassed. They don't need any monument after they are dead. Their sleep is just as sweet here as it would be in a beautiful city cemetery." Frank James pinched a twig from the great, green pine tree and walked away. "The marvel to me," he said to the *Herald* reporter, "is that I am not sleeping in a place like this. What have I been spared for when so many of my comrades were taken? 'Two men shall be working in a field, one shall be taken and the other left.' That's Scripture—you know my father was a Baptist preacher, a good man and a good preacher—it's Scripture and it's Life, too."

A brief stay was made at the farm house of William R. Jennings. Mr. Jennings helped bury the Federal dead the day after the battle. He could not remember the number but there were several wagon loads. "I felt sorry for one poor boy, hardly more than 17 years old, who had almost reached the woods in an attempt to escape. All the Federals," continued Mr. Jennings, "had been shot in the head. So unerring was the marksmanship of the bushwhackers that frequently we would find no wounds on the soldiers' bodies until we would turn back the eyelid or look into an ear and there would be a single little hole that brought death." When the old man closed his story the party turned to go. "Well," said Mr. Jennings, "I hope we'll meet in a better world than this." "I hope so," said Mr. James, "where there is no fighting."

HIS CONVERSATION WITH CITIZENS

In the afternoon at the Globe Hotel a large number of persons, men, women, and children, called, some from curiosity, others from genuine interest. Mr. James greeted all pleasantly. He did not seem to seek notoriety nor to shun it but accepted the inevitable. "They act like I was a wild beast," he smilingly said as a fresh crowd peered through the window. "And may be I was a little wild," he added—and then thoughtfully, "once. But it amuses them and doesn't hurt me."

Samuel Holland, employed by the Centralia Produce Company, remarked as he was introduced to James: "Major Johnson taught me the alphabet in my first school on Buckskin Prairie in Pike County, Missouri." "What kind of a man was he?" asked James. "He was rather short and stout with a sandy moustache. He liked to have his own way but was usually very shrewd." "Well, he acted foolishly at last," responded James.

A bright-looking boy, about twelve years of age, shook hands with Mr. James. "My name," he said, "is Marquette Richards. My grandfather, John Marquette, was the last man killed in the fight." James looked kindly at the manly little fellow. "Well, son, you may be proud of your grandfather. He was about the bravest in Johnson's command. He fought all the way. Arch Clements shot him near Sturgeon. He rode a dun horse which I learned down in Columbia the other day was afterwards bought by Dr. W. T. Lenoir." No contrast of the day was more striking than that of Frank James and the grandson of his old enemy, the grizzled veteran and the mite of a boy.

James R. Bryson, himself an old Confederate soldier, said: "You don't look as old as I expected you would." "Now this man is my friend," was the quick reply of James. "Any man who says I don't look old is my friend."

One lady said: "I hope you are a better man than when you were here before." Mr. James bowed courteously as he rejoined: "Well, madam, I was just as good a man that day as I knew how to be."

HOW THE GUERRILLAS LIVED

"We usually met," said Mr. James, "hospitable treatment through Missouri, Kentucky and states further south. There were enough southern sympathizers to give us a kind reception, and we had little trouble up to the last days of the war in getting enough food. We lived in the woods of course, that was our only home. We captured from the Federals clothes, horses and ammunition. We generally carried our coats and overcoats fastened on our saddles. Most of our clothing was the blue uniform of the Yankees. We wore vests cut low in the front and trimmed with gold lace. Each guerrilla carried two to four pistols. I nearly always carried two. I was small and slender and more than that number were too many for me.

"The stories about guerrillas riding with the reins of the horses between their teeth and firing with pistols in both hands is simply dime novel stuff. There was never any such thing. We always held our horses with one hand and the pistol with the other. It was as important to hold the horse as it was to hold the pistol.

"Anderson always made us keep our horses in good condition. If a man did not keep a good horse and good pistols he sent him to the infantry. I rode a horse named 'Little George' at Centralia.

"At night and when we were in camp we played like school boys. Some of our play was as rough as football. The truth was we were nothing but great big boys, anyhow."

SOME PERSONAL SKETCHES

"If you ever want to pick a company to do desperate work or to lead a forlorn hope, select young men from 17 to 21 years old. They will go anywhere in the world you will lead them. When men grow older they grow more cautious but at that age they are regular daredevils. Take our company and there has never been a more reckless lot of men. Only one or two were over 25. Most of them were under 21. Scarcely a dozen boasted a moustache. Wasn't it Bacon who said when a man had a wife and children he had given hostages to fortune?

"Arch Clements, who was the real brains of Anderson's command, was only 20. He, Payton Long and myself followed the Federals nearly to Sturgeon. He was First Lieutenant. Clements came from Kingsville, Johnson County. He was killed at Lexington.

"There were only two of the guerrillas who would fight in a battle just like in a personal difficulty, George Todd and Dick Kinney. They would get mad in a battle just like in a fist fight.

"Dave Pool was a born comedian. He could have gotten $500 a week on the stage.

"Up in the old German settlements of Lafayette County the mothers still quiet their children by telling them to be still or Dave Pool will get them. After the Centralia fight Pool walked across the dead bodies of the Federals stepping from one to another. Todd asked him what he was doing. 'Counting 'em.' 'But you needn't walk on 'em to count 'em,' said Todd, 'That's inhuman.' 'Aren't they dead?' replied Pool; 'and if they are dead I can't hurt them. I cannot count 'em good without stepping on 'em. When I get my foot on one this way I know I've got him.' Pool counted 130 dead bodies in one block.

KILLED 1,000 MEN IN TWO WEEKS

"The greatest raid made by the guerrillas was one in September, 1864. We were north of the Missouri river only about two weeks. We had with us never to exceed 250 men. We averaged a battle a day and we killed over 1,000 Federal soldiers besides destroying much Yankee property. The only battles in the world's history to surpass Centralia are Thermopylae and the Alamo. Next to the Centralia fight is the skirmish at Baxter Springs, Kansas, where we killed 130 of Gen. Blunt's bodyguard.

"Yes, I was at Wilson's Creek but that was a slow fight. The idea of that many thousand men fighting for hours and killing so few. I want results when I fight."

"We never met many Federal soldiers who would fight us on equal terms. They would either want to outnumber us or would run away. I have been amused to hear of the fellows in central Missouri who chased us. They always followed at a safe distance.

"The bravest Federal soldiers we met were Maj. Emery S. Foster's command and the Second Colorado commanded by Col. Ford. They were fighters, sure enough. Once while this Colorado regiment was chasing us they almost reached our rear guard. Dave Pool hollered to the Yankees, 'You cowards, you, if there wasn't so many of you, I'd stop and fight you. I'd fight any one of you.' To Pool's surprise they sent out one man and called back their other troops. And then those two men, Pool and the Yankee, sat on horseback and pecked away at each other until all their ammunition was exhausted. Pool had a slight flesh wound and the other man wasn't hurt. Pool always said he would have whipped him if he hadn't been afraid of the other Federals. But we made fun of him for inviting a fight and then getting licked."

THE WORST FRIGHT OF JAMES' LIFE

"The worst scared I ever was during the war was in the Fayette fight. That was the only time we ever got whipped, too. Bill Anderson managed this fight. Quantrill protested against it but finally told Anderson to go and he'd fight in the ranks as a private. We charged up to a blockhouse made of railroad ties filled with port holes and then charged back again. The blockhouse was filled with Federal troops and it was like charging a stone wall only this stone wall belched forth lead.

"On a slight rise a short distance from the blockhouse one of our men, Ol Johnson, fell. When we got back our captain asked for volunteers to go after Johnson's body. Sim Whitsett, Dick Kinney and myself started out. We got to the rise all right. There we were in plain view of the Federals and they simply peppered us with bullets. We got as close to the ground as we could. I was mightily scared. It was the worst fight I ever had. I knew if we raised up we would expose ourselves to the fire of the Yankees and we couldn't stay still.

"I tell you, Pride makes most of us do many things we wouldn't do otherwise. Many men would run away in a battle if the army wasn't watching them. Well, Pride kept us there until we got Johnson's body rolled up in a blanket and then we made tracks."

KILLED WITHIN SIGHT OF HOME

"I believe the saddest thing I know connected with the war," said Mr. James and the man of blood and iron showed much feeling as he told the story, "occurred at the battle of Franklin, Tennessee. Young Theodore Carter was fighting there. But a few yards away was his old home with his mother standing at the window, watching the battle and waiting for him. How bravely he fought that day and with eager anticipation he looked forward to the window where he knew his mother watched for him after years of absence. Almost within a stone's throw of his mother's door, within sight of the yard where he had played as a boy he was shot down and died.

"I visited the old battle-field some weeks ago and since then a friend has sent me a gavel made out of the old gin-house there. I cherish it for the memories it brings of that bloody day and of the gallant Theodore Carter."

CHARACTERISTICS OF THE MAN

Frank James would not be selected from a crowd as a desperate man. He is mild in manner, uses good English, does not swear, drink or chew. He wore on Sunday light gray trousers, black coat and vest, a slouch hat, a cheap necktie, a neat watch chain. There was nothing flashy or cowboy-like in his dress, talk or appearance. William R. Jennings, a good old farmer, mistook Editor Pool for the guerrilla and James for a reporter. His hair has begun to turn white and there are deep lines in his face but his step is as firm, vigorous and elastic as ever. Though he uses spectacles when he reads he can see a long distance without them.

Mr. James, his wife (formerly Miss Ralston, of Independence) and their one son, Robert F., a boy of 19 years, are keeping house at 4279 Laclede Avenue, St. Louis. He is a doorkeeper at the Standard Theatre. His son is employed in the auditor's department of the Wabash Railway. Saturday the lad was in a sprinting race in St. Louis and his father, who seems devoted to his family and proud of his wife and boy, was anxious to find out the result. He was gratified to learn he came in next to first among a dozen contestants and was only beaten by one yard. "I have been asked if I did not intend to send Robert to the State University. I wish I could afford to do so."

Mr. James is emphatic in his advocacy of temperance. "A man's a fool to drink," he said. "It takes away his money and his brains and does him no good in any way." He is a man of positive convictions on every subject. "Half way men are of no value to anybody even themselves," he said. "I like for a man to be all the way for or against anything." He manifests no resentment against any one except the detectives who threw hand grenades into his mother's home in Clay County, killed his little brother and tore off his mother's arm. He talks with bitterness of this event.

By a singular coincidence James Clark, engineer on the Wabash branch railroad Sunday, was the same man who took the ill-fated Wabash train into Centralia on the fatal September morning, 1864. As with James the snows of years have drifted on his head and he is an old man now.

Soon all the actors in this terrible drama of a day will meet again—at the judgment bar of Him who reads all hearts as an open book. And then?

THE KANSAS CITY WORLD, THURSDAY, FEBRUARY 23, 1899.

THE JESSE JAMES TRIAL HAS BEGUN.

Judge Shackleford Quickly Announced That No Further Delay Would Be Tolerated.

CONFESSOR W. W. LOWE IS ON THE STAND.

Prosecuting Attorney Says That Lowe's Confession Will Be Corroborated and Jesse's Familiarity With Kennedy Proved.

WALSH FOR DEFENSE.

HE CLAIMS THAT THE DEFENDANT'S PRESENCE AT THE ROBBERY WAS IMPOSSIBLE.

ARE MANY OBJECTIONS.

MR. WALSH OBJECTS TO REED'S ASSERTIONS AND MR. REED PROTESTS AT WALSH'S.

THEORY OF THE DEFENSE.

It Is That Detective Harbaugh Dictated the Confession of Lowe.

Judge Shackleford peremptorily refused to allow another delay in the Jesse James case, Thursday and ordered the counsel to proceed.

"The costs in this case are heavy. The witnesses are so many that if we don't proceed rapidly we will not finish this term, and the jury, being locked up, would suffer many inconveniences. This is not so in the other case in which the defendant's leading counsel is engaged. The costs are much smaller and the jury won't suffer. The defendant's counse must accommodate himself to the circumstances and get along as best he can. Mr. Prosecutor, make your opening statement to the jury."

"If your honor pleases," began Mr. Walsh, "I have a motion to make."

"Take out the jury," said the judge.

"I want to file a motion," continued Mr. Walsh, when the jurors had been removed, "to ask an order of the court, compelling the state to produce in court the depositions taken in the case of the state versus Andy Ryan. Mr. Reed subpoenaed the stenographer who took the depositions, before the grand jury, paid her for her work and made her file her note book. These depositions were taken by Attorney C. E. Blair before Notary Carnes about a month ago. They were filed with the clerk and taken away. I have subpoenaed Clerk Renick, but he hasn't them.

"I paid the young girl for her work because she hadn't been paid. She went to Judge Wofford, and he told her to file them. Then I paid her."

"I believe you had better turn the papers back to the clerk," said the judge, "and then the defense can examine them."

Mr. Reed produced the papers, but refused to turn them over to the clerk. He went out to Judge Wofford and secured an order withdrawing them from record. This put the matter out of Judge Shackleford's jurisdiction again.

ARGUED FOR AN HOUR.

Meantime, Mr. Walsh was urging Clerk Renick to demand the papers' return. The attorneys argued for an hour and then Mr. Reed agreed to give up that portion of the transcript he possessed, but retained the stenographers note book.

Then the defense served notice on Mr. Reed to produce the alleged confession made by W. W. Lowe. This confession, they claimed, is part of the evidence in the case, that it is in Mr. Reed's possession and must be produced.

Mr. Reed ignored the notice and refused to produce the document. The defense then announced that later in the day it would file a motion to force the state to bring the confession into court. Mr. Reed merely smiled at this.

Again Judge Shackleford ordered the case opened, but allowed Mr. Walsh 15 minutes to go to the circuit court and see what he could do in the Smith-Lowry case.

The jurors were evidently delighted at the break in their monotonous life of the past three days and settled themselves down to listen to the testimony.

USUAL HABITUES WERE THERE.

The announcement made by the defense, Wednesday, that Judge Shackleford had agreed to continue the case to oblige Judge Slover, and allow Attorney Walsh to continue in the Smith-Lowry case, had the effect of causing a very small attendance, while every seat in the room was filled when the case opened, the crowd was almost entirely composed of the usual criminal court room loungers—men and boys who have nothing to do, and who always spend their days there when cold or inclement weather makes life out of doors unpleasant. There were but five women present. One of these was Mrs. Joseph E. Broughal, whose husband is one of the 12. She was almost in hysterics and begged to see her husband. He had been away from her three days and while she knew he was on the jury, she had but a vague idea of what the duties of a juror were, and evidently expected him home each night. Judge Shackleford took pity on the young woman's forlorn condition and allowed her to see her husband a few minutes. She greeted him very affectionately and sobbed in his arms for the very joy of seeing him again.

The remaining four women were witnesses. Two of them were the daughters of old Caleb Stone, one of the men indicted with Jesse, and the other two were Mrs. Hollenbeck and daughter, who heard the bandits drive past her home the night of the robbery.

Jesse was as smiling and confident as ever. At his side, besides his attorneys, sat County Clerk T. T. Crittenden and his uncle, Frank James.

Marshal Chiles had taken precautions to handle a big crowd. At the door to the court room, he stationed Deputy Cass Welch: in the aisle, Deputy Wm. Buckner: at the bar entrance, Deputy Tom Pendergast, while Deputy Joel Mayes kept his watchful eyes on the jury.

OPENED BY MR. REED.

The Prosecuting Attorney Outlines the State's Case.

Mr. Reed opened the case by reading the formal indictment against Jesse James, charging him with "unlawfully and feloniously detaining and stopping a certain railway passenger, mail and express train" for the purpose of robbery. It charges him also with taking from Messenger Hill the sum of $29.

"I shall not attempt," said Mr. Reed, "in opening this case to go into all the details, but to assist you in comprehending them I shall briefly outline some of the most important points. The evidence will show you that on the night of Sept. 23, last, a Missouri Pacific train was held-up near Leeds by five men. Four of them wore masks and one had a white handkerchief over his face. They were all otherwise disguised. The exact spot of the hold-up was the Belt Line crossing. As it was coming to a stop, one of the men jumped on and set the air brakes. The first thing I want to do is to fix in your minds the exact geographical location at which transpired the various events we shall prove. I have here a map, made by a competent civil engineer from a survey. You can see on it Jesse James' home, Hill & Howard's drug store and Self's barn.

"The robbers met on Thirty-fifth-st, just back of Jesse's home, at the point marked with a cross. They fixed up there and left for the scene of the hold-up."

Mr. Reed then followed the course the robbers took, explaining it on the map.

"When they reached the track," continued the prosecutor, "they found a barbed wire fence. They cut the fence wires to aid them. They also cut the wires of the telepragh station and tore out the operator's instruments. I am not going to go into unnecessary details in this case. They simply cut the engine and express car off, ran them down the track, and blew the car to pieces. Then, the man who had the swag, accompanied by one of the others, went back the way they came through the weeds. The others turned the engine lose, got into their buggies and started for Kansas City. At least one of the buggies went on the run all the way to Thirty-fifth-st, distant 2½ miles to the scene of the robbery. At Thirty-fifth and Tracy, they hid their guns in the weeds--there were three men in the buggy. Then they drove over to Holmes-st and about Thirty-second-st to get a Holmes-st car. The others drove east on Thirty-second-st to Campbell, then north on Campbell a block. Then they got out, took the lap robe, wiped off the horse and turned it loose. One of the remaining men took the car, the other, the defendant, went home. The other man was W. W. Lowe and he happened to take the same car his confederate Andy Ryan took, and they were seen together. There was another buggy following behind this one, but it cuts little figure in this case.

"The entire distance is four miles and the roads were in splendid condition. I want to say, too, that I am convinced that the great mass of testimony will show beyond a doubt that the defendant is guilty.

"We expect to prove that this conspiracy began months before, when a Wabash train was selected. The conspiracy to hold up this train grew out of this other conspiracy. We will show that Jack Kennedy was in jail for the murder of Miss Schumacher, and——"

"I object; it's improper," from Mr. Walsh.

"W. W. Lowe, Jesse James and Andy Ryan were witnesses for him," went on Mr. Reed, ignoring the interruption.

BEGINNING OF THE INTIMACY.

"It was at this time that the intimacy between the men began which terminated in this crime. Both Andy Ryan, Jesse James and Mr. Lowe were together constantly during the progress of this case and that Jesse James began to talk with Mr. Lowe about how easy trains could be held up. In one of these, Jesse told Lowe he had heard of him from Kennedy and that Kennedy said he (Lowe) was all right. He continued these conversations often, and finally got an expression of confidence from Lowe. The latter told him this was no place to talk and Jesse said:

"'Come over to the court house and talk about it.'

"Lowe did so, and after some fencing, decided to hold up a train. Lowe still visited Kennedy and the latter told him that there would soon be a man in Kansas City who was an expert. He would be here early in September, he said. He wanted Lowe to take this man, whose name was Evans, to his house and he could tell him by opening his shirt and show where he was shot. Lowe declined, and Kennedy then said:

"'Tell the kid (Jesse), then.'

"Lowe did so. Later, Andy Ryan and Lowe discussed the holdup. They got into a dispute about the number of railroads near Leeds. He told Jesse of it and they decided to go out the next Sunday. That was on the 28th, and they did go out and looked the ground over. They went out again, one night, and found out just where the train stopped.

"They agreed to let Lowe manage the engines. They were to hold the train up early in September. Lowe went to the court house to talk it over and Jesse told him, for certain reasons, they could not do it.

NIGHT OF THE ROBBERY.

"On the night they went out to see where the train stopped, they saw a freight train going in and it at once occurred to them that if that train beat them to town the news would be there first. Then Jesse said he had two friends, Charlie and the old man, who had a horse and buggy and would get them. They could, by fast driving, get back first.

"Jesse told Lowe to meet him the night of the hold-up at his (Jesse's) house. Lowe went there and Jesse's mother and sister told him Jesse was at the car line, putting his aunt on the car. He returned in a moment, took Lowe through the house and pointed to the clump of trees on Thirty-fifth-st and said:

"'I telephoned for the horse and buggy, and it's there.'

"Lowe went there, found the horse restless and drove down on Troost-av. He met there 'Charlie' and the old man in a buggy. While they were introducing themselves Andy Ryan came up on foot. In a few minutes Jesse came up again, about 9:20, but again excused himself and went to the drug store, for the purpose, the state will contend, of proving an alibi."

"That's very improper," said Mr. Walsh. "It is wrong; it is arguing."

"It was an improper statement," said Judge Shackleford.

Then Mr. Reed went on to describe the details of the robbery.

"After two weeks' time Lowe was arrested and finally confessed. He will be put on the stand and his testimony will be corroborated by the best men in the county."

MR. WALSH'S STATEMENT.

He Says He Will Utterly Disprove Lowe's Confession.

Mr. Walsh made a brief opening statement:

"I believe the entire state's case is built on the testimony of a ——".

"I object," said Mr. Reed.

"He hasn't said anything yet," said the judge.

"——on the testimony," continued Mr. Walsh, "of a man named Lowe——"

"I object."

"——a self-confessed train robber.

"We will show that this boy had a splendid reputation, that to his family he was more of a husband and a father than a brother or son."

"I object," said Mr. Reed.

"It's incompetent," said the judge.

"I am going to show," went on Mr. Walsh, "if the state will let me, that this boy, 23 years old, who has grown up in this community, did go to the scene of the robbery, but not for the purpose of holding up a train. He went there with his sister and for an innocent purpose.

"We don't deny that Lowe came to Jesse's stand and talked to him. So he did to men in the collector's and as-

The nation was startled when it was announced in September 1898 that Jesse Edwards James, son of the bandit leader, had been arrested for robbing the Missouri Pacific Express at Leeds, on the outskirts of Kansas City. Young James insisted that he was innocent although police produced a bank robber named William Lowe who named James as the gang's leader. Attorneys for James charged there was "a conspiracy among certain policemen and detectives to convict James." The following March James was acquitted. *The James D. Horan Civil War and Western Americana Collection*

HEARTY

Cheers For the Verdict

That Acquitted Young Jesse James of Complicity in the Leeds Train Robbery.

KANSAS CITY, Mo., February 28.—Young Jesse James, son of the notorious bandit whose name he bears, was to-night adjudged not guilty of complicity in the robbery of a Missouri Pacific express train at Leeds, in the outskirts of Kansas City. The robbery which the police accused young James of leading was committed on September 23 last, and was the last of numerous robberies in the outskirts of Kansas City.

The jury was out less than an hour, and the verdict of acquittal was reached on the first ballot. The

COURTROOM WAS PACKED

With friends of young James, among them being his uncle, Frank James, of St. Louis, and the announcement of the verdict was the signal for applause and cheering that neither Judge nor bailiffs could suppress.

In returning their verdict of acquittal the jurors were compelled to discredit entirely the confession of Witness W. W. Lowe, who admitted being a member of the band, and who described the robbery in every detail, implicating as his accomplices young James, "Andy" Evans, alias Bill Ryan, and several others. After returning the verdict members of the jury stated that they could not accept the Lowe confession or the theory of the police, adding that the police located James in

TOO MANY PLACES

In a very brief time, and that they could not believe that a youth of his years could take such a part in a train robbery as the police charged, and appear in so many different places in less than an hour. The police were unable to show that James was away from his home in Kansas City a full hour on the night of the robbery, and witnesses for the defense made this time much briefer. Mrs. Samuels, the defendant's aged grandmother, even testifying that Jesse was sitting on the porch with her when the robbers exploded the dynamite that wrecked the safes, and that they heard the explosion.

A midwestern newspaper account of the acquittal of Jesse Edwards James on charges of train robbery. The jury, out for less than an hour, refused to believe the confessed train robber, William Lowe, and the police, who had young James "in so many places in less than an hour." *The James D. Horan Civil War and Western Americana Collection*

SON OF FAMOUS BANDIT LEADER WHO NOW IS A MEMBER OF LEGAL PROFESSION.

Jesse Edwards James by the grave of his father. *The James D. Horan Civil War and Western Americana Collection*

After his acquittal on charges of train robbery, young Jesse Edwards James attended law school with the help of former Governor Thomas Crittenden. Ironically, Crittenden had been elected on his promise to break up the James gang. The former chief executive's career had faded after he had been criticized by both parties of having "hired killers" to get the legendary bandit leader. *The James D. Horan Civil War and Western Americana Collection*

Legend has Belle Starr as the sweetheart of the dashing Cole Younger. Belle had been living with her family near Scyene, Texas, at the time Younger was there. Cole admitted in his late years that he had known her but denied that he was the father of her daughter, Pearl. Belle Starr maintained an ''outlaw's roost'' she called Younger's Bend in the early days of the Oklahoma frontier. *The James D. Horan Civil War and Western Americana Collection*

The *St. Paul Daily Globe's* 1889 headline and obituary of Belle Starr. *The James D. Horan Civil War and Western Americana Collection*

A STARR HAS SET.

Sudden Death of Cole Younger's Former Wife in the Choctaw Nation.

Special to the Globe.

FORT SMITH, Ark., Feb. 5.—Belle Starr, the former wife of Cole Younger, now serving a life sentence in the Stillwater penitentiary for bank robbery and murder at Northfield, Minn., died in the Choctaw Nation yesterday. The death of this notorious woman closes a remarkable and very interesting career, probably not equaled in romance by that of any other woman. Her whole life has been spent with desperate and lawless classes of men, and her own prowess as a crack shot and desperate woman has been for some years, the talk of the entire Southwest, where most of her life has been spent. Rumor connects her with the famous James and Younger gangs in Missouri, and with various latter day notorieties. For some years she had lived in the "Nation" and had been in Fort Smith on business and as a witness in the United States court. After the imprisonment of her husband, Cole Younger, she married Samuel Starr, and lived with him in the Choctaw nation. With her husband she was in Fort Smith about three years ago, and the two left for home in the evening, but on the way Starr was killed. They stopped at a dance across the river, where they met an old enemy named West. Starr pulled his pistol and shot West through the groin, but when in the death throes West managed to pull a pistol and shot Starr, both dying about the same time. Belle was in another room at the time, and upon hearing of the shooting, took two pistols, one in each hand, and went out to do her share of the killing. But when she arrived both men were dead. Soon afterward she married her late husband's cousin, James Starr, a tall, well formed Indian, with long hair falling over his shoulders. He was in town yesterday when the telegram announcing her death was received. There was bad blood in his eye when he heard the news, and without delay he saddled his horse, provided himself with a quart of whisky and struck out on the run for home, saying somebody was going to suffer. Belle Starr figured in the United States court in this city on several occasions, and was once sent to the penitentiary for selling whisky in the "nation." Dressed in men's clothes, mounted on a spirited horse, and armed with a brace of formidable pistols, she raided, caroused and participated in every form of outlawry prevalent in the nation. She rode with grace, shot with great skill, and with it all was a well educated and accomplished woman. Many citizens of Fort Smith have heard her play on the piano in this city. She leaves one daughter named Pearl Younger, a beautiful girl, possessing the mother's fire and father's reckless criminalities.

Warden Henry Wolfer, who became a friend and supporter of the Youngers. *The James D. Horan Civil War and Western Americana Collection*

Release of the Youngers

The fight to free the Younger brothers from the Minnesota State Penitentiary in Stillwater started in the 1880s and continued on into the new century. Influential men from both Missouri and Minnesota mailed thousands of pamphlets printed at their own expense and inundated the Minnesota Parole Board and governor's office with petitions.

Just as fierce in their determination that the outlaws should not be paroled were the Minnesota farmers, large numbers of whom rode into St. Paul on horseback and in wagons to protest against the freeing of the Youngers.[47]

After John Newman Edwards's death, his crusade on behalf of the James-Younger gang was picked up by Warren Carter Bronaugh, a former Confederate soldier and wealthy Henry County, Missouri, farmer.

Minnesotans, however, did not view the Jameses and Youngers through any romantic haze; the popular opinion was that the outlaws should have been hanged after their capture. In September 1889, Bob Younger died of tuberculo-

Warden Henry Wolfer, Minnesota State Prison at Stillwater, leading new prisoners to their cells at the time of the Youngers. *The James D. Horan Civil War and Western Americana Collection*

SUNDAY.
Breakfast: Baked pork and beans, light biscuits, *syrup*, BUTTER, coffee.
Dinner: Roast beef, mashed potatoes, mashed turnips, gravy, bread, *pickles, cake.*
Supper: Hot tea.
MONDAY.
Breakfast: Fried pork sausage, potatoes, gravy, bread, coffee.
Dinner: Vegetable soup, boiled fresh beef, bread, potatoes, *pickled beets.*
Supper: *Stewed Beans*, white and graham bread, tea.
TUESDAY.
Breakfast: Corned beef hash, *syrup*, bread, coffee.
Dinner: Boiled ham, cabbage, potatoes, gravy, bread, *bread pudding.*
Supper: *Apple sauce*, white and graham bread, tea.
WEDNESDAY.
Breakfast: Fried beef livers, potatoes, gravy, bread, coffee.
Dinner: Roast pork with dressing, mashed potatoes, gravy, pickles, *macaroni and tomatoes*, bread, cake, *cheese*, coffee.
Supper: Hot tea, prunes and bread.
THURSDAY.
Breakfast: Vienna sausage, potatoes, gravy, bread, coffee.
Dinner: Roast beef, potatoes, stewed beets, gravy, bread.
Supper: *Peach sauce*, white and graham bread, tea.
FRIDAY.
Breakfast: Fried bacon, potatoes, gravy, bread, coffee.
Dinner: Mutton stew, (potatoes, turnips and onions), bread.
Supper: *Oat meal and milk*, white and graham bread, tea.
SATURDAY.
Breakfast: Corned beef hash, *syrup*, bread, coffee.
Dinner: Boiled salt pork, potatoes, cabbage, gravy, bread, *bread pudding.*
Supper: Hot tea, dried peaches and bread.

A typical week's menu at Stillwater during the time the Youngers were there. *The James D. Horan Civil War and Western Americana Collection*

COLE YOUNGER

Cole Younger when he entered Stillwater on January 10, 1877, and when he left, July 14, 1901. *The James D. Horan Civil War and Western Americana Collection*

sis, whispering to Cole, "Don't weep for me." His body was removed to Missouri and buried at Lee's Summit, the Youngers' homestead.

During their years in Stillwater, Cole and Jim Younger were probably the best behaved and most popular inmates. Missouri politicians, old Confederate soldiers, social workers, and visitors to the penitentiary—all wanted to see "the notorious Youngers," as Cole wryly referred to himself and his brother.

One of Cole's visitors was Dr. George Morris, representative of the St. Paul chapter of the Phrenological Society. At the time the reigning fad in the United States was reading character from "the configurations of the human head." A chart showed from the bumps on the head how the mind worked; some firms even insisted that job applicants have their "head read" before they could be hired.

Dr. Morris was given permission to "measure" the heads of Cole and Jim to determine "their talents and inner secrets."

The mystified bandits sat in the warden's office while the professor put a papier-mâché mask over their heads and, with calipers, measured their bumps.

Later Doctor Morris sent a report of his findings to the St. Paul Phrenological Society.[48]

The Phrenological Study of Cole and Jim Younger

Yesterday at the prison with the Editor of the *Democrat*, we had an hour's talk with Coleman and James Younger. Cole said: "Sir, if you say anything bad about my head, I shall have my opinion of you, for your head is shaped like mine very much."

Cole's hair, what there is of it, is fine, every hair round, smooth and well formed and likes to have its own way. His skin [is] fair, soft and smooth. Eyes bright, features of the face very expressive. All these show fine quality. His head measures 23¾ circumference, by 14½ over Veneration.

Intellect good and practical.

Amativeness	4
Destinativeness	6½
Secretiveness	5
Spirituality and hope	5
Vitativeness	14
Alimentativeness	8
Confugality	4
Human nature	6½
Temperaments all	6

Conclusion: The subject is a natural leader: if he had been in the North and educated at West Point, he could have been useful a man as General Sheridan or General Hancock. He is a true friend but never forgiving. James is a natural gentleman, only lacks the faculty to get and keep money. He has considerable literary, artistic and mechanical talent.

Finally, with the turn of the century, the Minnesota State Legislature passed the Dening Act, which allowed the prison's Board of Managers the right to parole prisoners with the approval of the governor and chief justice of the state supreme court. On July 19, 1901, Jim and Cole Younger were paroled but confined within the state's borders.

Stillwater, Minn. May 6, 1890.

St. Paul Phren- Society,

Yesterday at 2 P.M. with the Editor of the Democrat we visited the Prison & had an hours talk with Coleman & James Younger. Cole said, "Sir, if you say any thing bad about my head, I shall have my opinion of you, for your head is shaped like mine very much." Cole has Organic Quality. His hair what there is of it is fine, every hair round, smooth & well formed & likes to have its own way. His skin is fair, soft, smooth & fine. Eyes bright &

He is a natural leader, & had he been born in the North & educated at West Point he could have been as useful a man as Sheridan or Hancock. He is a true friend, but never forgives. James is a natural gentleman, only lacks Cautiousness & the faculty to get & keep money. Head measures 22⅝ - by 14¼.

Excerpt from the phrenological report of Professor George Morris on his examination of the heads of Cole and Jim Younger in the Stillwater Prison in 1890. Morris said that Cole warned him that if "you say anything bad about my head, I will have my opinion of you." *Courtesy Minnesota Historical Society*

Professor Morris found Cole Younger a "natural leader" and ranked him with Sheridan and Hancock, but the professor decided that Jim Younger could not "get and keep money." *Courtesy Minnesota Historical Society*

MEMBER

Of Jesse James Gang.

Dick Liddell, Who Died of Heart Trouble

At Latonia, Was a Fugitive Bandit.

Once Indicted For Murder of Famous Robber,

With Whom He Fought a Terrific Battle.

Escaped Punishment and Started East With a String of Horses—His Long Record.

In July 1901 Dick Liddil died at a racetrack. Following the Frank James trials, he had vanished. Later he appeared at the Guttenberg, New Jersey, racetrack with what one newspaper called "a fine stable of horses," and then periodically visited various tracks around the country racing his horses. *The James D. Horan Civil War and Western Americana Collection*

FROM PRISON CELLS THEY RE-ENTER LIFE

Cole and Jim Younger Released After Twenty-five Years in State Penitentiary

Noted Survivors of the Desperate Band Calmly Receive the News —Come Out Changed Men.

After they had spent twenty-five years in the Minnesota State Penitentiary at Stillwater, Cole and Jim Younger were released in 1901. Here is the *St. Paul Globe*'s story of a reporter who interviewed the outlaws shortly after the announcement had been made. *The James D. Horan Civil War and Western Americana Collection*

COLE YOUNGER'S PARDON COSTS $60,000 IN VAIN

Chicago Syndicate Had Made Elaborate Preparations to Star Outlaw in a Sensational Melodrama.

CLAUSE IN RELEASE SPOILS THE SCHEME.

Famous Bandit Glad of It and Starts for Missouri Home to Live in Peace.

The pardon of Cole Younger, perhaps the most notorious bandit in the United States, and the last survivor of the Jesse James band of outlaws, by the Minnesota State Board of Pardons last Wednesday, caused the collapse of a Chicago syndicate organized to make money by exhibiting him, and resulted in the loss of more than $60,000 which had already been spent on a melodrama called "The Younger Brothers, Bank Robbers," which had been specially written to star him as an actor.

Strangely enough, the men who must suffer the losses are the ones who have exerted themselves most to obtain the paroled convict's absolute freedom. Most of it will fall upon R. L. Crescy, a Chicago real-estate man, who backed the enterprise. Two other Chicagoans, Ernest Stout and Ben H. Atwell, who wrote the play, have only waste paper on their hands and lithographs and posters picturing the ex-outlaw, to the value of $5,000 stored in Chicago, will never ornament the dead walls.

The reason is that the board in granting Younger's pardon added two clauses, one directing that he shall never return voluntarily to the State of Minnesota and the other ordering that he must not exhibit himself or appear as an actor in a public play. Younger is satisfied with the conditions. He is anxious to go back to his old home near Lee Summit, Mo., and end his days among his friends in peace. He is not perturbed over his failure to become an actor. He never had any heart in the matter, anyway.

His associates are all dead. His last and best friend, his brother, Jim Younger, committed suicide last October, and since then his health has slowly declined and his spirit has been broken by loneliness. Lately he has been cared for by his niece, Mrs. C. B. Hull, of St. Paul, the daughter of his sister.

How does a man feel who has just regained his complete liberty after being caged like a wild animal for more than a quarter of a century? Here is what happened:

Younger heard the first news of his pardon on his way to a newspaper office, where he had been summoned, with the announcement that the result would be immediately telephoned there from Governor Van Sant's office.

He was met by a friend who grasped his hand.

"Congratulations, Cole," he said.

The latter was surprised. "What for?" he asked. "Have they announced their decision?"

He was told they had. "Well, I—I'm glad," was all he could say for a moment. He continued on into the office, where many old friends had gathered to await the news.

"I am so happy," he said to them, "I can hardly say anything."

Then the conditions of his pardon were disclosed to him, but they did not affect him.

"The people of the State need not be ashamed of what they have done. I will be as good a citizen as any of them," he said.

"I would not allow myself to be exhibited in any event. I want to be a citizen like any one else, and that's all I ever asked. My future course will be that of which any man might not be ashamed.

"I am going back to old Missouri and my dear friends and relatives there. I will not come back to Minneapolis. But, nevertheless, I will always remember the people of this State. I know that I owe much to the people of Minnesota.

"I harbor no feelings of ill-will or malice against any one, least of all would I against the people of the State which has cared for me the past year and a half as it has.

"If I am able to do so, I will come back some day and show my appreciation. My best friends are here, and I will never forget them.

"I have expressed my sentiments to the people of the State before. I don't think I can say much more. My life

The Youngers' full pardon made national headlines in 1903. Here is the *New York World*'s story of how Chicago promoters lost sixty thousand dollars because the Minnesota State Board of Pardons made Cole promise "not to exhibit himself or appear as an actor in a public play." When Cole later joined Frank James in their Wild West show he sat in a box, signed autographs, and warned youngsters about the evils of drinking and gambling. *The James D. Horan Civil War and Western Americana Collection*

Ironically, their first job was selling tombstones for the P. N. Peterson Granite Company.

Part of the parole agreement stipulated that the Youngers write monthly reports of their activities for the parole board.

Cole's handwritten reports, sent in during the years 1901-03, were discovered in the files of the state penitentiary. They present a moving if sometimes humorous account of the one-time hard-riding guerilla and outlaw trying to adjust to the alien world of the twentieth century.[49]

Cole Younger's Parole Reports

Aug. 31, 1901:

I am working every day except Sunday selling monuments . . . my salary is sixty dollars a month . . . I spend my evenings trying to sell monuments . . . I go to church on Sunday and Sunday School Church . . . I have used tobacco with pleasure but no liquor, coffee is my strongest drink . . . I have been reading Shakespeare and all the newspapers . . . I went to the theatre to see *Uncle Tom's Cabin* and looked in at the dance at the hotel . . . my prospects are good and my surroundings pleasant . . . only I was shaken up in a coboose at the rear end of a fruit train getting from one train to another . . . I have been treated kindly and with courtesy by every and all over the state, by the rich and poor alike . . .

Jan. 20, 1902:

I am working in an office in St. Paul and have drawn pay every day . . . my salary is one dollar per day . . . I have spent some of my salary for tobacco and medicine for kidney [trouble] and rheumatism . . . on hand I have $50 with $25 due me . . . I spend my nights at the hotel but do not attend church regularly . . . I use tobacco but do not use liquor . . . I read the daily papers . . . I attended the annual supper of the Railroad Men in Minneapolis then went to the theatre on complimentary tickets . . . my prospects are good as I have prospects of a better job in the future . . . all is lovely as far as I am concerned. I am only working here waiting for a better job that [Police] Chief O'Connor is getting me . . .

Feb. 20, 1902:

I am assistant office manager working every day at $50 a month salary . . . I have spent $10 for clothes and tobacco. I expect to have a better job in March . . . I spend my evenings at home most of the time . . . I read the Crisis and the daily newspapers. I attended the smoke festivities of the newspapermen at the Elks Hall in Minneapolis and lectures and the theatre . . . my surroundings are good, my prospects bright. Everything is lovely. My health is good, my spirits happy. Everyone has been kind, there has been no trouble . . .

March 20, 1902:

I am still employed as Assistant Office Manager at $50 per month . . . I have a better thing in view . . . I spend my nights at home when not at the theatre. I read the Daily papers and a variety of Romances . . . I am in the best of spirits . . . with the warden's consent I will change work within a few days . . .

April 20, 1902:

I am employed by J. J. O'Connor, Chief of Police, St. Paul, Minnesota looking after his workmen at his house . . . my wages will be decided in the future . . . I

MONTHLY REPORT.

OF _____ No. _____

Paroled _____

N. B. Send copy of this report to F. A. Whittier, State Agent, Capitol Building, St. Paul, Minn.

To HENRY WOLFER,
WARDEN MINNESOTA STATE PRISON,
STILLWATER, MINNESOTA.

1. By whom have you been employed the past month? Ans. *T. N. Peterson Granite Co*

2. At what kind of work? Ans. *Traveling Sales man for T N Peterson*

3. How many days have you worked? Ans. *Every day Except Sunday*

4. What has been your wages per day or month? Ans. *Sixty Dollars per month*

5. How much of your earnings have you expended and for what? Ans. *Have not spent any of it* *Have not received it yet.*

6. How much money have you now on hand or due you? Ans. on hand $ ~~0~~ : Due me $ 60.00

7. If you have been idle during any portion of the month state why? Ans. *Have been at work or on duty Every day Since the 29 of July*

8. Are you satisfied with your present employment, if not, why not? Ans. *Yes I am all O.K.*

9. Where do you spend your evenings? Ans. *At Hotells and trying to sell Monuments*

10. Do you attend church? Ans. *Yes at Kendals went to Sunday School Church*

11. Have you used tobacco? Ans. *Yes with pleasure*

12. Have you used intoxicating liquor? Ans. *No Coffee has been my Strongest drink*

13. State what books, papers or magazines you have read. Ans. *No books Except Sketched the Late Senator C. K. Davis Shakespear and all Newspapers*

14. Have you attended any public meeting, dances, picnics or parties during the month, if so where and when? *I went to see Uncle Toms Cabin and looked on at them dance at the Hotell at Staples and at Lyons but did not dance*

15. State in a general way your surroundings and prospects. Ans. *Prospects good Surroundings Pleasant only when shaken up in a Caboos at the rear end of a frait train getting from one town to another*

16. Have you had any trouble or misunderstanding with anyone? If so, state full particulars. Ans. *No I have been treated kindly and with Courtesy*

Remarks: *by every one all over the State wherever I have been By the Rich and poor alike*

Dated at *Wadena* Minn., this *Aug 31* day of *1901*

(Signed) *Cole Younger*

STATEMENT OF EMPLOYER.

I have read the above statements of paroled prisoner and certify that to the best of my knowledge they are true.

Countersigned _____

When the Youngers were paroled they had to promise not to leave the state and to write monthly reports to the prison warden, Henry Wolfer. Here in Cole's unpublished first report he explains that he is working for T. N. Peterson's Granite Company, which ironically made tombstones. He also pointed out that coffee was his "strongest drink" and that he had gone to see *Uncle Tom's Cabin*. Courtesy Office of the Warden, Minnesota State Prison, Stillwater

MONTHLY REPORT.

OF .... No. ....

Paroled .... I ....

N. B. Send copy of this report to F. A. Whittier, State Agent, Capitol Building, St. Paul, Minn.

To HENRY WOLFER,
WARDEN MINNESOTA STATE PRISON,
STILLWATER, MINNESOTA.

1. *By whom have you been employed the past month?* Ans. *At the intrustery institute*
412 Rosabel St St Paul Minn.

2. *At what kind of work?* Ans. *In the Office*

3. *How many days have you worked?* Ans. *I have drawn pay every day*

4. *What has been your wages per day or month?* Ans. *One dollar per day Rito or well*

5. *How much of your earnings have you expended and for what?* Ans. *Tobaco and*
Medician pay Kidny & Rheumatism and
Griff and bar washing

6. *How much money have you now on hand or due you?* Ans. on hand $ 50; Due me $ 25

7. *If you have been idle during any portion of the month state why?* Ans. *I have had*
Griff and Rheumatism but did thy work

8. *Are you satisfied with your present employment, if not, why not?* Ans. *I am only working*

9. *Where do you spend your evenings?* Ans. *at the institute as stated*

10. *Do you attend church?* Ans. *Not often*

11. *Have you used tobacco?* Ans. *Yes*

12. *Have you used intoxicating liquor?* Ans. *No*

RECEIVED
NOV 22 1902
Minnesota State Prison

13. *State what books, papers or magazines you have read:* Ans. *Daily papers*

14. *Have you attended any public meeting, dances, picnics or parties during the month, if so where and when?*
Attended Annual Supper of Railroad men in
Minneapolis. Have went to theaters or camp

15. *State in a general way your surroundings and prospects.* Ans. *Surroundings good*
prospects better than the present as I have
in view a good Job in the near future

16. *Have you had any trouble or misunderstanding with anyone? If so, state full particulars.* Ans. *no*
All is lovely as fare as I am concerned

Remarks: *I am only working hear awaiting a good job*
that Chief Oconner is getting for me

Dated at *St Paul* Minn., this *Jun 20* day of *June* 1902

(Signed) *Cole Younger*

STATEMENT OF EMPLOYER.

I have read the above statements of paroled prisoner and certify that to the best of my knowledge they are true.

Countersigned ....

In this report Cole, whose spelling was not the best, reported he was spending his salary of a dollar a day on tobacco, laundry, and medicine to treat his rheumatism. In reply to the question about church attendance he wrote, "not often." *Courtesy Office of the Warden, Minnesota State Prison, Stillwater*

spend my evenings at police headquarters and at home . . . at Easter I went to hear the Archbishop . . . I went to one political [rally] and the theatre and one night I went to the Union Railroadmen's ball . . . I am happy and contented . . .

Nov. 20, 1902:

Laid off this month by the Hon. John J. O'Connor . . . due me . . . $100 . . . I have been [sic] past [sic] gravel [kidney stone] still weak but will soon be O. K. . . . I have been reading the daily papers together with fiction and magazines . . . my surroundings are good and prospects bright and hope for better things . . .

[This time Cole ended his report with:]

I would like to return to my childhood home . . .

During the campaign to parole the Youngers, volunteer committees had been formed in Minnesota and Missouri to send out letters to members of the legislature and distribute literature. One day in prison Jim met Alice Mueller, a pretty young volunteer from a prominent St. Paul family. They fell in love and planned to be married after Younger's release.

During the gunfight with the posse after Northfield, Jim had been severely wounded in the face. Part of his jawbone was removed while he was in prison and he suffered constant pain from the wound that periodically opened and drained.

Alice's parents fought against their daughter's plans to marry Younger, pointing out the "stigma" attached to marrying a notorious outlaw. When Alice insisted that she loved Jim, the family reluctantly gave their consent and invited Younger to live with them.

In March 1902, the happy couple went to the St. Paul county clerk to obtain a license. The clerk refused; the decision, he told them, would have to come from the state's attorney general.

After "spending days going over the musty tomes," Attorney General Douglass handed down the decision that since Younger was still under a life term he was legally dead, and "there was no law on the books to issue a dead man a license to marry."[50]

Jim besieged the governor and the state legislature but they refused to overlook the law. There was more family discussion and Jim angrily left the Mueller home to take a room in downtown St. Paul.

Younger moved from job to job, frantically trying to save money for the marriage he knew was rapidly slipping away. Everything went wrong: a job as a clerk in a grocery store and cigar stand ended, and then, one fall day, his fragile world fell apart when he received a note from Alice—his beloved "Lassie"—saying that at the insistence of her parents she was going to Boise, Idaho, to think things over.

Jim turned to Cole, demanding money from the amounts which had been sent them by well-wishers while they were in Stillwater. Cole protested that he had given him his share, but Jim insisted he "could have done more." They quarreled bitterly, with Jim vowing never again to speak to Cole.

He moved from St. Paul to Minneapolis, a gaunt, sad-eyed man who at

MONTHLY REPORT.

OF _____ No. _____

N. B.—Send copy of this report to F. A. Whittier, State Agent, Endicott Building, St. Paul, Minn.

To HENRY WOLFER,
WARDEN MINNESOTA STATE PRISON,
STILLWATER, MINNESOTA.

1. By whom have you been employed the last month? Ans. (Give name and address)
Hon. John J. Oconnor. St Paul. Minn.

2. At what kind of work? Ans. Laid off this Month.

3. How many days have you worked? Ans. (Give number of days) 0

4. What has been your wages per day or month? Ans. 0

5. Cash on hand and due me at date of last report. $30 — Due me 100.00

6. Give total earnings for month. $0

7. Expenditures:
   Board $0
   Clothes $1 - 50 cts
   Incidentals $10.   Total $11.50 cts.

8. Cash on hand ($25.00) Due me ($100.00)

9. If you have been idle during any portion of month state why? Ans. Sick
past gravle Still weak but will soon be O. K.

10. Are you satisfied with your present employment, if not, why not? Ans. Yes

11. Where do you spend your evenings? Ans. at my Nieces 571 Chl. St St Paul

12. Do you attend church? Ans. Not often 13. Have you used tobacco? Ans. Yes

14. Have you used intoxicating liquor? Ans. No

15. State what books, papers or magazines you have read. Ans. Dailys papers
togather with fiction and Magazines.

16. Have you attended any public meeting, dances, picnics or parties during the month, if so, where and when? No. Surroundings good
prospects bright and I hope for better things.

17. State in a general way your surroundings and prospects. Ans. " " "
" " " " " "

18. Have you had any trouble or misunderstanding with anyone? If so, state full particulars. Ans. All has been piece and
good will with me.

Remarks: I would like to return to
my Child hood home.

Dated at St Paul Minn., this 20 day of Nov 1902

Statement of Employer.
I have read the above statements of paroled prisoner and certify that to the best of my knowledge they are true.

Countersigned _____

(Signed) Cole. Younger.

Cole's last report to Warden Wolfer poignantly ended, "I would like to return to my childhood home." The following year he was granted a full pardon. But he returned alone to Lee's Summit, Missouri: his brother, Jim, had committed suicide. *Courtesy Office of the Warden, Minnesota State Prison, Stillwater*

JAMES YOUNGER COMMITS SUICIDE

SENDS A BULLET THROUGH HIS BRAIN

Paroled Prisoner Who Had Spent Twenty-five Years in Penitentiary Becomes Despondent—Has a Quarrel With His Brother Cole, and Ends His Own Life—Leaves Letter to the Public.

James Younger, the paroled prisoner, was found dead in his room in the Reardon block, Seventh and Minnesota streets, at 4:30 o'clock yesterday afternoon. The body was dressed in a suit of underwear. A 38-caliber revolver was clutched in the right hand and the left hand was covered with coagulated blood. He had evidently been dead for several hours, having shot himself in the right temple.

Dr. J. M. Finnell, acting for Coroner A. W. Miller, was called, and had the body taken to the morgue and afterwards the penitentiary during the quarter century. The pardon was hoped for at the last meeting of the state board, but the subject was not taken up by that body.

Quarrels With Brother.

The cause of the trouble between Jim and Cole Younger was money, Cole being the older of the brothers, has been the recipient of all money sent from friends in the South and elsewhere. Cole,

Disliked Notoriety.

Besides this it is said that he disliked the notoriety that attached to him. He felt that he was shunned and the object of observation everywhere. He became morose and often said that he had "no friends." He suffered constantly from a bullet wound in his face and had frequently consulted physicians concerning it since his parole.

The primary cause of the death of James Younger is thought to have been his infatuation for a young girl who is now in Boise City, Idaho. She became interested in his case and worked to secure his pardon. When Jim Younger was released he was admitted to her home. He fell in love with her and a quarrel with her relatives followed and he was told to find a home elsewhere.

He and she, it is said, wrote a book concerning the state penitentiary.

It is asserted that he hoped to get married as soon as a full pardon was granted to him, and intended then to publish the book covering the history of

---

Jim Younger, who suffered constantly from the bullet wound he had received in his jaw at Northfield, committed suicide in the fall of 1902, only a few months before Minnesota granted him and Cole a full pardon. Younger, who believed "he had no friends," refused to speak to his brother in his last days and became a recluse in a boardinghouse in St. Paul. This story of his suicide appeared in the *St. Paul Pioneer Press. The James D. Horan Civil War and Western Americana Collection*

times winced and closed his eyes from the intense spasms of pain in his face. Gradually he became a recluse, reading books on women's rights, spiritualism, and political philosophy, and occasionally writing to the governor or state attorney asking if there was any hope of a pardon.

During the early morning of October 19, 1902, in a new century which regarded him as an anachronism, Jim carefully put aside his books, finished writing a letter, then loaded a .38 caliber revolver and shot himself in the temple.

Younger lasted for some time, moaning in pain and dabbing helplessly at his bloody wound. Guests passing along the corridor and in adjacent rooms heard him but did not notify the police or the manager.

In the early evening a servant coming in to make up his room discovered the body.

Dr. J. M. Finnell, acting coroner, formally pronounced him dead and released the contents of Younger's pathetic note written to his "Lassie."[51]

Jim Younger's Suicide Note, October 18, 1902

Oct. 18. Last night on earth. So good by Lassie, for I still think of thee. Forgive me for this is the only chance. I have done nothing wrong.

But politics is all that Van Sant, Wolfer [the warden and parole board official] and others of their stripe, care for. Let the people judge. Treat me fair reporters for I am a square fellow, a socialist and decidedly in favor of Woman Rights.

Bryan is the brightest man these United States ever produced. His one mistake was not coming out for all the people and absolute socialism. Come out Bryan. There is no such thing as a personal God. God is universal and I know him well and I am not afraid.

I have no pity for the pardoning board. They do not stop to consider their wives or to think of the man who knows how to love and appreciate a friend in truth. Good-bye, sweet Lassie.

Jim Younger.

[On one side of the envelope he had written:]
To all that is good and true I love and bid farewell. Jim Younger.
[On the other side:]
Oh! Lassie! Goodbye. All relatives just stay away from me. No crocodile tears wanted. Reporters: Be my friends. Burn me up.

Ironically, not long after Jim's death the state granted a full pardon to Cole, who made the lonely journey to Lee's Summit.

In Missouri, Cole found Frank James working as a floorwalker in The Famous, a well-known St. Louis store, then later as a doorman for Ed Butler's Standard Theatre, a burlesque house in that same city. During the racing season he dropped the timer's flag at the Fair Grounds Track. Both were balding and portly, their bodies aching from rheumatism and old bullet wounds. Cole once estimated that he would carry eleven slugs to the grave.

In 1903 Cole joined Frank in the James-Younger Wild West Show. Under the terms of his parole Cole was not permitted to appear on the stage, but he sat in a reserved box, signed autographs, shook hands, and solemnly warned the young against the evil of whiskey.

Frank died in 1915; Cole lived on at Lee's Summit. In his last interview Cole revealed for the first time that the robbery at Northfield had backfired "because of a bottle of whiskey":

I didn't touch it [the whiskey] myself but Bob and two other men did and when they walked into the bank they were drunk. They forgot to close the door so they couldn't be seen from the street and they even let the cashier bang the door of the safe shut on all the money before they got close enough to prevent it. I had given instructions not to shoot to kill and if they had not been drunk the death of the banker would not have occurred. We followed the first three of our men into town, and when we rode around the corner they were to enter the bank and secure the money while we protected the outside. There happened to be an exhibition in town that day and the streets were crowded. Someone saw what was happening inside the bank and cries, "Robbers in the Bank!" were heard all over the town, while men were running for their guns. Three times I called for the boys inside the bank to come out but they didn't come and by this time the whole town was shooting at us. All of us were hit but we managed to get out of town by riding double. Then commenced the hunt for us.

It is significant that Cole made no mention of the confrontation between him and Jesse, when Jesse demanded they abandon Cole's wounded brother, Bob. From the day he was arrested until his death Cole never admitted that either Jesse or Frank was present at Northfield.

Cole then described how they were surrounded by the posse:

"Boys," I said, "those that want to, can surrender, for it is about sure death for us to do what there is to do. That is to wait until they are on top of us, then fire at them and break straight towards them and try to get through their lines."

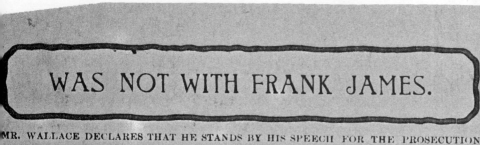

WAS NOT WITH FRANK JAMES.

MR. WALLACE DECLARES THAT HE STANDS BY HIS SPEECH FOR THE PROSECUTION
IN THE CELEBRATED TRIAL AT GALLATIN, MO.
[From the Kansas City Star, November 13, 1901.]

To the Star: In your issue of November 11, appears a statement which I am assured has gone broadcast through the state and which does me a great injustice. In an editorial in reference to the appearance of Frank James as an actor, you state that Mr. James should make his debut in Kansas City. This language is then used: "No doubt the boxes will be filled with former Missouri officials, with some present office holders and a number of distinguished laymen in the theater parties. Mr. William H. Wallace, candidate for United States Senate, who is now on a hunting trip with Mr. James in the Indian territory, would surely do his utmost to live down his record as the prosecuting attorney of Jackson county during the James regime."

I do not censure the Star for the statement that I was hunting with Frank James in the Indian territory, because I am assured by friends that it had been previously published—they do not recall in what paper—that such was a fact. Nor considering the lights before you can I object to the inference you draw, namely, that being a candidate for United States senator I was endeavoring in this way to obtain the favor and support of Frank James and his friends. But the fact is that your information was absolutely false. I have not been hunting with anyone for years, and never hunted in the Indian territory in my life. I have not seen Frank James, nor have I communicated with him, nor he with me, directly or indirectly, upon any subject whatever.

I have never gloated over the downfall of the Missouri bandits. This would be cowardly. But while this is true I defy any man to cite a single act or utterance of mine during the whole eighteen years that have elapsed since the destruction of the James gang, which could be tortured into the slightest apology for my official conduct. I spoke to a packed house at Liberty, in Clay county, the former home of the James boys, on the 4th of this month. I was told that there was in the audience a large number of men from the vicinity of Kearney, where Frank and Jesse James were raised. Before beginning my speech, word came twice from persons I knew were my friends, advising me to make no reference in my address to the Missouri bandits. These warnings assured me that it was thought there were some persons present who were opposed to me because of my prosecutions of train robbers. I stated to the audience that I devoted three years of my life to the work of assisting in the overthrow of one of the shrewdest and most desperate bands of outlaws known to modern times; that I had no apologies to make, and that if I had my official life to live over, my conduct would be precisely the same.

The Jameses and Youngers continued to shadow the life of William H. Wallace, prosecutor of Jackson County. In 1901 when he was running for senator, the *Kansas City Star* reported that he was hunting with Frank James "in the Indian Territory" and was "trying to live down his record" as the prosecutor who had put James on trial for murder. In this rare and unpublished pamphlet which he printed himself, Wallace denied the *Star* story. Wallace ran unsuccessfully for senator, congressman, and governor. He died in 1937. *The James D. Horan Civil War and Western Americana Collection*

In June 1902 Jesse James was reburied in a new grave next to his beloved Zee. In this dramatic story in the *St. Louis Post-Dispatch* Robertus Love, who had written many stories about the outlaws, described the events on that dreary, rainy day. As he pointed out, the state had not provided a metallic casket and the body of the bandit had not been embalmed in 1882. *The James D. Horan Civil War and Western Americana Collection*

JESSE JAMES'
BONES AT REST
IN NEW GRAVE

Comrades of Quantrell's Command Pallbearers at Reinterment,

AGED MOTHER SAW CHANGE

BULLET HOLE AND GOLD TEETH ESTABLISHED INDENTITY.

Post-Dispatch Correspondent Describes the Scenes Attending the Removal From Mother's Yard to Kearney Cemetery.

Jesse James had a wife;
She's a mourner all her life;
His children they were brave.
Oh, the dirty little coward who shot Mr. Howard!
And they laid Jesse James in his grave.
—From the Old Song.

BY ROBERTUS LOVE.

Special Correspondence of the Post-Dispatch.

KEARNEY, Mo., June 29.—"And they laid Jesse James in his grave," for the second and, doubtless, the last time.

Not as a bandit, but as a brother in arms, as a soldier, as a guerilla rough rider of the border warfare, as a fighter in the last cause, a squad of Quantrill's men, who rode and shot with the boy, Jesse James, in the last two years of the civil war, bore his bones this Sunday afternoon to his new grave between those of his wife and his little half-brother.

"Not a sound was heard, not a funeral note," not a word was spoken at the grave during the 20 minutes required for carrying the coffin from the hearse, lowering it into the earth, shoveling in the clay and rounding off the mound.

Yes, there was one sound—just for a moment or two—the sobbing of Jesse's mother.

It was a burial in silence. A preacher, in white necktie, stood in the crowd, but merely as a spectator. There was no religious ceremony, either at the farm house or at the cemetery.

came up, leaving the bottom to fall back into the grave, with the remains of Jesse James lying thereon.

The men stepped down into the grave and lifted the bottom of the casket to the top. The foot came up first and from the other end the skull rolled off into the grave. Zach Laffoon picked up the skull and replaced it.

As the coffin bottom was being turned around above ground the skull again fell off and dropped to the bottom of the grave. Zip Pollard jumped down and picked it up, placing it once more upon the old coffin bottom.

At this juncture John Samuel picked up the skull and began to turn it over in his hands, closely examining it.

BULLET HOLE IN SKULL.

"What are you looking for, John?" asked old Zach Laffoon.

"Bob Ford's bullet hole," replied the bandit's half-brother, "and here it is."

There it was, a little more than an inch behind the left ear and as large as a quarter. A small piece of the skull above it had broken in, otherwise the hole would have been round.

Young Jesse James looked curiously at his father's skull, glad to find the bullet hole and the gold-filled teeth, for those marks proved to him that the body of Jesse James never had been stolen and he could go back to his grandmother and allay her fears that, possibly, in spite of her twenty years' vigil, her son's grave had been violated.

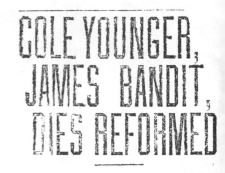
COLE YOUNGER, JAMES BANDIT, DIES REFORMED

Served in Quantrell's Guerillas, Robbed Banks and Fought Battles with Posses.

When Cole Younger died in March 1916 he was still national news. This is the *New York American's* account. *The James D. Horan Civil War and Western Americana Collection*

The account in the *Kansas City Times* of the death of Zerelda Samuel, mother of Jesse and Frank James, who died February 10, 1911, aboard a train while she was returning to Missouri after visiting Frank at his farm near Fletcher, Oklahoma. *The James D. Horan Civil War and Western Americana Collection*

No one would surrender and we tried the scheme but they shot down all of us before we could get through . . . I had eleven wounds and the others were as badly off . . .

We were wrong about the Northfield business . . . but for the rest I don't see how I could have avoided it . . . I am really happy now . . . I'm not afraid to be judged. I am getting to be an old man and I'm not afraid of death. If I had been wrong I would not have been permitted this happiness here in this life.

Then Cole lifted his infant nephew onto his lap, winked at the reporter, and filled his long-stemmed German-style pipe.

"What more could a worn-out old bandit ask beyond this?"[52]

Cole died on March 21, 1916, and was buried in the family plot at Lee's Summit.

A man and a time had been laid to rest.

Frank James and his horse, Dan, about the turn of the century. *Courtesy Jackson County Historical Society*

The last photograph of Frank James, taken outside the front gate of the family homestead. By now the visitor's fee had doubled. *Courtesy State Historical Society of Missouri*

"HANDS UP!"
Says Death
To Bandit Frank James
— By Nick Carter III.

FRANK JAMES ASKED CREMATION TO PREVENT AUTOPSY ON BRAIN

Believed it Was Permitted on Jesse; Ashes Will Be Sprinkled in Casket When Wife Is Buried.

By FRED T. BARTON.

It was fear—fear of science—that prompted Frank James, last of the James boys, to request that his body be hastened into dust by cremation. It was the result of a horror that had lived with him since the murder of his brother, Jesse James.

Frank James wanted to thwart any attempt by doctors to use his brain for scientific research.

Frank James had always believed his brother's brain was removed and given to scientists.

"Never let that happen to me," he often told his wife, and as a safeguard he made the request that his body be cremated.

As a further precaution he asked that members of his family remain with his body until it was converted into dust. In compliance, his son, Robert James, and his nephew, Jesse James, jr., followed his body to St. Louis last night and will not leave it until it has become ashes.

Held Autopsy on Jesse?

When Jesse James fell by the traitorous hand of Bob Ford government officials and Pinkerton men took charge of the body. Frank James believed an autopsy was permitted by officials before it was buried.

The request that his ashes be placed in a vault in Kansas City and kept there was an acknowledgement of his great devotion to a wrinkled old woman who wept beside his death bed —his wife. She married and clung to him when a price hung over his head and prison doors yawned.

"If I die first," he told the members of his family, "have my body cremated and the ashes locked in a safety deposit box. Then when mother dies sprinkle my ashes in her casket.

"If I survive her the safety deposit box will not be necessary—merely have my body cremated and placed in her grave."

Will Carry Out Request.

James' ashes, in accordance with his request, will only be preserved until his companion through those grim days of war and his latter days of peace shall have followed him. Then into her casket they will be sprinkled and the dust of one shall mingle with the dust of the other.

Never again will such an event transpire in the history of the West as was enacted at the little farm house on the old James homestead, two and one-half miles east of Kearney, Mo., yesterday. Missouri history was made when one of the James boys was sent to his eternal rest with all the good will and blessings of peace that old comrades, neighbors and friends could give.

In the little front room of the shambling yellow house where he spent the last years of his life his body lay in state in a plain black casket. Early in the morning there began a pilgrimage over the same roads that, could they talk, could tell of thundering hoofs, the clatter of guns and the spat of bullets.

From early morning the group in the front yard of the home of Frank James grew and scattered over the hills a[...]
many
Jes[...]

The *Kansas City Post*'s story of how Frank James, who had been haunted by the fear that his brain would be removed for "scientific research," requested that his body be cremated. *The James D. Horan Civil War and Western Americana Collection*

THE LAST HANDS UP!

Frank James, Bandit, Did Not Die with His Boots on

Passed Final Days of Life in Peace on the Farm

The *Boston Sunday Herald's* headline for the death of Frank James. *The James D. Horan Civil War and Western Americana Collection*

**Mrs. Ann Ralston James, Who
Married Frank Over Parental
Objections, Loyal to Her
Promise to the End.**

Mrs. Ann Ralston James, 91 years
old, widow of Frank James, notorious
Missouri outlaw, died today in a sanitarium at Excelsior Springs, Mo.

In ill health and blind several
years, Mrs. James until the last ad-
hered to her vow that the "true
story" of Frank and Jesse James
would die with her. Mrs. James
spent the last several winters in
Texas and the summer months at
the James farm, three miles east of
Kearney, Mo. Her son, Robert
James, lives on the farm. He is the
only survivor.

WAS MARRIED AT 22.

FOND OF VISITING

The Jameses had to a remarkable
degree the southern fetish for visiting their relatives. In 1879, when
their band had an international
notoriety, Frank James and his
wife left the farm near Nashville,
Tenn., where they were living under
assumed names, and came to Kansas City to visit his relatives and
Mrs. James's parents. Their visit
concluded, they started on foot to
the Missouri Pacific depot at the
foot of Grand avenue, where they
proposed to board a train for St.
Louis.

At the intersection of Fourth
street, a policeman was losing a
tussle with a drunken man. The officer called to James to help, but
the outlaw said he had to catch a
train. Instead, James offered $1
to a Negro to substitute for him, and
returned to his wife's side.

He was in Baltimore, where he
was living with his wife, a few
months later when an officer
stepped up and seized his elbow.
James was heavily armed; he said
he intended to kill the policeman
rather than submit to arrest. But
the officer only wanted him to serve
on a coroner's jury. James pointed
out he was only a visitor to the city
and went to his home, where he told
his wife of the incident. She immediately decided they could not stay
in Baltimore another day and they
departed that night for New York.

Cole Younger and a friend, Thomas Noland,
taken at Lee's Summit, Missouri, after Younger
returned from Minnesota. *Courtesy Jackson
County Historical Society*

Jesse James' Blacksmith Dies

By the United Press.

ST. PAUL, March 7.— James L.
Dewar, 79, who put "reverse" horse-
shoes on the mounts of Jesse James,
died yesterday after a long illness.

The James brothers were among
Dewar's best customers when he was
a blacksmith at Kansas City. He
once related:—

"When Jesse brought in his horses
I didn't have to be told what to do.
His mounts were always shod backward so it would appear they were
travelling in the opposite direction."

Dewar said Jesse's secret was well
guarded.

Jesse James has had an eternal attraction for
the American public. From the 1930s to the
1960s there have been many stories reporting
the deaths of relatives of the Ford brothers,
of men who supposedly ate with, or slept
alongside them, or played cards with Frank
James when he was a fugitive—even of a
man who owned a livery stable where the
outlaws kept their horses. Here is a 1939
account in the *New York World-Telegram*
of the death of "Jesse James' blacksmith."
*The James D. Horan Civil War and Western
Americana Collection*

The saga of Jesse and Frank
James ended in July 1944, when
Frank's wife, Annie, died in a
sanitarium at Excelsior Springs,
Missouri, vowing that the "true
story" of her husband and her
brother-in-law would die with
her. *The James D. Horan Civil
War and Western Americana
Collection*

THE DALTONS

LIKE THE JAMESES AND YOUNGERS, THE DALTONS WERE products of the violence, hate, and feuds that lasted for years in the Middle Border states following the end of the Civil War.

The father of the clan, James Lewis Dalton, was a jovial, footloose veteran of the Mexican war who liked to tell hair-raising stories of his war experiences, but the records show that he served only one year—and that as a fifer—in the Kentucky volunteers. His wife, and mother of the outlaw band, was Adeline Younger, a distant kin of the Youngers of Lee's Summit. In the 1850s Dalton, who had opened a saloon in Westport, now part of Kansas City, with the profits of a horse trade, met Adeline in Independence. From the meagre accounts extant she appears to have been a hard-working frontier wife and mother, burdened with a ne'er-do-well husband who liked racing horses, whiskey, and cards. When they were married she was fifteen, he was thirty-six.[1]

The Independence Youngers were regarded as a fairly well-to-do churchgoing family, and after their honeymoon Adeline tried to reform her husband. She insisted that he sell his tavern, swear off whiskey, and abandon his gambling and drinking companions. Dalton sold the saloon but soon drifted into the life of a transient horse trader who roamed around the Indian country swapping and selling horseflesh, and returning home only at intervals. Each time he left for another tour Adeline inevitably was pregnant.

[17] That I am _____ married; that the maiden name of my wife was *Adeline Younger* to whom I was married at *Jackson County*, in the State of *Missouri*, on the *12th* day of *March*, A.D. *1851.*; that my wife is now *living*, having died _____ on the _____ day of _____, A.D. _____, at *Vinita*, in the State of *Indian Territory.*; that I have _____ since remarried. That the name of my present wife is _____

That in support of my right to pension I tender herewith, under the regulations prescribed by the Secretary of the Interior, the following evidence: [18] *I had a Land Warrant for 160 acres issued to my the certificate for which was given to me when discharged* and the affidavits of *Albert G. Anderson a comrade of my Company we having been boys together at Mt. Sterling Kentucky where we enlisted together and came home together* *and of my son Littleton Dalton and refer to Wm. T. Wallace ex Chief Justice of California who a comrade of my Co.* [19] That I have *not* heretofore made application for pension or bounty land, which said claim is No. _____ [20] That I am *not* a pensioner of the United States under certificate No. _____, at the rate of _____ dollars per month. That since my discharge from said service I have resided as follows, to wit: *in Montgomery Co. Kentucky from discharge to 1851; in Jackson and Cass Counties Missouri from 1851 to 1880; in La Benton Co. Kansas from 1880 to 1883; at Vinita Indian Territory from 1883 to this time where my residence is now, being temporarily in California.* And my present post office address is *Vinita, Indian Territory.*

That I am not laboring under any political disabilities imposed by the fourteenth amendment to the Constitution of the United States. [And I hereby constitute and appoint Alexander M. Kenaday, of Washington, D. C., my true and lawful attorney, with full power of substitution and revocation to prosecute my claim and to furnish any additional evidence required.]

WITNESSES: *A G Anderson*
Littleton Dalton

Lewis Dalton
(Claimant sign here.)

Bob Dalton, leader of the Dalton band of train robbers. *The James D. Horan Civil War and Western Americana Collection*

Application for a Mexican War pension filed by Lewis Dalton, father of the Dalton brothers, listing the battles in which he fought. He states he can no longer do "hard labor." *Courtesy National Archives*

(3—243.)

MEXICAN WAR PENSION.

ACT OF JANUARY 29, A. D. 1887.

DECLARATION OF SURVIVOR FOR PENSION.

[1] State of *California*, County of *Fresno*, SS:

[2] On this *14th* day of *May*, A.D. 1887, personally appeared before me (full name of claimant), [3] *Lewis Dalton*, a resident of [4] *Vinita*, in the county of *Cherokee Indian Reservation*, in the State of *Indian Territory*, who, being by me first duly sworn according to law, deposes and says:

I am the identical [5] *Lewis Dalton*, who served under the name of [6] *Lewis Dalton*, as a [7] *Musician* in the company commanded by Captain [8] *McKenar Turbin* (If in Naval Service, name Vessel, etc.) in the [9] *2d* regiment of *Kentucky Infantry*, commanded by [10] *Col. Wm. R. McKee* in the war with Mexico; that I enlisted at [11] *Mt. Sterling Montgomery Co. Ky*, on or about the [12] *9th* day of *June*, A.D. 1846, for the term of [13] *twelve months*, and was honorably discharged at [14] *New Orleans Louisiana*, on the *9th* day of *June*, A.D. 1847.

First group of facts which will entitle to pension.

That being duly enlisted, as aforesaid, I actually served sixty days with the Army or Navy of the United States in Mexico, or on the coast or frontier thereof, or en route thereto, in the war with that nation, which service was as follows: [15] *I served with my Regiment from the place of enlistment to Brazos Santiago to Matamoras to Camargo Monterey Saltillo Agua Nueva Buena Vista, and back to New Orleans Louisiana*

(a.) That I am *61* years of age, having been born at [16] *Montgomery County Kentucky* on the *16th* day of *February*, 1826.

(or b.) That I am dependent on others than those legally bound for my support for my livelihood; that I have been so dependent since _____, and that the _____ upon whom I am dependent is _____ or _____, who has afforded me the following support: _____ (Here describe what has been done for your support.)

In his application for a pension, Dalton provided information on his marriage and indicated how he and his family had wandered after the Civil War. *Courtesy National Archives*

No. 7343

MEXICAN WAR.

Act of January 29, 1887.

WIDOW.

Adaline Lee Dalton

Widow of *Lewis Dalton*

Rank *Fifer*

Company *O.*

Regiment *2. Ky Vols*

Rate per month, $8.00.

Commencing ~~January 29, 1887~~ *July 17, 1890*

Certificate dated *Mch. 12, 1891,*

and mailed _____ 189__

Payable at *Topeka* Agency

Atty none

(8682—2,000.)

DEAD

Three years later Dalton was dead and his wife had been granted his eight-dollar-a-month pension. *Courtesy National Archives*

Gratton Dalton at about twenty-five. *The James D. Horan Civil War and Western Americana Collection*

Very rare photograph of the Dalton brothers as cowboys on the Bar X Bar Ranch near what is now Pawnee, Oklahoma. *The James D. Horan Civil War and Western Americana Collection*

She gave birth to fifteen children, ten sons and three daughters; two, name and sex forgotten, died in infancy. Those destined to form the core of the "Dalton gang" were Grattan, "Grat"; Franklin, or Frank; Robert Renick, or Bob, the most celebrated and the leader of the gang; William Marion, or Bill; and Emmett. The five other Dalton sons—the "honest" Daltons—were Charles, Ben, Littleton, and Henry. Simon, frail and sickly, died at the age of fourteen. The Dalton girls were Leona, Eva, and Nannie.

It was a hand-to-mouth existence, with Adeline moving her large brood about in wagons along the war-ravaged border where the gutted homes and deserted farms were grim memories of the raids by guerillas of both sides.

The heroes of the day were the Jameses and Youngers, and the Dalton boys were an eager audience for their father when he swaggered back home to boast of having met Jesse, Frank, or Cole in some frontier town.

Emmett recalled in his autobiography that he was twelve when he traded some coonskins to get his first weapon, "an old musket with the kick of a cannon." His brothers also had guns and they "riddled targets innumerable" to improve their marksmanship.

Emmett's greatest day came when two deputy United States marshals passed him on the street and observed:

"That Dalton boy is going to be a tough man to handle when he gets growed up."[2]

Emmett left home as a teen-ager to become a working hand on the Bar-X-Bar Ranch near Pawnee, Oklahoma. His saddle companions were Bill Doolin and Dick Broadwell. To the south on the Turkey Track spread were other friends: George Newcomb, Charlie Bryant, and Charlie Pierce. Newcomb, a happy-go-lucky cowhand, was variously known as "Bitter Creek" or "Slaughter's Kid" from having worked for John Slaughter, the rancher and famous Arizona sheriff. Bryant, whose powder-pocked face gave him the nickname of "Black Face Charlie," was a brooding young rider and expert marksman who boasted to Emmett that when he died it would be "in a hell-firing minute of smoking action." Doolin was slow, deliberate, and good-natured, with drooping mustaches and an unruly thatch of red hair. Dalton remembered him as having a "woebegone look . . . a six shooter always looked like a toy in his big paw. Not much to talk or boast; a droll, drawling range comedian when you got him started. Everyone laughed at Doolin's awkward antics and Bill grinned a little with them. But Bill Doolin became a sinister clown, and his six shooter a deadly toy. . . ."

While Emmett was throwing a riata on the Bar-X-Bar, Grat and Frank joined the Indian police that patrolled the badlands looking for whiskey smugglers.

Frank's ability as a lawman working with the Indians impressed John Carroll, marshal at Fort Smith, who appointed him a deputy attached to the court of Federal Judge Isaac Parker, known to the frontier as "Hanging Judge" Parker, whose court covered the largest and most dangerous jurisdiction in the West. Deputies paid by the fee system were allowed ten cents a mile one way, while serving papers or bringing in prisoners; forty cents a mile for feeding a prisoner while on the way to Parker's court; and two and a half dollars for "reading a warrant and the same amount for commitment." The guardsman who accompanied a deputy received two dollars a day.

It was a precarious life for a lawman in that wild land where cattlemen fought over choice grazing lands and Indians disputed prized hunting grounds. It was also the hideout for fugitives from many states and many warrants, the halfway station for horse and cattle thief trails, and the headquarters for whiskey peddlers and gun runners. Sixty-five out of two hundred and twenty-five deputies attached to Parker's court died in the line of duty—a record not matched even by the Texas Rangers.

In 1887 Frank died in a gun battle with a band of whiskey smugglers and Grat pinned on his dead brother's tin star. A few years later Bob took over as head of the Indian police and Emmett became his guardsman.

The trio not only engaged in rustling on the side but accepted bribes from the whiskey peddlers they caught selling colored alcohol to the Indians. When the tribal lands became Oklahoma Territory they turned in their badges, with Grat going to California to visit Bill and Littleton on the latter's ranch near Fresno. Restless Emmett and Bob finally had a posse on their heels for sticking up a faro game in New Mexico—a crime which Emmett admitted they had committed, but only after they had found the dealer cheating. Bob hid out with his brothers in California and Emmett returned to Oklahoma.

When the Southern Pacific train No. 17 was held up at Alila on February 6, 1891, a fireman was killed and the Wells Fargo messenger wounded. Bill and Grat were arrested and tried; Grat was found guilty and sentenced to twenty years, but Bill was acquitted. Both insisted that they had had nothing to do with the robbery.

Bill and Bob rejoined Emmett, and the three decided to go into outlawry. Their motive was revenge against the express companies that had falsely charged the Daltons with the California train robbery and had used their influence to send Grat to prison. They also planned, as Emmett claimed, to get enough money "to retire from our old haunts, to South America, perhaps, where we had vaguely contemplated cattle ranching . . ."

Other riders they recruited included Emmett's old friends from his cowboy days: "Bitter Creek" Newcomb, "Black Face" Charlie Bryant, Charlie Pierce, Dick Broadwell, Bill Powers, and the drawling, lanky cowhand who was an expert with a six-shooter, Bill Doolin. Train robbery became their specialty. They borrowed their technique from the Jameses and Youngers, but they also boasted that they never robbed a passenger—only the express car safes. By the 1890s they were charged with committing every train robbery in the West. For example, two trains were held up on a single night, one near St. Charles, Missouri, the other near El Paso, Texas. They were a thousand miles apart, but sheriffs in both communities announced that the Daltons were the robbers.

Bryant was the first to fall. He died as he wished, in a minute of "smoking action," trading shots with a deputy sheriff who had arrested him for train robbery.

The gang's biggest haul was in the Missouri, Kansas & Texas Railroad stick-up near Waggoner, western Oklahoma. Emmett Dalton claimed that the money taken from the express car amounted to $19,000 in bills and coins. After they divided the money into shares, Bob Dalton announced that he and Emmett were tired of running and intended to settle down. Doolin later formed his own gang with Newcomb, Pierce, Powers, and Broadwell. They were all hunted down and killed by the four great lawmen of the frontier: Bill Tilghman, Chris Madsen, Heck Thomas, and Bud Ledbetter.

After Grat Dalton escaped from prison in California, the Daltons joined together again and as Emmett put it, "We were Daltons together—one for all and all for one . . ."

The Santa Fe line in the Cherokee Strip at Red Rock was their first objective.[3] Bob, who had assumed leadership, refused to take the train when it appeared on schedule—a darkened coach made him uneasy. They let it pass and selected the next one. As Bob had surmised, the first train was a dummy, loaded with deputies; the second train netted the gang eleven thousand dollars.

Posses took up the chase but the Daltons covered their tracks by circling cattle and horse herds and splitting up into pairs.

In July 1892, the gang held up the Missouri, Kansas & Texas Railroad—the frontier's famous "Katy"—at Pryor Creek, a town south of Adair in the Indian Territory. However, Bob's sweetheart warned him that a posse was waiting at Pryor Creek so they boarded the train at the Adair depot. After a wild shoot-out with three deputies, the gang cleaned out the express safe of seventeen thousand dollars and made their getaway. In his autobiography Emmett estimated that the shooting and robbery had taken ten minutes. He was not hit in the wild fusillade.

"Born lucky", he wrote.[4]

The Daltons would have been just another band of train robbers in frontier history had it not been for their reckless and bloody raid on Coffeyville, Kansas, in October 1892—one of the most idiotic ventures in outlaw history. They were not only known to the citizens of Coffeyville, but their wanted posters had been posted throughout the area.

What, then, was their motive? I believe it was egotism: a fierce, twisted desire to be known as the greatest band of outlaws in America's Wild West. For not one bank but two would be robbed at the same time. One of the gang was quoted as saying that they would "outshine Jesse James . . . he never tried this!"

The citizens of Northfield, Minnesota, could have told them a different tale . . .

What happened on that fall morning was witnessed by David Stewart Elliott, editor of the *Coffeyville Journal*, who was in the town's plaza when the Daltons rode in. He not only took part in the gun battle, but wrote the most detailed and authentic account of it. His book was published shortly after the event had taken place.[5]

The Daltons Raid Coffeyville

The people of Coffeyville were never in the enjoyment of more peaceful or comfortable surroundings than on the eventful Wednesday morning of October 5th, 1892. People came and went and vehicles moved about in ordinary numbers until about fifteen minutes before ten o'clock, when the most remarkable occurrence that has ever taken place in the history of our country came upon the peaceful city like a flash of lightning from a clear sky.

A member of a well-known firm of general merchants was standing on the pavement in front of a dry goods store when men came out of the alley between the building and the drug store of Slosson & Co. The party passed within five feet of where he was standing. An oil wagon or tank of the Consolidated Company, drawn by two horses, pulled into the alley about the same time and was stopped in the neighborhood of one hundred feet from the front street. The gen-

The Dalton gang after their disastrous raid on the Coffeyville, Kansas, bank, October 5, 1892. *Courtesy Kansas State Historical Society*

tleman was close enough to detect the disguises on the men, and he recognized one of them by his well-known walk and the peculiar shape of the back of his head. After crossing the pavement the men quickened their pace, and the three in the front file went into C. M. Condon & Co.'s bank at the southwest door, while the two in the rear ran directly across the street to the First National Bank and entered the front door of that institution. The gentleman was almost transfixed with horror. He had an uninterrupted view of the inside of Condon & Co.'s bank, and the first thing that greeted his vision was a Winchester in the hands of one of the men, pointed towards the cashier's counter in the bank. He quickly recovered his lost wits, and realizing the truth of the situation, he called out to the men in the store that "The bank is being robbed!" Persons at different points on the Plaza heard the cry and it was taken up and quickly passed around the square. At the same time several gentlemen who saw the two men enter the First National Bank, suspecting their motive, followed close at their heels and witnessed them "holding up" the men in this institution. They gave the alarm on the east side of the Plaza. A "call to arms" came simultaneously with the alarm, and in less time than it takes to relate the fact a dozen men with Winchesters and revolvers in their hands were ready to resist the escape of the unwelcome visitors. Strange as it may seem, but nevertheless true, the citizens were wholly unprepared for an event of this kind. When the robbers were first discovered in the banks there was not an armed man any where upon the square or in the immediate neighborhood. The city marshal had laid his pistol aside and was totally unarmed when the crisis came. Every gun that was used, with the exception of a Winchester brought into action by one of the first victims of the robbers' bullets, was procured at the hardware stores and loaded and brought into action under the pressure of the great exigency that was upon the people. No one waited for the selection of a commander or the authority of a leader. Each individual formed himself into an independent commander for the avowed purpose of preventing the marauders from getting away with the money of the banks. The volunteer

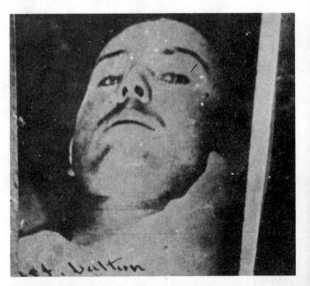

The bodies of Bob and Grat Dalton held up by the townspeople who had besieged the gang in the bank they were trying to rob. *The James D. Horan Civil War and Western Americana Collection*

Emmett Dalton, the youngest brother and only survivor of the Coffeyville raid. After he was released from prison, Dalton married his childhood sweetheart and went to California, where he became a successful contractor. Before he died in July 1937, Dalton returned to Coffeyville to shake hands with the aging men who had tried to kill him on that October day so many years before. *The James D. Horan Civil War and Western Americana Collection*

defenders of law were not impelled by a sentiment; they were inspired by a high sense of duty to their neighbors and the community.

The scene in Condon's bank and the interview that took place between the unwelcome visitors and the proprietors and officials of the bank were peculiarly exciting and intensely interesting. In view of the fact that a vast number of persons are unaware of the methods and manners employed by professional highwaymen and bank robbers to enforce their demands we shall attempt to describe what took place in this bank, as well as in the First National Bank, in the most careful manner.

The main entrances to the building occupied by C. M. Condon & Co., are on the southwest and southeast corners of the structure. The building faces directly to the south. The space between the doors on the south front is covered by two large plate-glass windows. Each entrance has double doors, with plate-glass in the upper portions. Entering the bank by the southwest door, the robbers found Mr. C. T. Carpenter, one of the proprietors, at the west front counter, engaged in making remittances. Mr. Tom C. Babb, the book-keeper, was at his desk, at the east front near the doors of the vault. Mr. Chas. M. Ball, the cashier, was in his private office, which occupies the northwest portion of the room, and has a door leading out to Walnut Street. The three men closed the front door after them as they entered, and quickly disposed themselves in different portions of the room. Mr. Carpenter, from his position, could not see the men as they came through the door. Attracted by their footsteps, he turned towards them, and was horrified to find the muzzle of three Winchesters pointed directly at his person. The man who acted as the leader, and who it was afterwards ascertained was Grat Dalton, called out in quick tones: "We have got you, G——d d——n you! Hold up your hands!" The other two men, who proved to be Bill Powers and Dick Broadwell, stopped in the front part of the bank, Broadwell being closer to the southeast entrance, and Powers stationed himself near the southwest door. Mr. Babb, the book-keeper, discovered the character of the men before they discovered him, and he quickly and quietly stepped into the vault. Mr. Ball, the cashier, hearing the noise in the front part of the bank, came into the room, and was at once put under the surveillance of the Winchesters in the hands of the daring men. Grat Dalton then ran to the private office door, passed through the office and into the front part of the bank, behind the counter. He had in his hands a two-bushel seamless grain sack, which he gave to Mr. Ball, with directions to hold it open, and at the same time he ordered Mr. Carpenter to put all the money on the counter and in the drawer into the sack. The latter reluctantly complied with the robber's request. After this was done, he asked: "Where is your gold?" Not receiving a satisfactory reply, he ordered Mr. Carpenter and Mr. Ball to go into the vault, and as they turned to comply he for the first time discovered the presence of Mr. Babb. He gave the young man a terrible cursing, and made him hold up his hands and come out from behind the book-rack, where he was secreted. The burglar-proof chest was closed and locked with the combination lock. The two front doors and the two sets of outside doors of the Hall burglar-proof safe were standing open. There were three canvas bags filled with silver, containing one thousand dollars each, in the safe. These fell under the eye of the robber, and he directed Mr. Carpenter to empty them into the sack which Mr. Ball was holding. While this was going on he asked: "What is that you are putting in there?" Mr. Ball replied, "Silver dollars." Looking around quickly and nervously at Mr. Ball, with an oath he said: "Open up the door," pointing to the burglar-proof chest. Mr. Ball replied: "It is not time for that to open."

Grat Dalton—"What time does it open?"

Mr. Ball—"Half past 9 o'clock," guessing at the time.

Grat Dalton—"What time is it now?"

Mr. Ball (looking at his watch)—"Twenty minutes after 9 o'clock."

Grat Dalton—"We can wait ten minutes."

It was actually twenty minutes of ten, and Mr. Ball had missed his guess just twenty minutes. In the meantime Mr. Carpenter had turned the handle of the door of the chest in order to show that it was locked. Waiting a moment or two with evident impatience, Grat Dalton exclaimed:

"G——d d——n you! I believe you are lying to me. I've a mind to put a bullet through you. Open it up or I will shoot you; you have been blowing too much about what you can do. Where is your gold?"

Mr. Ball—"We haven't any."

Grat Dalton—"How much is in this sack?"

Mr. Ball—"Four thousand dollars."

Grat Dalton—"How much cash did your books show last night?"

Mr. Ball—"Four thousand dollars; one thousand dollars in currency and three thousand dollars in silver, all of which you have in your sack. There is nothing in the burglar-proof chest except some nickels and pennies; we ordered some currency, but it has not been delivered yet; it is over in the express office."

In the meantime Mr. J. D. Levan and Mr. D. E. James, two customers of the bank, had entered at the southwest door, and had been captured by one of the fellows on the outside of the counter. Just at this critical juncture the citizens opened fire from the outside and the shots from their Winchesters and shot-guns pierced the plate-glass windows and rattled through the bank. Bill Powers and Dick Broadwell replied from the inside, and each fired from four to six shots at citizens on the outside. The battle then began in earnest. Evidently recognizing that the fight was on, Grat Dalton asked whether there was a back door through which they could go to get to the street. He was told that there was none. He then ordered Mr. Ball and Mr. Carpenter to carry the sack of money to the front door. Reaching the hall on the outside of the counter, the firing of the citizens through the windows became so terrific and the bullets whistled so close around their heads that the robbers and both bankers retreated to the back room again. Just then one at the southwest door was heard to exclaim: "I am shot; I can't use my arm; it is no use, I can't shoot any more." Grat Dalton then ordered Mr. Ball to go and bring the sack into the back room, which he did. He next ordered him to cut the string with which it had been tied shut, and take out the currency. Mr. Ball poured the contents on the floor and assorted the currency from the silver and handed the former to Grat Dalton, who immediately went out at the southwest door, by which he had entered, his companions following immediately after him. During the firing into the bank from the outside, the bankers and two customers, who had unwittingly fallen into the trap, were lying on the floor most of the time. The balls from one of the rifles passed in close proximity to Mr. Ball's head while he was engaged in taking the bag of silver from the floor. The interior of the bank shows the marks where several bullets struck, but strange as it may appear, neither of the bankers were injured.

At the First National Bank a similar scene was enacted. The two masked men came in at the front door, which was protected by a screen. They closed the heavy doors after them. Messrs. J. H. Brewster, A. W. Knotts and C. L. Hollingsworth, customers of the bank, were in the front part of the room at the time. Mr. J. E. S. Boothby stepped into the door a moment or two after the robbers, and was about to back out when one of them motioned to him with his Winchester to step inside, which he did. The tallest of the two men with his Winchester covered Mr. Thomas G. Ayres, the cashier, who was at his window, and with a horrid oath called upon every one present to hold up their hands. He ordered the customers present to stand still right where they were. The smallest one covered with his Winchester the teller, Mr. W. H. Shepard, who was at a desk near the vault, and also assisted in keeping those present in a state of nervous excitement by his dreadful profanity and the reckless manner in which he flourished his gun. These two men proved to be Bob Dalton, the leader of the gang, and his brother Emmett Dalton, the youngest member of the band. In describing their future movements we shall use their names. Leaving Emmett to take care of the men in front, Bob passed through the hallway into the private office in the rear of the bank room. This room has a door that opens into the lot that leads to the alley in the rear of the bank. The doorway is protected by a heavy iron grating with a spring lock on the inside. He found Mr. B. S. Ayres, the book-keeper, at his desk in the office, and peremptorily ordered him to go to the front, behind the counter, and hand out the bank's money. The young man obeyed, but not with sufficient alacrity to suit the Daltons, so they undertook to hurry him by swearing at him and threatening to shoot him. After young Ayres had handed over all the money on the counter and in the drawer, Bob ordered him to bring out the money in the safe. He told him that he did not know the combination. Turning to the cashier, Ayres, he said:

"Tom, you go and get it."

Mr. Ayres went and got some currency and put it in a sack which the men had brought with them. Bob asked them if that was all. Mr. Ayres replied that there was some gold in the vault, and asked if he wanted that. Bob replied:

"Yes; every d——n cent of it."

Mr. Ayres then got the gold and gave it to him. He inquired a second time if that was all. Mr. Ayres pushed the safe shut and replied that it was. Determined to see for himself, Bob went into the vault, opened the safe doors, and taking out two packages of currency containing five thousand dollars each, he inquired:

"What's this?"

He threw them into the sack, and turning again to the vault, emptied the silver on the floor, but did not take any. He picked up a box containing gold watches that belonged to a customer, but the bankers told him there was nothing but papers in it, and he placed it back again. He then ordered the three bankers to walk out from behind the counter in front of him, and they put the whole party out at the front door. Before they reached the door, Emmet called out to Bob to "Look out there at the left." Just as the bankers and their customers had reached the pavement, and as Bob and Emmett appeared at the door, two shots were fired at them from the doorway of the drug store of Rammel Bros., which adjoins the bank on the north, by George Cubine, from a Winchester and C. S. Cox from a revolver. Neither one of them was hit. They were driven back into the bank and Messrs. B. S. Ayres and W. H. Shepard sprang in after them. Bob stepped to the door a second time, and raising his Winchester to his shoulder, took deliberate aim and fired in a southerly direction. Emmet held his Winchester under his arm while he tied a string around the mouth of the sack containing the money. They then ordered the young men to open the back door and let them out. Mr. Shepard complied and went with them to the rear of the building, when they passed out into the alley. It was then that the bloody work of the dread desperadoes began.

The hardware stores, where guns and ammunition are kept for sale, quite naturally became the rallying points for the alarmed citizens. The store of Isham Brothers & Mansur, hardware merchants, is a large one-story brick building, with basement and heavy plate-glass windows and doors. The front is protected by an awning supported by iron columns. It is situated on the east side of Union

Street, immediately opposite the bank of C. M. Condon & Co., and adjoins the First National Bank on the north. It has two entrances from Union Street, and when the fight began the heavy front doors were all wide open. The men who visited the First National were compelled to pass immediately in front of this store on their way to the bank. The store of A. P. Boswell & Co., hardware merchants, is a large two-story brick, with basement. The lower front is of plate-glass, and is protected by an awning similar to that of Isham Bros. & Mansur. The proprietors of these stores most willingly passed out their guns and ammunition to the eager citizens. John J. Kloehr, of the firm of Lewark & Kloehr, livery-men, was among the first to obtain a Winchester at the store of Boswell & Co. Some one handed him the gun and he went behind the counter and selected his own cartridges and loaded the piece. In company with several others, he took a position on the pavement in front of the store, where a good view of the Condon bank could be had, and from this point a number of shots were fired at the robbers in that building and as they passed out. Parker L. Williams secured a Colt's forty-four calibre revolver and got out upon the awning in front of Boswell's, from which point he opened up on the robbers in Condon's bank. The one who stood at the southwest entrance, and who afterwards turned out to be Richard L. Broadwell, alias "Texas Jack," placed the muzzle of his Winchester against the heavy glass in the door and fired at Mr. Williams, but missed. A second shot from his gun, through the hole made by the first, passed into an open window on the second floor of the clothing department of the firm of Barndollar Brothers, next door to the hardware store, and lodged in some queensware stored on the shelves. Mr. Williams then abandoned his conspicuous position, but not until his enemy on the inside of the bank was seen to drop his gun and grasp his right arm. Several citizens, who modestly refused to make the fact known, used shot-guns with good effect from this point.

Charles T. Gump, who was driving his team on the street at the time, sprang from his wagon when the alarm was given, ran into Isham's store, seized a double-barreled shot-gun and returned to the outside edge of the pavement and took a position behind the iron awning post, facing the First National Bank. He held his gun in a position of "ready" and awaited the exit of the robbers. A shot from Bob Dalton's rifle, and the first one fired by that individual, struck Mr. Gump on the hand with which he had the gun clasped, cutting away the wood surrounding the pinion on which the gun was operated in loading, and made a dent in the barrel. The gun fell in several pieces at his feet, and Mr. Gump was seized by friends and drawn into the store. His hand was torn by the bullet, and he was found to have sustained a severe wound. He retired as the first victim of the dreadful fight that followed. About the time that Mr. Gump was wounded, Lucius M. Baldwin, a clerk in the store of Read Brothers, general merchants, a noble, generous-hearted, brave and loyal young man, came from his employer's store on the west side of the Plaza, and entering Isham's store, siezed a small revolver that came within his reach, and passed out at the back door of the store, into the alley. As he reached the alley, Bob and Emmet Dalton came to the rear door of the First National Bank, having Mr. Shepard, the teller, in charge. The latter opened the door for them and they passed out. Mr. Baldwin, holding the pistol down at his side, started forward with the evident purpose of joining the men, when both leveled their Winchesters at him and commanded him to stop. He either did not hear the command or else failed to understand it, and continued to move toward them. His attitude was not hostile, but the fact that he carried a pistol sealed his fate. "I'll have to get that man," exclaimed Bob Dalton, and his deadly rifle rang out upon the morning air a second time. Young Baldwin fell bleeding and dying within fifty feet of his assassin, a bullet having pierced his left breast and passed through his body, near his warm and tender heart. As the Daltons turned and ran northward on the alley and disappeared on Eighth Street, friends tenderly gathered up the unconscious young man and carried him to a place of safety. He regained consciousness and lived for three hours, when his young life went out in triumph and he died, the first martyr in the battle against the unholy designs of his wicked slayers. There is some controversy as to which of the Daltons did the fatal shooting that followed on their part. It is safe to say that they each took a part in the bloody work, and we shall treat their future operations accordingly. Reaching Eighth Street, the Daltons turned west toward Union. Arriving at the corner of the street, they both quickly glanced up the pavement and two shots were fired from this point without any results, and evidently for the purpose of intimidation. Moving on westward to the middle of the street their practiced eyes fell upon the brave and intrepid Geo. B. Cubine, who was standing in the doorway of the drug store of Rammel Bros., which adjoins the First National Bank on the north, with a Winchester in his hand and his gaze fixed intently on the doors of the First National Bank. Four shots rang out, and the dauntless Cubine fell dead upon the pavement with a bullet through his heart, one through his left thigh and another through his ankle. The other ball crashed through the bottom sash of the plate-glass window and fell on the floor inside. Charles Brown an aged gentleman whose place of business was immediately north of the drug store, was the first person to approach the prostrate form of Mr. Cubine. Discovering that his fellow-mechanic was dead, he seized his gun and turned upon his slayers. Four more shots came from the middle of the street below, and the brave old veteran fell bleeding and dying within two feet of the prostrate form of his friend. He lived three hours in dreadful agony, and then peacefully passed away. He made the fourth victim of the deadly rifles of the daring bandits. All of this bloody work was accomplished in an incredibly short space of time. The shots were fired by the Daltons at a distance of from forty to fifty yards from the objects of their aim. When Tho. G. Ayres, the cashier of the First National Bank, was turned out of the bank by the Daltons, he immediately ran into Isham's store, and seizing a Winchester, took a position in the north doorway of that establishment where he could command a view of the front of the bank. He expected the Daltons to force their way out by the front entrance, and he intently fixed his eyes upon the doors of the building where he had left them a few moments before. In the meantime they had passed around the north end of the block and had accomplished the death of three men in their hasty movement. They had reached the west side of Union Street and were ascending the steps to an elevated pavement that surrounds the brick building in the center of the Plaza, when Bob's keen eye caught sight of Mr. Ayres in the door. Taking deliberate aim, at a distance of over seventy-five yards, he sent a ball crashing through the face of the brave cashier who was willing to fight for the preservation of his rights and the protection of his property. The bullet entered below Mr. Ayres's left eye and came out near the base of his skull. He fell bleeding and unconscious to the floor. Just at this critical moment Grat Dalton and his companions reached the alley in their efforts to escape, and before the prostrate form of Mr. Ayres could be removed the fleeing robbers fired nine shots into the front of the building where he lay, several of which passed in close proximity to his person.

Bob and Emmet Dalton disappeared behind the buildings and were not seen again until they reappeared at the junction of the two alleys, at a point near where the band went down under the unerring aim of the citizens who were intent on preventing their escape and avenging the death of their friends.

When the alarm was first given that the banks were being robbed, Henry H. Isham, the senior member of the firm of Isham Bros. & Mansur, was at his desk, receiving payment of a note from a customer. Two of the clerks in the store, Lewis A. Dietz and T. Arthur Reynolds, were waiting upon other customers in the front part of the store. Mr. Isham dismissed his customer, closed his safe, and grasping a Winchester, stationed himself near a large steel range in the front part of the store, where he could see all that was going on in the front of Condon's bank, and at the same time command an excellent range of the alley on the opposite side of the Plaza. Mr. Dietz seized a revolver and stationed himself close to Mr. Isham.

The intrepid Reynolds, having observed the robbers enter the banks, was so eager to prevent their escape that he grasped a Winchester and ran out upon the pavement and commenced firing at the robber who occupied the position at the southeastern door. A shot from the rifle of the latter struck some intervening object and glanced and hit Mr. Reynolds in the right foot at the base of the little toe and came out at the instep. His friends on the inside had endeavored to keep him with them, and he was now forced to leave the field. He made the third wounded man in the store. Each one bled profusely and the floor of the store room was bespattered with human blood. M. N. Anderson, a carpenter, who was at work two blocks away, had arrived at the store in the meantime, and he took up the Winchester that Mr. Reynolds had been using, and stationing himself near Mr. Isham, performed valiant service from that time till the close of the engagement. Charles K. Smith, a young Kansan and the son of the proprietor of a barber shop near Isham's store, procured a Winchester and joined the forces in the hardware store in time to help in the work of exterminating the bandit gang. From five to nine shots were fired by each man who handled a Winchester at this point. The principal credit for the successful and fatal work that was accomplished from the store is due to Mr. Isham. He is a trained marksman and none of his shots were thrown away. Cool and self-possessed, he gave directions to his companions, and at the same time kept his own Winchester in action.

The moment that Grat Dalton and his companions, Dick Broadwell and Bill Powers, left the bank that they had just looted, they came under the guns of the men in Isham's store. Grat Dalton and Bill Powers each received mortal wounds before they had retreated twenty steps. The dust was seen to fly from their clothes, and Powers in his desperation attempted to take refuge in the rear doorway of an adjoining store, but the door was locked and no one answered his request to be let in. He kept his feet and clung to his Winchester until he reached his horse, when another ball struck him in the back and he fell dead at the feet of the animal that had carried him on his errand of robbery. Grat Dalton, getting under cover of the oil tank, managed to reach the side of a barn that stands on the south side of the alley about two hundred feet from Walnut Street. The point where he stopped was out of range of the guns at Isham's to some extent because of an obstruction in the shape of an outside stairway to the second floor of Slosson's drug store building. Here he stood for a few moments, either waiting for Bob and Emmet to join him, or else because he was unable to go any further. He fired several wild shots from where he stood, one of which passed very close to the heads of several gentlemen who were standing in a group in front of Masonic Block, on Ninth Street, and lodged in the frame of the doorway leading to the second story of a building. After the robbers entered the alley at Slosson's, they were lost to the sight of the men at Boswell's store. John J. Kloehr, the liveryman, Carey Seamen and Marshal Connelly, who were on the south side of the Plaza, near Read's store, started up Ninth Street for the purpose of intercepting them before they could reach their horses. Marshal Connelly was in the hall on the third

floor of an adjoining building when the firing commenced. He had left his revolver at his residence that morning; hence was wholly unarmed. As they were
passing up the street he told Mr. Kloehr that he was defenseless and must have a
gun and when the latter passed into his livery barn, the faithful and courageous
marshal ran to the machine shop of Swisher Bros., a short distance west, and procured a small Winchester. Nothing daunted, he ran across the vacant lot to an
opening in the fence at the alley, right at the corner of the barn where Grat Dalton
was still standing. The marshal sprang into the alley with his face towards the
point where the horses were hitched. This movement brought him with his back
to the murderous Dalton, who was seen to raise his Winchester to his side and
without taking aim fire a shot into the back of the brave officer. Marshal Connelly fell forward on his face within twenty feet of where his murderer stood. He
breathed his last just as the fight ended. Dick Broadwell in the meantime had
reached cover in the Long-Bell Lumber Company's yards, where he laid down for
a few moments. He was wounded in the back. A lull occurred, in the firing after
Grat Dalton and Bill Powers had fallen. Broadwell took advantage of this and
crawled out of his hiding-place and mounted his horse and rode away.

A ball from Kloehr's rifle and a load of shot from a gun in the hands of Carey
Seamen overtook him before he had ridden twenty feet. Bleeding and dying he
clung to his horse and passed out of the city over a portion of the route by which
the party had entered not more than twenty minutes prior to that time. His dead
body was subsequently found alongside of the road a half-mile west of the city,
and his horse and trappings captured near where he fell. Almost at the same
moment that Marshal Connelly went down before the deadly rifle of Grat Dalton, the two brothers in crime, Bob and Emmet Dalton, emerged from the alley
by which they had left Eighth Street in their effort to join the rest of the party at
the place where their horses were secured. They had not met with any resistance
in passing from where they had shot Cubine, Brown and Ayres. The firing on
the south part of the Plaza had attracted the attention of most persons to that locality. The alley over which they passed before reaching the "alley of death" is a
private thoroughfare that runs north and south in the rear of a block of brick
store buildings. Its southern termination is directly opposite the rear end of Slosson & Co.'s drug store. When the two Daltons reached the junction of the alleys
they discovered F. D. Benson in the act of climbing through a rear window with
a gun in his hand. Divining his object, Bob fired at him point blank at a distance
of not over thirty feet. The shot missed Mr. Benson, but struck the window and
demolished the glass. Bob then stepped into the alley and glanced up towards the
tops of the buildings as if he suspected that the shots that were being fired at the
time were coming from that direction. As he did so, the men at Isham's took deliberate aim at him from their position in the store, and fired. The notorious leader of the Dalton gang evidently received a severe if not fatal wound at this
moment. He staggered across the alley and sat down on a pile of dressed curb-
stones near the city jail.

True to his desperate nature, he kept his rifle in action and fired several shots
from where he was seated. His aim was unsteady and the bullets went wild.
While sitting on the rocks he espied John Kloehr on the inside of the fence near
Slosson's store. He tried to raise his Winchester to his shoulder, but could not,
and his shot, intended for Mr. Kloehr, struck the side of a small building and
failed in its intended mission. The Dalton then made his supreme effort. He arose
to his feet and sought refuge alongside of an old barn west of the city jail, and
leaning against the southwest corner, brought his rifle into action again and fired

two shots in the direction of his pursuers. A ball from Mr. Kloehr's rifle struck the bandit full in the breast and he fell upon his back among the stones that covered the ground where he was standing. He bled profusely from his first wound and the stones on which he sat were covered with his blood. After shooting Marshal Connelly, Grat Dalton made another attempt to reach his horse. He passed by his fallen victim and had advanced probably twenty feet from where he was standing when he fired the fatal shot. Turning his face to his pursuers, he again attempted to use his Winchester. John Kloehr's rifle spoke in unmistakable tones another time, and the oldest member of the band dropped with a bullet in his throat and a broken neck. He fell within a few feet of the dying Marshal Connelly. Emmet Dalton had managed to escape unhurt up to this time. He kept under shelter after he reached the alley until he attempted to mount his horse. A half-dozen rifles sent their contents in the direction of his person as he undertook to get into the saddle. The two intervening horses, belonging to Bob Dalton and Bill Powers, were killed by some of the shots that were intended for Emmet. The two horses attached to the oil tank, being directly in range, also received fatal wounds. Emmet succeeded in getting into the saddle, but not until he had received a shot through the right arm and one through the left hip and groin. During all this time he had clung to the sack containing the money they had taken from the First National Bank. Instead of riding off, as he might have done, Emmet boldly rode back to where Bob Dalton was lying, and reaching down his hand, attempted to lift his dying brother on the horse with him. "It's no use," faintly whispered the fallen bandit, and just then Carey Seamen fired the contents of both barrels of his shot-gun into Emmet's back as he was leaning over the prostrate form of his leader and tutor in crime. He dropped from his horse, carrying the sack containing over twenty thousand dollars with him, and both fell near the feet of Bob, who expired a moment thereafter. Citizens who had followed close after the robbers, and some who were near by when they fell, surrounded their bodies.

Emmet Dalton readily responded to the command to hold up his uninjured hand and made a pathetic appeal for mercy. Lynching was suggested for the wounded one, but wiser counsel prevailed and he was taken to a surgeon's office and his wounds dressed. Willing hands tenderly carried the form of Marshal Connelly to an adjoining drug store, but he expired before reaching the place. Indignation and sorrow commingled in the breast of every man and woman in the city, and the whole population went into mourning. Stalwart men wept great tears of grief, whilst the women and children cried and wrung their hands in agony. Business was suspended and groups of excited men gathered at every convenient point. The dreadful occurrences of the day were discussed with bated breath and in tones of sorrow.

The scene that was presented in the "alley of death" was ghastly beyond human conception. A moment or two passed after the cry went up, "They are all down!" before anyone ventured to approach the prostrate forms of the dead and dying. Just as soon as their work was finished, the citizens ceased firing, shouldered their guns and gathered around those who had fallen in the alley. Three men lay dead in an almost direct line with each other, a fourth was in the last throes of death, and a fifth was helpless and bleeding from a number of dreadful wounds. Three dead horses, smoking Winchesters, the hats of the fallen, and other evidences of a bloody conflict, were scattered over the ground where the bandits made their last stand. Grat Dalton had kept his false whiskers on his

The Condon Bank of Coffeyville, Kansas, target of the Dalton gang. *Courtesy Kansas State Historical Society*

face, and when these were removed the ghastly features of the man, who had a number of acquaintances in the city and neighborhood, were revealed. The currency which he had secured from Condon's bank, amounting to nearly eleven hundred dollars, was found on the inside of his vest, where he had evidently stuffed it in a hasty manner. His Winchester, which was lying by his side, gave evidences of having been fired a number of times, but the pair of immense Colt's revolvers that were in his belt had not been discharged. Bill Powers, better known as Tom Evans, had thrown off the mask which he wore while in the bank, and his empty Winchester showed that he had taken an active part in the fight. He had neither money nor valuables of any kind on his person, and nothing to show his identity or reveal his antecedents. Bob Dalton had taken off his mask, and he was dead when the first man reached him. His rifle was empty, but the revolvers in his belt had not been discharged. Emmet Dalton denied his identity at first, and gave his name as Charley McLaughlin. He fell with his Winchester in his hand, the smoking muzzle of which showed that it had been very recently used. His two revolvers were in his belt, fully loaded. Each of the men had belts around their waists, containing a supply of rifle and pistol cartridges.

They were all closely shaven, had on clean and comfortable clothing, and were booted and spurred in accordance with the style so prevalent in the West. The bodies of the dead raiders were picked up and carried into the city jail and a guard placed over them.

It is simply impossible to describe the scenes that followed. Excited and indignant men, weeping women and screaming children thronged the Plaza and crowded the alley in which the last scenes of the fight had taken place. A few cool-headed citizens kept disorder from ensuing. The dead and dying citizens were removed to their homes or other comfortable locations. The citizens who were not in the fight congratulated those who had a part in the engagement, and condoled with those who had lost relatives and friends in the bloody affair. Guards were thrown out, and the city sat down in sackcloth and ashes to mourn for the heroic men who had given their lives for the protection of the property of the citizens and the maintenance of law in the community.

Less than fifteen minutes elapsed from the time the raiders entered the banks until four of their number were dead and the remaining one severely wounded and in the hands of the officers. It was just twelve minutes from the time the first shot was fired until the last one resounded a victory for the citizens. The bullets of the Daltons found their victims in some of the best citizens. The country is rid of the desperate gang, but the riddance cost Coffeyville some of its most precious blood.

The bullet-shattered front doors of the Condon Bank of Coffeyville, vivid evidence of the intense gun battle waged between the Daltons and the townspeople. *Courtesy Kansas State Historical Society*

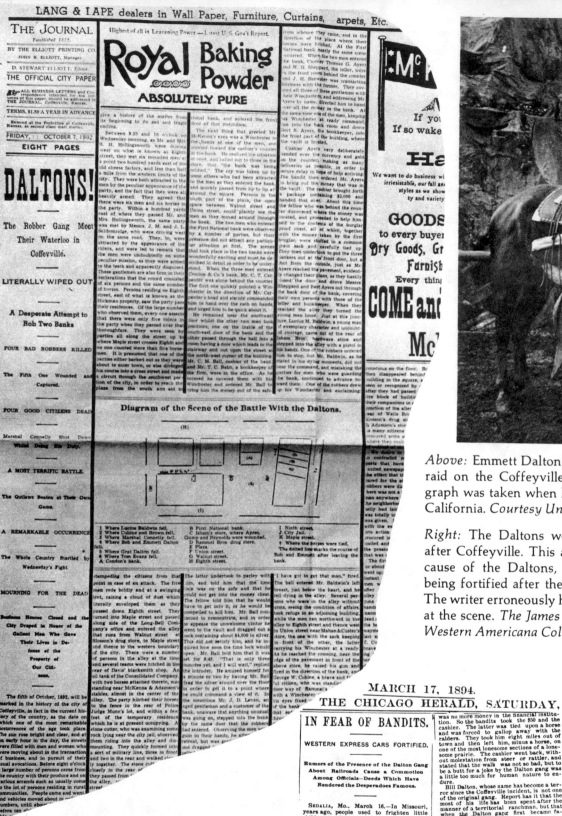

THE JOURNAL

Established 1875.
BY THE ELLIOTT PRINTING CO.
JOHN B. ELLIOTT, Manager.
D. STEWART ELLIOTT, Editor.
THE OFFICIAL CITY PAPER

Highest of all in Leavening Power — Latest U. S. Gov't Report

Royal Baking Powder
ABSOLUTELY PURE

ALL BUSINESS LETTERS and Correspondence intended for the columns of this paper, should be addressed to THE JOURNAL, Coffeyville, Kansas.

TERMS, $1.50 A YEAR IN ADVANCE

Entered at the Postoffice at Coffeyville, Kansas, as second class mail matter.

FRIDAY, : : OCTOBER 7, 1892.

EIGHT PAGES

DALTONS!

The Robber Gang Meet Their Waterloo in Coffeyville.

LITERALLY WIPED OUT

A Desperate Attempt to Rob Two Banks

FOUR BAD ROBBERS KILLED

The Fifth One Wounded and Captured.

FOUR GOOD CITIZENS DEAD

Marshal Connelly Shot Down Whilst Doing His Duty.

A MOST TERRIFIC BATTLE.

The Outlaws Beaten at Their Own Game.

A REMARKABLE OCCURRENCE

The Whole Country Startled by Wednesday's Fight.

MOURNING FOR THE DEAD

Business Houses Closed and the City Draped in Honor of the Gallant Men Who Gave Their Lives in Defense of the Property of Our Citizens.

Diagram of the Scene of the Battle With the Daltons.

1 Where Lucius Baldwin fell.
2 Where Cubine and Brown fell.
3 Where Marshal Connelly fell.
4 Where Bob and Emmett Dalton fell.
5 Where Grat Dalton fell.
6 Where Tom Evans fell.
A Condon's bank.
B First National bank.
C Isham's store, where Ayres, Gump and Reynolds were wounded.
D Rammel Bros drug store.
E Plaza.
F Union street.
G Walnut street.
H Eighth street.
I Ninth street.
J City Jail.
K Maple street.
* Where the horses were tied.
The dotted line marks the course of Bob and Emmett after leaving the bank.

MARCH 17, 1894.
THE CHICAGO HERALD, SATURDAY,

IN FEAR OF BANDITS.

WESTERN EXPRESS CARS FORTIFIED.

Rumors of the Presence of the Dalton Gang About Railroads Cause a Commotion Among Officials—Deeds Which Have Rendered the Desperadoes Famous.

SEDALIA, Mo., March 16.—In Missouri, years ago, people used to frighten little children to sleep with the names of the James boys. In these days they still call Fear to the aid of Morpheus, but it is by mentioning the bandits whom criminal history knows as the Dalton gang. Fit successors of Missouri's famous bandits, these products of Kansas border life began a reign of terror in the nation, as the Indian Territory was known within its old confines, that received no serious check until the Coffeyville bank robbery was planned and executed Oct. 5, 1892. This event might be called the Waterloo of the original gang of bandits, but enough of them were left to continue, with the aid of kindred spirits, a career of lawlessness which has made them feared in Kansas and Missouri by the officers of the law as much as by the people whom they choose to visit.

As is only natural, every deed of crime with particular features of boldness which occurs in the sections frequented by the desperadoes is ascribed to them. Just now the cars of the express companies on the lines of railroad in Missouri, Kansas and Oklahoma are being fortified after the fashion of the arsenal. To be sure the companies have not as yet mounted Gatling guns, but they have armed their messengers to the teeth, doors and cars are being made bullet proof, and a time giant powder or...

The Coffeyville Robbery.

By far the most notable event in the career of the bandits was the robbery of the two national banks at Coffeyville, Kan., where four of them were killed. It was a desperate fight in which death came to them, for an equal number of residents of Coffeyville received fatal wounds at the same time.

The visit of the Daltons to Coffeyville was not wholly unexpected. The town was once their home and they were well known there. Some nights before the battle Bob Dalton awoke a local druggist and demanded whisky. This man had none and Bob, with many threats and flourishing his six shooter, went on to another store. There he got his liquor and rode out of town. The people who then knew that the gang heeded the warning, their Winchesters, and stood partias this the attack...

...while given the alarm, and men had hastily secured weapons and were rushing to the scene. As Bob and Emmet Dalton emerged from the bank Pacific Express Agent C. S. Cox and George Cubine opened fire on them, wounding Emmet. The brothers turned back, and running through the bank came out of a side door. There they met and mortally wounded Lucius Baldwin. Coming out on the street they returned the fire of Cubine, instantly killing him, and wounding Charles Brown so badly that he died at 1 o'clock the next afternoon. The elder Ayers started to run, but a volley from the robbers in the other bank, who fired through the windows, struck him, and he fell seriously wounded. Bob and Emmet quickly joined the rest of their band and started for their horses, but they were then the targets for a fusillade. Bob and Grattan Dalton and Texas Jack were killed at the mouth of the alley, not, however, before Bob had killed City Marshal Connelly. Tom Evans and Gge mounted their horses and dashed out town, but Evans was hit hard and fell from his horse half a mile away. Escaped. From the First National robbers got $20,000 and from Co $3,000, but were compelled booty, and every cent was r Emmet Dalton made a before his death that same which robbed the on the Missouri, Kailroad at Adair stati in July, 1892, and robberies. The Parsons shortly eral Superin' Kansas and cial car, in zens with to Coffe perado rival th b

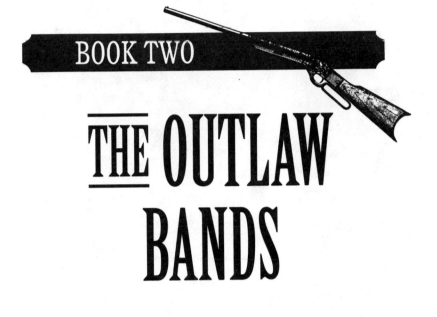

BOOK TWO

THE OUTLAW BANDS

JOAQUIN MURIETA

In the summer of 1853 most of San Francisco was closely following the adventures of Captain Harry Love. A former Texas Ranger, Love had been appointed by the legislature to head a mounted troop of twenty rangers assigned to capture or kill "the five Joaquins," all Mexican outlaws of the same first name, who had been terrorizing the ranches and gold camps. Love and his men were to be paid a thousand dollars for each Joaquin.

Love's rangers were not all pure knights: one had murdered the leader of the expedition that had discovered Yosemite Valley; another, to show his contempt for poor dining room service, had killed his waiter.

For two months the residents of San Francisco avidly read the "letters" sent in by correspondents following Love's manhunt. But both the legislature and citizens grew restless when Love and his band failed to find even one Joaquin.

Then in July, Love's troopers came upon a band of Mexicans. There was a shootout and Manuel Garcia, alias "Three-Fingered Jack," was killed. As proof, a finger was cut off and preserved in alcohol. The head of another, said to be a leader, was also preserved in an alcohol-filled jar. Prisoners were turned over to the Sheriff of Mariposa and the victorious band returned to Sacramento with the head of the bandit chief and finger of his follower.

San Francisco newspapers hailed Love for killing "the notorious bandit chief, Joaquin," but nowhere in those early accounts does the bandit's last name appear. Evidently no one cared; rustling and highway robbery stopped and that was what was important.

The delighted legislature not only paid Love and his men the thousand-dollar reward, but gave them a four-thousand-dollar bonus.

The editor of the San Francisco *Alta* was not satisfied, however; his investigative reporting and subsequent stories amused the city and angered the legislature.[1]

Whose Head Is It? Joaquin Murieta's?

It affords amusement to our citizens to read the various accounts of the capture and decapitation of "the notorious Joaquin Murietta." The humbug is so transparent that it is surprising any sensible person can be imposed upon by the statements of the affairs which have appeared in the prints.

A few weeks ago a party of native Americans and Sonorians started for Tulara Valley for the expressed and avowed purpose of running mustangs. Three of the party have returned and report that they were attacked by a party of Americans and the balance of their party, four in number, had been killed; that Joaquin Valenzuela, one of them, was killed as he was endeavoring to escape and that his head was cut off and taken as a trophy.

It is too well known that Joaquin Murietta was not in the party nor was he the person killed by Captain Harry Love's party at the Panache Pass. The head recently exhibited in Stockton bears no resemblance to that individual, and this is positively asserted by those who have seen the real Murietta and the spurious head.

All the accounts wind up by recommending the continuing of Love's Company in service. All right. The term of service was about expiring, and although I will not say that interested parties have gotten up this Joaquin expedition, yet such expeditions can generally be traced to have an origin with a few speculators.

At the time of the murder of General Bean at Mission San Gabriel, Murietta was strongly suspected of the crime and efforts were made to arrest him but he escaped. Since then every murder and robbery in the country has been attributed to "Joaquin." Sometimes it is Joaquin Carrillo that had committed all these crimes; then it is Joaquin Murietta, then Joaquin something else but always Joaquin! The very act of the Legislature authorizing a company to capture "the five Joaquins" was in itself a farce and these names were inserted in order to fill the bill.

Despite the *Alta*'s skepticism, the preserved "head of Joaquin Murietta" made the rounds of saloons, bars, gambling halls, and museums.

At about the same time, Louise Amelia Knapp Smith Clappe, wife of a physician stationed at the Rich and Indian bars of the Feather River's gold camps, had submitted the first of twenty-three letters written from the camps to *Pioneer Magazine* in San Francisco.[2] The editor, Steven Massett, one of California's great journalists, sensed immediately that he had a literary find. The letters would become a famous source describing life in the gold camps.

In letter nineteen, Mrs. Clappe describes how the camp's Vigilante Committee convicted "five or six Spaniards" on charges of starting a riot in the camps and sentenced them to be whipped.

The first story of the killing of "Joaquin, the notorious robber and murderer," by Captain Love's Rangers. It appeared in the San Francisco *Alta*, July 29, 1853, and was sent into the newspaper by its Quartzburg correspondent. *Courtesy Bancroft Library, University of California, Berkeley*

The story of the killing of the "famous bandit Joaquin, whose name is associated with a hundred deeds of blood," which appeared in the San Francisco *Herald*, July 1853. The writer reported that the bandit's head had been cut off by the Rangers and "placed in spirits." The alleged "Head of Murieta, the Outlaw" was exhibited for many years in San Francisco saloons and museums but was never accepted as that of the bandit. The *Alta* called it "humbug." *Courtesy Bancroft Library, University of California, Berkeley*

Less than a month after the capture and the beheading of the "notorious bandit, Joaquin Murieta," the San Francisco *Alta* voiced suspicion that the whole affair was an attempt to have the legislature extend the term of Captain Love's company of Rangers. The writer pointed out there were so many "Joaquins" that some residents with that name were preparing to change it. *Courtesy Bancroft Library, University of California, Berkeley*

WILL BE
EXHIBITED
FOR ONE DAY ONLY!

AT THE STOCKTON HOUSE!
THIS DAY, AUG. 12, FROM 9 A. M., UNTIL 6, P. M.

THE HEAD
Of the renowned Bandit!

JOAQUIN!
AND THE
HAND OF THREE FINGERED JACK!
THE NOTORIOUS ROBBER AND MURDERER.

"JOAQUIN" and "THREE-FINGERED JACK" were captured by the *State Rangers*, under the command of Capt. Harry Love, at the Arroya Cantina, July 24th. No reasonable doubt can be entertained in regard to the identification of the head now on exhibition, as being that of the notorious robber, *Joaquin Murietta*, as it has been recog- nised by hundreds of persons who have formerly seen him.

Poster announcing the exhibition of the head of "Joaquin." *Courtesy J. E. Reynolds*

A staff artist of the *Overland Monthly* claimed to have sketched the outlaw's head, which was preserved in a bottle of alcohol. As the *California Alta* commented: "Joaquin is a fabulous character; only that is well known." *Courtesy California State Library*

Residence in the Mines
From Our Log Cabin, Indian Bar, August 4, 1852

One of these unhappy persons was a very gentlemanly young Spaniard who implored for death in the most moving manner. He appealed to the judges in the most eloquent manner—as gentlemen, as men of honor, representing to them that to be deprived of life was nothing in comparison to the never-to-be-effaced stain of the vilest convict's punishment—to which they had sentenced him. Finding all his entreaties disregarded, he swore a most solemn oath, that he would murder every American that he should chance to meet alone, and as he is a man of the most dauntless courage, and rendered desperate by a burning sense of disgrace, which will cease only with his life, he will doubtless keep his word. . . .

In a strange way Mrs. Knapp's letter helped to launch the saga of Joaquin Murieta . . .

John Rollin Ridge and the Murieta Legend

It was the worst of times when John Ridge, son of Major Ridge, the Cherokee leader, brought his young white bride to his father's home in Georgia's beautiful Ookellogee Valley.

Reverberations from White Path's rebellion still echoed across Georgia, and the United States was demanding that the Cherokee Nation surrender its land and move across Mississippi. Delegations had been sent to Washington, and while the Great White Father made many promises, the Cherokee leaders soon realized that they were written in smoke.

The times were dangerous and uncertain, but for young John Ridge it was an opportunity to display his charm and leadership. Colonel Thomas Loraine McKenney, the nation's first head of the Indian Bureau, said of him: "He had youth, education, talents, piety, enthusiasm, and was a son of the race out of which it was proposed to rear a new nation."

And of his wife, McKenney said:

"She loved the young Indian . . . and there is reason to believe that her example and her counsels were eminently useful to her adopted countrymen. . . ."

The great Cherokee, Sequoyah, had given his people the gift of unification and by the time young Ridge returned to his people, the first issue of the *Cherokee Phoenix* had been published in a log cabin from type shipped from Boston and sent two hundred miles in a wagon over the mountains.

Young Ridge used the newspaper to further his father's argument that removal was the only way for the Cherokee to survive. He was bitterly opposed by John Ross, Chief of the Nation. Ridge became secretary and interpreter for the Cherokee delegation sent to Washington to make a final appeal to the President, and there he was a familiar figure in the White House and Senate. However, the protests and appeals of the Cherokee delegation were ignored: the Nation was forced to give up its lands and move along The Trail of Tears into the barren, hostile Indian Territory across the Mississippi.

John Rollin Ridge (Yellow Bird), the Cherokee journalist who created the Joaquin Murieta legend. *Courtesy California State Library*

After a short time jealousy, greed, and ambition accomplished the white man's ultimate goal—to force Cherokees to fight Cherokees.

In the struggle for national leadership, Ridge and his father were murdered as outlaws who had betrayed their people.

The white wife of Ridge, who had come to the beautiful Georgia valley as his bride, who had survived the savage tribal feuds, power struggles, and the terrible winter journey to what the white man had promised would be their Promised Land, sadly packed her belongings and left for Arkansas with her son, John Rollin Ridge.

After she died her son moved to California and became a journalist and free-lance writer, often using his Cherokee name, "Yellow Bird." He wrote short stories, articles, and poems, but only a small amount of his work appeared in print.

Sometime during the winter of 1853-54, he read the newspaper accounts of Captain Love's capture of "Joaquin Murietta" and Shirley Knapp's letters to the *Pioneer Magazine*, which he visited frequently, trying to sell his material.

He became fascinated with the idea of a bold, handsome Robin Hood, driven into outlawry by the lash of the hated Yankee miners who had accused him falsely of a crime. By spring he had finished what he called *The Life and Adventures of Joaquin Murieta, Celebrated California Bandit.*[3]

It was a preposterous, completely fictionalized, slim paperback published by a San Francisco printer, but it created the legend of Joaquin Murieta.

Ridge's timing was perfect. It was an era of outlawry among the native Californians, who had watched the blue-eyed gringos tearing apart the earth in search of gold and gradually destroying their pastoral way of life. Since the discovery at Sutter's Mill there had been a cultural and economic clash between the strangers and the natives. Governor Pio Pico summed up the growing tension:

"We find ourselves suddenly threatened by hordes of Yankee immigrants who have already begun to flock into our country and whose progress we can't stop. . . ."

The Treaty of Guadalupe Hidalgo, signed on May 20, 1848, concluded the cession of California to the Americans, but the army of tough, extremely ruthless gold seekers ignored the promise of the treaty makers that the rights, liberty, and freedom of the native Californians would always be protected by the power of the United States.

The feudal economy of the large *ranchos* began to disappear; villages, towns, gold camps—all American in style—emerged, leaving the original residents adrift: first bewildered, then angry and full of hate for the brash, unthinking Yankees.

The gold rush frontier cried out for a Robin Hood, a dashing outlaw figure who could capture the imagination of this new land. Ridge recognized this urge. His completely fictitious Joaquin was in the classic style: "gracefully built and active as a tiger" with a melodramatic and accepted motivation for turning outlaw—his beautiful bride, Rosita, had been raped by a band of evil American miners while he was forced to watch; his brother had been lynched; and he had been whipped by the laughing, contemptuous gold seekers.

With some variations to fit the area and time, the same tale was told about Jesse James and most of the other western outlaws in the *Police Gazette* read by countless millions in saloons, barbershops, and gambling halls—and by armies of small boys in barns and privies . . .[4]

In Ridge's version, after the whipping Murieta swears a terrible oath of vengeance and takes off to the mountains with his bride and faithful band, including Three-Fingered Jack. This Jack is not a deadly rogue and horse thief, as was the real Garcia, but is rather a knight of the forest whose heart is filled with love and admiration for his gallant leader.

For the rest of the tale Murieta wades in blood as he robs and kills to avenge his honor but also does many deeds to protect the weak, usually beautiful maidens and those who aid him. The motivation is revealed when Murieta discovers an old American friend from the gold camp where he was flogged. As they embrace, Murieta sadly explains:

A conception of Joaquin Murieta, painted in the Civil War period by Charles Christian Nahl. It now hangs in San Francisco's Union League Club. The romantic and completely fictitious Murieta was created by John Rollin Ridge, son of the famous Cherokee leader, John Ridge. *The James D. Horan Civil War and Western Americana Collection*

"I am not the man I was. I am a deep-dyed scoundrel. But so help me God! I was driven to it by oppression and wrong!"

Seven thousand copies of the book were sold, but all Ridge had left were his old debts and poor credit; the publisher slipped out of San Francisco with the profits, leaving Ridge, as he wrote to a friend, "to whistle for our money." He added that he was planning to have the book republished in "the Atlantic States," but apparently he became so disgusted that he abandoned the project.

Five years passed. During that period Ridge's Murieta became California's Robin Hood. Then, in the autumn of 1859, the editor of the California *Police Gazette* decided to resurrect the bandit for his readers. He assigned someone to rewrite Ridge's slim paperback, altering a few fictional "facts" such as changing the name of Ridge's Rosita, wife of the outlaw, to Carmela. The serial ran for ten issues with illustrations by the noted California artist Charles Christian Nahl. From the serial came another paperback, and sales soared.

During the Civil War years Ridge's "life story" of Murieta was lifted by writers and publishers in many countries; in Spain he became as legendary as in California.

Charles E. B. Howe of San Francisco wrote a five-act play, *Joaquin Murieta de Castille*. Now Ridge's original Rosita became Belloro, which the author explained meant "Golden Bell." Although the play was published, there is no evidence that it was ever produced.

Ridge, meanwhile, was understandably bitter. He constantly complained of the literary piracy but apparently didn't take any legal moves to collect damages. But he did bring out a new edition with an angry foreword, denouncing the "spurious edition" of his work which had been published and complaining that his authorship had been damaged by the "crude interpolations."

However, as Joseph Henry Jackson points out in his excellent *Bad Company*, the other writers had actually improved Ridge's fiction; purple passages were trimmed, Three-Fingered Jack's passionate orations were cut to the bone, and the entire narrative was tightened.

Ridge never lived to see his new version of Murieta; he died in 1871 in San Francisco shortly before the book was published.

The poets next discovered Ridge's tale. Cincinnatus Hiner Miller composed an atrociously bad poem called "California," which was published in the Northwest and later in England; Miller made Rosita a descendant of Montezuma. Next came the Beadle Dime Library. That firm's prolific Joseph E. Badger wrote *Joaquin, the Saddle King*, and this one was pirated by another paperback firm as *Joaquin: The Claude Duval of California: A Romance Based on Truth.*[5]

By the 1870s Ridge's original and plagiarized versions of Murieta had made the fictitious outlaw a popular folklore figure in the United States and throughout Europe.

Finally the outlaw's story became history. In 1888, Hubert Howe Bancroft, whose California histories are still reference sources, incorporated Murieta into his *California Pastoral: 1769-1848.*[6]

Bancroft took his version from Ridge, adding some fictitious dialogue when needed.

Joaquin Murieta: The Terror of the Stanislaus

Joaquin Murieta, the terror of the Stanislaus, has a history, which, though crimson with murder, abounds in dramatic interest. He was a Mexican of good blood . . . , born in the department of Sonora, and received an ordinary education in the schools of his native country. In his youth he is said to have been mild, affectionate, and genial in disposition, the pet of the maestro, and a favorite among his fellows of the playground. Yet, while acknowledging the pulpy sweetness of his boyhood, it is safe to presume that there was a dash of bandit blood in the veins of Joaquin, which was eventually to fire his heart with the madness for an outlaw life. As Joaquin and his Rosita reached the new El Dorado, the first flash of the great gold fever was then spreading over its wild ranges. In the memorable spring of 1850 we find him engaged as an honest miner among the Stanislaus placers, where he had a rich claim, and was fast amassing a competency, when, one evening, a party of some half dozen American desperadoes swaggered into his little cabin where with Rosita he was resting after a hard day's work.

Five years after John Rollin Ridge published his fictitious account of Joaquin Murieta, the editor of the *California Police Gazette* rewrote Ridge's book, using the original dialogue, and serialized it in the *Gazette* in ten installments. He then brought out a paperback book illustrated by the famous California artist Christian Nahl. This is the cover of the exceedingly rare book published by the *Gazette* in late 1859. *Courtesy Bancroft Library, University of California, Berkeley*

This engraving of the fictitious Joaquin Murieta by Thomas Armstrong, a staff artist for the *Sacramento Union*, became the model for all conceptions of later Murieta paintings and sketches. It first appeared in the *Union* on April 22, 1853. This print is from an original copy of the newspaper's "Steamer Edition." *Courtesy California State Library*

"You don't know, I suppose, that greasers are not allowed to take gold from American ground," began the leader insolently.

"If you mean that I have no right to my claim, in obtaining which I have conformed to all the laws of the district, I certainly did not know it," answered Joaquin with quiet dignity.

"Well, you may know it now. And you have got to go; so vamoose, git, and that instanter, and take that trumpery with you," jerking his thumb toward Rosita. "The women if anything are worse than the men."

Joaquin stepped forward with clinched hand, while the hot blood mantled his face: "I will leave these parts if such be your wish, but speak one word against that woman, and though you were ten times an American, you shall rue it."

Scarcely were these words uttered when another of the party reached over and struck Joaquin a severe blow in the face. The latter sprang for his bowie-knife, which he had thrown upon the bed on returning from his work, when Rosita, instinct with the danger such rashness threatened, threw herself before him, and seizing him in her arms, frantically held him. For the intruders to thrust aside the woman and strike the unarmed man senseless was the work of a moment. When Joaquin awoke to consciousness, it was to find Rosita prostrate, her face buried in her clothes, sobbing hysterically. Then he knew the worst.

Fleeing from his outraged home on the Stanislaus, Joaquin and his devoted companion sought refuge on a modest little rancho, hid away in the rugged seclusion of the Calaveras mountains. His dream of peace was soon broken, however, by the sudden apparition of two bearded missionaries, whose monosyllabic warning, "Git!" threw down his hopes and household gods once more into the dust. The hapless twain were driven out from the shadows of Calaveras, and once more became fugitives in the land. We next find Joaquin working as a miner at Murphy Diggings; but luck was against him in the placers, and he finally assumed the gay and remunerative occupation of monte-dealer, a department of industry at the time deemed respectable, even for Americans, not a few of them being thorough adepts in the art of "layouts," and both swift and relentless in catching their customers "in the door."

The new vocation was well-suited to the suave young Sonorense, and fortune for a while seemed to befriend him, the uncoined gold of the miners rolling into his ever thickening purse. But his pathway was destined to blush with redder hues than rosy fortune wears. While riding into town a horse that he had borrowed from a half-brother of his who lived on a rancho nearby, he was accosted by an American claiming the animal to have been stolen from him. Murieta pleaded that it was not his, but borrowed. This, however, availed him not. Indeed, it seems that the claim was a well-founded one, and Murieta was charged with the theft, the penalty whereof was death. A half-drunken crowd soon gathered around, and Murieta's protestations of innocence, and offers of money for a respite until witnesses could be forthcoming to prove the truth of his statement, were disregarded. He was pulled down from the saddle, and amid cries of "Kill the thief! Hang the greaser!" they hurriedly carried him to the rancho of his brother, whom they summarily launched into eternity from the branch of a neighboring tree. Joaquin was stripped, bound to the same tree, and flogged. While the heavy lash was lacerating his back, a demoniac expression appeared upon his face; he looked around and stamped the features of each of his persecutors on the tablets of his memory. When the executioners had finished their work, they departed, leaving him with his dead. It was then that Joaquin Murieta registered his oath of vengeance which he so relentlessly kept, rarely sparing even the innocent. From that hour he was the implacable foe of every American, and even of every being that bore the resemblance of a gringo. Lucifer had him now for his own.

Within a few months the dashing boy was at the head of an organized band of highwaymen, which ravaged the country in every direction. This band consisted sometimes of twenty, and at other times of as many as eighty. The boy leader gave proof every day of possessing a peculiar genius controlling the most accomplished scoundrels that had ever congregated in Christendom. He was their master; his word was their law, and woe betide him who dared to disobey, while to break faith with a fellow-robber was quick death. A member of the band, perforated by four bullets, was captured in February, 1853, at Los Muertos, near Los Angeles, brought to San Andreas, tried, and hanged by the people. He was but an humble member of the profession, and when he saw that death was certain, he was induced to talk a little. He said that no member of the fraternity was much respected who had not killed his man, and each ranked in importance according to the number that he had slain. This was something as it is in the army. Every member was bound under most solemn oaths, first, to obey his superiors. Disobedience was punished with death. There was hardly one chance in a hundred that a traitor could escape; for it was the duty and pleasure of the betrayed whose lives were jeopardized by the treachery to hunt and slay the informer.

This completeness of organization, coupled with the awful power wielded by the leader, enabled the band during nearly three years to carry on its operations, and its boyish chief to flit between towns and country, flipping his fingers in the face of police and people, while throughout the length and breadth of the Californian valley, from Shasta to Tulare, and along the coast line of missions the country was wailing its dead and ringing with rewards. The modus operandi to accomplish the purposes of the organization was as follows: Each subaltern was restricted to certain limits beyond which he dare not step. He had to be at all times ready to receive an order from any captain or lieutenant of the band. His eyes and ears were to be always open, and his mouth closed; passing events were to be narrowly observed, such as the yield of the various mining claims, the drift of the gold dust, where a company kept their money, or certain Chinamen had hidden theirs. It was, moreover, his duty to shelter and protect any of the brotherhood needing his assistance; to warn them of danger, and provide horses and aid to escape; and generally, to assist them in all their undertakings.

Joaquin was always splendidly mounted; in fact much of his success depended on his horses. It was the special business of a certain portion of the brotherhood to keep the company well supplied with the best horses in the country. There were, also, members living in towns, and among the peaceable inhabitants, pursuing honest occupations, who were spies, and kept the officers of the band advised of matters they were desirous of knowing.

To relate the hundreds of incidents in which Joaquin and his chief captains and lieutenants personally displayed their skill and courage, would occupy more space than I can devote to the matter. I will, however, narrate some of the most daring deeds of the young leader.

In 1851 while sojourning in a secluded part of San José, he attended a fandango, where he became involved in a fracas, for which he was arrested and fined $12 by the magistrate. Being in charge of Deputy Sheriff Clark, who was not aware of his being the robber chief, he invited the latter to go with him to his house for the money. Clark had become obnoxious to Murieta for his vigorous pursuit of the band. On reaching an unfrequented place the robber suddenly turned upon the officer, and with a smile said, "Accept the compliments of Joaquin," and drove his jeweled poignard to the hilt in his breast. In the autumn of the same year Murieta and his band were at the Sonoran camp near Marysville, where they committed a number of robberies, and five murders, every one of the murdered men bearing on his neck the fatal mark of the flying noose. All had been lassoed, and dragged at the saddle bow by the lariat. In the wild region west of the white pyramid of Shasta, the band roamed many months engaged in horse-stealing, with now and then a murder. Once, while two of the band were galloping near the town of Hamilton, an elk rushed past them, hotly pursued by a beautiful girl mounted on a fine steed. She hurled her lasso at the animal and secured it, only to find herself in turn held fast by the lariats of the two banditti. Her terror was distracting. She implored them not to harm her, but little did they care for her entreaties. There was only one voice on earth which they would heed, and that came unexpectedly, as if from another world. "Restore that girl to her horse instantly." It was Joaquin who spoke.

One evening not long afterward, Joaquin was sitting at a monte table in a small town on the Feather River, when an American boastfully offered to bet $500 that he would kill the scoundrel Joaquin the first time he met him. Carried away by one of his dare-devil impulses, Joaquin sprang upon the table, and thrusting his pistol in the man's face cried, "I take the bet; Joaquin is before you"; then tossing the corner of his serape over his shoulder, he jumped down, strode out of the room, mounted his horse and rode away with some of his henchmen at his heels.

In the spring of 1852 Murieta drove 300 stolen horses through Southern California into Sonora. On his return after a few weeks, he was quartered at the Arroyo de Cantúa, situated between the Coast Range and the Tulare lake. It is possible that it was just previous to this that they sojourned for a while in Los Angeles and vicinity. Riding with some of his men toward San Luis Gonzaga, and his purse being light, Murieta, after the manner of Robin Hood, resolved to rob the first man that came along. The victim happened to be a young fellow named Albert Ruddle, who was driving a wagon loaded with groceries. Joaquin requested the loan of what money he had, promising to return it at an early opportunity. Ruddle made a movement as if to draw a weapon. He was told to keep quiet or he would be killed, but as he persisted, Joaquin with a muttered imprecation, slashed him across the neck with his knife, almost severing the head from the body. After rifling the dead man's pockets, the robbers rode off.

While in Los Angeles for a few days, he heard that Deputy Sheriff Wilson of Santa Bárbara was on his trail, with the avowed intention of taking him dead or alive. He got up a sham fight between two Indians in front of the hotel where Wilson was staying. The latter came out to see the fight, when Joaquin rode swiftly to him, and hissing his own terrible name in his ear, drove a bullet through his head and drove away.

Riding one day alone toward the town of Los Hornitos, the chief met young Joe Lake, a playmate of his boyhood. In the course of their conversation Joaquin revealed his present mode of living, and said, "Joe, you are the only American whose good opinion I crave. Believe me my friend, I was driven to this by hellish wrongs." "Why don't you leave the country, and abandon your criminal life?" answered Joe. "Too late, Joe, I must die now as I live, pistol in hand. Do not betray me; do not divulge having met me here. If you do, I shall be very sorry," significantly tapping the stock of his revolver. Lake deemed it his duty to apprise the authorities of Murieta's presence, and the usual persecution began. The next morning a portly ranchero came up to Lake, and saying, "You betrayed me, Joe!" plunged a knife into his breast, and rode away unharmed.

One evening, Joaquin rode into a camp where about 25 miners were at supper, and sitting sideways on his horse entered into conversation with them. It so happened that a man who knew him by sight soon after came from the creek, and on seeing him called out, "That is Joaquin; why, in the name of God don't you kill him?" Putting spurs to his horse with one bound he cleared the camp and dashed down the cañon. Finding his way blocked there he returned toward the camp, to avail himself of a narrow coyote trail around the brow of a precipice that overhung the awful depths of the cañon below. A shower of bullets greeted his reappearance, but none touched him, as he dashed up and along that dizzy path, waving his dagger and shouting defiance.

In the early part of March, 1853, Joaquin, unattended, visited a large Mexican camp on Burns creek, about twenty miles from the town of Mariposa. He presented the appearance of a dashing cavalier, with plumed sombrero, gold laced cloak, and gayly caparisoned steed, as he slowly rode down the principal thoroughfare of the camp, tinkling his spurs to the measures of some lively fandango, and was the cynosure of many admiring glances from the eyes of the señoritas. Passing in front of a saloon he called for a drink, and was just lifting it to his lips, when an American, one of two who were standing together and had recognized him, drew his revolver and fired a shot that cut the plume of the brigand's hat. The drink was never taken, but Joaquin, after having wounded one of the Americans in the arm and the other in the abdomen, galloped away without a scratch.

Later in the same month, Murieta and three or four of his men robbed a Chinese camp at Rich gulch, not far from San Andreas, of about $10,000, leaving three dead and five wounded. The next morning they entered another Chinese camp at the foot of the mountains, gashed the throats of three of the Chinamen, mortally wounded five others, and carried off some $3,000 in gold. They next visited several other Chinese camps, all of which they desolated, the cries of their victims being heard at long distances. Finding themselves pursued by a party of Americans, they calmly continued their devastation, until the pursuers were within half a mile of them, when they mounted their steeds, and rode away with the speed of the wind.

On one occasion, Murieta riding leisurely in disguise through Stockton, he saw the hand-bills offering $1,000 for his capture. Taking from his pocket a pencil, he wrote on the margin beneath one of them, "I will give $5,000. Joaquin," and quietly rode away.

One night a cattle-dealer, whose name was Cocariouris, was camping with one companion on the San Joaquin, when they were visited by several Mexicans, splendidly mounted and gaily attired, who asked for supper and a place to sleep. Their occupation being quite evident, they were treated with much politeness, and their requests promptly complied with. In the morning the robber was cordially greeted by the cattle dealer:

"And how does Señor Joaquin this morning?"

"You know me, then," replied the robber.

"I knew you the moment I saw you," said Cocariouris.

"And why did you not kill me last night when I slept, and secure the reward?" demanded Joaquin.

"I do not like to kill men; I do not care for the reward," replied the host. "Besides, you never injured me; you asked for food; if every man deserving to be hanged went supperless, there would be an empty chair at more tables than mine."

"True," replied Joaquin, meditatively, "and I will see that you lose nothing by your broad philosophy."

Cocariouris was often on the road with large herds of stock, not one head of which was ever, to his knowledge, touched by any of Murieta's band.

At last, the people throughout the state were aroused to the importance of suppressing this overwhelming evil. For three years this bloody work had been going on—a long time in that rushing epoch—and it was a reflection on the manhood of California that the robbers should go so long uncaught. At length, on the 17th of May, 1853, the legislature of California passed an act authorizing Harry Love to bring his mountaineer's experience, bravery, and tested nerve into action, with a well-organized and equipped body of twenty mounted rangers, to hunt the marauders down. Love was soon in the field, and lost no time in getting upon the track of the brigands.

Poor Joaquin! Love encompassed him without and within. For his girl, Antonia la Molinera, who went about with him dressed in men's clothes, proved false, having run away with a traitorous member of the band, Pancho Daniel. Murieta swore he would kill both of them; and Antonia when she heard of it, and knowing him so well, and realizing that her life was not safe for a moment as long as he was at liberty, resolved to betray him into the hands of justice.

Murieta sent first Vergara to kill her, but Vergara proved false, and let the girl live, abandoning the banditti, and going to work on the rancho of Palos Verdes, where was later Wilmington. Murieta sent another member of his band to bring back Vergara, but a few days thereafter the messenger was found murdered in the street in Los Angeles. Likewise, others of Joaquin's girls were giving him trouble. Thus discord was in the camp, men proving traitorous and women false, which shows that the life of a robber is not always a happy one.

Stealthily enough Harry Love, with his fierce eyes and flowing hair, followed upon the trail of Joaquin, spying upon him by night, and keeping under close cover by day, thirsting for the blood-money, thirsting both for the blood and the money, eager to slay the slayer and rob the robber.

Thus the toils which must inevitably sooner or later end such a career were closing round Joaquin. In the latter part of July, with eight of his rangers, Love came upon a party of Mexicans in camp near the Tejon pass. Six of them were seated round a small fire, where preparations for breakfast were going forward, while the seventh, he of the slender figure, and graceful limbs, and large black eyes, and long black hair, a perfect Apollo, richly dressed, blooming in the pride of health and manly beauty, was washing down a superb bay horse, at a little distance from the fire, with some water which he held in a pan. Joaquin was unknown to the rangers, who dashed into the camp before they were discovered, and succeeded in cutting the robbers off from their horses. Captain Love rode up to the one standing by his horse, and enquired whither they were going.

"To Los Angeles," the chief replied.

Turning to one of the others, the captain put the same question when an entirely different answer was returned. Joaquin bit his lip and spoke angrily, "I command here; address yourself to me." He then moved a few steps toward the fire, around which lay the saddles, blankets, and arms of the party. He was ordered to stop, and when he did not heed, Love cocked his revolver upon him and told him to stand or he would shoot. The chief tossed his hair back scornfully while his eyes blazed with the lightnings of his wrath, and stepping backward, he stood again by the side of his handsome steed, his jeweled hand resting lightly on its mane. Three-Fingered Jack stood a little distance away, fully armed and waiting for his chief. At this critical moment Lieutenant Byrnes, with whom Joaquin was well acquainted, moved up, and Joaquin, realizing that the game was up, called out to his followers to save themselves the best they could, and threw himself upon the back of his charger without saddle or bridle, and sped down the mountain like a tempest. He leaped his horse over a precipice, when he fell, but was on his feet again in a moment, and remounting, the daring rider dashed on.

Close at his heels came the rangers, firing as they rode, and soon the gallant steed, struck in the side, fell to the earth, and Joaquin ran on afoot. Three balls had pierced his body, when he turned with a lifted hand toward his pursuers, and called out: "It is enough; the work is done,"—reeled, fell upon his right arm, and, sinking slowly down before his pursuers, gave up the ghost without a groan.

Three-Fingered Jack, cornered, fought like a tiger, but the end was at hand. And so with others of the company. Claudio had fallen some time before. The bandits, now left without an efficient leader, and admonished by the swift and sorrowful fate of Joaquin, broke up the organization, and stole away from the theatre of their crimes. For purposes of identification, the head of Joaquin, and the mutilated hand of Three-Fingered Jack, were severed from the bodies, and, preserved in spirits, were brought to San Francisco in August, 1853, by Black and Nuttall, two of Harry Love's rangers. The head was placed on exhibition, as the following notice, which appeared in the papers of the city on the 18th of August, and for several days following, will show: "Joaquin's Head! is to be seen at King's, corner of Halleck and Sansome streets. Admission one dollar." Then followed certificates of persons who had known Joaquin, as to the identity of the head. No money was recovered, though one of the prisoners declared that Jack had thrown away a heavy purse of gold during the chase. It is probable that others did the same, as the heavy operations of the band must have kept them well supplied with dust and coin. The growth, after death, of the hair on the head of Joaquin, and the fingernails of Jack's hand, caused quite a sensation among those not accustomed to such phenomena.

Another California historian, Theodore Hittell, also gave Murieta's story the stamp of truth when he included the tale of the outlaw in his works. However, he was more cautious than Bancroft, pointing out that while he quoted Ridge, the sources on Murieta were "unreliable."

The majority of California's county historians also accepted Ridge's version, with the usual "pioneers" contributing "eyewitness accounts" of the outlaw's robberies and Robin Hood deeds.

Illustrations for all the works were difficult; the early *Police Gazette* used Nahl's drawings, but there were no daguerreotypes or photographs. As Murieta "biographies" increased, so did the versions of his likeness; they ranged from crude woodcuts to Nahl's classical painting of the outlaw: handsome, daring, black eyes flashing fire as he thunders across some unknown landscape. Curiously, no one had photographed "Murieta's head" while it was exhibited in side shows or museums, although ads show that it was still being exhibited as late as the time of San Francisco's earthquake in 1906.

Ridge's fictionalized hero, plagiarized, rewritten, and distorted, went from the printing presses to the stage and finally into films.

After the early moviemakers graduated from the Coney Island "peep show" era and moved to a quiet California suburb named Hollywood, writers began hunting for romantic heroes. Murieta, of course, fitted every specification; he was not only a handsome, brave cavalier who had conquered evil in the Wild West, but the motivation that had driven him into a life of outlawry—the rape of his beautiful bride, and so forth—was superb.

The scriptwriters blew the dust from Ridge's books, the *Police Gazette* serials, and the many volumes which followed, then typewriters began clicking. When they finished, Ridge and his imitators would never have recognized their originals: Joaquin Murieta—the Napoleon of Banditry, Marauder of the Mines, the Saddle King, the Claude Duval of California—was now embroidered beyond belief. The script was based on Walter Noble Burns's "biography," *The Robin Hood of El Dorado*. Burns had written other popular books on western figures such as Billy the Kid, and his book on Murieta became a best seller. It was quickly sold to Hollywood and four years later it reached the screen.

In 1936 Warner Baxter, playing the bandit's role, rode across a thousand movie screens to thrill and entertain a weary nation slowly emerging from the Depression. It was a highly improbable tale filled with villains, heroines, and thrilling chases all surrounding the dashing, handsome Baxter.

The saga of Murieta has continued with novels, newspaper series, and books perpetuating the fiction of the harassed Cherokee writer, John Rollin Ridge.

He was the West's first outlaw image maker, who turned legend into history. Many followed his example.

TIBURCIO VASQUEZ

THERE WAS NO JOHN ROLLIN RIDGE TO ROMANTICIZE Tiburcio Vasquez. He was as deadly as a knife blade and his story is as grim as a lynching.

For more than twenty years he killed, robbed, and plundered in California, escaped numerous posses, and left behind him a trail of dead men—most of them gunned down without a chance to defend themselves.

In the 1870s he was an anachronism, a throwback to the California gold rush frontier when outlaws robbed stagecoaches and mining camps. The state's era of lawlessness ended when he was finally captured and executed, and his band dispersed.

In an interview Vasquez said he was born on August 11, 1835, in Monterey. At fifteen, when the police came to question him as one of three suspects in the dance hall stabbing death of Constable William Hardimount, Vasquez fled to the interior of Monterey. It was the time when "the five Joaquins" were terrorizing the towns and gold camps and Mexicans, who watched helplessly as their land was stolen by invading hordes of American miners.

The morning after Hardimount's death vigilantes lynched the owner of the dance hall. Young Vasquez knew that he could expect little justice in the *gringo*'s court, so he hid out until friends advised him that the incident had been forgotten. He came home only to find the police waiting.

There was a gunfight and Vasquez escaped. As he later told his interviewer:

Exceedingly rare and unpublished photograph of Tiburcio Vasquez, California's legendary outlaw. After coolly inspecting the coffin he had ordered, Vasquez went to the gallows in San Jose, Santa Clara County, California, on March 19, 1875. He had been captured by a Los Angeles posse. This mounted photograph taken after the Civil War is believed to have been owned by Undersheriff Peter Warner, who knew Vasquez and headed many posses that hunted him. *The James D. Horan Civil War and Western Americana Collection*

"I went to my mother and told her I intended to commence a different life. I asked for and obtained her blessing and at once I commenced the career of a robber."[1]

Vasquez's claim that "from the beginning I had confederates with me but I was always recognized as the leader" appears to be mere boasting; there is evidence, instead, that he served his apprenticeship in the outlaw bands of Juan Soto and Tomaso Rodundo, alias "Procopio."[2]

In addition to riding in the large, organized bands he also became an expert horse thief and rustler. Extant records disclose that he was twenty when he was sent to prison for horse stealing. In the celebrated San Quentin prison riot of 1859 he made his escape, returned to stealing horses, and within a few months was back in the state penitentiary. This time he served four years and was released in the summer of 1863. He next appears as a suspect in the murder of a miner in the quicksilver camps of New Almaden near San Jose, but the case was dropped because of flimsy evidence.[3]

Although Vasquez was a small, slender man with a dark, sullen face, he gained a reputation as a frontier Don Juan, surrounded by an air of danger that captivated the wives, daughters, and sisters of miners and ranchers. One story has him running away with the daughter of a rich rancher near Mount Diablo. The father chased and shot Vasquez, then brought his daughter back home. There are several versions of this incident, but apparently it has some basis in fact, as evidenced by newspaper articles of the time.

Between his romances Vasquez increased his rustling. Near Sonoma, in the area of San Francisco Bay, he ran off a large herd of cattle but was captured by a posse and returned to San Quentin, this time for three years.

Shortly after his release Vasquez formed a band of rustlers and stagecoach robbers. They made their first strike near Soap Lake when they held up the Hollister stage. The driver threw down the box and the passengers yielded a hatful of cash and jewelry. On the way back to their hideout the bandits met Thomas McMahon, who unfortunately was carrying the weekly proceeds of his store, and Vasquez took that. But McMahon recognized him and alerted Sheriff Harry N. Morse of Alameda County, one of the finest, if little known, lawmen of the West.[4]

Morse set out after Vasquez, but in the meantime the constable of Santa Cruz had a confrontation with the gang, killing two and seriously wounding Vasquez. Weak from loss of blood, and clinging to his saddlehorn, he managed to make his way to the hills, where he was hidden by friends. During his recovery Vasquez staged raids on stagecoaches and ranches. Once, when he was advised that a sheriff's posse was staying at the New Idria mines, Vasquez slipped into the camp at night and stole the posse's horses.

His braggadocio and triumphs over the hated gringos caught the imagination of the Mexicans. In the spring of 1873 he formed a new gang and started a series of robberies. This time he had a first-rate lieutenant, Cleo Vara Chavez, a small, dark-skinned, violent man who dismissed Vasquez's former casual planning: now every strike had to be exact to the smallest detail.

Their first successful raid—on the large general store at Firebaugh's Ferry—was followed by a number of robberies of stagecoaches, inns, stores, and cattle camps from San Jose to Gilroy. Success bred recklessness; despite the warnings of Chavez, Vasquez swaggered down the muddy streets of New Idria, confident that his countrymen would not betray him.

Early photograph of San Quentin Prison when Vasquez was there. This photograph was taken by G. E. Watkins, who gained international fame from his pioneering photographs of Yosemite, then called Yo Semite. *The James D. Horan Civil War and Western Americana Collection*

In 1873 the gang turned to train robbery, but the episode became a farce. Without stopping, the fast Southern Pacific ploughed through the gang's obstacles of logs laid across the tracks, leaving the bandits—mouths open, six-shooters in hand—sprawled in the brush. Chavez, for all his cunning, should have served an apprenticeship with the James-Younger gang or the Wild Bunch.

That summer the gang returned to robbing general stores. On August 28 they rode into Tres Pines, Monterey County, to conduct what they thought would be a leisurely robbery of Andrew Snyder's general store. The five outlaws tied their horses outside and, guns drawn, walked in as Snyder was talking to a customer.

Vasquez, after being assured by Chavez that all was going well, joined his horse holder. Inside the store his gang quickly filled grain sacks with cash, food, and jewelry of the customers. The town lay quiet in the heat; nearby two teamsters, unaware that a robbery was taking place, prepared to hitch up their horses.

Suddenly a sheepherder appeared, walking toward the store. As he came closer, Vasquez barked a command to halt. The sheepman, either confused or not understanding, kept walking and Vasquez killed him.

The shot alerted the teamsters, who started to run. When they ignored Vasquez's order to halt, he clubbed one into unconsciousness with his six-shooter and killed the other. A. M. Davidson, owner of a boardinghouse, saw the shooting and started down the street, calling out a warning to his wife as she opened their front door. When he refused to halt, Vasquez killed him with a rifle shot.

A small boy darted out the rear door of the store only to be tripped by Chavez, who then cold-bloodedly clubbed the child into unconsciousness with the butt of his gun.

The gang rode out of town, grain sacks bulging with loot, leaving behind them three dead men and the unconscious teamster and child lying in the dusty street.

The "Tres Penes Massacre" horrified California's frontier. Posses combed the hills and valleys without finding any sign of Vasquez and his men.[5]

Then, in December, Vasquez led his band, now numbering eleven riders, into Kingston, a small town in Fresno County. He took over the entire community, keeping thirty-five men tied hand and foot while the gang plundered two stores and the hotel, escaping with two thousand dollars in cash and jewelry.

For the first time, reward posters appeared; within a few months Governor Newton Booth offered eight thousand dollars for the capture of the bandit leader. But Vasquez, Chavez, and their men were elusive as shadows in a forest. In February 1874 they surrounded the Coyote Hole Station and held up the Los Angeles and Owens stagecoach. The following day, in a countryside alive with posses, they robbed another line.

Meanwhile, Sheriff Morse of Alameda County was quietly gathering dossiers of information on every Mexican bandit in the territory. Unlike many sheriffs, who staged flamboyant but unsuccessful raids, Morse would ride alone into the hills, studying the haunts of the outlaws and the general topography of the area. Along the way he would make friends among the Yankee ranchers and the terrorized Mexican farmers. He also corresponded with other sheriffs and wardens of jails to learn the habits and weaknesses of the territory's more notorious outlaws.

The clannish Mexicans were not suspicious; they saw only a beardless young gringo riding about the foothills seeking range for his stock.[6]

Finally Morse would move, obtaining warrants and arresting the wanted men and outlaw leaders, most often going alone and handcuffing them at gunpoint in dance halls, backwoods saloons, and fandangos.

As a magazine writer described him:

"The audacity of the man and the rapidity of his movements bewildered the outlaws. No one could tell when he was safe or when he might be free of the searching eye of the tireless official. Little by little the beardless boy assumed the proportions of a relentless terror to the criminal community, and outlawry no longer stalked defiantly through its old haunts. . . ."[7]

In March 1874, Governor Booth appointed Morse to form a company of eight expert manhunters to hunt down Vasquez, and persuaded the legislature to appropriate five thousand dollars for his expenses. As soon as the winter rains were over, Morse led his band into the mountains. A precise man, Morse logged the miles they traveled: from March 12 to May 12 they rode 2,700 miles, making a daily average of over 45 miles through some of the wildest country in the West.

While Morse and his deputies fought their way through the brush of southern California, Vasquez's band raided the Repetto sheep ranch near the San Gabriel Mission.

In what must be one of the extraordinary scenes in western outlawry, Repetto argued with the outlaw chieftain that while it was true he had received ten thousand dollars for a recent sale of sheep, he had used the money to buy land.

"Very well," Vasquez told him, "if you can prove it by your books and statements I will excuse you."[8]

Repetto then produced his ledgers. While the gang waited outside, Vasquez and Repetto went over the entries. It took hours but finally Vasquez was satisfied; Repetto had proven that he had used the ten thousand dollars to buy land.

Vasquez congratulated Repetto on his honesty, then asked for a loan! Repetto agreed to let him have a few hundred dollars. He wrote out a check and gave it to a member of his family, who was to bring it to the bank and return with the cash. However, the bank's officer became suspicious and alerted the sheriff. A posse rode up to the house but was spotted by Vasquez's lookouts. The outlaws were trailed to Arroyo Seco but escaped the posses.

There are two versions of the capture of Vasquez in May 1874; one by Morse, the other by Sheriff William Rowland of Los Angeles. Morse claimed that by paying what he called "a consideration" to a Mexican in Los Angeles, he located Vasquez's hiding place in Alison Canyon; the bandit leader was staying at the home of a wealthy rancher, "Greek George" Allen. Out of courtesy, Morse says, he met with Sheriff Rowland and told him that he planned to raid Allen's adobe house with his posse. The Los Angeles sheriff insisted

Rare early photograph of Los Angeles at the time of Tiburcio Vasquez. It was then a farming community of stables, dirt streets, a "billiard saloon," and an occasional windmill. *The James D. Horan Civil War and Western Americana Collection*

Los Angeles Daily Star

FRIDAY..........MAY 15, 1874

THE HUNT ENDED.

THE BANDIT IN THE TOILS.

VASQUEZ CAPTURED AT LAST.

FULL PARTICULARS OF THE HUNT.

As the clerk of the City Council was about to read the last communication to that body yesterday, about 4:30 P. M., an unusual stir about the front attracted some attention, and in a moment more, City Fathers, City Clerk, City Surveyor, City Reporters and everybody else in the room, were making for the front door. Instinctively we supposed Vasques had something to do with the fuss. We were right. Vasques was lying pale and bloody in a light wagon, in front of the entrance to the city jail. A surging crowd was gathering around. Two men who were taken in his company, at the time of the capture, were taken into jail and locked up. In a moment after Vasques himself was lifted from the wagon and was borne into the city prison. Dr. Wise presented himself; and, assisted by several medical gentlemen of this city, rendered the wounded robber such surgical services as he required. The result of the examination showed a buckshot in his left arm, one in the left leg, one in left side of head, one in front of the pectoral region, passing out under the left arm, and one in the left arm. The balls were extracted, the wounds pronounced not dangerous and opinion expressed that he would be well in a few days.

During the time referred to Mr. Miles, who lent Vasques his watch out in the San Gabriel region last April, came into the room. He was at once recognized by the wounded man—in fact the recognition was mutual. Mr. Hartley, the Chief of Police, had taken Mr. Miles' watch into his keeping. It was returned to the proper owner. Mr. M.'s chain was missing, however; Vasques said nothing about it at the time, but after Dr. Wise and his associates had dressed his wound he requested Dr. Wise to take his porte-monnaie from his hip pocket. It was done and Vasques opened it and handed the missing chain to Dr. W. and requested him to return it to its rightful owner. He remarked "it belongs to him *now*," emphasizing the last word as much as to say, "he might have whistled for it if they had not caught me." While his wounds were being dressed Mr. B. F. Hartley, Chief of Police, one of his captors, asked him why he (Vasques,) had asked him (Hartley,) what his name was. Quoth Vasques, "Usted es un hombre valiente lo mismo con yo." (You are …

… come afoot or on horseback, with three hours the start of his pursuers, Cuban bloodhounds would have compassed his capture. A sudden, well arranged surprise was the only chance to secure him. It has been effected, and in the manner hereinafter related.

After the futile pursuit of the robber up the Tejunga pass, and over the ground described by the STAR, in its full account of the chase inaugurated after the Repetto robbery, Mr. Wm. Rowland, Sheriff of this county, came to the conclusion that any further prosecution of the quest in that manner and direction was a waste of time, energy and money. His subordinates were ordered to desist, and many and loud were the complaints lodged against him for inaction and inefficiency.

Mr. Rowland, however, kept on the even tenor of his way, and availing himself of every possible source of information, at length became satisfied that the long sought for prize was within his grasp, and he quietly arranged for his capture. On Wednesday night he received positive information of the whereabouts of Tiburcio Vasquez. He had kept for sometime a list of names from which to choose a party to undertake the arrest. He organized his party as follows: Mr. Albert Johnston, Under Sheriff; Major H. M. Mitchell, attorney at law of this city; Mr. J. S. Bryant, city constable; Mr. E. Harris, policeman; Mr. Thos. Rogers, of the Palace Saloon; Mr. D. K. Smith, a citizen of this county; Mr. B. F. Hartley, Chief of Police and deputy City Marshal, and Mr. Beers, of San Francisco and special correspondent of the San Francisco Chronicle. Sheriff Rowland intended to accompany the party, but his informant told him emphatically that if he left the city and was not seen early in the morning, unless Vasquez was captured at the earliest hour, the game would break cover and be over the hills, and far away. The sequel as shown by the arrest of Greek George, which we will refer to again, proved the soundness of the advice. The horses for the pursuing party were sent one by one on Wednesday evening to the corral of Mr. Jones, on Spring street, near Seventh. One by one the above party met at the rendezvous, and at 1:30 A. M. on Thursday the party of eight were in the saddle and on their way to the spot, which for many years will be pointed out as the scene of the capture.

Greek George's ranch lies about ten miles due west from Los Angeles. It is situated at the base of a mountain, one of a series of semi detached spurs between which there are a dozen trails, known only to the *habitues* of that section, which afford egress to the San Fernando plains. The dwelling house on the ranch is an old adobe, forming a letter L, the foot of the letter facing the mountain range, the shank lying north and south. Behind the house and but a short distance from it runs a comparatively disused road, leading from the San Vincente through La Brea rancho, and thence to this city, behind this road the mountains, and in front of the house a small monte of willows grown up around a spring and beyond these a rolling plai… stre ching to the … ern end … u…

… there was another man (also a native,) was driven up, from the direction of Greek George's. It was a box wagon. It was not long before the plan of capture was decided upon. Six of the party remained. The extra man with the wagon made seven. Mr. Hartley, who speaks Spanish fluently, was instructed to inform the driver that he was to turn his horses heads, allow all six of the party and his extra man to lie down in the wagon bed and then drive back to Greek George's and as close to the house as possible; that if he gave a sign or made an alarm his life would pay the forfeit. In due time the house was reached. In a moment the party were out of the wagon and on their feet with shot guns and rifles cocked and ready for what might offer. Mr. Hartley and Mr. Beers went to the west side of the house, the other four to the southern passing around the eastern end. The foremost of the party had hardly reached the door opening into the dining room when a women opened it partly. Seeing the armed party of four approaching she gave an exclamation of fright and attempted to close it. The party burst in, Mr. Harris leading the way and seeing the retreating form of the prize they sought leaving the table and plunging through the door leading into the kitchen.

Harris was close upon his heels and Vasques with the agility of a mountain cat had jumped through the narrow window or rather opening which admitted the light, when Harris fired at the vanishing form with his Henry rifle, exclaiming "There he goes through the window." The party left the house as precipitatedly as they entered it. Vasques stood for a second of time irresolute. Whether to seek cover in the monte or rush for his horse seemed the all important question. He seemed to decide for the horse—doubtless he would have given ten kingdoms if he had had them, to be astride of him—and started, when Mr. Hartley fired; turning, he sought another direction, when one after another, shot after shot, showed him the utter hopelessness of escape. He had already been wounded, just how severely we have already told. He had fallen but recovered himself; blood was spouting from his shoulder and streaming from his wounds. He threw up his hands, approached the party and said with a cold, passionless smile wreathing his thin lips, "Boys you have done well; I have been a d—d fool; but it is all my own fault." He was taken to the courtyard on the southern side of the house, and laid upon an extemporized pallet. Not a murmur, scarcely a contortion of the visage, bespoke either pain, remorse, or any other emotion of the mind or soul.

The house was entered and a young man whose name is supposed to be Labrado, was captured in the north room before described. This was the arsenal of the robber gang. T… Henry rifles and one Spenc… latest patterns and … ship, besides other … there and taken … Mitchell a… the p…

… pared to "welcome them with bloody hands to hospitable graves," nobody could know, but determined to capture him if possible they "went for him," and they got him.

His coolness in the hour of capture, the fortitude and the uncomplaining stoicism with which he bore his wounds, all go to show that whatever opinion as to his bravery may have become current with the public, he is a man who would have sold his life dearly if he had had a ghost of a show. We verily believe that if he had had a knife or pistol on his person he would have sought and found death rather than capture. No posse of armed men could have approached the well chosen fastness which he had selected. Strategy and a fortunate concurrence of circumstances placed him in the power of the law.

While being brought into town he exchanged notes with Major Mitchell relative to the Tejunga Pass pursuit. He told the Major that twice during the pursuit he was near enough to kill him and his party if he had desired so to do and convinced Major Mitchell of the truth of his assertion. Vasquez protested that he had never killed a man, that the murders at Tres Pinos were committed before his arrival; but he admitted that he led the party who committed the outrages away from that point. After his capture he enquired who was the leader of the party and upon being told that Mr. Albert Johnson was, he delivered to him his memorandum book and commenced to make a statement to him, not knowing at the time but that his wounds were mortal.

His first declaration related to his two children, when the preparations for the march to the city being completed the record was abruptly brought to a close. He showed Mr. Johnston the photographs of the children, and enclosed in the same envelope with them was a wavy tress of black and silky hair, bound in a blue ribbon. This he requested Mr. Johnston to preserve carefully and return to him when he should require or demand it. What secret heart history is bound up with this mute memorial of days when perhaps the outlaw had his dream of home and all that makes life beautiful, no one can tell. At a late hour we visited him in prison. Lying upon his pallet, to all human appearances a doomed man, a price set upon his head, an outlaw and an outcast, he received us and a number of other visitors with an ease and grace and elegance which would have done no discredit to any gentleman in the land, reclining upon his *fauteil* in his dressing room.

After answering quietly and politely a number of questions, he requested those present to retire, as he had … thing to communicate to … relative to certain … cepting us. … the …

Major Mitchell, soldier, law… miner, apiarist and journalist, … young man of talent and educa… With what valor and intrepidity … followed the flag of the Southern Confederacy may be seen in his persistent and unrivalled pursuit of the robber chief, from the Repetto event until the achievement yesterday.

Mr. Thomas Rogers is a young man of thirty-two years of age, twenty-four of which he lived in San Francisco. He has been associated with the Sheriff's party from the start, and is as brave as he is genteel and unostentatious. He is part proprietor of the Palace saloon, and has made hosts of friends here since he took up his residence among us.

Mr. Smith is, we believe, a farmer, and resides outside of the city. When Mr. Smith went to Greek George's house, a few days ago, to inquire if h… wanted any barley cut, the latter … in the least suspected that the woul… hay maker was taking a survey … premises for Mr. Rowland; so th… the time arrived for the a… could be made without conf… without loss of life, if possi… besieging party.

Mr. Beers, the corresp… Chronicle, is represente… gallant as his fellow … up to the scene of att… hand prepared for an…

Thus endeth the ch… suit and capture of TI… QUEZ!

The *Los Angeles Daily Star*'s story of Friday, May 15, 1874, announcing the capture of Vasquez. Note the ad of the enterprising clothier who rushed into print with the endorsement from the outlaw. *Courtesy Los Angeles Public Library*

Harry Nicholson Morse, one of the finest but least-known lawmen of the Wild West, who chased Vasquez for months and supplied information to the Los Angeles sheriff that led to the capture of the outlaw leader. Morse singlehandedly captured or killed many early California outlaws. This photograph was taken in 1880. *Courtesy California Historical Society, San Francisco*

that there was nothing "in the clue" and suggested that Morse return to searching the hills northward from Tejon. As soon as Morse left, Rowland gathered a posse and captured Vasquez.

Rowland's version is that after the Repetto robbery he ordered his men to stop searching the hills with posses "as it was a waste of time and energy. . . . Loud were the protests." He kept on his "own even tenor," gathering information on Vasquez from friendly Mexicans until he pinpointed where Vasquez was hiding in Alison Canyon.[9]

A century later it is difficult to determine which story is true. However, it must be pointed out that Morse was a man of great integrity and modesty, and it is difficult to question his veracity; Rowland, on the other hand, had no previous reputation as a manhunter, although the outlaw bands had committed a number of holdups in his county.

Yet, whether he acted on his own information or had simply accepted what Morse had to offer, Rowland's carefully planned strategy worked, and the elusive Vasquez was finally captured after years of freebooting and murder.

Beers, the correspondent of the *San Francisco Chronicle*, was a member of the posse, but the anonymous reporter for the *Los Angeles Star* wrote the most detailed and accurate account of the planning, storming of the ranch house where Vasquez was hiding, and the gunfight which took place on that wild morning.[10]

Capture of Tiburcio Vasquez, May 15, 1874

As the clerk of the City Council was about to read the last communication to that body about 4:30 P.M. yesterday, an unusual stir about the front caused a great deal of attention and in a moment more City Fathers, City Clerks, City Surveyors, City Reporters and everybody else in the room was making for the front door. Instinctively we knew that Vasquez had something to do with the fuss.

We were right, Vasquez was lying pale and bloody in a wagon in front of the jail. Two men who were taken in his company were taken into the jail, and locked up. A moment later Vasquez himself was lifted from the wagon and taken to the jail.

Dr. Wise presented himself and with the assistance of several medical friends in the community, rendered the wounded robber what services he required.

The examination showed buckshot in his left leg, in his left arm, in the left side of his side, one in the pectoral region, passing out the left side and in the left arm. The balls were extracted and the opinion given the wounds were not serious and he would be well within a few days.

During the time referred to, Mr. Miles who lent Vasquez his watch in the San Gabriel region last April, came into the room.

He was at once recognized by the wounded man and in fact the recognition was mutual. Mr. Hartley, the chief of police, had taken Mr. Miles' watch into his possession. His chain was missing but Mr. Miles did not say anything about it at the time but after Dr. Wise had his assistants dress his wounds, the outlaw requested Dr. Wise to take his *porte monnaie* from his pocket. It was done and Vasquez took from it the missing chain and requested Dr. Wise give it to the proper owner. He remarked "It belongs to him now," emphasizing the last word as if to say, "He might have whistled for it had they not captured me."

While his wounds were being dressed, Chief of Police E. F. Hartley, one of his captors, asked him (Vasquez) why he had asked him (Hartley) his name.

Quote Vasquez: "Usted es un hombre valiente lo mian o con." (You are a brave man like myself.)

He bore the probing and opening of his wounds without a murmur. In personal appearance the robber chieftain is anything but unusual. Take away the expression of his eyes, furtive, snaky and cunning, and he would pass unnoticed in a crowd. Not more than five feet seven inches in height and of spare build, he looks little like a man who could create a reign of terror. His forehead is low and slightly retreating to where it is joined by a thick mass of raven black, coarse hair, his moustache is by no means luxuriant, his skin whiskers are passably full, his sunken cheeks are only slightly sprinkled with beard, his lips are thin and bloodless, his teeth white, even and firm. His feet and hands are small, perhaps 130 pounds is all that he weighs. His light build made it easy for the horses to perform forced marches.

The history of the capture of Vasquez forms one of the most interesting chapters in criminal matters that has ever been written. The captured robber had defied pursuit, mocked at strategy and eluded for months the skill of the bravest and most celebrated detectives in the West. We do not believe that once afoot or on horseback, with three hours the start of his pursuers, Cuban bloodhounds would have compassed his capture. A sudden, well arranged surprise was the

Los Angeles Daily Star

SATURDAY........ .....MAY 16, 1874.

VASQUEZ.

AN INTERVIEW WITH THE NOTED BANDIT.

HIS BIRTH, PARENTAGE AND EARLY LIFE.

THE CAUSES WHICH LED TO HIS CAREER.

JEALOUSY AND REVENGE.

A LONG CAREER OF DELIBERATE CRIME.

We interviewed Tiburcio Vasquez yesterday. He seemed but little the worse for his wounds. Sheriff Rowland has provided him with a comfortable spring mattress and the dinner which was brought to him during our stay in his cell, or rather room, "was good enough for anybody. He was as communicative as one could wish. He laughed and talked as gaily and unconstrainedly as if he were in his parlor instead of in the clutches of the violated law. In reply to our questions he gave the following account of himself, substantially:

"I was born in Monterey county, California, at the town of Monterey, August 11th, 1835. My parents are both dead. I have three brothers and two sisters. Two of my brothers, reside in Monterey county; one unmarried and one married, the other resides in Los Angeles county; he is married. My sisters are both married; one of them lives at San Juan Baptista, Monterey County, the other at the New Idria Quicksilver Mines. I was never married, but I have one child in this county a year old. I can read and write, having attended school in Monterey. My parents were people in ordinarily good circumstances; owned a small tract of land and always had enough for their wants. My career grew out of the circumstances by which I was surrounded. As I grew up to manhood I was in the habit of attending balls and parties given by the native Californians, into which the Americans, then begining to become numerous, would force themselves and shove the native born men aside, monopolizing the dance and the women. This was about 1852. A spirit of hatred and revenge took possession of me. I had numerous fights in defence of what I believed to be my rights and those of my countrymen. The officers were continually in pursuit of me. I believed that we were unjustly and wrongfully deprived of the social rights which belonged to us. So perpetually was I involved in these difficulties that I at length determined to leave the thickly settled portions of the country, and did so. I gathered together a small band of cattle, and went into Mendocino county, back of Ukiah, and beyond Fales Valley. Even here I was not permitted to remain in peace. The officers of the law sought ____ in that remote region and

violence, as when I arrived I would be the judge, and if any body had to be shot I would do the shooting. When I arrived there with Chavis, however, I found three men dead and was told that two of them were killed by Leiva and one by another of the party named Romano, the rest of the men in the place were all tied. I told Leiva and his companions that they had acted contrary to my orders, that I did not wish to remain there long. Leiva and his men had not secured money enough for my purposes and I told a woman, the wife of one of the men who was tied, that I would kill him if she did not procure funds. She did so and we gathered up what goods and clothing and provisions we needed and started for Elizabeth Lake, Los Angeles county. On the way there I seduced the wife of the man Leiva. He did not discover our intimacy until we had pitched camp at the Lake. He at once rebelled and swore revenge. He left his wife at Heffner's place on Elizabeth Lake and started to Los Angeles to deliver himself up as well as to deliver me to the authorities if he could do so. Sheriff Rowland, however, was on my track, and in company with Sheriff Adams of Santa Clara county, and a posse of men endeavored to capture Chavis and myself at Rock Creek. We fired at them and could have killed them if we had wished to do. We effected our escape and arriving at Heffner's I took Leiva's wife behind me on my horse, and started back in the direction I knew Rowland and Adams and their party would be coming, knowing that I would hear them approaching on their horses. I did so, and as they drew near I turned aside from the road. The Sheriffs and their posse passed on and I took Leiva's wife to a certain point, which I do not care to name, and left her in the hills at a sheep ranch, while I went out and made a raid on Firebaugh's Ferry, on the San Joaquin river, for money to send her back to her parents house. I did so and have not seen her since. I provided for all her wants while she was with me. I tied ten men and a Chinaman up at Firebaugh's Ferry in the raid above referred to.

Here we digress a moment, to tell what befell Sheriffs Rowland and Adams and posse. They went straight to Heffner's, found their game had broken cover. They found Vasquez' camp, captured 30 horses and the greater part of the goods, clothing and provisions taken from Tres Pinos, and then divided, Sheriff Rowland returning to Los Angeles with the horses, all of which have been returned to their owners, except two. While at the camp Leiva came up, and was arrested by Sheriff Rowland, on suspicion; was by him turned over to Mr. Wasson, the Sheriff of Monterey county, and, as above stated, is now in jail at San Jose, awaiting the action of the law in the premises. Sheriff Adams and his party kept up an unsuccessful search for the bandit for several days, and finally abandoned it. We now resume the narrative where it was left off.

"After sending Leiva's wife home, I went to King's River, in Tulare county, where, with a party of eight men besides myself, I captured and tied up thirty-five men. There were ____ and a hotel in the ____ plunder ____

wrapped our guns in our blankets, retaining only our pistols, and I went toward the house, where I met the sheep herder and commenced talking about business. Asked him if Repetto wanted herders or shearers, how many sheep could he shear in a day, etc.; speaking in a loud tone in order to let Repetto hear us and throw him off his guard. I had left my men behind a small fence, and being told that he was at home I entered the house to see if I could bring the patron to terms without killing him. I found him at home, and told him I was an expert sheep shearer and asked him if he wished to employ any shearers; told him that my friends, the gentlemen who were waiting out by the fence, were also good shearers and wanted work. All were invited in, and as they entered surrounded Repetto. I then told him that I wanted money. At this he commenced hollering, when I had him securely tied and told him to give me what money he had in the house. He handed me eighty dollars. I told him that that would not do, that I knew all about his affairs; that he had sold nearly $10,000 worth of sheep lately, and that he must have plenty of money buried about the place somewhere. Repetto then protested that he had paid out nearly all the money he had received in the purchase of land; that he had receipts to show for it, etc. I told him that I could read and write and understood accounts; that if he produced his books and receipts and they balanced according to his statements, I would excuse him. He produced the books, and after examining them carefully I became convinced that he had told very nearly the truth. I then expressed my regrets for the trouble I had put him to, and offered to compromise. I told him I was in need of money, and that if he would accommodate me with a small sum I would repay him in thirty days, with interest at 1½ per cent. per month. He kindly consented to do so, and sent a messenger to the bank in Los Angeles for the money, being first warned that in the event of treachery or betrayal his life would pay the forfeit. The messenger returned, not without exciting the suspicions of the authorities, who, as it is well known, endeavored at that time to effect my capture but failed. But you know all about the Arroyo Seco affair. After my escape I wandered for a while in the mountains; was near enough to the parties who were searching for me to kill them if I had desired so to do. For the past three weeks I have had my camp near the place where I was captured, only coming to the house at intervals to get a meal. I was not expecting company at the time the arrest was made or the result might have been different.

The above is a very fair paraphrase of the recital made to us by Vasquez, in the presence of Sheriff Rowland. Almost all of it, except his version of the Tres Pinos affair, we know to be true. Only the leading events of his long career of brigandage and ____ ry are described. Our ____ draw their own ____ manner of ma____ He pro____

The *Star's* fascinating interview with Vasquez in which the outlaw tells his life story. *Courtesy Los Angeles Public Library*

only way to secure him. It has been effected and in the manner hereinafter related.

After the futile pursuit of the robbers up Tejunga pass after the Repetto robbery, Mr. William Rowland, sheriff of this county came to the conclusion that any further persecution of the quest in that direction, was a waste of time, energy and money. His subordinates were ordered to desist, and many a complaint was lodged against him for inaction and inefficiency.

Mr. Rowland, however, kept on the even tenor of his way, and availing himself of every possible source of information, became satisfied that the long sought after prize was within his grasp, and he quietly arranged for his capture.

On Wednesday night he received positive information of the whereabouts of Tiburcio Vasquez. He had kept for some time a list of names from which to choose a party to undertake the arrest. He organized his party as follows: Mr. Albert Johnson; Under Sheriff Major H. M. Mitchell, attorney of law of this city; Mr. J. M. Bryant, constable of this city; Mr. E. Harris, policeman; Mr. Thomas Rogers of the Paris Saloon; Mr. D. K. Smith, a citizen of this country; D. F. Hartley, chief of police and Deputy County Marshal and Mr. Beers, of San Francisco and special correspondent of the *San Francisco Chronicle*. Sheriff Rowland intended to accompany the party but his informant told him emphatically that if he left the city and was seen early in the morning, if Vasquez was not captured in the earliest hour, the game would break cover and be over the hills and far away.

The sequel as shown by the arrest of Greek George who we will refer to again, proved the soundness of the advice. The horses for the pursuing party were sent out, one by one, on Wednesday evening to the corral of Mr. Jones on Spring Street, near Seventh. One by one, the above party met at a rendezvous at 1:30 A.M. On Thursday the party of eight were in the saddle and on their way to the spot which will be pointed out for many years as the scene of the capture.

Greek George's ranch lies about ten miles due west of Los Angeles. It is situated at the base of a mountain, one of a series of detached spurs between which there are a dozen trails known only to the habitues of the region, which afford egress to the San Fernando plains. The dwelling house on the ranch is an old adobe, forming the letter L, the foot of the letter facing the mountain range, the shank lying north and south.

Behind the house and running a short distance from it lies a disused road, leading from the San Fernando to the LaBrea rancho, and thence to the city, behind this road the mountains, and in front of the house a small monte of willow groves grown up around a spring and beyond them a rolling plain stretching on to the ocean. On the northern end of the building was a room used by the robber as a storeroom and as a lookout. A window on the north afforded him a lookout for miles to the east (toward the city) and for a good distance west. No chance for a surprise for armed horsemen from either direction. The middle section of the western part, the shank of the house, was used as a dining room where the bandit was eating, surprised and captured.

A small apartment at the house was used as a kitchen in which was a small opening through which Vasquez made a leap for life when he found himself in the toils. His horse was staked out a few rods to the northwest of the building when the event occurred. Let us see how the capture was effected.

As stated above, the party left Los Angeles Thursday at 1:30 A.M. At 4 A.M. they arrived at the ranch of Major Mitchell, one of the party. There they had breakfast and held a council of war. The ranch is in a small canon, off the usual lines of travel, visited occasionally by neighboring ranchers for wood. After consultation Messrs. Albert Johnson, Mitchell and Sam Bryant, left the party and followed a mountain trail about one mile and a half until they came to a point opposite Greek George's ranch. Turning square north they climbed a point, where with a field glass, they could obtain an unobstructed view of the cover. A heavy fog rendered satisfactory observation impossible for hours. When it lifted they saw enough to convince them the game was at the very point designated.

A horse of the very description ridden by the outlaw was picketed outside. Twice they saw a man answering the description of Vasquez, lead him to the monte and returning, picketed him outside. Another man went in pursuit of a white horse answering the description of a horse used by the gang. Various plans were discussed for the capture of Vasquez by the trio, but it was finally decided that Mr. Johnson should ride to the ranch and marshall his forces while Mitchell and Smith should ride in pursuit of the horseman referred to above who they believed to be Chavez, the lieutenant of Vasquez.

Arrived there, unexpected, and it almost seems providentially sent allies, presented themselves. A wagon driven by a Californian and in which there was another man (also a native) was driven up from the direction of Greek George's.

It was a box wagon. It was not long before a plan was decided upon. Six of the party remained. The extra man, the driver of the wagon, made seven. Mr. Hartley who speaks Spanish fluently, was instructed to inform the driver to turn his horses' heads, to allow all six of his party and to allow the extra man to lie in the wagon's body bed and then to drive back to Greek George's, and as close to the house as possible, and if he made a sign or gave an alarm his life would be in forfeit.

In due time the house was reached. In a moment the party was out of the wagon with shotguns and rifles cocked ready for what might offer. Mr. Hartley and Mr. Beers went to the west side of the house, the other four to the southern, passing around the eastern end.

The foremost of the party had hardly reached the opening into the dining room when a woman opened it partly. Seeing the armed party of four approaching she gave a cry of fright and attempted to close the door. The party burst in with Mr. Harris leading the way and seeing the retreating form of the prize they sought, leaving the table and plunging through the opening to the kitchen.

Mr. Harris was close upon his heels and Vasquez with the agility of a mountain cat, leaped through the narrow window or opening to admit the light, when Harris fired at the vanishing form with his Henry rifle exclaiming, "There he goes through the window."

The party left the house as they had entered it. Vasquez stood for a second of time irresolute. Whether to seek cover in the monte or rush for his horse seemed the all important question. He seemed to decide for the horse—doubtless he would have given ten kingdoms if he had them, to be astride of him—and started when Mr. Hartley fired; turning he sought another direction when one after another, shot after shot, showed him the utter hopelessness of escape. He had already been wounded, just how severely we have already told. He had fallen but recovered himself, blood was spurting from his shoulder and streaming from his wounds. He threw up his hands, approached the party and said with a cold, passionless smile on his thin lips, "Boys, you have done well, I have been a d—— fool but it was all my own fault."

He was taken to the courtyard on the southern side of the house and laid upon a pallet. Not a murmur, scarcely a contortion of his face, bespoke either pain, remorse or any other emotion of the mind or soul.

Beers, the shotgun-equipped correspondent for the *Chronicle*, had been following the trail of Vasquez for months, joining posses, interviewing lawmen, and promising his readers that one day he would be present when the outlaw was taken. Sheriff Rowland had undoubtedly included Beers in his posse not only because of the newspaperman's seniority, but also because of his knowledge of Vasquez's habits.

But Rowland also realized that he would have to live with the *Los Angeles Star* long after Beers had departed; he hoped to run for reelection and he knew that an angry reporter assigned daily to cover him and his office could do irrefutable damage.

On the day following Vasquez's capture, in what may have been a peace offering, Rowland gave permission to the *Star*'s reporter to obtain an exclusive interview with the outlaw in his cell.

The newsman found Vasquez "as communicative as one would wish." The outlaw, the *Star*'s man observed, had been equipped with "a comfortable spring mattress, and the dinner which was brought to him in the cell during our stay was good enough for anybody."

Vasquez, who "seemed but little the worse for his wounds," spoke freely and at times during the interview "laughed and talked as gaily and unconstrained as though he was in his own parlor." Fortunately, the *Star*'s man let the outlaw chieftain talk. The result is a fascinating autobiography of California's legendary bandit.[11]

Vasquez: *An Interview with the Noted Bandit, May 16, 1874*

I was born in Monterey County, in Monterey California, August 11, 1835. My parents are both dead. I have three brothers and two sisters. Two of my brothers reside in Monterey County; one unmarried, the other married. One of them lives in San Juan Baptiste, Monterey County, the other at the New Idria Quicksilver Mines. I was never married but I have one child, a year old, in this county.

I can read and write having attended the school in Monterey. My people were people in ordinarily good circumstances, owning a small tract of land and always had enough for their wants. My career grew out of the circumstances with which I was surrounded.

As I grew up to manhood I was in the habit of attending balls and parties given by the native Californians, into which the Americans, then becoming numerous, would force themselves and force the native-born men aside, monopolizing the dance and the women.

This was about 1852. A spirit of hatred and revenge began to take possession of me. I had numerous fights in defense of what I believed were my rights and those of my countrymen. The officers were constantly in pursuit of me. I believed we were unjustly deprived of the social rights which rightly belonged to us. So perpetually was I involved in these difficulties that I at length finally determined to leave the thickly settled portion of the country and did so.

I gathered together a small band of cattle and went into Mendocino County, back of Ukiah and beyond Falis Valley. Even here I was not permitted to remain in peace. The officers of the law sought me out in that remote region and started to drag me before the courts. I always resisted arrest. I went to my mother and told her I intended to commence a different life. I asked for and obtained her blessing and at once commenced the career of a robber.

My first exploit consisted of robbing some peddlers in Monterey County of some money and clothes. My next was the capture and robbery of a stage coach in the same County. I had confederates with me from the first and was always regarded as leader. Robbery after robbery followed each other as circumstances allowed, until 1857 or 1858 I was arrested in Los Angeles for horse stealing, convicted of grand larceny, sentenced to the penitentiary and was taken to San Quentin and remained there until the term of my imprisonment expired in 1863.

Up to the time of my conviction and imprisonment, I had robbed stagecoaches, wagons, horses, houses, etc., indiscriminately, carrying on my operations for the most part in daylight, sometimes however, visiting homes after dark.

After my discharge from San Quentin I returned to the home of my parents and endeavored to lead a peaceful and honest life. However, I was soon accused of being a confederate of Procopio and Soto, both noted bandits, the latter of whom was killed by Sheriff Harry Morse of Alameda County.

I was again forced to become a fugitive from the law officers and driven to desperation left home and family and commenced robbing whenever the opportunity offered. I made but little money by my exploits. I always managed to avoid arrest. I believe I owe my frequent escapes solely to my courage (mi valor). I was always ready to fight whenever opportunity offered but always endeavored to avoid bloodshed.

I know of nothing worthy of note until the *Tres Pinos* occurred. The true story of that transaction is as follows:

I, together with four other men, including Chavez my lieutenant, and one Leiva who is now in jail at San Jose, awaiting an opportunity to testify, he having turned state's evidence, camped within a short distance of *Tres Pinos*. I sent three of the party, Leiva included, to that point making Leiva the captain.

I instructed them to take a drink, examine the locality, acquaint themselves with the number of men around and wait until I came. I told them not to use any violence, as when I arrived I would be the judge, and if anybody had to be shot, I would do the shooting.

When I entered there with Chavez, I found three men dead and I was told that two of them had been killed by Leiva and another by a man named Romano, the rest of the men in the place were all tied.

I told Leiva and his companions that they had acted contrary to my orders, that I did not wish to remain there long. Leiva and the men had not secured enough money for my purposes, and I told a woman, the wife of one of the men who was tied, that I would kill him if she did not procure funds.

She did so and we gathered up what goods and provisions we needed and started for Elizabeth Lake, Los Angeles County. On the way there I seduced the wife of the man named Leiva.

He did not discover our intimacy until we had pitched camp at the lake. He at once rebelled and swore revenge. He left his wife at Heffner's place on the lake and started for Los Angeles to deliver himself up as well as to deliver me to the authorities if he could do so.

Sheriff Rowland, however, was on my track and in company of Sheriff Adams of Santa Clara County and a posse of men endeavored to capture Chavez and myself at Rock Creek. We fired at the party and could have killed them if we so desired.

We effected our escape and arriving at Heffner's I took Leiva's wife behind me on my horse and started back into the direction I knew Rowland and Adams and their party would be coming, knowing that I could hear them approaching on their horses. I did so and as they drew near I turned aside from the road.

The Sheriff's posses passed on and I took Leiva's wife to a certain point, which

I do not care to name, and left her in the hills at a sheep ranch, while I went out and made a raid on Firebaugh's Ferry, on the San Joaquin River, for money to send her back home to her parents' home. I did so and have not seen her since. I provided with all her wants when she was with me. I tied ten men and a China-man at Firebaugh's Ferry, the raid above referred to.

[We here digress for a moment to tell what happened to Sheriffs Rowland and Adams and their posse. They went straight to Heffner's and found their game had broken cover. They found Vasquez's camp, captured thirty horses and the greater part of the goods, clothing and provisions taken at *Tres Pinos*, and then divided, Sheriff Rowland returning to Los Angeles with the stolen horses, all re-turned to their rightful owners except two. While at the camp Leiva came up, was arrested and turned over by Sheriff Rowland to the sheriff of Santa Clara County where he is now in jail at San Jose, waiting the action of the law. Sheriff Adams and his party kept up an unsuccessful hunt for the bandit for several days and finally abandoned it. We now resume the narrative of Vasquez where he left off.]

After sending Leiva's wife home I went on to King's River, in Tulare County, where with a party of eight men besides myself I captured and tied up thirty-five men. There were two stores and a hotel in the place. I had time to plunder only one of the stores as the citizens aroused themselves and began to fight.

The numbers were unequal and I retired. I got eight hundred dollars and con-siderable jewelry by this raid. I went from there to a small settlement named Panama on the Kern River where myself and my party had a carouse for three days, dancing, love making, etc. El Capitan Vasquez was quite a favorite with the senoritas. It was well known to the citizens of Bakersfield which is only two or three miles from Panama, that I was there, and the arrangement was made for my capture but the attempt was not made until I had been gone for twenty-four hours.

Then they came and searched the house in which I was supposed to be con-cealed. When I left Panama I started for the Sweetwater Mountains, and skirted their base never travelling along the road but keeping alone in the direction of Lone Pine. I returned by way of Coyote Hole where the robbery of the stage took place.

Here Chavez and myself captured the *diligencia* and sixteen men. Chavez held his gun over them while I took their jewelry and money. We got about 200 dollars, some pistols and jewelry, watches etc. also a pocket book belonging to Mr. James Craig containing about $10,000 in mining stock which I threw away.

One man was disposed to show fight and to preserve order I shot him in the leg and made him sit down. I got six horses from the stage company, two from the station. I drove off four in one direction and went in another direction to elude pursuit.

I wandered around after that in the mountains until the Repetto robbery. The day before that occurrence I camped at the Pietra Gordo at the head of the Ar-royo Seco. I had selected Repetto as a good subject. In pursuance of the plan I had adopted, I went to a sheep herder employed on the place and asked him if he had seen a brown horse which I had lost, required if Repetto was at home and took in all the surroundings.

I told the man I had to go to the Old Mission on very important business, that if he would catch my horse I would give him $10 or $15. I then returned by a roundabout way to my companions in the Arroyo Seco. As soon as it was dark I returned with my men to the neighborhood of Repetto's and camped within a few rods of the house. The next morning about breakfast we wrapped our guns in our blankets retaining only our pistols and I went toward the house where I met the sheep herder and commenced talking about business.

Asked him if Repetto wanted herders or sheep shearers, how many sheep could he shear in one day, etc. speaking in a loud tone in order to let Repetto hear us and throw him off guard. I left my men behind a small fence and upon being told he was home I entered the house to see if I could bring the patron to terms without killing him.

I found him at home and told him I was an expert sheep shearer and asked him if he wished to employ any shearers; told him my friends who were the gentlemen who were waiting by the fence were all good shearers and wanted work.

All were invited in and as they entered they surrounded Repetto. I then told him I needed money. At this he commenced hollering. When I had him securely tied I told him to give me what he had in the house. He gave me eighty dollars. I told him that was not enough, that I knew all about his affairs, that I knew he had sold $10,000 worth of sheep lately and he must have plenty of money buried around someplace.

Repetto then protested that he had paid out nearly all the money in the purchase of land, that he had receipts to show it. I then told him that I could read and write and I understood accounts, and if he produced his receipts and they balanced according to his statements I would excuse him.

He produced the books and after examining them carefully I became convinced that he had told very nearly the truth. I then expressed my regrets for the trouble I had put him through and offered to compromise.

I told him I was in need of money and that if he would accommodate me with a small sum I would repay him in thirty days with interest at 1½ per cent per month. He kindly consented to do so and sent a messenger to the bank in Los Angeles for the money, being first warned that in the event of treachery or betrayal, his life would pay the forfeit.

The messenger returned not without exciting the suspicions of the authorities, who as is well known, endeavored at this time to effect my capture but failed. But you know all about the Arroyo Seco affair. After my escape I wandered for a while in the mountains, near enough to the parties who were searching for me to kill them if I had desired to do so.

For the past three weeks I have had my camp near the place where I was captured, only coming to the house at intervals to get a meal. I was not expecting company at the time the arrest was made or the result might have been different. . . .

Vasquez was charged with the murder of the two men in Tres Pinos and remanded to the San Jose jail. He issued an appeal to his countrymen and enough money was collected to hire two attorneys. Vasquez, fast becoming a legend, attracted lines of the curious, including "many adoring women" who filed into the jail to see and talk to the bandit leader. His cell was filled with food, flowers, and jugs of fine wine.

Vasquez's trial began on January 5, 1875, with the local newspaper indignantly reporting that the gallery was "filled with ladies representing the elite and respectability of the city . . . Vasquez unblushingly directed his glances upon them. . . ."

Two weeks later the packed courtroom heard the jury return a guilty verdict after a brief deliberation. The judge sentenced the outlaw chief to the gallows remarking, "Your life has been one unbroken record of lawlessness and outrage, pillage and murder. . . ."[12]

An appeal was entered, and while it was being considered a letter supposedly written by Chavez was found in the Wells Fargo Express Company's mailbox. It was rambling and bombastic, threatening the people of San Jose that if "my captain" died on the gallows, "you will have to suffer as in the time of Joaquin Murieta. . . ."

Once again John Rollin Ridge's fictional hero was riding to avenge his countrymen. The letter, which created a sensation in the city, undoubtedly was spurious; there is no evidence that Chavez could read or write.

On March 12, Vasquez's final appeal was denied and Santa Clara County Sheriff Adams began making preparations for the execution on March 19. San Jose did not have a gallows, so Adams borrowed one from Sacramento. He also sent out formal invitations ("Not Transferable") and wrote the bandit's last two messages. One asked pardon "from each and every one I have in any way injured" and expressed gratitude to Adams, his staff, and the defense lawyers. The second was to his riders, proudly pointing out that at no time had he weakened and betrayed them, and urging them to mend their ways or they, too, could be walking up the gallows' steps.

His last request was to see his coffin. It was brought to his cell. He admired the satin lining, then exclaimed:

"I can sleep here forever very well!"

On the morning of his execution he awoke at 2 A.M., drank a glass of wine, smoked a cigar, and talked for a few minutes to the son of Sheriff Adams, who was on guard. When Adams asked him if he believed in life after death, Vasquez nodded and said fervently:

"I hope so, for in that case by tomorrow I will see all my old sweethearts together!"

He finished his cigar, said goodnight, and in a moment was sound asleep.

The execution was scheduled for 1:30 P.M., but crowds gathered at dawn. Shortly after 1 P.M., Sheriff Adams read Vasquez the death warrant, then solemnly announced:

"Vasquez, the time has come!"

Vasquez calmly put out the cigar he was smoking and they left the cell—the deputies leading, Vasquez between Father Sorda, the local priest, and Sheriff Adams.

On the scaffold his knees and arms were strapped and the noose was adjusted.

"Pronto!" Vasquez snapped, and the trap was sprung. He was pronounced dead at 1:47 P.M.[13]

Vasquez was quietly buried by his family, with one San Francisco reporter pointing out in his story the final irony: for twenty years Vasquez's name had been in the newspapers across the state as he plundered and killed, but now in death he was treated with "utter indifference."

The mythmakers would soon arrange for Vasquez to join the company of legendary outlaws of the American West; within a year the *Police Gazette* and job printers were picturing the squat, unattractive man as a handsome, gallant Lochinvar who had ridden out of the hills to avenge the wrongs of his people . . .

SAM BASS

Sam Bass was born in Indiana, it was his native home;
And at the age of seventeen young Sam began to roam;
Sam first came to Texas, a cowboy for to be—
A kinder-hearted fellow you seldom ever see . . .

A FEW MINUTES AFTER HE WHISPERED, "THE WORLD IS bobbing around me," Sam Bass died in a shack in Round Rock, Texas. It was 3:58 P.M., Sunday, July 21, 1878—his twenty-seventh birthday.

Not long after the gravediggers had patted down the small mound, Sam began to live in song and legend. Old cowmen insisted that the ballad sung about him by the night guards soothed most of the herds of longhorns moving north to the Kansas cowtowns; Charlie Siringo, the cowboy-detective, called Sam "the hero of more Texas cowboys than any other bad man."

Folklore pictures Sam as a smiling, reckless young lad who remained true to his friends to the last, shared his stolen gold with the poor, was a gallant with the ladies, loved children and horses, and was lured to his death by a Judas in his ranks—in brief, the classic western Robin Hood.

Not long after his death cowboys were reading paperback biographies of Sam and singing about him around their campfires or as they slowly rode on the fringes of the uneasy herds, calming them as thunder rumbled in the distance or wolves ran a prey to its death.

Behind the myth and folklore was an illiterate, likable cowboy and teamster who drifted into the "robbing business," as he called it, as an easy method of getting money without working too hard.

He was a charismatic leader who won the admiration of young cowboys, ranchers, and farmers for his daring robberies of the hated railroads. He was no Robin Hood; Sam spent his money freely but only on whiskey, elaborate gifts to his friends, dance-hall girls, and horses. He was only a fair shot but the rangers and posses weren't much better. Volley after volley was fired in the "war" on Sam, but casualties on both sides were few.

It was primitive law enforcement that allowed Sam to operate as long as he did; the holdups of the Deadwood stage are an excellent example. Sam and his gang held up the stage with such regularity that they became known to the drivers, who would call out to their passengers, "The boys are here again."

The gang easily outrode or outwitted the posses of miners who halfhearted-ly chased them. It wasn't until they killed a popular driver that the mining camp rose up in anger. Then Sam ordered his men to forget about the poorly paying stage—they once got a handful of peaches as loot—and concentrate on the Union Pacific and the Texas railroads.

It was then that the legend of Sam Bass was born.

Sam was not a native Texan, but was born July 21, 1851, on a farm near the town of Mitchell, Indiana. His mother, Jane, died in 1861; his father, Daniel, followed her three years later. Sam, his two brothers, and four sisters were raised by their maternal uncle, David L. Sheeks.[1]

The story of Sam's early years is the familiar one of a frontier farm boy who detested school but loved fine horses, hunting, and cards. It wasn't until he reached Denton, Texas, that he learned to write his name. His tutor was Charles Brim, a young schoolboy; Sam was twenty-three.

In Denton he worked as a teamster for Sheriff W. F. Egan, who would become his fiercest adversary. Sam's biographer, Denton County Court Judge Thomas E. Hogg, recalled Sam as about five feet eight inches in height, slender, with dark hair and hazel eyes.

Egan, known to the townspeople of Denton as "Dad Egan," was not a strict employer, but Sam soon tired of hauling firewood and provisions for ranchers, or being hired out to cut grain or build fences. He never hid his dream of get-ting some "easy money." Like Jesse James, he loved racehorses, and when the opportunity came to buy a chestnut-sorrel mare from a neighboring farmer, Sam went to Armstrong B. Egan, the sheriff's younger brother, with an offer to become a partner in a horse he predicted would be the champion of the Denton County tracks.

Sam had seen and admired the two-year-old mare he had heard came from the strain of Steel Dust, a famous Kentucky thoroughbred in the decade before the Civil War.

He named the mare Jenny and began training her on the Denton dirt track just outside the town.

Sheriff Egan, however, frowned on his brother's becoming a part of the rac-ing and gambling crowd. He insisted that Armstrong sell his share in Jenny and even advanced Sam the money to buy out his brother.

Sam quit his freighting job to become the full-time owner of a one-man rac-ing stable. His jockey was a reed-thin black named Charley Tucker, who had worn the silks of a prominent racing family. Jenny's fame spread; with the black man up, she won race after race.

Sam's first experience with the law took place in 1874 when he raced his mare against a horse owned by Marcus Millner, a deputy constable for Parker

A photograph of a rather formal Sam Bass, the legendary Texas outlaw leader. Charlie Siringo, the cowboy whose autobiography is a classic of western frontier literature, once said that the story of Sam Bass, crooned by the night watch, helped to calm more herds moving north to the Kansas cowtowns than any other cowboy ballad. *Courtesy University of Texas*

County. Each wagered a horse corralled about a mile from Denton. Millner won the race but Sam refused to pay his bet, claiming that Millner had fouled his mare. When the deputy ignored Sam's protest and took the horse, Bass insisted that Denton's marshal, William Fry, arrest Millner as a horse thief.

Fry and Sam found Millner at a Parker County dance and forced him to give Sam back his horse. Millner sued in civil court but Sam, who knew that Millner had to travel fifty miles for every hearing, kept postponing the case until the deputy constable ran out of funds to pay his lawyers and dropped the suit. At the time Sam laboriously signed the court papers "Sam B Ass." Judge Hogg, Sam's biographer, explained, "Sam used a capital B and a capital A in Bass and separated them so far apart as to make the B appear as an initial."[2]

Sam soon became an excellent judge not only of horseflesh but also of women and cards. He could be seen almost any night bucking the tiger in the frontier saloons or whirling a partner about in rough dance halls.

Jenny had changed his personality; instead of the worn, dusty clothes he had worn as a teamster, he now dressed in suits made of the best cloth, rode in a carriage, and proudly showed a diamond stickpin; both the carriage and the stickpin were won in races.

He no longer slouched, head hung down with his battered hat pulled to eye level. He was cheerful, always happy, generous with his winnings, and an eternal optimist.

"I got the world by the tail with a downward pull," he would cry as he raised a glass to the cheers of the crowded saloons.

One of his closest friends in Denton was Henry Underwood, son of a farmer and millowner in Jennings County, Indiana. Underwood, slightly older than Sam, had fought with Jennison's Jayhawkers in the Civil War. After killing a man in a Kansas gunfight he had fled to Texas, where he established a freighting business in Denton, hauling firewood and provisions from Denton to Dallas. He was described as about the same size as Sam, but "quick and nervous in his movements and while free from anger . . . quick tempered and daring to resent an affront. . . ."[3]

In 1874 Sam and Underwood became embroiled with a group of blacks who had laughed because Sam had dropped a large watermelon when his horse suddenly reared. Denton's Deputy Sheriff Tom Gerren attempted to arrest Underwood, but he fled after a gunfight. A posse later found their camp and Sam and Underwood held them off with rifle fire before they rode out of the county—Sam to San Antonio to race his mare, and Underwood to continue rustling and committing small robberies.

In San Antonio Sam met Joel Collins, a handsome and reckless young cowboy and temporary bartender who had made four cattle drives from Texas to the Kansas cowtowns from 1871 to 1874.

Collins discarded his bartender's apron to form a partnership with Sam. They devised this scheme: Collins would appear as Jenny's owner, while Sam, posing as a racetrack tout, would select a horse he knew Jenny could beat and advise the animal's owner that he knew the mare would fade before the finish. Collins would bet what money they had, then split the winnings with Sam.[4]

For over a year the pair traveled about the Texas frontier race-track circuit until the professional horsemen caught on to their scheme. Sam sadly sold Jenny and told Collins, "The jig is up in this country . . . I don't believe we can do anything. . . ."

But Collins had another plan. He was well known in the area and had no difficulty in buying a herd of several hundred cattle by signing notes to be paid after the cattle were sold. Joined by Jack Davis, who Judge Hogg described as "another bird of like feather," the trio drove the herd north, first to Dodge City and then to Ogallala in the valley of the South Platte, where they sold it for eight thousand dollars.

Gold, not cattle, was all men talked about in the crowded saloons and dance halls. There was so much in the Black Hills all a man had to do was pick up the nuggets and fill a wheat sack. Deadwood was the principal camp where the latest lodes had been found.

The trio decided it was a chance of a lifetime; they split the money and headed for Deadwood in the fall of 1876.

Snow and freezing rains made mining impossible, so they settled down in the roaring camp jammed with thousands of whores, pimps, gunmen, thieves, amateur miners, and professional gamblers.

Davis built an "elegant" house for a prostitute named Maud who had caught his eye, while Sam and Joel, after losing steadily at the poker tables, decided to use the remainder of their money to establish a freighting outfit, hauling between Deadwood and Cheyenne. On their first trip their expenses exceeded their profit by sixty dollars.

"It's pretty hard to quit our old trade and go into a business that don't pay any better than this," Sam pointed out. Collins agreed and Sam decided they had better go into the "robbing business."[5]

They gathered about them a gang: Tom Nixon, a Canadian; Bill Heffridge, a Pennsylvanian down on his luck; and Jim Berry, who had left his wife and four children in Missouri to hunt for gold. The Deadwood stage was to be their first target. They held up the stage four times, from July to August 1877, with seven peaches and less than $50 as their total loot—Sam complained to the passengers and drivers at the "cheapness of their trade." He agreed to try once more when Collins learned that a shipment of $150,000 in gold dust was to leave the mining camp.

The holdup was a failure. Ten miles from Deadwood they rose out of the brush, the usual kerchiefs masking their faces, and ordered the driver to "throw down the box." But guards inside the coach started shooting and John Slaughter, the driver, began whipping the team. Collins and Heffridge fired, and Slaughter was killed. Sam and the gang raced after the stage, careening down the narrow rocky trail, and a running gunfight took place. But after several miles they gave up and fled into the brush.

Deadwood, which had been curiously phlegmatic about the robberies, rose up in anger over the killing of the popular Slaughter. Posses were formed and miners' committees began investigating. Sam decided it was time to leave; in September 1877 he told his riders that the Union Pacific would be more profitable.

The gang's first train robbery was its most successful. At Big Springs, Nebraska, the loot was sixty thousand dollars in gleaming new twenty-dollar gold coins from the San Francisco mint. The passengers turned over an additional four hundred dollars in cash and several gold watches.

After dividing their loot, the gang split up. Sam and Davis headed for Texas, Collins and Heffridge moved along the Republican River into Kansas, and Berry and Nixon rode into Missouri.[6]

In late October 1877, after outwitting a patrol of cavalry, Sam and Davis entered Texas at the Red River Station, and on November 1 rode into Denton.

Collins and Heffridge were not as lucky. They were also headed for Texas, but apparently stopped along the way. The Union Pacific "by some means known only to themselves" had learned that Collins was one of the robbers and had posted a large reward for his capture. Sheriff Bardsley of Ellis County, Kansas, a ten-man patrol of cavalrymen from Fort Hays, and a railroad detective trailed the gang to the Platte River crossing, then to the Republican. They made their camp at Buffalo Station, sixty miles west of Hays City, and started to search the wild empty land for the train robbers.

On October 26 Collins and Heffridge, carrying the gold coins in a pair of pants, the legs tied at both ends, rode up to the station. In a few minutes, after a brief gun battle, they were dead.

The *Kansas City Times* gave an account of the shooting, based on interviews with Sheriff Bardsley and the cavalry officer.[7]

The Death of Joel Collins and Bill Heffridge

They rode in from the north, coming in boldly from a high ridge of open prairie. They led between them a pony loaded down with something [that] while it was not bulky, seemed to tax the strength of the pony to carry it.

The men were dusty and travel stained. They appeared to be and might have been Texas cowboys out on a hunt for cattle or on their way to join a herd. Had they rode straight across the track and continued their journey without stopping, no suspicion would have been aroused, but they were led instinctively to their death.

They rested their jaded horses to the shady side of the principal building of the station and one of the two dismounted, leaving his partner in charge of the horses and pack pony. The man left in charge of horses said they were Texas cattlemen on their way home and inquired their way to Fort Larned. The dismounted man walked up to the station agent and inquired the way to Jim Thompson's Store.

The building was pointed out to him, but as he stood conversing, he took out a handkerchief which revealed a letter in his pocket on which was plainly visible the superscription "Joel Collins."

This was the name of the leader of the Union Pacific train robbers, and the brands on their horses assured the station agent that these were the men wanted by the sheriff and the soldiers encamped only a few hundred yards away.

Sheriff Bardsley was notified at once and he came up to the station, examined the horses and made other satisfactory observations. He conversed with the robber chief for some time, and asked many questions which were answered freely.

They walked together to the station and took a drink and conversed on many and various inconsequential topics. Collins made no attempt to hide his real name. He had no suspicion that the telegraph had given his name and description at that little station in the middle of the Buffalo plains. Bardsley then left his prey and started back to the camp of the soldiers, who were under the command of Lieutenant Allen, and ordered them to saddle up and follow him and he would bring back the Texans.

In the meantime the two horsemen, with their overburdened pony, had started out on the open plains southward. Sheriff Bardsley and his party started out in pursuit. When Collins and his companion saw the sheriff and his blue-coated posse appear on their trail, they manifested no excitement. They did not even attempt to run. On the contrary they rode leisurely on the Texas trail until Sheriff Bardsley rode up and halted them.

Even then they gave no sign of trepidation or excitement. Collins looked at Sheriff Bardsley with the coolest effrontery and demanded his business. Said Sheriff Bardsley:

"I have a description of some train robbers which answers well to your appearance. I want you and your partner to return with me to the station. You need fear nothing if you are innocent but if you are the man I want, then I am $10,000 better off. Please come back to the station, gentlemen."

"You are mistaken in your men, gentlemen," replied Collins laughingly. "But of course there is no use to object. We will go back and have the mistake explained. We are Texas boys going home, that's all."

They then turned their tired horses back toward the station. As they turned they exchanged a few brief words which were undistinguishable even by the nearest trooper. They rode a few miles over the level plains toward the solitary station, when suddenly the leader, Joel Collins, broke the silence. Turning to his companion he said:

"Pard, if we are to die, we might as well die game."

Then he drew his revolver. His partner followed his example but before either could fire the troopers had fired a volley into them and they fell from their horses riddled with bullets. The robbers died instantly and were taken to the station for burial but afterwards taken to Ellis Station where an inquest was held and where the bodies were buried. About twenty-five thousand dollars in twenty dollar gold pieces were found upon the pony. The coins were of the mintage of 1877.

The wealth weighed nearly one hundred pounds and was tied up in a pair of

Left to right: Jim Murphy, Sam's friend who led him to his death at Round Rock, Texas; Sam Bass; and Sebe Barnes, one of his riders. This photograph was taken by H. B. Hillyer, who started a gallery in Austin in 1857 and was appointed official photographer for Texas during the Civil War. At the time of his death at Bowie, Texas, in 1903 Hillyer had become a famous frontier photographer. *The James D. Horan Civil War and Western Americana Collection*

old trousers with the lower ends tied together and thrown over the pony's back with blankets spread over it.

Berry was killed a short time later in Anderson County, Missouri. Lawmen discovered that he had exchanged several thousand dollars in gold coins for currency and had "ordered an elegant suit of clothes" before leaving town. He refused to surrender to a posse and was killed. Nixon, who did not reveal his affluence, successfully made his way to Canada, where he vanished.

From Denton, Sam and Davis went on to Fort Worth, where they separated, Sam hiding out in Cooke County and Davis going to New Orleans. A short time later Sam reorganized his gang, recruiting Frank Jackson, known as "Blockey," who had been working as a tinsmith in Denton.[8]

Sam continued to visit Denton at night and one old friend he saw was Jim Murphy, who looked wide-eyed at the pile of gold pieces Sam laughingly jiggled in his cupped hand. He told Murphy he was now "in funds" and had struck it rich in the Black Hills.

After buying two horses from Murphy, Sam joined Henry Underwood and Jackson and the trio headed for San Antonio for what Bass later called "a general carousal."

Underwood returned to Denton to see his family on Christmas Eve of 1877, only to be arrested by a posse under Sheriff William C. Everheart of Grayson County, directly north of Denton, and Tooney Waits, a Pinkerton detective who had mistakenly identified Underwood as Tom Nixon.[9]

Based on a warrant signed by Waits, the protesting Underwood was taken to

Nebraska and jailed as Nixon, with the five-hundred-dollar reward paid to Sheriff Everheart. Although Underwood summoned citizens from Denton who positively identified him, the obvious power of the Pinkertons kept the Texan in prison for months. It was some time before he escaped to rejoin Bass and Jackson.

In Texas, Sam and Jackson twice held up the Fort Worth stage, their loot amounting to eighty-one dollars and three gold watches. In February 1878 Sam returned to train robbery; the Texas Central Express was selected as the next victim. An account in the *Galveston News* identified train No. 4 out of Denison as the one held up at Allen Station in Collin County, eight miles south of McKinney. On this raid Sam had two new recruits, Seaborn "Sebe" Barnes, a restless young Texan nicknamed "Nubbins Colt," and Tom Spotswood, rustler and killer. The train robbers cut loose the express car and threatened to burn it unless James Thomas, the Texas Express Company messenger, rolled back the door.[10]

Thomas obeyed Sam's order but fired at the first robber to enter the car. A gun battle took place, but both sides were miserable shots and no one was wounded. Thomas finally surrendered and the gang looted the car, leaving with what Sam later estimated was $1,280.

Spotswood returned home to McKinney, in the eastern section of Denton County, while Bass, Jackson, and Barnes hid out in Cove Hollow, Cooke County.

In March the *Denton Monitor* reported the arrest of Spotswood by George Drennan, "the gallant deputy sheriff of Denton County." Drennan brought the Texas Express messenger to Denton, where he identified Spotswood, who was put in the county jail to await the grand jury action.

Sam was disgusted after reading the *Monitor's* account.

"Any man who robs a train in fifteen minutes of his home and then returns home and trys to play old solid, ought to be captured," he told his riders.[11]

Cove Hollow, in the southwestern section of Cooke County and extending into Wise, was a formidable hideout. The six-mile-long deep ravine was filled with oak, and walnut trees, and a junglelike tangle of vines and shrubs. The only inhabitants of the wet limestone caves were rattlesnakes and copperheads. At high noon the sun barely penetrated the thick roof of trees, and for the occasional visitor it was like moving across the bottom of a motionless sea. The hollow was only forty-three miles from Denton, which could be easily visited at night. Other advantages were the nearby Murphy ranch run by Bob Murphy, and Jim, Bob's brother and Sam's old friend, who lived in a cabin on the edge of the hollow. Bass knew that both would alert him if strangers appeared.[12]

That same year the trio held up the Houston & Texas Central train at Hutchins. An eyewitness left a vivid account of what happened at the lonely station.[13]

Sam Bass and His Gang Rob the No. 4 Houston & Texas Central Train at Hutchins

The robbers who understood their business well had evidently planned the assault deliberately, and the manner of its execution was prompt and effective.

They first took into their possession the railroad agent at Hutchins and a negro, then captured the engineer and fireman of the train. They also captured two tramp printers from Dallas who were stealing a ride on the front of the locomotive, and added them to the crowd.

This squad they marched in front of them to the express car door, so that should the messenger aboard the train fire, the discharge would take effect, not on the robbers but on the innocent agent, negro, fireman, engineer or puncture the valuable epidermis of the newspaper fraternity.

The messenger barred the door and extinguished the lights but the robbers soon burst asunder the door. The messenger then fired into the mob with what effect is not known but the fire was returned and the messenger was wounded in the face.

Also one of the printers was wounded in one of the limbs, which for the present operates a serious check to his perambulatory tendencies.

Messenger [Henry] Thomas, being wounded and seeing the futility of attempting any further resistance surrendered to the mob. The sack was rifled of its contents and the mail car was ransacked for whatever plunder the robbers saw fit to appropriate. In regard to the amount of money taken from the sack, there are many rumors.

One is that they only obtained a small amount, the express manager having secreted the bulk of the money and valuables in the store while the lights were out. Another rumor is to the effect they obtained several thousand dollars.

Messenger Thomas continued on to his route to Corsicana, where he stopped off on account of his wound. He is the brother of the agent who was in charge of the car which was robbed in Allen Station.

Word of the robbery was dispatched to all stations, but up to noon today no trace of the scoundrels had been obtained.

The passengers aboard the train were not molested. The robbers, it was said, after finishing their business, took off for the Trinity Bottoms but the attempt to trail them for any distance has failed. Later reports confirm the statement that the robbers obtained a small amount of money, not more than $300.

For the first time suspicion now pointed to Sam Bass as the leader of the train robbers.[14] With the consent of United States Commissioner Alexander Robinson, Denton County Sheriff Egan hired William Miner as an undercover agent. Miner first sought out Scott Mayes, who owned a livery stable and hotel in Denton. One of the attractions of Mayes's "one-horse saloon" was the ten-pin alley, where the local sports gathered to lay wagers. Egan believed that Mayes selected potential robbery victims for the gang.[15]

Official Texas was also moving against the Bass gang. Captain Junius (June) Peak had been summoned to Austin and ordered by the governor to form a special task force of manhunters to capture or kill Sam and his riders, while United States District Attorney Andrew J. Evans and United States Marshal Stilwell R. Russell had set up headquarters in Tyler with a special grand jury to begin investigating the train robberies and how the gang was obtaining horses and supplies from friends in Denton County.

Peak, City Recorder of Dallas, was a popular choice to head this frontier command. He had been one of General John Hunt Morgan's troopers when that brash Confederate cavalryman had tried to invade Ohio, only to end up in the Ohio Penitentiary. But Peak had escaped and made his way through the

Union lines to reenlist in Forrest's command. He was twice wounded at Chickamauga.

After the war he served as deputy sheriff of Dallas, then served for four years as city marshal. He was a well-known buffalo hunter and in 1872 had been selected by a group of cattlemen to end rustling in Billy the Kid's country in New Mexico.

In April 1878, he and Major John B. Jones, the Ranger commander, organized a group of thirty rangers with an enlistment for a month.

While Peak and Jones were training their new rangers, Miner, Sheriff Egan's "spy," was spending most of his time in Mayes's "one-horse saloon." Another deputy, W. R. Wetsel, persuaded Sheriff Egan that he knew Sam from his freighting days and could probably get him to "come in" and answer the suspicion that he was the leader of the train-robbing gang.

An incredible scene took place when Wetsel rode into Sam's camp. Bass, Barnes, and Jackson were sleeping, but the deputy woke them up and suggested a game of cards. The sleepy outlaws agreed and they played "Schneck's Favorite" all day. They continued until dark, then rode into Bolivar where they "kept 'schnecking' the greasy old cards" until dawn.

Wetsel tried to get them to talk about the robberies but Sam and his boys ignored the questions. The following day Jim Murphy brought the stirring news that Henry Underwood had escaped from the Nebraska prison and was back in Denton with another outlaw he had recruited, Arkansas Johnson.

When Underwood appeared with Johnson, Wetsel reached into his boot and took out a warrant for Underwood's arrest for rustling. While the gang listened impassively, he read the formal charge and demanded that Underwood post a bond to insure his appearance in Denton's circuit court!

Bass and the others argued with the deputy, Sam at one point taking Underwood aside and advising him of his rights. After conferring with his leader, Underwood returned and told Wetsel he "would not fill it out now but would in a week or so."

Wetsel reluctantly agreed and left the camp.[16]

The days dragged on in the dim, green world of Cove Hollow. Frank Jackson, chaffing at the inactivity, told Sam he had decided outlawry left a great deal to be desired and he was going to rejoin his family and return to farming.

Bass lectured him severely on the dangers of the outside world.

"Hold on," he said, "that won't do now. They'll hang you. You can't get protection elsewhere than with me. See, Arkansas and Underwood are with us now—we'll have a livelier time and better trade. We know Henry—he's O.K., but we must try Arkansas and see if he is a thoroughbred. Henry says he is all right, but I want to know if he has any business in him."

Sam then revealed that he planned to hold up the Texas & Pacific railroad at Eagle Ford. But Jackson still insisted that he wanted to pass on this one, and Underwood told Sam he had to spend some time with his family. Sebe Barnes had returned home, so Bass selected Arkansas Johnson, "to see if he is a thoroughbred," and two local recruits who have never been identified.

Jackson, Underwood, and Barnes, he said, "would be conspicuous in Denton at the time of the robbery to ward off any suspicions that they were in on the robberies."

Just before midnight, April 6, 1878, Sam, Arkansas Johnson, and the two other riders held up the westbound Texas & Pacific train at the tiny Eagle Ford station. They marched the station agent, engineer, and fireman back to the depot, where they were held under guard while Sam broke down the heavy wooden door of the express car with a log. No shots were fired, and after scooping up about fifty dollars in gold eagles the gang rode off.

The morning after the robbery, a Dallas posse led by Sam Finley, the well-known express company detective, and Ranger Commander June Peak picked up the trail of the gang.

Another casual encounter between the manhunters and the outlaws took place when they found Underwood and Frank Jackson asleep in the woods. As Underwood later told the story, no shots were fired as Peak and his men crept up on them, seized their rifles and six-shooters, then demanded their names.

"Jones," the imperturbable Jackson replied.

"Well, we don't want you," one of the leaders said. They returned the rifles and revolvers to the outlaws and "asked that they not shoot at them as they rode off."

Underwood and Jackson graciously gave their promise.[17]

A few days later Sheriff Egan's deputy, Tom Gerren, volunteered to find Sam's camp. Egan warned him that Sam would probably kill him, but when Gerren insisted, he reluctantly gave his permission.

Gerren, who knew Sam, found the outlaw's camp on the outskirts of Denton. He rode in, dismounted, and shook hands with the most wanted man in Texas. They talked "reservedly" until Gerren turned and found himself staring into the barrel of a Winchester held by a man sitting near a tree.

He didn't know Arkansas and asked Sam: "Who is that fellow, Sam?"

Bass grinned. "Oh, he's a fellow that stays around here."

Gerren, as he later reported, "took my leave."[18]

A week later Sam told the gang they were going to rob the Texas & Pacific railroad again, this time at the Mesquite station. Recruits were flocking into Sam's camp; to the regulars he added Sam Pipes, Albert Herndon, William Collins, and William Scott, with "nine other citizens of Denton County" held in reserve. All were young farm boys "chaffing for adventure." They had heard wild tales of the golden eagles Sam supposedly had taken from the express cars, and they winked and laughed when Sam insisted that the loot had been disappointingly small and "the business is dangerous."

Billy Collins was sent into Mesquite "to see how the land lay." For most of the afternoon he loafed about the sleepy little prairie town, twelve miles east of Dallas. Only the measured sound of the blacksmith's hammer broke the stillness. Even the town's one saloon was quiet, with only a few horses hitched outside. But young Collins did notice one thing: on a sidetrack near the station was a special train housing prisoners working on construction gangs for the railroad. Armed guards could be seen.

When he reported this, Sam only shrugged and pointed out that the few guards would never turn their backs on their very tough charges because they knew they would be killed in a mass escape.

Just about midnight, the gang clambered aboard the westbound train at Sam's command: "On to her, boys!"

As usual, an eyewitness to the robbery hurried to the offices of the *Denton Monitor* to give his account of what one victim called a "hilarious" robbery.[19]

Sam Bass Holds Up the Texas & Pacific Railroad at Mesquite

As the train stopped Mr. [Jake] Zurn, the agent stepped from the depot and was in the act of handing a paper aboard when he was saluted with the order: "Hold up your arms!"

The truth that this emanated from the robbers flashed across his mind at once but he obeyed knowing that resistance was useless. At this time Mr. [Daniel] Healey came off the train to speak to Mr. Zurn. He was ordered to stop and throw up his hands, and disregarding the order they hit him over the head several times with their pistols.

He at last effected his escape, losing his hat which was found this morning with a bullet hole through it. In the meantime the engineer had been secured. The fireman escaped and hid under some trestle work.

Mrs. Zurn was on the platform. At the first intimation of danger she started to go in, but was arrested by one of the ruffians who ordered her to throw up her hands, but she showed a great presence of mind, and a contempt of danger truly admirable, paid no attention to him, but went in and locked the door, whereupon they fired a volley at the door which had no effect except to make a loud noise and wake up the town.

They commenced the effort to get into the express car. But to all their commands and threats the messenger, who was quite cool all the time, refused their requests.

Then came a regular fusillade and enough shots were exchanged to kill every man there. During the firing Finellen, one of the guards, fired several times and hit one of the fellows. They then made the engineer give them oil, which they poured on the steps of the express car and set it afire.

After repeating this they at last got out the express messenger, his guard, the baggage master, mail agent and brakeman, who were all in the same car and from whom they got from between one hundred and one hundred and fifty dollars.

They got seventy-five cents from the brakeman but when he told them this was his last "red cent" they gave it back to him. Then they told Mr. Towers, the express agent, to go into the car with them and give them the registered package.

The robbers threatened to turn the convicts loose and for that reason the guards could render no assistance.

Mr. Gross, the enterprising merchant in Denton, hearing the noise got his gun and started to the scene of the action. He saw a man, the fireman, hiding under the bridge and taking him for one of the bandits, made him throw up his hands.

He then approached the station as prudently as possible and after waiting a while he heard the agent laugh.

The laugh was caused by the remark of the express messenger who asked the robbers after they went through him, "if they were not going to give him a receipt for the money."

Thinking the danger was over he went to them. They no sooner saw him when they drew their guns on him and made him surrender.

After they got all they wanted they marched the men out onto the prairie, told them to " 'bout face and to go double quick. . . ."

V. D. Lacy, a leading dry goods merchant of Ozark, Arkansas, the son of Mrs. S. E. Lacy of Denton was on the train. He did not know any of the robbers but believed by the remark made by one of them that they were from Dallas.

For instance when the peanut vendor on the train appeared with a pistol, one of the robbers cried out:

"We don't want any peanuts—get back!"

This indicated to Mr. Lacy that the robbers were not strangers to the employees of the train. He says the peanut boy, the messenger and the conductor displayed a great deal of pluck.

Conductor (Julius) Alvord emptied his pistol and during the time was recipient of a running spit-spat denunciation from the train robbers who were firing at him.

Said one robber: "You are a brave dog but you are my meat."

The conductor made no reply but appeared to be in good humor as were the robbers.

The messenger saved fifteen hundred dollars by putting it in his boots. He held out to the last minute, and the passengers thought he would be hung by the robbers, on account of having killed one with his shotgun.

Mr. Lacy said the whole affair was conducted by the train robbers in a quiet manner. The chief of the gang gave his orders in a low tone and they were executed with promptness and dispatch. At times there was gusty laughter from among them from remarks made by the employees.

The robbery, Mr. Lacy said, was conducted and ended with a hilarity more peculiar to a dancing party than a robbery . . .

Despite the "hilarity," for the first time there were injuries among Sam's riders: Sebe Barnes had been wounded four times, three shots in the leg and one in the thigh; Sam had been hit by a "timtit vest pocket revolver"—the ball, stopped by his coat, freakishly traveled down his arm to fall out in his hand; one of his men died of wounds. Sam's epitaph for the victim, as repeated by Jim Murphy, was:

"I'm sorry for it, he was a fine looking young man but I warned them all it was a dangerous business, that they had better stay at home but they all wanted to learn the game of making money easy as times were getting hard and crops short, and [they] persisted in going."

Mesquite was Sam's last train robbery; after that he was on the run. For the first time Sheriff "Dad" Egan was issued a United States warrant for the arrest of Bass, Underwood, Barnes, and Jackson for train robbery. Denton County was virtually crisscrossed by posses under Egan and Sheriff Everheart of Grayson County, and Rangers under captains Lee Hall and Peak.

On Sunday morning, April 29, Jim Murphy in his shack on the outskirts of Cove Hollow warned Sam that Sheriff Everheart's posse and a company of Rangers were approaching. Sam roused his men. The combined posses galloped across the prairie to line up on one edge of the deep ravine, facing the outlaws on the opposite bluff. Five hundred yards separated them.

Sam, in front of his men, yelled: "Stand up and fight like men," and fired at Everheart.

Both sides opened up with rifles and six-shooters; gunfire echoed across the empty land while a thick pall of gunpowder clung to the trees and brush of the hollow.

Ranger Sergeant Parrot waited patiently until he caught Sam in his sights. He fired two shots in rapid succession; one tore the cartridge belt from the outlaw leader's waist, the other shattered the stock of his Winchester. Sam then decided on a valorous retreat.

"They hit me at last, boys," he shouted. "Let's get away from here."[20]

A few days later it was Royal Wetsel, Sheriff Egan's "spy," who found the gang "camped by Hard Carter's house." He fired a signal to alert the other members of the posse, bravely dismounted, and calmly exchanged shots with Sam and the gang as they pounded past. Both sides missed.

The "war" continued for days, Egan's posse conducting a running fight with the outlaws. When word was passed from ranch to farm that "Dad Egan's treed Sam," riders galloped from Dallas, Denton, and other towns to be in on the kill. But Bass knew the land as well as he did the back of his own hand. Outlaws and possemen fought across the prairie, in hollows, thick cross timbers on the banks of streams, and finally into a dense swamp where the sheriff wearily told his men the trail was lost.

They returned to Denton, where Egan conferred with Peak, who had just returned from a futile search of the heavily wooded area along Hickory Creek, between Lewisville and Denton. As Judge Hogg, Sam's biographer, depicted the town, Denton was an armed camp. Every man within fifty miles who owned a shotgun and a horse was in town, boasting how he would capture or kill the outlaw leader whose fame was spreading across the West.

In the morning Egan and Peak had agreed on a plan: the Rangers would guard Dallas Road, several miles below Denton, while the sheriff would divide his men into several groups, each to search a section of the county.

The area was now filled with volunteers and the inevitable happened: one man shot off his toe, another arrested a passing farmer for Sam Bass, and cattle were killed.

While the posses were chasing Sam, United States marshals were arresting anyone suspected of aiding the gang. Pipes and Herndon were jailed, and Henderson Murphy and his son Jim were picked up in the roundup and charged with harboring fugitives. It was a time of official hysteria; indictments were "ground out wholesale against people, many of whom had as little to do with Sam Bass as the judge or district attorney. . . ."

Denton was terrorized by federal marshals dragging men and women from their stores, beds, and homes to be sent to the federal jail at Tyler. Many were held for exorbitant bail and remained imprisoned for a long time until the charges were dismissed.

Sympathy turned to Sam, with the embittered ranchers, farmers, and townspeople viewing the government agents and possemen from Dallas as dangerous interlopers. The witch-hunt finally died down, but Egan, Peak, and Sheriff Everheart of Grayson County doggedly kept on Sam's faint trail.

On May 7 Bass and his men left their swamp hideout to ride to Big Caddo Creek, where Frank Jackson had relatives, to get provisions and fresh horses.

A "suspicious woman from the neighborhood" alerted Stephens County Sheriff Barry Meadows, who blundered into the outlaws' camp. A fight took place with many bullets fired, but the marksmanship on both sides was so poor that there were no casualties.

Meadows sent a telegram to Denton, and Captain Peak and his rangers hurried to the scene. A gun battle on horseback took place from Sunday to the following Tuesday, with Sam leading his men across ravines, rivers, creeks,

L. B. Blair, Deputy Sheriff of Erath County, Texas, celebrated Indian fighter and lawman who was a member of the posse that ambushed Sam Bass. Blair, "known all over western Texas as the greatest terror to evildoers," as a frontier newspaper noted, at one time had in his jail three murderers and seven rustlers whom he had captured. *The James D. Horan Civil War and Western Americana Collection*

and up and down hills. The frustrated Captain Peak told Sheriff Meadows that he would capture or kill Bass "if he lost half his men in the attempt."

But Sam, still cheerful and defiant, stopped off at a general store to leave word with the owner that they were ready to face Peak and his rangers "in a desperate fight and he did not propose to be bull-dozed any longer. . . ."

Shortly after the gang rode off they came upon four farmers, all armed with shotguns. They told Sam that they were after the great Sam Bass and intended to "share one fourth of the glory and one fourth of the reward money."

It was too much for Sam. He slapped the manhunters on the back, declared that they, too, were searching for the great Sam Bass, and proposed a partnership. The quartet agreed and Sam and his grinning riders returned to the general store, where Sam, at gunpoint, forced the four to drink enough whiskey "that the four heroes were so drunk they were ready to go to bed on the ground and cover [themselves] with a plank."

Sam, who loved good horseflesh, brooded over the loss of his mounts to Egan's and Judge Hogg's posses. When he learned that the animals were in Work's livery in Denton, he boldly raided the town and recaptured both horses.

"Damn 'em, we'll show 'em they can't steal anything from us that we can't get back!" Underwood shouted as they galloped down the main street. As they passed Sheriff Egan's home, Sam saw the lawman's eight-year-old son walking toward the barn. When he had worked for Egan, young John had been his favorite.

"Hello, Little Pard," he shouted and waved as they passed.

When a courier arrived with the news Mrs. Egan refused to awaken her husband, who had only just returned after days of chasing the outlaws. But when a posse rode up she finally roused the sheriff, who wearily put on his boots, saddled his horse, and again led the angry townspeople after Sam.

A posse under Deputy Sheriff Clay Withers first clashed with the gang. When Sam forced the fight, the posse finally retreated with one man wounded. A few hours later Egan and his men joined Withers, and the chase continued.

For most of the day it was hounds and hare. The manhunters now numbered more than forty; outlaws and possemen swayed in their saddles as the relentless running fight went on "with the temperature at 95 degrees in the shade," as Judge Hogg recalled.

But the chase was beginning to show on Sam. At Davenport Mills he rushed into a general store where the clerk was waiting on two lady customers. When Sam called out for provisions, the clerk snapped: "Just a moment, sir, I must attend to these ladies."

"Goddammit!" the usually gallant Sam shouted. "I'm in a hurry and I want you to wait on me. I'm Sam Bass!"

"Excuse me, ladies," the clerk said and hurriedly gave Sam his provisions.[21]

The hunt continued for days with the posses always in sight of the outlaws, who stole horses from ranches or forced riders to turn over their reins. On June 12 Captain Peak discovered the saddle-weary gang camped on Salt Creek in southwestern Wise County. This time Peak led his men in a wild, galloping charge. Volleys were exchanged and Arkansas Johnson fell. The rest of the gang, now on foot except for Underwood, who had reached the horses to make his escape, were forced into a clump of trees and tangled brush. Here the battle reached an impasse; for some reason Peak did not order an advance on the hideout. The furious possemen retreated, leaving Sam and his men to escape once again.[22]

While the posses were chasing Sam, Jim Murphy's father was arrested and confined in the Tyler prison as an accessory. Many of Denton's leading citizens protested that the senior Murphy was a "man of honor and integrity," but Captain Peak and Sheriff Egan pointed out that someone in that law-abiding and honorable family had been harboring the gang and warning them when the posses neared Sam's hideout in Cove Hollow.

Jim brooded about his father's confinement and blamed not himself but Sam for his family's disgrace. He later told Judge Hogg that he had known Sam, Underwood, and Jackson for years, and while he had given them food and shelter he had never taken part in a train or stage robbery.

Captain Peak then ordered the arrest of Jim, who was confined in Sherman. When he was transferred to Tyler by Deputy U. S. Marshal Walter Johnson, he offered to lead Sam and his men into an ambush if all charges were dropped against him and his father. Johnson brought the proposal to Major Jones, the Ranger commander who had questioned Sam. Satisfied that Murphy was sincere, he arranged with United States District Attorney Andrew J. Evans of the Western District of Texas to have Jim and his father released on a "straw bond." Evans signed a secret consent agreement protecting Jim's bail bondsman and dismissing all charges pending against the Murphys if Jim would assist the government law enforcement agencies in securing the arrest of the gang.[23]

Only Sheriff Everheart of Grayson County had been informed that Jim was now playing the role of a traitor; curiously, the aggressive and honorable Sheriff Egan, who had chased, fought, and trailed Sam for months was not told of the arrangement by the federal lawmen.

While the trap was being planned for their capture or death, Sam and Frank Jackson came out of the brush and rode into Dallas, where they bought guns, ammunition, provisions, and fresh horses. On June 15, 1878, they returned to their favorite hideout, Cove Hollow. As they rode in, they met Murphy in his cabin on the outskirts of the Hollow. As Murphy described the reunion, "Sam and Frank shook hands and took on over me terribly."

"Well, old fellow, how do you like to play checkers with your nose?" Sam asked, referring to Murphy's recent stay in jail.

"Not at all," Murphy replied.

"That's h——l, ain't it, Jim?" Sam said sympathetically. "Well, old fellow, you have better come and go with me and you won't have to play checkers with your nose. We have lots of fun and plenty of money in camp."

"Well, I had thought of going with you boys," Murphy said, "but I have about given it out and thought I would go back and stand my trial and come clear."

"Yes, Jim," Sam answered, "that's very nice, but you won't have a show with the United States, with the prejudice there is against you. There is no showing for you boys because they think you are friends of mine, and I tell you the best thing you can do, is to go with me and make some money, and we will send the money to pay off your bond as soon as we make a strike."

Jim made a great show of considering the proposition, then said:

"Well, Sam, if you will wait until I thresh my wheat tomorrow, maybe I'll go."

"All right," said Sam, "if you will go, we will wait. We need you in our business."

And to prove his affluence he gave Murphy a twenty-dollar gold eagle and asked him to cash it in town.

The wheat was threshed and Jim Murphy rode off with Bass and Barnes, who told him they were on a tour looking to make another "strike," preferably a bank.

In late 1878, Murphy gave Judge Hogg a long statement detailing his move-. ments with the gang and how he set up the ambush at Round Rock. It is the most accurate version of the outlaw leader's last days. The simple, day-to-day account has a marvelous sense of the tension, frustrations, and near-misses that any informer suffers in his final act of betrayal. There was no remorse, no compassion, in Murphy's deadly game of self-survival.

He told Hogg that it was an aimless tour. Sam, still the cheerful, happy-go-lucky leader, took his men in and out of the small towns, passing fields and farmers for whom he had worked as a hired hand and insisting that his men practice their "shoot."

"You had better practice," he warned Jackson and Murphy, "for I tell you, if old Dad [Sheriff Egan] gets after us you will have to shoot—for we mean business now."

He pointed to a log three or four hundred yards away and told Murphy:

"Watch me hit that piece. If that was old Judge Hogg [who would write his biography] how easy could I bust his leather! I would make him wish he had never saddled old Coley [one of Sam's horses taken by the posse]—the blamed old rascal. He ain't able to buy him a good horse, so he must step around and pick up my boys' horses. I took my gun down off of him once but I will never do that any more."

Egan seemed on his mind; as he rode he told the men that they had to be alert for Egan and his possemen "and that blasted Clay Withers—is some h——l too as you go along but all we got to do is to kill a few horses, then retreat and they'll kind o' go slow and won't crowd us much more." Like Egan, Withers, a deputy sheriff of Elizabethtown, in Denton County, was constantly trailing Sam.

There was one poignant moment. When two small boys walked into the outlaws' camp, Sam told them:

"Well, boys, I am looking for a sheep ranch, and if these old grangers will let me alone, I will move in here, be a neighbor to you and go to raising sheep."

Murphy told Judge Hogg:

"That tickled the boys and they went away, laughing. Then Sam said as we rode off: 'What would I give to be in their places! I would give all the gold I ever saw, and more too if I had it. But it's too late now to think of that . . . it all goes in a lifetime . . . I will make some old banker pay for my troubles because money will sweeten anything."

On the road and over the campfires, Sam and Barnes described for Murphy the details of the various robberies they had committed and the gun battles which had taken place.

In Dallas County they stopped at a country store, where Sam, the most wanted man on the southwestern frontier, bought a bag of candy which he shared with a farm boy. While the boy munched the candy, he boasted to the loungers how he intended to hunt down Sam Bass, collect the mounting rewards, and live a life of luxury. Sam solemnly wished him luck.

Along the road they were joined by two new friends of Sam, who openly accused Murphy of being a traitor and urged Sam to "kill him right now."

The frightened Murphy turned to Jackson.

"Did you hear that, Frank?"

Jackson nodded. "Yes, Jim h——l is up! Just be easy. I won't let them hurt you."

Despite the security measures the United States District Attorney's office in Tyler had taken, news of Murphy's role as a traitor had leaked out. Before they left, the two strangers, never identified, warned Sam that he was riding to his death. Only Jackson defended Jim. One time Murphy awoke to find Bass and Barnes, six-shooters cocked, "ready to blow out my brains," but again Jackson, this time at gunpoint, warned his leader that he would have to face him in a gunfight if he harmed Murphy.

Sam hesitated. For a long moment in the fresh dawn they faced each other with drawn guns while the man who was planning to betray them cowered in his blanket, begged for his life, and swore to his friendship and loyalty.

Finally, reluctantly, Sam and Barnes holstered their guns, the glowering Barnes warning Murphy that he would watch his every step, "because the word has come down to us that one of Murphy's boys is ready to betray us and I don't trust you any more."

Evidently Murphy persuaded Sam and Barnes, the "Nubbins Colt," that he was eager and ready to rob the strongest bank or the most heavily guarded train. Like traitors from the beginning of time, he finally groveled, protested, and lied their suspicions away.

As the days passed, Sam lost some of his charisma; he tried to recruit new riders but the young cowboys and farmers shook their heads.

Once, while riding to Rockwall, they stopped dead in the road; directly in front of them was a gallows. As Murphy later learned, it had been built only a few weeks before for the execution of an outlaw who cheated the law by committing suicide in his cell.

The three horsemen silently studied the stark gibbet outlined against the lowering evening sky. Sam dismounted, told the others to make camp, then slowly walked up to the gallows.

He returned, "looking very serious." "Boys, that makes me feel bad," he told Barnes and Murphy. "That is the first one of them things I ever saw, and I hope it will be the last."

They ate a hasty supper and despite the darkness rode off, leaving behind the gallows splashed with the light of the rising moon, its ugly rope swaying in the evening breeze.

But the next morning Sam had regained his cheerfulness. He urged them to saddle up and ride into the frontier town of Kauffman "to look over the pickings."

But the tiny settlement didn't have a bank, so the gang rode on. Sam, an extrovert, attracted a strange collection of casual friends along the way: the ferryman who insisted on letting them in on his secret plans to capture the great Sam Bass; the farmer who invited them to celebrate July 4th by eating watermelons and listening to his philosophy that all railroads were robbing the poor and he didn't care how many trains Sam Bass robbed as long as he "let the citizens alone"; the lonely, talkative schoolteacher who stuck so close to them that they had to take the wrong pike to get rid of him; the farm boy who gave them peaches and amused Sam with his wild boasting of how he was going to trap the wily Sam Bass.

Murphy, still wary of the quick-tempered Barnes, realized that he had to get word to Sheriff Everheart or Major Jones. He tried several times to send a note or telegram but failed.

In Ennis, Sam sent Murphy and Barnes into town to "look at the bank." The building looked too formidable, so Sam reluctantly called off his strike. In Waco, Bass treated Murphy and Jackson to a shave, haircut, dinner, and fresh horses.

"Jim, this is putting on a heap of style for highwaymen, ain't it?" Jackson observed as they walked down the town's main street. While waiting to change a bill in the Waco Savings Bank, Jackson nudged Murphy; on the counters were piles of greenbacks and gold eagles.

"If we mean business, this is the place to commence, Jim," Jackson whispered.

Sam, impressed by Jackson's excited report, went back into Waco for a personal inspection. He returned and announced that he was ready "to hit the bank."

The frightened Murphy demurred; escape routes had to be planned, provisions gathered, and the best horseflesh bought. Jackson waved away his suggestions.

"Jim," he said, "we're going to take that [bank] as easy as to take a drink of water. We will scare those town folks so bad they won't know what is up until we have the money and be gone."

Murphy kept pointing out the dangers of hitting a large town unprepared.

They argued for hours over the campfire until Bass announced that he would give his decision in the morning. After breakfast he grudgingly announced that he agreed with Murphy, but then he startled the traitor by telling him that he was giving him the honor of selecting the bank they would next hit.

Thinking fast, Murphy, who knew the layout of Round Rock, announced that he selected the Williamson County Bank, one of the largest in the territory. They bought provisions and beer, with Sam announcing they had spent their last golden eagle.

"I'll get some more in a few days," he predicted. "Let it gush! It all goes in a lifetime."

Barnes stole a horse that afternoon and spent most of the evening bragging how they would make Sheriff Everheart, Clay Withers, or Dad Egan and their posses run after they took the bank. But Sam soberly warned him that while he could stand off the Denton lawmen "with a wooden gun," they might face stiffer opposition in Round Rock.

They stopped off at Belton, a small town where Murphy managed to write a few frantic lines to Sheriff Everheart and Deputy Marshal Johnson, "telling them for God's sakes to come at once to Round Rock." At Georgetown he sent another note, this time to Major Jones. Finally they reached the outskirts of Round Rock. Bass went into town alone and soon returned.

"Jim," he said, "you were right about coming to this place. We can take that bank too easy to talk about."

A short time later, Sam Bass led Jackson, Barnes, and Murphy into town.

Judge Hogg interviewed Jim Murphy, Major Jones, and the seriously wounded Deputy Sheriff Maurice Moore shortly after Sam's last raid, to leave this account.

The Battle of Round Rock and the Capture of Sam Bass

Major Jones received Murphy's letter from Belton and at once repaired to Round Rock in company with Maurice Moore, Deputy Sheriff of Travis county, to meet the Robbers. Lieut. [N.O.] Reynolds was ordered to Round Rock with a detachment of his rangers [from Company E]. Maj. Jones notified the banker of the plan of the bandits and of the measures he had on foot to arrest them. The arrangements of Major Jones did not mature, but a collision was precipitated by the mistake of Deputy Moore and [Deputy Sheriff A.W.] Grimes, of Williamson county, the particulars of which, as detailed by Moore, who was severely wounded in the left lung, are here given. He says:

"About 4 p.m., I was standing in front of Smith's livery stable, and three men passed up the street. Smith remarked to me, 'There go three strangers.' I noticed them carefully and thought one of them had a six shooter under his coat. The others were carrying saddlebags. They looked at me rather hard and went across the street into a store. I walked up the street to where Grimes was standing, and remarked to him, 'I think one of those men has a six shooter on.' Grimes remarked that he would go and see. We walked across the street and went into the store. Not wishing to let them know I was watching them, I stood up inside the store door with my hands in my pockets, whistling. Grimes approached them carelessly and asked one if he had not a six shooter. They all three replied, yes, and at the same instant two of them shot Grimes and one shot me.

After I had fired my first shot I could not see the men on account of the smoke. They continued shooting and so did I, until I fired five shots: as they passed out I saw one man bleeding from the arm and side; I then leaned against the store door, feeling faint and sick, and recovering myself, I started on and fired the remaining shot at one of them.

"Having lent one of my pistols to another man the day before, I stopped and reloaded my pistol, went into the stable and got my Winchester and started in pursuit of them, and was stopped by Dr. [A. F.] Morris, who said, 'Hold on; don't go any further, for if you get over-heated your wound may kill you.' I stopped and gave my Winchester to another man. Grimes did not have time to pull out his pistol; six bullet holes were put through his body.

The rangers hearing the firing came upon the scene and fired upon the robbers as they retreated. Major Jones reached the place in time to engage in the fusilade. The whole village was thrown into a tumult of excitement, and the citizens who could procure arms joined in the affray. The robbers taking cover behind houses and fences, and firing back at every opportunity, retreated down an alley towards their horses. Early in the engagement Bass had received a shot through the hand, and as they retreated down the alley a ranger, George Harrall, shot him in the back, inflicting a mortal wound. He, however, reached and mounted his horse. Barnes was shot by Geo. Ware, a ranger, through the head, just as he mounted his horse, and fell dead on the spot. Jackson and Bass rode off together. Major Jones, Ware and Tubbs fired at them as they left. F. L. Jordon and Albert Highsmith, citizens of Round Rock, joined in the fight and did their best to lift the robbers out of their saddles. Major Jones, Capt. Lee Hall and three rangers gave chase on horseback, but the bandits had the start of them too far, and they lost the trail and returned to the town. That evening Lieut. Reynolds with ten rangers, from San Saba, and Lieut. [John B.] Armstrong, from Austin, with a squad, arrived at Round Rock. After Bass and Jackson had gone several miles from the scene Bass' wounds began to grow so sore that he found he would have to stop. Jackson wanted to stop and remain with him, but Bass told him no—that he was seriously wounded and must stop, and that Frank must take care of himself. He gave Jackson all the money he had, his horse, arms, and ammunition and enjoined him to go and leave him. Jackson took his departure from Bass and left him there alone. After Jackson left Bass went to a house to get some water. He was bloody and looked very feeble; this attracted the attention of the lady of the house who gave him the water. After he got the water he left afoot and the lady saw the direction he went. Next morning she informed his pursuers of the incident and by this means he was found. We give below an extract from a letter from Travis county, written to the *Galveston News* and clipped from the *Denton Monitor* of August the 2d, '78, as follows:

"Later in the evening Lieut. Armstrong's party from Austin arrived. Next morning Sergt. [C. L.] Neville, of Lieut. Reynolds' company, with eight men and Deputy Sheriff [Milt] Tucker, of this county, took the trail of Bass and Jackson where it had been lost the evening before, but soon found that the two had separated.

After hunting around awhile they found Bass lying under a large tree in the edge of the prairie. As the sergeant approached, he held up his hand and said, "Don't shoot; I am unarmed and helpless; I am the man you're looking for; I am Sam Bass."

He had lain in the brush all night, but crawled out to the tree in the prairie about daylight, and hailed a negro who passed him, and tried to bribe him to haul him off and secrete him. Information of the capture was brought to Major Jones, who went out, accompanied by Dr. [C. P.] Cochran, and brought the prisoner in.

The news of the capture of Sam Bass flew across the frontier. Major Jones sent a telegram to Attorney General William Steele and a speaker at the State Democratic Convention in Austin interrupted politics to announce that the famous outlaw was in custody. Sam by now was a legend, and the delegates refused to believe the news. The Attorney General telegraphed Jones to confirm the arrest by telegram and, if possible, to bring Bass in irons to Austin.

While the delegates rose to cheer the news, Sam was dying in a small shack near the Hart House in Round Rock. After he had examined the outlaw leader, Dr. Cochran solemnly shook his head; Sam didn't have much time, he told Major Jones.

Bass continued to hold on as the curious poured into the town by train, wagon, and on horseback. Crowds swarmed to the shack hoping to catch a glimpse of Sam. The correspondent of the *Galveston News*, then the leading newspaper in the state, was permitted to interview Sam.

He admitted that he was Sam Bass and said he had intended to "make a raise on the bank here and then go to Mexico." He also told the reporter, "I'm shot to pieces and there's no use to deny it."[24]

While Sam clung to life, Deputy Sheriff Grimes and Sebe Barnes were buried—Grimes given an elaborate funeral and Barnes unceremoniously put into a cheap pine box and buried in a corner of the Round Rock graveyard.

Although Sam refused to make a formal deathbed confession, Major Jones kept a copybook at the outlaw's bedside with orders to his men to take down everything Bass said.

Judge Hogg copied "verbatim" Sam's last words from that book.[25]

The Last Words of Sam Bass

Joel Collins, Bill Heffrige, Tom Nixon, Jack Davis, Jim Berry and me were in the Union Pacific robbery. Tom Nixon is in Canada; haven't seen him since that robbery. Jack Davis was in New Orleans from the time of the Union Pacific robbery till he went to Denton to get me to go in with him and buy hides. This was the last of April, 1878.

Grimes asked me if I had a pistol. Said I had, and then all three of us drew and shot him. If I killed him he was the first man I ever killed. Am 25 years old, and have two brothers, John and Linton; have four sisters. They all live at Mitchel, Ind. Have not seen Henry Underwood since the Salt Creek fight. Saw the two Collinses at old man Collins, since I left Denton.

Have been in the robbing business a long time. Had done much of that kind of business before the U. P. robbery last fall.

First time I saw Billy Scott was at Bob Murphy's; last time was at Green Hills. Saw him at William Collins', but do not know the date; do not pay any attention to dates. Never saw him but those three times. I will not tell who was in the Eagle Ford robbery besides myself and Jackson, because it is against my profession. Think I will go to hell, anyhow, and believe a man should die with what he knows in him.

I do not know. They were with us about six months. Henry was with me in the Salt Creek fight, four or five weeks ago. Arkansaw Johnson was killed in that fight. Do not know whether Underwood was wounded in the Salt Creek fight or not. Sebe Barnes, Frank Jackson and Charley Carter were there. We were all set afoot in that fight, but stole horses enough to remount ourselves in three hours, or as soon as dark came, after which we went back to Denton, where we stayed till we came to Round Rock.

Q—Where is Jackson now?

A—I do not know.

Q—How did you usually get together after being scattered?

A—Generally told by friends. [Declined to tell who these friends were.]

Q—How came you to commence this kind of life?

A—Started out on sporting horses.

Q—Why did you get worse than horse-racing?

A—Because they robbed me of my first $300.

Q—After they robbed you what did you do next?

A—Went to robbing stages in Black Hills—robbed seven. Got very little money. Jack Davis, Nixon and myself were all that were in the Black Hills stage robberies.

Speaking of Bass' caution in not compromising himself or his friends, Maj. Jones, who had him in charge, says: "I tried every conceivable plan to obtain some information from him, but to no purpose. About noon on Sunday, he began to suffer greatly and sent for me to know if I could not give him some relief. I did everything I could for him. Thinking this an excellent opportunity, I said to him, "Bass, you have done much wrong in this world, you now have an opportunity to do some good before you die by giving some information which will lead to the vindication of that justice which you have so often defied and the law which you have constantly violated." He replied, "No, I won't tell." "Why won't you," said I. "Because it is agin my profession to blow on my pals. If a man knows anything he ought to die with it in him." He positively refused to converse on religion, and in reply to some remark made, he said, "I am going to hell anyhow." I made a particular effort to obtain some information from him in regard to William Collins. I asked him if he was ever at Collin's house? He said no. I then put the question in a different form, saying, "Where did you first see Will Scott?" He replied at Bob Murphy's. I then said, "You saw him at Green Hill's, too, didn't you?" He replied yes. These answers were not of any consequence, but I then said, "When did you see him at William Collins." He said, "I don't remember, as I never paid attention to dates, being always on the scout, I only saw him these three times." This answer was important, as it fixed the fact that Bass was at Collin's house. But this was the only statement of any importance which he made. All his other statements were of facts well-known or concerning individuals beyond the reach of future justice."

Bass clung to the hope of life to the last extremity. While suffering the most excruciating anguish from his wounds he hugged the delusion of recovery. At last when his physician told him that death was fast approaching, and that he would soon be gone to eternity he said "Let me go!" Then closing his eyes for a few moments, he opened them and exclaimed to his nurse, as if startled, "The world is bobbing around me!"

These were the last words of Sam Bass.

Sam's grave was unmarked for a year. Then, in the summer of 1879, his sister came from Indiana and erected a tombstone. Sebe Barnes's grave, in the same cemetery, had a small sandstone marker with this tribute:

"He was the right bower to Sam Bass."[26]

Souvenir hunters chipped away at both markers until they vanished. In the late 1920s S. E. Loving, a local monument maker, placed a simple concrete slab over both graves.

After Sam's death reward-hungry sheriffs and deputies continued to hunt down members of the gang. Henry Collins, Joel's nineteen-year-old brother, who had briefly ridden with Bass, was killed by a sheriff shortly after the Round Rock battle.

Billy Collins, who had jumped bail in Tyler after being indicted as an accessory to Sam in the Mesquite train robbery, died from his wounds after killing Deputy Sheriff William H. Anderson of Dallas, who had tenaciously trailed him to the tiny farming town of Pembina, Dakota Territory, near the Manitoba border.

Underwood never again appeared after the Salt Creek battle with June Peak's rangers. Legend claimed that he later rode with Jesse James, which is not true. Frank Jackson, who stayed with Sam until there was no more hope, briefly appeared in Denton County after the Round Rock shooting, then vanished. Charlie Siringo claimed that Jackson was an honest rancher in Montana, and other frontiersmen placed him in various sections of the West working as a cattleman or a peace officer.

The naïve young farm boys Sam Pipes and Albert G. Herndon, Sam's raw recruits who wanted to learn "the robbing business" and ended up in prison instead, were pardoned by President Grover Cleveland after volunteering to work as nurses in a plague ship quarantined in New York harbor.

Tom Nixon, who helped Sam hold up the Union Pacific at Big Springs, Nebraska, safely made his way to Canada and vanished with his share of the golden eagle loot; Jack Davis, another member of the gang, fled to South America.

Like all informers and traitors, Jim Murphy suffered the worst. Less than a week after Sam was buried, United States Attorney Evans kept his word and dismissed the indictment against Jim and his father. Murphy returned to Denton, but life was never the same. Scarcely a day went by that he didn't receive a threat or word passed from some kindly law officer that a wild young cowboy eager to make a reputation as a gunfighter was on his way to Denton to kill him.

One letter he wrote to Major Jones shows how the gang crumbled after Sam's death. He told the Ranger commander that stalwart Frank Jackson was eager to set up a trap for Underwood and the other remaining fugitive members of the gang in return for dismissal of all charges against him. It was the only thing Murphy could do for Jackson, who undoubtedly had saved his life on that aimless tour of the Texas towns when Sam was looking to make another "raise."

Jackson vanished and Murphy stayed on in Denton, frightened and alone, scorned by his fellow townsmen. At one time there were so many threats against his life that he lived in the county jail.

Then, a year after the Round Rock battle, Murphy accidentally swallowed atrophine, a poisonous crystalline alkaloid he had been using for an eye disease. After a day of agony and convulsions, the man who had "sold out Sam and Barnes and left their friends to mourn" finally answered Gabriel's horn to get a "scorching," as the ballad said . . .

THE JOHNSON COUNTY WAR, THE WILD BUNCH, BUTCH CASSIDY AND THE SUNDANCE KID

THE WILD BUNCH, THE LARGEST BAND OF OUTLAWS IN THE history of the Wild West, was born of a depression in the cattle country that followed the disastrous blizzard of 1886-87. In affluent times rustling had been tolerated by the big cattle syndicates. But a combination of a declining eastern beef market, the steady advance of small ranchers, sheepmen, fences and plows ended the free range and forced the barons to view steer stealing and mavericking—putting your brand on stray young cattle that you knew did not belong to you—as major crimes.

When jobless, rootless cowboys drifted into the desolate Hole-in-the-Wall country and began to prey on the decimated herds, the cattlemen struck back.

They started with vigilante hangings. Their first victims were Jim Averill and his common-law wife, "Cattle Kate" Watson. Averill had maintained a small store in which he sold whiskey and supplies and fenced stolen cattle; Kate traded sex for steers. Together they acquired a sizable herd.

Then Averill, already under suspicion, began writing indignant letters to the local newspapers denouncing the large cattle interests as tyrants who were forcing out the smaller rancher and settler. One hot July night a posse took Jim and Kate into quiet Spring Creek Canyon on the Sweetwater and hanged them from the small trees.

An organization of gunmen recruited by the cattlemen and dubbed the

Fort McKinney W.T.
May 3rd. — 1880;
Judge Andrews.
  Laramie City Wyo.
  Dear Sir:
    You will no doubt be surprised to hear of my having shot Charley Johnson. but I was compelled to do so or be shot myself; according to his own words which were not only spoken to me, but to others and the people at large. I sincerely regret that such things had to happen — but I avoided it by keeping out of his way since March 20. until yesterday when he met me where I could not get out of his way in safety. You know the character of this man.

    I want to know when you will be here and if you can assist

Jim Averill, who died a rustler's death at the end of a rope on the Sweetwater. *Courtesy Collection of Fred and Jo Mazzulla*

A letter written by Jim Averill to a Laramie City judge offering to surrender for killing a man in what he claimed was self-defense. *Courtesy Collection of Fred and Jo Mazzulla*

me by counsel I would like to see you here, and if you had have here this awful affair would not have happened as you know I intimated to you that I wanted to put him under bonds to keep the peace and leave me alone.

    Please let me hear from you soon as possible and your advice be of assistance to me I believe
    Respectfully Your
    James Averill

Spring Canyon on the Sweetwater and the tree vigilantes used to hang Cattle Kate Watson and Jim Averill in July 1889. *Courtesy University of Wyoming Library*

A vigilante committee of the Wild West with its ropes. *The James D. Horan Civil War and Western Americana Collection*

Cattle Kate Watson, who traded her favors for stolen cattle. Vigilantes hanged her and Jim Averill on the Sweetwater. *Courtesy University of Wyoming Library*

Lynching Rustler

Last week we remarked that the failure of the courts to convict and punish cattle thieves would result in stockmen taking the matter into their own hands, and this prediction has been verified right speedily. Last Sunday night James Averill and an abandoned woman who lived with him as his wife were hanged near Independence mountain on the Sweetwater in Carbon county. The Cheyenne *Leader* gives the following particulars:

Averill and the woman were fearless maverickers. The female was the equal of any man on the range. Of robust physique she was a daredevil in the saddle, handy with a six-shooter and an adept with the lariat and branding iron.

The thieving pair were ordered to leave the country several times, but paid no attention to the warnings, sending the message that they could take care of themselves, that mavericks were common property and that they would continue to appropriate unmarked cattle.

Lately it has been rumored that the woman and Averill were engaged in a regular round up of mavericks and would gather several hundred for shipment this fall. The ugly story was partially verified by the stealthy visit of a cow boy to their place Saturday. He reported that their corral held no less than fifty head of newly branded steers, mostly yearlings, with a few nearly full grown.

The statement of the spy circulated rapidly and thoroughly incensed the ranchman, who resolved to abate the menace to their herds. Word was passed along the river and early in the night from ten to twenty men, made desperate by steady loss, gathered at a designated rendezvous and quietly galloped to the Averill ranch. A few hundred yards from the cabin they dismounted and approached cautiously. This movement was well advised, for Averill had murdered two men and would not hesitate to shoot, while the woman was always full of fight.

Within the little habitation sat the thieving pair before a rude fireplace. The room was clouded with cigarette smoke. A whisky bottle with two glasses was on the deal table, and firearms were scattered around the interior so as to be within easy reach.

The leader of the regulators stationed a man with a Winchester at each window and led a rush into the door. The sound of "Hands up!" sounded above the crash of glass as the rifles were leveled at the strangely assorted pair of thieves. There was a struggle, but the lawless partners were quickly overpowered and their hands bound.

Averill, always feared because he was a murderous coward, showed himself a cur. He begged and whined, and protested innocence, even saying that the woman did all the stealing. The female was made of sterner stuff. She exhausted a blasphemous vocabulary upon the visitors, who essayed to stop the vile flow by gagging her, but found the task too great. After applying every imaginable epithet to the lynchers, she cursed everything and everybody, challenging the Deity to cheat her enemies by striking her dead if he dared. When preparations for the short trip to the scaffold were made she called for her own horse and vaulted to its back from the ground.

Ropes were hung from the limb of a big cottonwood on the south bank of the Sweetwater. Nooses were adjusted to the necks of Averill and his wife and their horses led from under them. The woman died with curses on her foul lips.

A point overlooked by the amateur executioners was tying the limbs of the victims, and the kicking and writhing of these members was something awful.

Monday morning the bodies were swayed to and fro by a gentle breeze which wafted the sweet odor of modest prairie flowers across the plain. The faces were discolored and shrunken tongues hung from between their swollen lips, while a film had gathered over the bulging eyes, and the unnatural position of the limbs completed the frightful picture.

The coroner's jury investigated the case and returned a verdict charging the hanging of the rustlers to John Durbin of Cheyenne, Robert Galbraith of Rawlins, Tom Sun, A. J. Bothwell, Terence McLean and Robert Connor. A Rawlins telegram says that all the men were arrested by Sheriff Hadsell of Carbon county and given a preliminary yesterday afternoon. Bail was fixed at $5,000 each and surety promptly furnished.

Eyewitness account of the lynching of Jim Averill and Cattle Kate Watson from the *Cheyenne Leader*, July 1889. *The James D. Horan Civil War and Western Americana Collection*

A letter from Wyoming's Governor Francis E. Warren to the Rawlins coroner who had charged, in his official report of the hanging of Averill and Cattle Kate, that the vigilantes would not be tried because Warren was "standing in with the accused." The coroner's prophecy proved to be true: there were no trials. *The James D. Horan Civil War and Western Americana Collection*

of it which are to be deplored.

The Carbon Lynching.

The lynching of Averill and Cattle Kate continues to be the leading subject of interest in Carbon county and throughout the territory. Coroner J. A. Bennett of Rawlins wrote a full and detailed statement of the affair to Governor Warren, in which he brands the affair as a cold blooded, wanton murder and protests letting it go unpunished.

To this letter Governor Warren replies as follows:

EXECUTIVE DEPARTMENT, }
CHEYENNE, Wyoming, August 2, 1889. }

J. A. BENNETT, Coroner, Rawlins, Wyoming Territory.

DEAR SIR:—Your long communication of July 28 is received, and contents very carefully noted. I do not, however, understand the following language, quoted from your letter: "Third, that since the lynching rumor has it that nothing can be done because the governor of Wyoming and the officers of the county of Carbon are interested parties, and for this reason are standing in with the accused." I beg to assure you that the governor of Wyoming is not an interested party in anything concerning this lamentable affair, except that the laws of Wyoming may prevail and that law breakers may be brought to justice and fully punished. The governor of Wyoming desires to execute the laws of Wyoming fully and impartially, whether it be for him a popular or unpopular move. His action a few years since in the Chinese riot at Rock Springs should be sufficient proof of this.

Concerning the officers of Carbon county, I have had no communication with them since this crime was committed. I have understood they were prepared to do their full duty in the premises, as I shall certainly do mine.

There are no two sides to this, as those who commit murder should pay the penalty whether it be called lynching or by any other name, and whatever may have been the circumstances preceding the crime.

Very Truly Yours,

FRANCIS E. WARREN,
Governor

TERRITORY OF WYOMING,

COUNTY OF CARBON, } ss.

AT AN INQUISITION

Holden at _Averill Ranch_, in _Carbon_ County, on the _Twenty third_ day of _July_ A. D. 18 _89_ before me, _J. H. Bennett_ Coroner of said County, upon the body of _James Averill and Ella Watson_ lying dead, by the Jurors whose names are hereto subscribed, the said Jurors upon their _oath do say_

We came over to Averill Ranch arriving here on the night of the 22nd of July also _in the morning of the 23rd day of July 1889_ Organized and found according to testimony given. The bodies of James Averill & Ella Watson were buried at Averill Ranch and were not fit to be exhumed.

From the evidence given we the Jurors summoned by J. A. Bennett, Coroner of Carbon Co. Wyo., find from the evidence given that James Averill, and Ella Watson came to there death from hanging by parties unknown to us.

In Testimony Whereof, _The said Jurors have hereunto set their hands the day and year_ _aforesaid._

JURORS.

A. R. Gates.

H. L. Mead

George Birmingham

L. L. Hitshew

William Granger

Neff May

_____ J A Bennett _____ Coroner.

Attest: A. R. Gates Clerk.

The findings of the Carbon County Coroner's inquest into the lynching of Jim Averill and Cattle Kate Watson. _Courtesy Mrs. Ruth M. Cables, Carbon County clerk_

Regulators selected as their next victims Thomas Waggoner, who operated a horse ranch forty miles southwest of Newcastle; Nate (Nat) Champion, one of the best horsemen and gunfighters in the territory; Orley (Ranger) Jones, a rancher from Buffalo; and another rancher, John A. Tisdale.

Waggoner was hanged in June 1891. Champion drove off the cattlemen's mercenaries with rifle fire. Jones was shot and killed fifteen miles south of Buffalo. Tisdale was killed by a sniper as he drove home with his children's Christmas toys.

Frightened and infuriated homesteaders, small ranchers, and rustlers banded together to fight their mutual enemy, the cattle kings. Threats were exchanged but six-guns remained in holsters. Then on April 5, 1892, a cattlemen's "army" of hired gunfighters invaded Wyoming's Johnson County to take over Buffalo, the "Rustler's Capitol"—its courthouse, records, and weapons of the militia stored there—and to arrest those they considered to be rustlers.[1]

Generalship of the group was shared by Major Frank Walcott, a small, dapper Civil War veteran, and Frank Canton, one of the most incredible figures in the Wild West. Rancher, stockmen's detective, Deputy U. S. Marshal, bounty hunter, and killer, he left dead men and legends from Wyoming to the Klondike.

On April 7 the invaders stormed Champion's two-room log cabin on the Nolan KC Ranch, located on the Middle Fork of the Powder River. This time they killed both Champion and his partner, Nick Ray. Champion immortalized the day-long battle in a terse diary written under gunfire. The final entry reads:

"The house is all fired . . . goodby boys if I never see you . . ."

Champion and Ray were dead, but news of the invasion had spread across the county with the speed of a prairie fire. Sheriff Red Angus gathered together a striking force that swooped down on the hired gunfighters and drove them into a barn on the TA Ranch on the Crazy Woman River. Portholes were cut in the walls and the battle continued. However, the riders out of Buffalo had cut off the mercenaries' supply wagons and they were soon without food and water.

During the battle the county's defenders constructed mobile forts on wagon beds. Rustlers, homesteaders, and ranchers used them like tanks to storm the barn. When this tactic was unsuccessful, the forts were turned into fire wagons. Loaded with bales of flaming hay, the wagons slammed into the barn but burned out before the walls caught fire.

Three days later troops of the 6th Cavalry from Fort McKinney, near Buffalo, rescued the invaders. Fifty prisoners were taken to the fort and charged with murder. After many court battles, and with the county admitting that it had run out of funds and could no longer care for the prisoners, they were released in January 1893.

The rustlers and ranchers with a "long rope" (the range term describing the stealing of steers) continued to defy the cattle barons. Hole-in-the-Wall soon became the headquarters for large bands of cattle and horse thieves.

About fifty miles south of Buffalo and a day's hard ride to Casper to the north, the barren, desolate Hole was the perfect setting for an outlaw society.

Major Frank Walcott, an officer in the Civil War and a former United States Marshal, shared the leadership of the cattleman's "army" in the "invasion" of Wyoming's Johnson County, April 1892. *Courtesy University of Wyoming Library*

Ben Morrison, a well-known stockmen's detective who accompanied the Johnson County invaders. This photograph was taken by C. D. Kirkland, known for his pictures of the cattle country. *Courtesy University of Wyoming Library*

Nate Champion, behind the cowhand with the gauntlet, during a roundup of the Bar C Ranch in 1884. Champion was killed in the gun battle at the KC Ranch during the Johnson County "invasion." *Western History Research Center, University of Wyoming*

Frank Canton, killer, sheriff, stock detective, deputy U. S. marshal, who was known and feared in Texas and Oklahoma, where he died in 1927. Canton shared leadership of the raiders with Major Walcott. *Western History Research Center, University of Wyoming*

The dugout of Nate Champion and Nick Ray, where they were killed by the cattlemen's hired killers. *Courtesy Peter Decker*

RUSTLERS WANT BLOOD.

MAY MURDER CAPTURED CATTLEMEN.

A Thousand Armed Men Waiting for an Opportunity to Shoot the Prisoners Down—Thrilling Narrative of the Campaign Against Thieves.

BENTWOOD JOE, A RUSTLER CHIEF.

A RUSTLER SCOUT.

Johnson County Sheriff W. G. (Red) Angus, who rounded up the force that finally besieged the invaders in the barn on the Crazy Woman Ranch. *The James D. Horan Civil War and Western Americana Collection*

The barn of the Crazy Woman Ranch, where the Johnson County raiders were besieged by the combined forces of rustlers, small ranchers, and homesteaders. *Courtesy Peter Decker*

RUSTLERS AND CATTLE MEN AT CLOSE QUARTERS

A front-page story of the Johnson County invasion by Samuel Travers Clover of the *Chicago Herald*, who accompanied the raiders. Although Champion's diary cannot be found in Wyoming's archives, Clover's story presents impressive evidence that it existed and is not a myth. *Courtesy Chicago Public Library*

THE

Banditti of the Plains

— OR THE —

Cattlemen's Invasion of Wyoming in 1892

———

[THE CROWNING INFAMY OF THE AGES.]

———

By A. S. MERCER.

The title page of Asa Mercer's book, which exposed the Johnson County invasion. The book was suppressed by the powerful cattle interests, Mercer's printing plant was burned, and even copies in the Library of Congress were stolen. *The James D. Horan Civil War and Western Americana Collection*

The letter of President Harrison to the Secretary of War ordering him to preserve peace in Johnson County. The President was awakened in the early hours of the morning by Wyoming's Washington representatives, who asked him to intervene to save the lives of the invaders besieged in the barn on the Crazy Woman Ranch. *Courtesy National Archives*

Arapaho Brown, who invented the mobile forts mounted on wagons used to charge the cattlemen's army of invaders. *The James D. Horan Civil War and Western Americana Collection*

It had been a prehistoric lake and during the course of centuries the water had eaten its way through one end to form an outlet. As age after age passed, the outlet became a deep gorge. The lake finally disappeared, leaving a sloping grassy valley fed by mountain streams and hemmed in by sheer red cliffs. Unlike the outside plains there was no high keening wind here, only an eerie silence. In the summer there was the smell of hot rock, and in the strong sunshine tule grass gleamed like polished brass. Winter brought a dead silence. The only entrance and exit was the gorge: Hole-in-the-Wall.

The growth of the Hole after the Johnson County War was rapid. It was soon a community of homeless, jobless cowhands, drifters, killers, and wanted men. From this valley an outlaw trail ran south, a trail as marked as the Wilderness Road or the Natchez Trace. It wound through canyons, across deserts, over mountains, and beyond the plains to New Mexico, with stations on the way such as Brown's Hole, lying partly in Wyoming, Colorado, and Utah, and Robbers Roost in southeastern Utah.

When George (Flat Nose) Currie, long recognized as the Hole's leader of the rustlers, was killed, Harvey (Kid Curry) Logan, a fugitive from Montana, took over the loosely organized groups. Using Brown's Hole and Hole-in-the-Wall as alternative hideouts, Logan added bank and train robbery to the gang's activities.[2]

At this time Robert LeRoy Parker, who would be immortalized as Butch Cassidy in the history of the Wild West, had joined the McCarty band of bank robbers. Their leader, Tom McCarty, was a careful tutor; Butch was an eager pupil.

The Johnson County "army" after they had surrendered to the cavalry and been escorted to Fort McKinney. The deadly Frank Canton is No. 34 and Ben Morrison, the stockmen's detective, is No. 21. *Courtesy Western History Research Center, University of Wyoming*

"THE INVADERS"
JOHNSON COUNTY CATTLE WAR. TAKEN AT Ft. D.A. RUSSELL
(FRANCIS E. WARREN) MAY 4TH 1892

NO.1 TOM SMITH
" 2 A.B.CLARKE
" 3 J.N. LESLIE

NO.8 A.R. POWERS
" 9 A.D. ADAMSON
" 10 C.A. CAMPBELL

NO.15 W.C. IRVINE
" 16 BOB TISDALE
" 17 JOE ELLIOTT

NO.22 W.J. CLARKE
" 23 L.H. PARKER
" 24 TESCHMACHER

NO.29 J. BARLINGS
" 30 M.A. McNALLY
" 31 MIKE SHONSEY
" 32 DICK ALLEN

NO.36 JEFF MYNETT
" 37 BOB BARLINGS
" 38 S. SUTHERLAND
" 39 BUCK GARRETT

Interior of a covered wagon, typical of those guided across the western wilderness by Maximilian Parker, father of Robert LeRoy Parker, who became Butch Cassidy. *Courtesy National Archives*

Desolate Hole - in - the - Wall, Wyoming, headquarters of the Wild Bunch. *Courtesy Wyoming University Library*

Robert LeRoy Parker, Butch Cassidy of the Wild West, taken in his late twenties. For years he was called "George" in frontier histories, but Moroni Gillies wrote a memoir of his cousin for the author in which he supplied the outlaw's correct name. *The James D. Horan Civil War and Western Americana Collection*

In the days when the Wild Bunch riders ruled the outlaw Wild West, some of the best working cowboys were black. A few became outlaws; one of these was Isom Dart, a former slave named Ned Huddleston, who became a well-known rustler in the outlaw community of Brown's Hole. But the majority of black cowboys became top hands on major ranches of the West and skilled wild bronc riders who were featured in early rodeos. Here, in this rare action photograph, the frontier photographer L. A. Huffman caught a black cowboy "cutting out" a steer on the range. *The James D. Horan Civil War and Western Americana Collection*

On June 24, 1889, after much careful planning, Tom McCarty led Cassidy, Matt Warner, and Bert Madden, a bartender-turned-outlaw, into Telluride, Colorado, and robbed the San Miguel Valley Bank of $10,500. McCarty always insisted that his men use fine horses, and they soon outdistanced the posse.

They hid out that winter of 1889-90 in Star Valley, an isolated region which lies partly in Wyoming and partly in Idaho just south of Jackson Hole.

In the spring Tom led his band, now including his brother Bill and Bill's seventeen-year-old son, Fred, to the northwest, to rob the Wallowa National Bank, Enterprise, Oregon, on October 8, 1891, but Cassidy remained behind. On September 3, 1893, the citizens of Delta, Colorado, killed Bill and young Fred McCarty after the gang had robbed the Merchants Bank. Tom escaped and apparently abandoned outlawry. No one knows where or how he died.

In the meantime Cassidy became an itinerant cowhand, working on ranches in Utah and Wyoming. Using his share of the Telluride robbery and what he could save from his wages, he bought a horse ranch in Wyoming's Wild River country with another cowboy named Al Hainer.

In 1893 they were arrested for horse stealing, but acquitted. The following year a sheriff caught them with a stolen herd. In July 1894 Hainer was acquitted, but Cassidy was found guilty and sentenced to two years in Wyoming's State Prison. He was twenty-seven. After a year and a half he was pardoned by Governor William A. Richards on his promise "to keep out of Wyoming." On January 19, 1896, Cassidy walked out of prison. He drifted into Brown's Hole, where he organized his own outlaw band and eventually joined up with Kid Curry: thus was born the Wild Bunch.[3]

Cassidy and the Kid shared leadership. Butch was the personality, while the deadly Kid Curry was the bold planner. They were vivid contrasts: Cassidy, likable, good-natured; the dark-skinned Kid, impassive, completely devoid of fear, and contemptuous of his own life and of those who foolishly challenged his fast draw.

The core of the Wild Bunch would always be:

Harry (The Sundance Kid) Longbaugh, who "looked like a morose Swedish or German carpenter out of a job." He was handsome, of medium height, slightly bowlegged, surly at times, and very precise. He carefully stitched "HL" on everything he wore from shirts to underwear. He had sandy hair and mustache, and cold blue or gray eyes. He is said to have been born in Trenton, New Jersey, Wyoming, Utah, or Montana. He could have gotten his name from Sundance, Wyoming, where he was captured as a horse thief.

Curiously, the favorite meal of the Sundance Kid was Ralston's breakfast food. As one man recalled, "He is always talking about its benefits."

Ben (The Tall Texan) Kilpatrick, born into a Texas outlaw family, most of whom were horse thieves or rustlers. He was the tallest of the Wild Bunch riders. Like Cassidy, he was happy-go-lucky, liked practical jokes, and was not a killer. He was illiterate and never ordered anything but ham and beans in frontier saloons because he was unable to read the menus, whitewashed on the mirror behind the bar. He attracted women. Kid Curry admitted in Knoxville, when he was captured and temporarily jailed, that "the Texan was the lady

The cabin where Butch Cassidy spent his boyhood. The homestead is about a mile south of the southern Utah town of Circleville. *Courtesy Frank T. Jensen, Cedar City, Utah*

Bill McCarty of the McCarty gang who, with his brother Tom, taught Butch Cassidy how to rob a frontier bank. Bill McCarty and his teen-age son, Fred, were killed while holding up the Farmers and Merchants Bank, Delta, Colorado, on September 6, 1893. *The James D. Horan Civil War and Western Americana Collection*

Robert LeRoy Parker—Butch Cassidy—one of the best-known outlaws in the Wild West. His grandfather, Robert Parker, who came to the West from Preston, England, was one of the leaders of the Mormon's Hand Cart Expedition of 1856. His son, Maximilian, who later guided Mormon emigrant trains to Utah, became the father of seven children, the eldest of whom was Robert LeRoy Parker, the outlaw. *The James D. Horan Civil War and Western Americana Collection* and *Victor J. Hampton*

TEMPLE BLOCK, SALT LAKE CITY.

A colorful photograph taken by C. R. Savage of "The Dragon" featured in Salt Lake City's Jubilee parade in Butch Cassidy's time. Note that most of the parade watchers had turned to stare at a passing column of Indians in blankets and hats, some with feathers stuck in the crown. One Indian is carrying a fan. *The James D. Horan Civil War and Western Americana Collection*

East Temple Street, Salt Lake City, as Butch Cassidy knew it. Note on the left the early office of Studebaker Brothers, "Carriages and Buggies." This is one of a series of photographs taken by C. R. Savage, the celebrated frontier photographer. There is hardly a textbook on American history that does not have a reproduction of Savage's famous photograph of the meeting of the railroads at Promontory Point, Utah, May 10, 1869. His works are rare. *The James D. Horan Civil War and Western Americana Collection*

The Children's Day Parade of the Jubilee celebration taken by C. R. Savage in Butch Cassidy's day. Note the photographer perched on the crossbar of the telegraph pole. *The James D. Horan Civil War and Western Americana Collection*

C. R. Savage's photograph of the Mormon Temple Block, Salt Lake City, as Butch Cassidy knew it. *The James D. Horan Civil War and Western Americana Collection*

Hall of Relics, Salt Lake City, at the time of Utah's Mormon Pioneer Jubilee, when Butch Cassidy was one of the most wanted men in the Wild West. Photograph by C. R. Savage. *The James D. Horan Civil War and Western Americana Collection*

IN OGDEN CANYON.

Above: Ogden Canyon, Utah, when Butch Cassidy was driving herds of stolen horses from Utah to New Mexico. *Below:* Observatory Peak, Ogden, as Butch Cassidy and his Wild Bunch riders knew it. *The James D. Horan Civil War and Western Americana Collection*

killer." This was grudging admiration from Curry, who was never without a woman when he was on the dodge.

Bill (Tod) Carver, a handsome daredevil, fast with a gun, and a killer when cornered. Like his fellow Texan, Kilpatrick, he was jovial but liquor made him moody and dangerous.

Camilla (Deaf Charley) Hanks, a strange, quiet man with a mouth like a trap, close-cropped auburn hair, many scars from bullet and knife wounds, and a habit of cocking his head slightly to the left to favor his good ear. He was raised near Las Vegas, New Mexico, in the closing days of the Civil War and knew Lincoln County well. After he killed his first man in a brawl he headed north to work as a cowboy in Wyoming and Montana. He was a skillful rider, once leaping onto the back of a nag pulling an ice wagon to outride a St. Louis posse in buggies. He was a cool man with a gun. As Kid Curry said of him: "I brought Charley in because he was a good man on the outside [of the train being held up]."

Elza Lay, also known as William McGinniss, could be called the "educated rider" of the Wild Bunch. A slender, handsome man with melancholy dark eyes, he later studied geology under a Yale professor while they were hunting oil fields in the badlands. Later still, under the federal Placer Mining Act, he staked out the Hiawatha field which presently supplies Salt Lake City.

Tom (Peep) O'Day was the court jester, general utility man, lookout, and sometimes horse holder. When he was sent to prison for stealing horses the judge told him: "Tom, you ought to have quit when the rest of the boys did."

In a time when hard drinking among cowboys was commonplace, Joe Chancellor was a teetotaler. He had a chalk-white face that never took on color in all the years he was on the range. In addition to his skill in blowing express safes with dynamite and Hercules powder, he was also a fanatical poker player who could sit in the same chair for days, hat tilted back on his head, a brown paper cigarette hanging from his lips, his dead-white face never showing emotion. One man who knew Chancellor said that he could easily roll his cigarettes on horseback while fleeing from a posse or pushing a herd of stolen cattle down to the Bunch's favorite market: Alma, New Mexico.

"One thing you noticed with Joe was those brown cigarettes," he said, "and how his fingers were stained from the constant use of that brown paper."

Jim Lowe, whose name Butch Cassidy would use in South America, was the smallest of the Wild Bunch riders. In between stealing cattle and horses and robbing trains, he was a bartender and looked the part. He carefully parted his dark hair in the middle and favored a white shirt and tie complete with stickpin, instead of the garb of a working cowhand.

Jesse Linsley was a handsome man until he smiled, revealing that most of his upper front teeth were missing. He had once worked for a railroad and the Bunch used his knowledge of engines and trains. He never wore a beard or mustache and was considered a dapper dresser.

William (Bill) Cruzan was probably the best horse thief in the Wild Bunch. He knew the hidden canyons where a stolen herd could be kept, was skillful as an Apache in covering his trail, and had enormous physical stamina. Charlie Siringo confessed that he had trailed Cruzan and Kid Curry for thousands of

A rare photograph of the Tall Texan (Ben Kilpatrick), who was the bicycle rider of the Wild Bunch, not Butch Cassidy. *The James D. Horan Civil War and Western Americana Collection*

ENTIRE TOWN ARMED TO RESIST FRIENDS OF TOM O'DAY.

JAIL GUARDS INSTRUCTED TO SHOOT PRISONER RATHER THAN DELIVER HIM.

CASPER, Wyo., Nov. 26.—(Special.)— Sheriff Webb to-day received word that 200 or 300 heavily armed outlaws and cowboys had left the Hole-in-the-Wall rendezvous and were marching on Casper with the avowed intention of raiding the town and delivering Tom O'Day, the notorious outlaw captured a few days ago, from the county jail. Sheriff Webb immediately swore in 150 deputies, and to-night every road leading into the town from the north and west is patrolled by posses awaiting for the first signs of the outlaws.

A hundred deputies surround the jail and about O'Day's cell are stationed trusted men with instructions to shoot the prisoner if an attack comes and promises to be successful. Every citizen of the town owning a gun is in the readiness to repel an attack and a warm reception awaits the invaders.

The Hole-in-the-Wall is 70 miles from Casper, and the outlaws left there this morning. They are well mounted and should reach Casper some time between midnight and morning, as they are reported to have passed the McDonald ranch, nine miles from the Hole-in-the-Wall, shortly after daylight.

Every outlaw of central Wyoming has been summoned to assist in the rescue of the leader. From Thermopolis, where the Hot Springs reservation, which is neither under county nor federal authority, has long afforded a refuge, the desperadoes of half a dozen counties rode to the Hole-in-the-Wall as soon as news of O'Day's capture reached them and joined the gang already gathered there. In case of a repulse and the following pursuit they have made preparations to stand a siege in the Hole-in-the-Wall, which is a natural fortress.

The country between Casper and McDonald's is sparsely settled and there are no telephones, so the first news of the approach of the outlaws is expected to come from pickets stationed far out on the roads. If the jail is attacked a sanguinary battle will be the result, and there is talk of lynching O'Day and removing the prime cause of trouble in advance. Sheriff Webb has taken a determined stand, and will defend the prisoner against all comers, whether friends or infuriated citizens. The outlaws are led by Jack Smith, a notorious bad man.

Story in a Denver newspaper of the "army" of outlaws supposedly riding out of Hole-in-the-Wall to storm the small Casper, Wyoming, jail, seventy miles away to free Tom (Peep) O'Day, who had been arrested by Casper's sheriff, Frank K. Webb, with twenty-three stolen horses. When Judge Craig sent him to prison he said: "Tom, you ought to have quit when the rest of the boys did." *The James D. Horan Civil War and Western Americana Collection*

James Lowe, whose name Butch Cassidy used when he worked on the WS Ranch in New Mexico. *The James D. Horan Civil War and Western Americana Collection*

Tod Carver, a close friend of Kid Curry (Harvey Logan). Carver and Curry killed Sheriff Jesse M. Tyler and Deputy Sam Jenkins near Moab, Utah, in May 1900. Carver was arrested the following year for Tyler's murder but was released for lack of evidence. At the time he gave his name as T. C. Hilliard. *The James D. Horan Civil War and Western Americana Collection*

Ben Cruzan, the Wild Bunch's best horse thief. Trailed by Charlie Siringo, Cruzan and Kid Curry drove a herd of stolen horses from Utah to New Mexico. Although the pair was burdened by the logistics of feeding, hiding, and moving the herd, Siringo admitted he could never catch up with them. *The James D. Horan Civil War and Western Americana Collection*

miles but although the pair was burdened with a herd of stolen horses, he could never catch up with them.

All that is known of Dave Atkins is that he killed at least one man in a gunfight and walked with a peculiar slouch. By the time he joined the Bunch, the sheriff of San Angelo, Texas, had posted a $300 reward for him and described him as dangerous.

Walter Punteney (Wat the Watcher) was the reconnaissance man for the Wild Bunch. He was an excellent horseman, good shot, and apparently ordinary enough to blend into any frontier town he visited. He lived until the 1950s and gave me his terse explanation of how the Wild Bunch operated:

"Cassidy and Longbaugh—they were not murderers. They would slip in some town and get the money and slip out again and they didn't want to hurt anybody. . . ."

Willard E. Christiansen, who left his mark in the Wild West as Matt Warner, was the son of a Mormon convert and brother-in-law of Tom McCarty, leader of the McCarty gang. Warner, as a teen-ager, fled to Brown's Hole after he mistakenly thought he had killed a playmate in a fight. He rustled cattle and later joined his brother-in-law's gang when they temporarily put aside bank robbery to drive a stolen herd of cattle into Mexico. He died in 1938.

Bob Meeks, a likable Utah cowboy, friend of Elza Lay and Cassidy, was in his early twenties when he started to ride with the Wild Bunch. He had always existed on a cowboy's wages and his sudden affluence, after taking part in a few bank robberies, was so overwhelming that it eventually led to his arrest and a tragic end.

The majority of the Wild Bunch riders were in their mid-thirties. Nearly all had been cowboys, several were wanted for murder, stealing horses, or rustling cattle. There were many who appeared briefly, only to disappear when they had made their "raise." They are only names in fading reports written by stockmen's detectives or in frontier newspapers. A few became ranchers or saloon owners who were always prepared to provide information, provisions, shelter, weapons, or horses for their former comrades.

There were women, too: Laura Bullion, gum-chewing, fast-talking—"she talks like a machine gun," one reporter observed—who rode with the gang. In contrast to her there was Etta Place, a striking woman with lustrous reddish-brown hair, soft brown eyes, a quiet smile, and gleaming Tiffany gold watch on her bosom. Despite the many stories and movies which picture her as a schoolteacher on the lonely frontier who fell in love with the Sundance Kid, Etta was a prostitute.

Cassidy once described her as "a fine housekeeper but a whore at heart." Frank Dimaio, the veteran detective who chased Cassidy and the Sundance Kid in South America, said that Etta was one of the girls in Fanny Porter's Sporting House, where the gang hid out after every robbery.[4]

One of the most interesting women connected with the Wild Bunch was pretty red-haired Annie Rogers, who also used the names "Maud Williams" and "Maud Rogers." Annie, who worked in Fanny's house, Hell's Half Acre in San Antonio, was Kid Curry's favorite.

In the summer of 1900, Annie and Lillie Davis, another of Fanny's girls, accompanied the Kid and Will Carver on what must have been one of the most

WANTED!

Nativity, American; complexion, dark; age, 32; height, 5 ft. 11 in.; weight, 175; size of shoe, 7; eyes, light hazel; hair, black and thin. Marks and scars: Two scars on forehead over left eye, three scars on left thumb, two scars on the right thumb, three scars on the left knee and one scar on left ankle in front.

This is a splendid likeness of Henry Meek, alias "Bob" Meek, who escaped from the Idaho State Prison's barn yard at 1:40 p. m. on December 24, 1901. The Governor of Idaho offers a reward of $100 for his apprehension.

Notify me by wire or 'phone, at my expense, if you have seen this man.

CHAS E. ARNEY,
Warden,
IDAHO STATE PENITENTIARY,
BOISE, IDAHO.

Henry "Bob" or "Bub" Meeks, the horse holder for two Wild Bunch bank robberies: Montpelier, Idaho, and Castle Gate, Utah. He was sentenced to a long term in the Idaho penitentiary but escaped after serving a few months. He was recaptured and in a second escape attempt was wounded in the leg so severely that the limb had to be amputated. In 1903 this one-legged outlaw successfully escaped from the State Hospital and vanished. *The James D. Horan Civil War and Western Americana Collection*

hilarious incidents in all the history of western banditry.

They started with a visit to the San Antonio Fair, then went on to Denver, Shoshone, Idaho, and back to Denver (with a brief interlude while the Kid and Carver joined other Wild Bunch riders in robbing a bank), finally returning to Texas so Lillie and Carver could be married. The tearful bride had informed her outlaw groom she couldn't stand not being "respectful."

During their grand tour they took in all the tourist sights, such as the Shoshone Falls. However, the outlaws had a problem—they were troubled with their luggage, which included, as Annie later recalled, "six or seven bags of gold." Carver also had difficulty between drinking and dancing with Lillie "in the best hook shops" in watching over his trunk filled, as Annie said, "with paper money."

In addition to his sacks of gold, the Kid carried his favorite six-shooter in a small valise, but despite their tight security, someone stole the valise while they were "riding the cars." Kid Curry raged at his loss. It was hard to believe, he told Annie, that someone could be as cheap as to steal a man's gun!

In Denver the Kid, one of the deadliest men on the frontier, and his regal-looking girl friend shared the finest suite the Brown's Hotel Palace could offer. Annie was dressed in the latest fashion, whereas Logan wore a conservative dark blue suit, winged collar, and polished boots.

The pair looked like a banker on holiday with his wife, who could have been the president of the ladies' auxiliary and a church organist. Annie drank nothing but champagne and the Kid sipped sedately at his favorite drink, apricot brandy. Before they left Denver they visited what police later described as the city's "finest men's shop," where Annie helped the Kid select several sets of expensive underwear and dress shirts.

In August 1900 the Kid kissed Annie good-bye, explaining that he and Carver "had to go up the road for a while." The "road" was to Tipton, Wyoming, and train No. 3 of the Southern Pacific, held up by the Wild Bunch riders.

The outlaws returned with more sacks of gold, but Annie, wise in the ways of the West, asked no questions of the impassive dark-skinned man she both liked and feared.

On the way back to Fanny's place the quartet stopped off at Fort Worth, where Carver and Lillie were married, with the bride quickly recovering the wedding certificate to send to her father in Palestine, Texas, "to clear my name and to show I was married."

After holding up the Great Northern Train near Wagner, Montana, on July 3, 1901, the Kid picked up Annie at Fanny's place and they began another tour, this time of the South. In December Annie was arrested in Nashville and charged with trying to cash forged banknotes taken in the Wagner robbery. A short time later the Kid was captured in Knoxville. In jail he made an affidavit absolving Annie of any knowledge of the forged notes and the robbery, and Annie was acquitted.

Giers, one of the best-known photographers in the South, was charmed by Annie when taking her photograph for the Nashville police rogues' gallery. She told him she had worked as a secretary, then as a photographer in Texas, and seemed surprisingly knowledgeable about photography. At one point she said that the only disagreeable part of the business was the developing process; "very sloppy work," she concluded. Giers found her pretty, well spoken, witty, and bubbling with good humor.

In her love letters smuggled in to the Kid in the Knoxville jail, Annie proved that, like her lover, she was a realist—the game was up, she told him, and there was nothing she could do for him. Visiting the jail would only mean being tailed by "snoopy" detectives. She denounced the press and its reporters, who pictured her man as "the most desperate train robber and outlaw in the West," wished him well, and returned to San Antonio. But with the Wild Bunch shattered, Fanny's place wasn't the same. Annie hocked the diamond ring the Kid had given her with "Kid Fox," the local fence, announced that she was tired of "the life," and intended to go home to St. Louis, where her family owned a department store. She was never seen again.

Laura Bullion, alias Della Rose, the Tall Texan's sweetheart, who was arrested with him in St. Louis in 1901. After serving a five-year term she opened a boardinghouse in Atlanta and waited for the Texan's release. At the time of her arrest the *St. Louis Times* described her as a "soft spoken, well dressed slender woman with a graceful figure who protested gently that she was innocent." *The James D. Horan Civil War and Western Americana Collection*

HARVEY LOGAN, TRAIN ROBBER, LASSOES GUARD AND ESCAPES

Secures Revolver, Terrorizes His Keepers, and Rides Away on the Sheriff's Horse--- Posse in Pursuit.

• • • • • • • • • •
• Was Under Sentence for •
• Train Robbery in Montana •
• and Was Wanted for Similar •
• Job in Wyoming. •
• Record of the Most Daring •
• Criminal in the West's an- •
• nals—Head of the "Hole in •
• the Wall" Gang. •
• • • • • • • • • •

Knoxville, Tenn., June 27.—Harvey Logan, the Montana train robber, over whom is hanging a sentence to a federal prison aggregating twenty-five years, escaped from Knox county jail this afternoon at 4 o'clock. Logan has been confined in a separate corridor under a special guard. The guard, Irwin by name, left his pistols at one end of the corridor in the outside row of cells, and went to the other end to look out of a window. While he was at the window Logan stealthily lassoed him with a wire clothesline he had in his cell upon which to hang his bedding. Logan threatened to choke Irwin to death if he screamed, and Irwin submitted. By means of a pole he had in his cell, Logan reached through the bars and pulled Irwin's two revolvers to him. With these in hand, Logan called the jailer, Bell, to come and give him medicine.

Logan having been under a doctor's care, the jailer responded, and as he entered the corridor, the bandit covered him with the pistols and demanded to be released from jail. Bell submitted, and Logan walked out of the jail, defying everyone in his path. He went to a stable in the rear of the jail, mounted Sheriff Fox's horse and rode away, going south across the Tennessee river bridge in the direction of the mountains. A posse was at once organized and [...]

The *Denver Post*'s story of how the Kid escaped from the Knoxville jail. *The James D. Horan Civil War and Western Americana Collection*

While the Wild Bunch was fading into frontier history, Kid Curry was leisurely traveling about the South with Anna (Annie) Rogers, a pretty redhead. She was arrested in Nashville, Tennessee, while passing forged bank notes, the loot of a train robbery, but the Kid escaped. He was finally captured by a Knoxville posse after he had shot two policemen. *The James D. Horan Civil War and Western Americana Collection*

The *Knoxville Daily Sentinel*'s page one story of Kid Curry's capture. *The James D. Horan Civil War and Western Americana Collection*

MONTANA TRAIN ROBBER WHO SHOT POLICEMEN NOW BEHIND THE BARS

Arrested Sunday Afternoon Near Jefferson City and Brought to Knoxville==Showed no Resistance, Was Not Armed. His Identity Has Been Established.

Anna (Annie) Rogers, the sweetheart of Kid Curry at the time she was indicted in Nashville for passing forged bank notes. The Kid, however, signed a deposition in the Knoxville jail that she did not know his real identity and he had told her he had won the notes gambling. The deposition won her acquittal. The author has copies of her love letters smuggled in to the Kid. In one, she denounced the press of her time: "I would burn them all in a bundle along with their darn reporters . . . Oh, if it was only me in that place instead of you . . . you must believe I have been a good girl for you ever since I was released . . . I know we will be together soon . . ." But Anna never met the Kid again. She returned to Texas and vanished. *The James D. Horan Civil War and Western Americana Collection*

The cold snap of yesterday finished the job begun Friday night by the "billies" of Patrolmen Dinwiddie and Saylor and drove the suspected Montana train robber and assailant of the police officers into the hands of the law. He was arrested near Jefferson City (Mossy Creek) about 4 o'clock in a sinkhole in a field where he was forced to build a fire or freeze. Here he was found almost starved and benumbed with the cold, but still in possession of his nerve. He was brought to the city last night and lodged in the Knox county jail.

A companion giving the name of John Dreeso was also brought to the city, but he is thought to be a moulder and had no connection with the desperado.

There is little doubt that this man is Harvey Logan, the leader of the desperate band of outlaws who robbed the Great Northern train in Montana in July. Altogether there has been about $9,000 of the Montana bills recovered from this man. If he was not one of the original band he has secured some of the money.

The description of Logan furnished by Pinkerton is as follows:
Name, Harvey Logan, alias Harvey Curry, "Kid" Curry, Bob Jones and Tom Jones. Residence, last known, Landusky and Harlem, Montana. Nativity, Dodson county, Missouri. Color, white. Occupation, cowboy, rustler.

Criminal occupation, bank robber, train robber, horse and cattle thief, rustler, "hold up" and murderer. Age, 36 years (1901). Eyes, dark. Height, 5 feet 7 1-2 inches. Weight, 145 to 160 pounds. Build, medium. Complexion, dark, swarthy. Nose, prominent, large, long and straight. Color of hair, dark brown, darker than mustache. Style of beard, can raise heavy beard and mustache, color somewhat lighter than hair. Marks, has gunshot wound on wrist; talks slowly; is of quiet reserved manner. Harvey Logan is a fugitive from justice, having murdered Pike Landusky at Landusky, Montana, December 25, 1894, and since then has been implicated in a number of robberies, among them the robbery of a Union Pacific railway train at Wilcox, Wyoming, June 2, 1899, a posse overtook Logan and his band near Casper, Wyoming, and in an attempt to arrest them, Sheriff Joseph Hazen, of Converse county, Wyoming, was assassinated.

This tallies with the man in arrest, as far as mere observation can go. As yet he has not been measured as he will be when the Pinkerton representative arrives.

If he is Logan, he is the leader and one of the most desperate of the entire gang, and is therefore one of the biggest catches ever made in this country. When arrested in the sinkhole, the suspect had on his person nearly

$2,000 of the Montana bank notes. In his pocket he carried two checks. These were in a pocketbook which was turned over to Lieut. McIntyre. After putting the man in jail last night Lieut. McIntyre opened the pocketbook and found $50 in cash, $240 of the Montana bills, and some small change. With them were baggage checks.

Later the officers went to the baggage room and were shown the grips for the checks. The grip being opened in the private office of Baggagemaster Gore, and $3,130 more of the Montana bills found. These bills were wrapped in a newspaper of the date of December 4. There was writing material and a pen in it also, but nothing that would lead to the man's name. Some of the bills were signed by various names as president and cashier and some in the large package had never been cut apart. In the other grip was a lot of wearing apparel and a big 45 Colts revolver. One of the features was a reversible suit. It could be turned inside out and a different colored suit entirely made of it.

The baggage was brought from Chattanooga on train No. 36 last Thursday. They were claimed by two men, one filling the description of the suspect now under arrest. They took some articles out of the grips and rechecked them.

The first bank robbery committed by the Wild Bunch was not for money but to help a fellow rider.

When Matt Warner was jailed for participating in the murder of two prospectors, Butch Cassidy decided, out of loyalty, that Warner had to be defended by the best lawyer in the territory. To finance his plan Cassidy recruited Meeks and Lay to rob the Montpelier, Idaho, bank on the afternoon of August 13, 1896.

Cassidy now adopted McCarty's technique: the trio reconnoitered the isolated town during the time they worked on a nearby ranch. Then, on August 13, 1896, they moved in on the bank. They rode out with loot variously estimated from six to sixteen thousand dollars.[5]

The loot financed Warner's team of defense lawyers, headed by Douglas V. Preston, an outstanding frontier lawyer. Warner was convicted but Preston's eloquence persuaded the judge to sentence him to the comparatively light term of five years in the state penitentiary.

Cassidy sent a message to Warner that he would ride in with the "boys" and take the jail apart if necessary. But Mrs. Warner pleaded with her husband not to have anything to do with the plan. Warner sent word to Cassidy to call off his jail delivery.[6]

The next Wild Bunch rider to be jailed was Bob "Bub" Meeks, who had been the horse holder in the Montpelier bank robbery. Meeks used his share of the robbery to buy a silver bridle, elaborate saddle, and numerous drinks for friends in the local saloons. Word was sent to Sheriff John Ward of Fort Bridger. He arrested Meeks, who protested that he was only a hard-working cowboy.

Ward produced A. N. Mackintosh, the bank's cashier, who identified Meeks as the gang's horse holder, with the result that Meeks was indicted for the bank robbery. He was convicted and sentenced to thirty-two years at hard labor—the state's maximum term for the crime.

The confinement drove Meeks into making a desperate bid for freedom. On Christmas Eve, 1901, he made his first break but was recaptured the following day. In the winter of the following year he made his second bid, but during the escape attempt was shot in the leg; the bone was so badly shattered that the limb had to be amputated. A few months later he was confined to Idaho's state asylum, only to escape again, this time into oblivion.

Kid Curry next led his riders into South Dakota to rob the Belle Fourche National Bank on June 28, 1897. Kid Curry, the Sundance Kid, Walter Punteney, and Peep O'Day backed cashier Arthur Marble and the other employees up against a wall, then swept a stack of bills into a bag. The loot was a sad hundred dollars.

The gang terrorized the town with gunfire and then rode off, but O'Day's horse bolted, leaving him on foot. He attempted to cut a mule from a wagon but was recognized by a minister, who summoned the sheriff. O'Day was captured and put in the Deadwood jail, the newspapers explaining that "the Butte County jail [had] been destroyed by fire only a few weeks before the robbery. . . ."[7]

A month later a posse led by Stock Inspector Long captured Kid Curry, the Sundance Kid, and Punteney.

That same summer, under pressure of the cattle barons, Sheriff A. L. Sproul of Buffalo led a large posse into Hole-in-the-Wall to move out all stolen cattle.

Before, there had been watchers on the rim of the towering red walls to warn the outlaw community that the law was approaching. Riders would summon the armed gangs, who usually drove off the posses without too much trouble. But this time Sproul's men outnumbered the lawless; not a shot was fired as the rustlers' cattle was driven out through the Hole.

Before he left, Sheriff Sproul made it clear that he would return with armed men any time he heard that there were stolen cattle in the valley.[8]

Kid Curry and Butch Cassidy, now aware that the outlaw community was no longer impregnable, abandoned the Hole for Powder Springs, a few miles north of Brown's Hole. It was a grim journey; the bloodlust was up in the Kid —he robbed every sheep camp they passed and ruthlessly slaughtered the flocks.

The Wild Bunch next held up train No. 1 of the Overland Flyer, near Wilcox, Wyoming, at 2:30 A.M. June 2, 1899. The technique was classic Wild West: Engineer W. R. Jones had seen a red light waving at the entrance to a small bridge; when he stopped, two men with guns climbed aboard and ordered him to take the train across the bridge; when he hesitated, the outlaws knocked him unconscious.

One of the robbers then took over the throttle and the train slowly chugged across the bridge, which was immediately blown up by two other members of the band.

The four went to the express car, two on either side, and shouted demands to Express Messenger Woodcock to open the door. When he refused, a stick of dynamite blew open the door. Woodcock was hurled outside and ten pounds of dynamite was placed on top of the heavy safe. The explosion tore a ten-inch hole in the heavy iron box and reduced the rest of the car to rubble. The ground was littered with banknotes smeared with the remnants of a consignment of raspberries.

The gang quickly collected the sticky bills, which amounted to nearly thirty thousand dollars, and rode off.

While the Wild Bunch riders were picking up their loot, a brakeman escaped to signal the second section of the train before it reached the blown bridge.

Union Pacific Railroad detectives and a number of deputies boarded a special train at Cheyenne and took after the train robbers. They were trailed to the Platte at Casper, where the manhunters were joined by another posse under Converse County Sheriff Joseph Hazen.

A running gunfight took place between the combined posses and the gang near Teapot Creek, about thirty miles north of Casper. Finally the gang made a stand in a small canyon. Rifle and six-shooter fire became intense; men dodged from rock to rock, the bullets chipping and ricocheting from the canyon walls. Hazen led his men so close, some possemen recalled, that they could hear the curses and comments of the outlaws. Finally Hazen was hit and died as his men were removing him to the rear.

The gunfight continued all that afternoon and through the night. At dawn, when the posse rushed forward under a heavy covering fire, they discovered that the Wild Bunch riders had slipped through their lines and escaped.[9]

$2500 REWARD.

will be paid by us for the capture of the four men hereinafter described. $625 reward will be paid for each man. These men are wanted for attempting to rob this bank on Monday June 28, 1897.

Description.

GEO. CURRIE—About 5 ft 10 in., weight 175, age 27, light complexion, high cheek bones, flat forehead, flat pug nose, big hands and bones, stoops a little, long light mustache, probably clean shaven.

HARVE RAY—About 5 ft 8 1-2 in., weight 185, age 42, dark complexion, round full faced, bald headed, heavy long dirty brown mustache, might have heavy beard, dark gray eyes, hair quite gray above ears and inclined to curl, bow legged.

— ROBERTS—About 5 ft 7 1-2 in., age 32, rather small, weight about 140, very dark complexion, possibly quarter breed Indian. Formerly from Indian territory.

--- ROBERTS---Rather small man. About 5 ft 6 in. weight 130. age 28, very dark, probably quarter breed Indian, large upper front teeth protruding from mouth.

$100 reward for information leading to their arrest. Please destroy former circulars.

BUTTE COUNTY BANK,
Belle Fourche, S. D.

July 28th 1897.

Wanted poster issued by the Butte County Bank, Belle Fourche, South Dakota. The bank was held up in July 1897 by Kid Curry, Flat Nose George Currie, and Tom (Peep) O'Day. *The James D. Horan Civil War and Western Americana Collection*

$18,000.00 REWARD

€€

Union Pacific Railroad and Pacific Express Companies jointly, will pay $2,000.00 per head, dead or alive, for the six robbers who held up Union Pacific mail and express train ten miles west of Rock Creek Station, Albany County, Wyoming, on the morning of June 2nd, 1899.

The United States Government has also offered a reward of $1,000.00 per head, making in all $3,000.00 for each of these robbers.

Three of the gang described below, are now being pursued in northern Wyoming; the other three are not yet located, but doubtless soon will be.

DESCRIPTION: One man about 32 years of age; height, five feet, nine inches; weight 185 pounds; complexion and hair, light; eyes, light blue; peculiar nose, flattened at bridge and heavy at point; round, full, red face; bald forehead; walks slightly stooping; when last seen wore No. 8 cow-boy boots.

Two men, look like brothers, complexion, hair and eyes, very dark; larger one, age about 30; height, five feet, five inches; weight, 145 pounds; may have slight growth of whiskers; smaller one, age about 28; height, five feet, seven inches; weight 135 pounds; sometimes wears moustache.

Any information concerning these bandits should be promptly forwarded to Union Pacific Railroad Company and to the United States Marshal of Wyoming, at Cheyenne.

UNION PACIFIC RAILROAD COMPANY.
PACIFIC EXPRESS COMPANY.

Omaha, Nebraska, June 10th, 1899.

A wanted poster for the Wild Bunch riders who held up the Union Pacific's Overland Flyer. When the express messenger refused to open the door, the gang blew it open with dynamite. Among the robbers were Flat Nose George Currie, Kid Curry, and Elza Lay. *The James D. Horan Civil War and Western Americana Collection*

Office of the stockmen's detectives for the Wyoming Stock Growers Association. In this headquarters the men who hunted Butch Cassidy, Kid Curry, the Tall Texan, Tod Carver, and other members of the Wild Bunch had established a rogues gallery of every known rustler, horse thief, and outlaw in the Wild West. Their cases were marked "closed" only after a reward-conscious sheriff had sent them a photograph of a fugitive's bullet-shattered body tied to a board, resting against a rock, or in the case of Kid Curry, disinterred from a frontier cemetery. *Courtesy Western History Research Center; University of Wyoming*

Great Northern Express Co.

ST. PAUL, MINN., JULY 4, 1901.

$5000 Reward

The Great Northern Railway "Overland" West-bound Train No. 3 was held up about three miles east of Wagner, Mont., Wednesday afternoon, July 3, 1901, and the Great Northern Express Company's through safe blown open with dynamite and the contents taken.

There were three men connected with the hold-up, described as follows:

One was, height 5 feet and 9 inches, weight about 175 pounds, blue eyes, had a projecting brow and about two weeks growth of sandy beard on chin, wore new tan shoes, black coat, corduroy trousers, and carried a silver plated, gold mounted Colt's revolver with a pearl handle.

Second man, height 6 feet, weight about 175 pounds, sandy complexion, blue eyes, not very large with slight cast in left eye; wore workingman's shoes, blue overalls over black suit of clothes, had a boot leg for cartridge pouch suspended from his neck.

Third man resembled a half breed very strongly, had large dark eyes, smoothly shaven face, and a very prominent nose; features clear cut, weight about 180 pounds, slightly stooped in shoulders, but very square across the shoulders, and wore a light slouch hat.

All three men used very marked Texas cowboy dialect, and two of them carried Winchester rifles, one of which was new.   One had a carbine, same pattern as the Winchesters.   They rode away on black, white, and buckskin horses respectively.

The Great Northern Express Company will give $5000 reward for the capture and identification of the three men, or a proportionate amount for one or two and $500 additional for each conviction.

D. S. ELLIOTT,
Auditor.

Approved:

D. MILLER,
President.

The Great Northern's poster for Butch Cassidy, Kid Curry, and the Sundance Kid, who held up the train east of Wagner, Montana, on July 3, 1901. The poster overlooked Deaf Charley Hanks, the fourth man and horse holder. *The James D. Horan Civil and Western Americana Collection*

LOUIS (LONIE) CURRY.

[FROM A RECENT PHOTOGRAPH.]

The Lewistown Argus has the following in its last issue concerning the Curry brohers:

"A Pinkerton detective connected with the case was in Lewistown about Christmas and was accompanied to Gilt Edge by Sheriff Shaw. where the fact was ascertained that Loney and Bob Curry had been in Gilt Edge shortly before the robbery occurred and had left there by private conveyance for Rocky Point in time to have reached the scene of the robbery by the date it occurred. The detective said that detectives were engaged on the case. Sheriff Shaw is very much surprised that the men should have been permitted to leave Harlem. Tuesday the sheriff received from the Union Pacific officials a circular giving a description of the men and renewing the reward of $3,000 each which was offered for the robbers last summer—dead or alive."

The Lewistown Democrat says that Loney Curry was in that town about the 15th of May for the purpose of buying the Shufelt quartz mill to operate in the Little Rockies mining district. About the 28th of the month according to the files of this paper. he came to Harlem. leaving here a day or two later for a purported

The Wild Bunch was breaking up fast as the century turned. The *Harlem* (Montana) *Enterprise* reported that handsome Lonny Logan, brother of Kid Curry, had slipped out of Harlem shortly before lawmen arrived to arrest him for train robbery. He was later killed by a posse outside his aunt's house in Dodson, Missouri. *Courtesy Montana Historical Society*

In February 1900, stolen banknotes were discovered in the vicinity of Dodson, Missouri, where the Logans had lived with "Mrs. Lee, an aunt on Troast Avenue."

The "Lee house," as it was called, was located on a slight elevation, and according to one account, "The house afforded an excellent strategic point from which the wanted man could detect anyone approaching the premises, there being no cover which could conceal the officers."

Pinkerton Detective W. O. Sayles and Kansas City Police Detectives McAnnay, Kashlear, and Hickman left their carriages a half mile from the house and moved forward on foot through the deep snow.

Lonny Logan suddenly rushed out the rear door and headed for a strip of woods. When Hickman called out an order to halt, Lonny dived behind a small mound of snow. The barrel of his revolver slid over the rim of the tiny fort and a bullet plucked a hat from the head of one of the Kansas City officers.

The battle in the snow lasted for about twenty-five minutes. During a brief lull, Sayles shouted for the outlaw to surrender. But there was no surrender in the handsome, dark-skinned outlaw from Hole-in-the-Wall. He suddenly sprang to his feet, blazing away with his six-shooters as he stumbled through the snow toward the kneeling, exposed lawmen.

Sayles and the others immediately opened fire at the lunging target. Logan slowly slumped to his knees, then fell over on his side, his blood crimsoning the snow. As he stood over the dead outlaw, Sayles thoughtfully fingered the sleeve of his coat: one of Logan's bullets had traveled along the cloth without scratching the skin.[10]

Around the same time, Bob Lee, a cousin of the Logans who had left Dodson with them to go west, was arrested in Cripple Creek and sent to the Wyoming State Prison for a long term.

After Wilcox, Flat Nose George Currie told his riders that he had had enough of train robbery and returned to rustling. On the afternoon of April 17, 1900, he was working a running iron, changing brands of steers belonging to the Webster Cattle Company near Castle, Utah, when he was discovered by sheriffs Tyler of Moab and Peerce of Bernal, who had been scouting for rustlers who had plagued the Webster herds.

Currie, an expert horseman, mounted and got off a shot that made a hole in the peak of Peerce's hat. A running gunfight followed, with Tyler finally killing the rustler.

The next train robbery committed by the Wild Bunch took place at Tipton, Sweetwater County, Wyoming, when the gang held up the Union Pacific on the evening of August 29, 1900. The scene and the players were the same. After the outlaws stopped the train they demanded that the express messenger open the door. It was young Woodcock again and he refused, but when Conductor Edward J. Kerrigan saw the gang preparing a charge powerful enough to blow the car to bits, he persuaded Woodcock to slide back the door.

The safe was blown apart, but this time the loot only amounted to $50.40—they had missed a $100,000 gold shipment which had passed the same spot only a few hours before.

Railroad detectives identified Cassidy, the Sundance Kid, Kid Curry, the Tall Texan, and William Cruzan as the train robbers.[11]

Cassidy, a wise leader, knew that the days of the Wild West were over; barbed wire now cut up the open range, the telegraph was everywhere. Also to be considered was the railroad's new strategy, in which detectives loaded their horses aboard a special train to head off the Wild Bunch riders trying to reach their hideouts in New Mexico. Cassidy's new goal was the wild frontier of South America, where there was homesteading—and many banks and gold trains . . .

To help finance his plans, Butch and Kid Curry led their raiders into Winnemucca, Nevada, on September 19, 1900. It was a busy Saturday afternoon and the streets were crowded with visiting ranchers and their families.[12]

Three customers were lined up at the teller's cage when the outlaw trio walked into the Winnemucca First National Bank.

As Tom Nixon, the bank's president, and his cashier, bookkeeper, and stenographer were filling the wheat sack with $32,640 from the vault, a terrible odor filled the air. One of the bank's customers, his hands still held above his head, wrinkled his nose in disgust.

"My God, what's that smell?" he complained.

Cassidy and the others moved away from an uneasy Bill Carver.

"What happened to you?" Butch asked.

"I met a skunk on the way here," Carver explained.

The sack was filled and the outlaws ran for their horses. As they galloped out of town Bill Carver seemed to be several paces in the rear.

A wonderful account of the robbery given to a detective by an informant describes the battle between Bill Carver and the skunk.[13]

Bill Carver's Battle with the Skunk

Jim Lowe [Butch Cassidy], Harry Longbaugh [the Sundance Kid] and Bill Carver . . . met a man they knew who told them about the Winnemucca Bank being an easy one. This man worked for a time for old Senator Nixon and I think he was in a position to know something about the bank's affairs. So Jim Lowe, Longbaugh and Carver came and stayed at a ranch near the river close to town and watched things.

The morning they came into town to rob the bank, they crossed a field and cut the wire of a place their friends had told them about so they could pass through. Carver had a couple of blankets rolled up and tied with a strap. He had on hobnailed shoes and certainly looked like a tramp. Inside this roll of blankets he had a 30-30 carbine. After cutting the fence they separated. Jim Lowe and Longbaugh came into town first. Carver stopped on the way to kill a skunk but got the worst of the battle. After killing the skunk he came into town and tied his horse and stood near the bank (I think near a watering place). Anyway he was there waiting for the signal that the coast was clear. During the time Carver was standing there an old lady and an old man came by to talk to him to "roast" the town for "being so slow."

They said it should be dead and buried. Then Carver told them that if they waited around for awhile things would be pretty lively.

The old man looked at Carver and said: "Say, mister, what's goin' to happen, an earthquake or somethin'?"

Just then Carver got the signal from Jim Lowe and Longbaugh that the coast was clear and the boys walked in. The Sundance Kid and Lowe went in first. Carver went in last with his roll of blankets and sat them on one end between his legs and began fumbling around in his pockets while the other two covered the outfit and went to work.

Jim Lowe climbed over the railing and gathered in the dough. As they came out of the bank, the old party before mentioned sees them and yells "robbers" so Longbaugh dropped a couple under the old man's feet. The old man and the old lady began tearing up the street with the old lady yelling for them "not to shoot pa as he won't hurt you-uns."

Carver later said the old gent's coattails were sticking out straight behind.

The boys said the clerks in the bank began sniffing when Carver came in and Carver said he could hardly stand it himself. This was on account of his battle with the skunk. They dropped one sack of money on the street and Jim Lowe went back to get it. When the people saw him coming they all broke for cover as though they thought he was coming back to kill them so they got out of his way.

The boys rode all that day and cached their money and changed their clothes and separated, each going his own direction to meet later. Carver's clothes stunk like hell.

After the Winnemucca robbery the gang met at Fanny Porter's Sporting House, where during a friendly scuffle some of their felt hats were damaged.

They "repaired to a hat store" and seeing some derby hats in the window,

David A. Trousdale, the express messenger who killed the Tall Texan with a heavy mallet and then shot Buck with the Texan's gun. *The James D. Horan Civil War and Western Americana Collection*

The bodies of the Tall Texan and Ole Buck being held up against a baggage cart near Sanderson, Texas, after they had been killed on March 13, 1911, while holding up a train. *The James D. Horan Civil War and Western Americana Collection*

"KID" CURRY IN CITY OF DENVER

Montana Outlaw Identified by an Old Friend at the Hotel at Which He Had Stayed and Immediately Makes a Getaway—Fugitive Had Stolen Bank Bills With Him.

Traveling alone and with no food, Kid Curry somehow crossed the Tennessee wilderness known as "Jeffrey's Hell" to appear suddenly in a fashionable Denver hotel carrying two grips filled with "new currency," as this story in the *Great Falls* (Montana) *Tribune* reported. He escaped, but a few years later committed suicide when he was trapped in a canyon near Rifle, Colorado. He was buried in Glenwood Springs. *Courtesy Montana Historical Society*

"decided as a jest to attire themselves in this headgear which was unusual in the West at that time."

Dressed up as dudes, Kid Curry, the Tall Texan, Butch Cassidy, and Bill Carver stopped off at the photographic studio of John Swartz, 705 Main Street, Fort Worth, to have their picture taken as a group. The result was impressive.

Sitting demurely in the front row were the Sundance Kid, the Tall Texan, and Cassidy, while standing in the rear, their hands reposing in the approved fashion of the time on the shoulders of those in front, were Kid Curry and Carver.

The joke was to boomerang for the Wild Bunch riders: the photograph fell into the hands of detectives trailing the gang and the photos were widely circulated throughout the country and across South America.[14]

After their last spree at Fanny's place, the Wild Bunch scattered. Cassidy, the Sundance Kid, and Etta Place headed for New York City, and later South America.

DOOM OF THE "WILD BUNCH" HOLD-UP MEN
THE "HOLE IN THE WALL"

WHEN "Kid" Curry, cornered in a Colorado gulch by a sheriff's posse a few weeks ago, turned his weapon upon himself there came to an untimely end almost the last and perhaps the greatest of the "Wild Bunch," the most desperate band of outlaws that ever held up a train or robbed a bank.

Then 'neath trap that civilization sets for the feet of the transgressor has found them, or is finding them, one by one. The rope, the knife, the bullet, the dry rot of the jail are civilization's answer to the hail of the "hold up" man.

The beginning of the "Wild Bunch" is not less interesting than its end. They came together from all corners of the West for mutual protection and combined plunder. Hunted from place to place for individual crimes that ranged from train holds ups to murders, but included nothing petty, they were "rounded up" at last in that wild section of the Big Horn Mountains in Wyoming known as the "Hole in the Wall."

From this natural stockade they defied authority, issuing forth from time to time to prey upon stage coaches, express trains, small banks, and, indeed, country towns. Then followed dashing rides, sometimes for hundreds of miles, back to the Hole in the Wall—immune from arrest when once hid within its impenetrable fastnesses.

They formed, as nearly as such a thing can be, a trust in outlawry, and it is significant that the forces of law and order, slowly, surely, inevitably closed in upon them and one by one made them pay the penalty.

Their resistance was futile. Out of all the unflinching men that formed the "Wild Bunch" and made their home in the Hole in the Wall only two remain at large—"Butch" Cassidy and Harry Longbaugh, "the Sundance Kid"—and these two have driven from this country. Even in [the] [la]nds they are pursued, and since [Rob]son, writing not long [since] at the ...

sassinated by the outlaws and many deputies, detectives, policemen and private citizens wounded. Whatever records there may be now are incomplete and await returns from Mr. Cassidy and Mr. Longbaugh, still at large.

When, driven further and further from civilization, these robbers, "hold-ups" and murderers by common consent finally selected the Hole in the Wall for their rendezvous they chose of all places in this or perhaps any other country the one most admirably suited for such a purpose. Here ten men can defy a thousand and one man elude a hundred for months. It is worthy of observation that of all those of the "Wild Bunch" who have been "rounded up" by law and order not one has come to his reckoning in the Hole in the Wall. It may be that within its walls there still lurk some minor members of the band who no longer dare to risk a fight in the open. It may be that several are living within the fortress—perhaps even under the leadership of "Bill" Cruzans. Report has it that "Bill" Cruzans died fighting, but Western sheriffs whose lives may depend upon knowing such things shake their heads and say, "We are not certain." If any are hidden in the Hole in the Wall they can stay there and die there, for no one ever went into that place for the purpose of reprisal and returned to tell of it. The footsteps of these lead all one way.

Formation of "The Hole."

Specifically it is a part of the United States and of the Territory of Wyoming, a district of the Big Horn Mountains, known colloquially at this part as the Tetons, and is about fifty miles south of Buffalo, Wyo., and eighty miles northwest of Casper.

In prehistoric times it was evidently a great lake. In the course of centuries the waters ate their way by a narrow stream through one end and formed an outlet ...

through him came the first positive information regarding the formation of the "Wild Bunch." Hanks was born and brought up after a fashion in Yorktown, Texas, and early in his history he became a fugitive from there for murdering a ranchman and attacking his wife. He escaped a mob, and was next heard from in New Mexico, where he murdered a woman. These were old records and practically forgotten when Hanks was captured in 1892. He was tried for the robbery of the express train and sentenced to ten years in the penitentiary at Deer Lodge, Mont. He was the first of the "Wild Bunch" to pay the law's penalty, and when he had served his sentence he congratulated himself upon the lightness of it and immediately upon his release made his way to the Hole in the Wall and joined his old companions, who in the meantime had not been idle.

One of the leaders, "Lonny" Logan, alias Lee, a brother of "Kid" Curry, whose real name was Harvey Logan, came with the "Kid" to visit their home in Dodson, Mo. While there Pinkerton detectives who had been waiting for such a visit, together with members of the Kansas City p[olice] force, surrounded the house. In th[e fight] that followed "Lonny" Logan w[as killed], but "Kid" Curry escaped, de[...] Missouri and fled back to W[yoming].

In the "Wild Bunch" be[sides Lo]gan's death were "Tom[...]" known as "Black Jack[,..." ...] of the band; "Sam [...] the two Logans; "[...] Carver, a sneer[ing ...] who feared n[othing ...] at nothing: [...] Nose Ge[orge ...] Curry, [...] "Ber[...] a [...]

The death of Kid Curry produced countless feature stories about him and the Wild Bunch in the nation's large newspapers. Here is one in the *New York Herald* about "the most desperate band of outlaws that ever held up a train or robbed a bank . . ." *The James D. Horan Civil War and Western Americana Collection*

Kid Curry's gun and holster, owned by E. Dixon Larson of Orem, Utah. Mr. Larson, a nationally known expert on western frontier arms, supplied impressive evidence that the body exhumed from the Glenwood Springs, Colorado, grave at the turn of the century was that of Kid Curry. A single-action Army Colt No. 147144, factory-engraved, was taken from Charles Judd, a Colt salesman, by Kid Curry during the Wilcox robbery. The same revolver, pictured above, was removed from the Kid's body by Deputy Fred D. Carlson of Glenwood, after the outlaw committed suicide near Rifle, Colorado. Mr. Larson points out that Curry's holster is very unusual in cut and style. Although the holster had been squared off at the top, exposing more of the gun, there had been no effort to further expose the trigger guard. It has an effective hammer keeper that can be drawn quickly into place by a saloon token. Mr. Larson believes that Curry used this innovation to keep his gun from being dislodged from the holster during hard riding. *Courtesy E. Dixon Larson*

Butch Cassidy, the Sundance Kid, and Etta Place in New York City

The final chapters of the lives of Butch Cassidy, the Sundance Kid, and Etta Place, his common-law wife, move from the Wild West to New York City at the turn of the century, and finally to South America, where this strange pas de trois introduced outlawry, western-style, to the pampas and jungle.

While it is an extraordinary true story, once again we find Hollywood, as a twentieth-century mythmaker, distorting the facts for the convenience of the camera. For example, Cassidy, the Sundance Kid, and Etta never saw a movie in the jungle about the exploits of the Wild Bunch. As I wrote in the 1962 revised edition of my *Desperate Men*, Percy Seibert, the American engineer and employer of Cassidy and the Kid at the Concordia Tin Mines in Bolivia, saw the pioneering film in Coney Island shortly before he left the States for South America, where he met Cassidy for the first time in La Paz. Etta, the heroine, did not return to the States because her outlaw lover refused to abandon a life of banditry but for the more prosaic reason that she had acute appendicitis and refused to risk an operation in the primitive jungle hospital. The story of how the Kid accompanied her back to the States is both hilarious and dramatic, better than Hollywood's fiction.[15]

Here, then, based on eyewitness interviews and official documents, is what

The Sundance Kid (Harry Longbaugh), one of the most wanted men in the Wild West, in formal dress with a top hat, and the pretty Etta Place, "a good housekeeper but a whore at heart," as Butch Cassidy described her, taken when they were staying in New York City before leaving for the Argentine Republic. Cassidy had returned to the West to stage his last robbery to finance their long stay in South America. The watch on Etta's bosom was bought for her at Tiffany's by the Kid and Cassidy. This photograph is by Joseph DeYoung, a well-known New York City photographer. *Courtesy Pinkertons, Inc.*

actually happened to Cassidy, the Sundance Kid, and Etta Place after they left the Wild West in its closing days.

They arrived in New York City in February 1901. Posing as cattlemen from the West, they rented rooms on the first floor of Mrs. Julia Taylor's boardinghouse at 235 East Twelfth Street. The Kid and Etta used the names "Mr. and Mrs. Harry A. Place," and Cassidy posed as "Jim Lowe." During his stay in Manhattan he also used the alias "Jim Ryan."[16]

For the next twenty days the most wanted men in the West casually wandered about the city as tourists and bought Etta a hundred-and-fifty-dollar gold watch at Tiffany's on Fifth Avenue. Then, as the evidence indicates, Cassidy returned to the West to take part in the last train holdup staged by the Wild Bunch.

During their stay in Manhattan the Sundance Kid and Etta Place visited the studio of society photographer Joseph DeYoung at 826 Broadway and had a series of photographs taken. Both were dressed in evening clothes; in one the Kid holds a top hat.

Later they traveled to Dr. Pierce's Medical Institute in Buffalo, probably to

OUTLAWS READY FOR DESPERATE WORK

Story From Rock Springs, Wyo. Relates of Preparations of Hole-in-the-Wall and Robbers' Roost Gang and of Their Intentions --- Daring Deeds of "Butch" Cassidy's Bad Gang.

According to Francis D. Harper, who was in Anaconda yesterday from Rock Springs, Wyo., indications point to a thorough reorganization of the famous "Butch" Cassidy gang of robbers, murderers and thieves which has terrorized the West and Northwest for so many years.

Mr. Harper is authority for the statement that the gang has increased and strengthened its forces and power in numerous ways and that it has in contemplation the wholesale raiding of the country about its territory during the coming two years.

Mr. Harper states that "Butch" Cassidy was recently in Rock Springs for the purpose of communicating with the outlaws who have promised to organize under him as leader.

The last few years have seen the capture and conviction of a number of the most efficient and noted members of the gang. Among the more or less famous of the bandits thus retired from criminal activity can be mentioned Tom Tracy, now in the Oregon penitentiary; Eliza Lay, serving a sentence in Arizona; Bob Meeks, convicted for participation in the Montpelier, Idaho, bank robbery; Harvey Logan, alias "Kid" Curry, now held in Tennessee; Ben Kilpatrick, "the Tall Texan," now in a southern prison; Bill Carver, killed at Sonora, Tex., while resisting arrest for murder, and "Bob Lee," serving a sentence in Montana.

Short Some Old

In addition to the gang is short the Sam," or ...

The Winnemucca Bank Robbery.

In that instance the daring thieves, in the light of day, rode into that town, which is located on the Southern Pacific railroad. Deliberately dismounting within a short distance of the banking house, located in the very heart of the town, the thieves entered the establishment with drawn guns. Three customers were at the paying teller's window transacting business, but soon realized the situation and were content to line up against the wall with upstretched hands. Bank Cashier George S. Nixon, a nervy, shrewd and thoroughly fearless man, sized up the situation in an instant and looked for an avenue of escape. The thieves outnumbered his total strength, even though the assistants were armed to the teeth. He calmly resolved to make the effort to save his bank's money if such a thing was possible, but a sharp command from the leader of the gang, which had so unceremoniously interrupted the ordinary proceedings of the business life in the small town, brought vividly to Mr. Nixon's mind the fact that resistance would be foolhardy. He therefore obeyed the command of the robber, who kept his gun cocked and leveled in a threatening manner. The looters secured about $40,000 and in a twinkle had mounted their horses and were off. A posse, headed by the bank cashier himself, started in pursuit of the robbers and for days the search was continued. Over mountain and through valley followed the determined men of Winnemucca in their effort ... the desperate cha...

Harry L... hand and as dange' intellect Harry L alias H alias F Kid," an 1' Wyo but Lon and Mo Ma ten esc as Los alla Bel of the hau cape Lont O. Hank Charl the L for m in the for p Mont from 1901 ...

A story in the *Anaconda Standard* reporting Butch Cassidy's plans to "reorganize" the Wild Bunch. By this time Cassidy was on his way to South America. The last robbery he staged was of the Great Northern near Wagner, Montana, 196 miles east of Great Falls. *The James D. Horan Civil War and Western Americana Collection*

WOMAN'S CONFESSION
LATE THURSDAY AFTERNOON
BETRAYS LONGBAUGH

Laura Bullion Admits to Chief Desmond That She Months Ago Believed Her Companion to Be the Desperate Great Northern Bandit.

SHE FORGED SIGNATURES TO THE BANK NOTES

At 4 o'clock Thursday afternoon Laura Bullion began to make admissions to Chief of Police Desmond which he says amount to a confession that her male companion is the bandit Henry Longbaugh who is known to have been one of the Great Northern train robbers.

The woman said that in Fort Worth shortly after her first meeting with her companion, who then called himself Cunningham, she discovered in his pocket a dictionary on the fly leaf of which was written:

HARRY LONGBAUGH,
WAGNER, MONT.

She further told Chief Desmond that when "Cunningham" gave her $7000 in unsigned Helena National Bank notes she was convinced that he was Longbaugh the train robber.

She said that she never mentioned her suspicions to "Cunningham" because "she was too wise."

She confessed to the chief that she had forged the name of J. W. Smith, cashier of the National Bank of Helena, to the notes found so signed in her possession.

The maximum penalty for the offense charged is 15 years in the penitentiary.

The case will be called to the attention of the federal grand jury. That body is now in session and an immediate indictment against the woman is considered probable.

In that event she will go to trial before Judge Adams of the United States District Court within the next two weeks.

Since death is the penalty for train robbery in Montana, the federal government is willing to let the man be tried there.

"It is not improbable that Laura Bullion, disguised as a boy, took active part in the Montana train robbery," said Chief of Detectives Desmond to the Post-Dispatch Thursday morning.

"I wouldn't think helping to hold up a train was too much for her. She is cool, shows absolutely no fear, and, in male attire, would readily pass for a boy.

"She has a masculine face, and that would give her assurance in her disguise.

... after them.

"The gang was in hiding, and Carver and another member of the gang had to go to Sonora, Tex., to get supplies. They were recognized and the sheriff got a posse together and gave chase. There was a fight, and Carver was killed. This was on April 2 of this year.

"Bill Cheney was a member of the gang. He knew that I was stopping with an uncle, James Lambert, in Douglas, Cashise County, Arizona, and after Bill was killed he came to me and told me all about it, and told me he had another sweetheart for me.

"He told me that this new man was in Forth Worth, Tex., and he gave me money to go there. He accompanied me there and introduced me to Longbaugh. We lived in Hyde's flats there for several weeks.

SHE ASKED NO QUESTIONS.

"We went by the name of Cunningham there. Then we went to Memphis and half a dozen other towns. We always changed names wherever we went. He had plenty of money and I never asked him any questions as to where he got it.

"He gave me the money that was in my possession when I was arrested. I don't know where he got it. I never asked him and he never told me. I don't know anything about that Wagner robbery.

IMPORTANT ADMISSION.

An important development last night was the man's admission that he did not obtain

---

The *St. Louis Post-Dispatch* story of the arrest of Laura Bullion and the Tall Texan in St. Louis, November 1901, while trying to pass forged bank notes—the loot of the Great Northern train robbery. The Texan refused to talk and police at first identified him as the Sundance Kid. Laura, believed to be part Indian, had been living earlier in the year with Bill Carver when he was killed by Sheriff Ed Bryant in Sonora, Texas. *The James D. Horan Civil War and Western Americana Collection*

be treated for venereal disease. They also visited a New York physician, Dr. Weinstein, at his office at 174 Second Avenue.[17]

On February 20, 1901, the Sundance Kid and Etta Place sailed aboard the Lambert & Holt liner *Soldier Prince* for Buenos Aires; Cassidy meanwhile was gathering his Wild Bunch riders for their last strike.

In the spring of 1901 Cassidy was reportedly seen with Bill Carver at Sonora, Texas, but left for Arizona after Carver was killed by lawmen on April 2. In May, Butch was in Globe, Arizona, using the name "Jim Lowe" and preparing to leave for Alma, New Mexico, presumably to pick up the Tall Texan, Kid Curry, and Deaf Charley Hanks to hold up a Great Northern train between Malta and Wagner, Montana, on the morning of July 23, 1901. Black powder or dynamite was used to blow a hole in the heavy safe so that the gang could scoop out forty thousand dollars—some estimates are as high as eighty thousand—in Helena banknotes.

After the loot was divided, the Wild Bunch scattered for the last time; the Tall Texan would be arrested in St. Louis with Laura Bullion and sentenced to fifteen years in Atlanta, while Laura got five. After his release, the Texan was killed, in March 1912, while holding up a Southern Pacific train near Sanderson, Texas. Bill Carver had been killed by Sheriff E. S. Briant in Sonora, Sutton County, Texas; Deaf Charley, after stealing an ice wagon to escape a posse, was later killed in San Antonio, Texas, on April 17, 1902; Bob Lee was in the Wyoming penitentiary; Elza Lay was serving a life term in the New Mexico penitentiary for the murder of a sheriff; Bob Meeks was in prison in Idaho planning his escape, which would leave him a cripple.[18]

In November 1902, Kid Curry made his dramatic escape from the Knoxville jail after he had been sentenced to twenty years at hard labor in a federal penitentiary and fined five thousand dollars for forging and passing the Helena, Montana, banknotes taken in the Wagner robbery. Somehow, on foot, in poor physical condition from his long confinement and with a small amount of food, he made his way across a tract of mountain wilderness known as Jeffrey's Hell and eventually reached the West. He was later seen in a Denver hotel with two suitcases filled with money, but he fled before police arrived.

On June 7, 1904, he was trapped in a canyon by a posse after robbing the Denver & Rio Grande Railroad at Parachute, Colorado, and he committed suicide. Although he was buried under the name of Tap Duncan, an itinerant cowhand, his body was disinterred and identified by Pinkerton detective Lowell Spence.

The Wild West was finished; Cassidy headed for the Argentine.

When the Sundance Kid and Etta Place arrived in Buenos Aires, the Kid opened an account in the London River Platte Bank, whose records disclose he had deposited twelve thousand dollars in Bank of England notes and had given their address as the fashionable Hotel Europa. Witnesses saw them in formal clothes strolling across the lobby on their way to dinner. They stayed at the Europa for two weeks, then disappeared.

Where Cassidy joined them and where and how they spent that first year is not known. The outlaw trio next appeared in Buenos Aires at the colonial land office on April 2, 1902, to file claim for "Four Square Leagues" of government land for homesteading in the Province of Chubut, District 16 of Octubre, near Cholilo. In their formal petition they also asked the right to buy the land after they had improved it. The petition was signed by the Kid under the name "Harry E. Place" and by Cassidy as "Santiago Ryan."[19]

That same day they visited the London River Platte Bank and withdrew $3,546 with a check "made by one, signed by the other." The Kid and Etta Place, still traveling as "Mr. and Mrs. Harry E. Place," booked passage on the *Soldier Prince*, arriving in Manhattan some time in late April 1902. Cassidy remained behind. The Kid and Etta did not return to Mrs. Taylor's boarding-house on Twelfth Street; where they stayed in the city is not known.

They came back to the city for medical reasons, possibly for treatment of a recurrence of chronic venereal disease. On May 10 they traveled to Buffalo and again entered the Pierce Institute.[20] After a few days' treatment they returned to Manhattan. One wonders if their luggage contained several bottles of Dr. Pierce's famous "Favorite Prescription," an elixir that promised to cure anything from "an object stuck in the windpipe to snakebite." For two months they lost themselves in the then bustling city of three million. In that year every New Yorker was a sidewalk superintendent, watching the crews dig the deep holes for New York's first subway. Perhaps one of the West's most famous outlaws and his pretty lady watched in awe as the gigantic machines, never seen before in the city, scooped up the mounds of dirt and slime from Manhattan's insides.

But the Kid was uneasy; he probably possessed that singular intuition of the hunted and sensed that the law was closing in. Early in June he appeared at the Lambert & Holt Lines office to book passage back to Buenos Aires, again on the *Soldier Prince*, but this time he was disappointed—he had waited too long and missed the sailing. The only available transportation was on the freighter *Harorious*, which did not officially carry passengers.

The Sundance Kid was determined to get back to the open spaces of South America; he accepted a tiny cabin on the freighter for himself and Etta; they were listed on the ship's crew as: "Harry E. Place, Purser, and Mrs. Place, Stewardess." The freighter sailed from New York on July 10, 1902. The pair left just in time: two weeks later detectives picked up their trail in New York City.

In an urgent message sent from his Manhattan office, Robert Pinkerton alerted all branch offices of his agency that Cassidy, the Sundance Kid, and Etta Place—who was then a new name—the most wanted trio in the American West, had finally been located on their way back to South America after a brief stay in New York City.[21]

It is puzzling to discover that the Pinkertons did not cable the police agencies in the Argentine Republic, warning them that a pair of much-wanted fugitives would be landing in their city within a few days. Robert Pinkerton's "alert" to his offices was sent out on July 29, 1902; Etta and the Sundance Kid did not arrive in the South American city until August 2. That same day they checked into the Hotel Europa, where they remained for three weeks. Had they been warned, the Buenos Aires police could have captured the pair.

The Pinkertons' delay in contacting the South American police may be explained by their very makeup. Their agency was a private, profit-making organization; no one was paying them to chase the Wild Bunch riders outside the United States, at least at that time.

On August 14, 1902, the Sundance Kid appeared at the London River Platte Bank to withdraw a balance of $1,105.50 and close his account. The Kid had originally deposited $12,000. He had withdrawn $3,546 for the trip to New York and return, leaving a balance of $8,454. In their absence Cassidy may have used the remainder to stock the homesteading ranch with thirteen hundred sheep, five hundred head of cattle, and thirty-five horses—all recorded in the land office records.

The day after he had closed their bank account, the Sundance Kid and Etta Place booked passage on the coastwise steamer *Chubert* for Puerto Madryn in the gulf of Neuvo, two hundred fifty miles south of Buenos Aires. There they hired horses and rejoined Cassidy at the homesteading ranch in the interior.

It took a year for the Pinkertons to move. On March 8, 1903, Frank Dimaio, a superb operative, received a cablegram at his hotel in Sao Paolo, Brazil, ordering him to proceed to the Hotel Metropole in Buenos Aires, where he would find a letter of instructions. Dimaio, who was trailing an international forger, turned what information he had over to the local police and took up his new assignment. More than twenty-five years ago in a series of interviews held in his Dover, Delaware, hotel room, Dimaio described to me how he had trailed Butch Cassidy, the Sundance Kid, and Etta Place across South America.[22]

Frank Dimaio's Story

After I received the cablegram from the home office I proceeded at once to book passage on the French steamer *Chili* [sic] which sailed from Rio de Janeiro on March 10; I arrived in Buenos Aires on the 16th and immediately went to the Hotel Metropole. Waiting for me was a small package. Inside was a letter from RP [Robert Pinkerton] ordering me to locate Harry Longbaugh, alias Harry E. Place, alias the Sundance Kid, his alleged common-law wife, Etta Place, and George Parker, alias Butch Cassidy, all members of the Wild Bunch, the outlaw gang in the West.

Of course I had heard of these men, but I had never heard of the woman. The package included copies of photographs of Cassidy, Longbaugh, and Etta Place. The Kid and Etta had had their pictures taken by a New York photographer and the New York office had found them.

Now in those days the Argentine Republic's interior was a pretty wild place, large enough to swallow up an army without leaving a trace. I started at a logical beginning, the United States Legation. I had no illusions that Cassidy and the Kid had left their calling cards but there were small, tightly knit American colonies in the South American countries and word somehow always seems to move along the jungle telegraph when new white faces appear, and that word eventually got back to the legation or the leaders of the colonies in the big cities.

I wanted to see Mr. Lord, United States Minister to the Argentine, but I discovered he was old and ill and Secretary Eames was taking his place. Eames gave me letters of introduction to Dr. Robert Newberry, a dentist and the leader of the American colony in Buenos Aires, and Dr. Francis Beasley, Chief of Police of Buenos Aires.

Dr. Newberry was most helpful. When I first asked about the Kid and Cassidy —I used their aliases of Place and Ryan—he immediately informed me that they had the ranch next to his at Cholilo, Province of Chubut, District 16 de Octubre. I can recall him saying at the time, as if it were today:

"Oh, Harry Place and Jim Ryan are good fellows. They have improved their ranch and doubled their stock within the past year. Mrs. Place is a very pretty woman. In fact she's the only white woman in the whole Province."

Then I took out the pictures of the Kid, Etta, and Cassidy and asked him to identify them. He did so as Mr. and Mrs. Place and Jim Ryan. When I told him

Frank Dimaio in what he told the author was his "Mafia uniform." In the 1880s, posing as a convicted New York counterfeiter, he was put in the New Orleans prison to get evidence on eleven Mafia leaders awaiting trial for murdering New Orleans Police Chief David Hennessy. Dimaio did get one to confess. *The James D. Horan Civil War and Western Americana Collection*

that they were Cassidy and Longbaugh, western outlaws wanted for among other things, the robbery of the First National Bank of Winnemucca in Nevada, he was shocked.

"I can't believe they are robbers," he said, "they seem like such nice people."

But when he was convinced they were fugitives wanted by the law back in the States, he promised to do anything to help in their apprehension.

When I told him I intended to buy equipment and start out after them, he shook his head.

"You can't go in after them, Dimaio," he said.

"Why not?" I asked.

"It would be impossible," he said. "The rainy season has started in the jungle and the country out there is so flooded it would be impossible to get through a horse or mule. In fact I don't think you could even hire a guide."

Then he took out a map and showed me how to get to Cholilo. I would first take the steamer to Puerto Madryn, which was about 250 miles south of Buenos Aires. There I would have to hire horses, equipment, and a guide. The only way to get to Cholilo was by riding at least fifteen days across very rough country.

At Cholilo, he said, there was a small army garrison where I could get help from the commandant. He advised me strongly to wait until the rainy season was over.

Dr. Newberry also made a sketch for me of the outlaws' ranch. The main building, he said, was a log structure and the smaller one, a bunk house, was nearby. There was also a corral. Several natives worked on the ranch as cowboys and sheepherders, he said.

When he finished making the sketch he studied it thoughtfully. "You know, Dimaio," he said, "there has always been one thing in the back of my mind."

"What's that?" I asked.

He pointed to the main log house of the ranch. "I had the idle thought when I rode over there to pay them a visit and to welcome them to the Province, that they had built their place as though they were building a fort. I thought perhaps they were afraid that the Indians here were like those on the Plains in the West, and as I recall I even joked about it and assured them there was no trouble like that as long as everyone treated the natives decently . . ." He looked at me. "Maybe they had people like you in mind, Dimaio."

I was still determined to go in after them so I paid a visit to Chief Beasley. He was a fine gentleman and very cooperative. He also advised me very strongly not to try to move through the jungle to Cholilo. He posed the same arguments as Dr. Newberry. There was a possibility, he said, that I would be stuck in Puerto Madryn because no native would enter the flooded areas.

I finally accepted both their advice and continued my investigation in Buenos Aires. When I found Cassidy, the Sundance Kid, and Etta Place had stayed at the Hotel Europa, I talked to Americans who had seen them in formal clothes, walking to the dining room and sitting in the lobby. Evidently Cassidy at one point was introduced by the Kid as his brother.

Later I visited all the banks in the city. At the London River Platte Bank I met the manager and showed him the pictures of the Kid, Etta, and Cassidy. He identified them as Harry E. Place and his wife, and James Ryan. He checked his account records and showed me where the Kid had deposited twelve thousand dollars in gold notes on March 23, 1901. He said he recalled Butch Cassidy because one time when he entered the bank with Longbaugh, Cassidy asked if he could inspect the bank's vault.

The manager thought that was peculiar but he wanted to humor his new American customers so he gave them a tour of the vault.

"Why, señor, do you want to see our vaults?" he asked Cassidy.

"Well, sir," Cassidy said with a straight face, "we've worked hard for this money and we're afraid of robbers."

The manager told me he hastened to assure them there were no bank robbers in Buenos Aires.

The manager's records showed that the Kid cashed a check for $13,546 dated April 2, 1902, endorsed by one Angelo M. Bottaro, Argentine Republic, who the manager assured me was a respectable rancher and well known in Buenos Aires. On April 14 Longbaugh withdrew the balance of the account of $1,105.50 and it was then worth, as I recall, $.44 to the American dollar in gold. The manager said he had no further record of any other transactions but from what he had heard in the bank, the trio was still ranching at Cholilo.

When I informed him who Place and Ryan were, and of their background as bank and train robbers, the manager almost swooned.

By this time I had enough information on their location and activities and this I cabled New York. A few days later I received instructions not to proceed into the interior but to canvas the coast with wanted posters and to arrange with Chief Beasley to send to New York any further information he received on the Kid, Cassidy, and Etta.

My next stop was to check the steamship lines. I discovered that the Kid and

LOS RETRATOS, SEÑAS PERSONALES Y LA HISTORIA CRIMINAL DE CADA UNO DE LOS INDIVIDUOS SOSPECHOSOS, SE DAN Á CONTINUACIÓN.

HARRY LONGBAUGH.
Retrato tomado el 21 de Noviembre de 1900.

NOMBRE......Harry Longbaugh, (a) "Kid" Longbaugh, (a) Harry Alonzo, (a) Frank Jones, (a) Frank Body, (a) el "Sundance Kid."
NACIONALIDAD......sueco-americano........PROFESION......Vaquero; tratante
OCUPACIÓN CRIMINAL......Salteador de caminos, ladrón de bancos, de ganado y de caballos.
EDAD......35 años..................ESTATURA......5 pies 10 pulgadas
PESO....de 165 á 175 libras..............CONSTITUCION..........Buena
OJOS........Azules ó pardos...............COLOR..........Trigueño claro
BIGOTE Ó BARBA......[si tiene] castaño natural con matiz rojizo.
FACCIONES......tipo griego..............NARIZ......Más bien larga
COLOR DEL PELO.........castaño, puede habérselo teñido; se peina pompadour.

ES ESTEVADO Y TIENE LOS PIES MUY SEPARADOS.

OBSERVACIONES........Harry Longbaugh estuvo 18 meses cumpliendo sentencia en la cárcel de Sundance, Condado de Cook, Wyoming, cuando era muchacho, por robo de caballos. En Diciembre de 1892, Harry Longbaugh, Bill Madden y Henry Bass asaltaron un tren del Ferrocarril "Great Northern" en Malta, Montana. Bass y Madden fueron juzgados por este crimen y sentenciados á 10 y 14 años de presidio, respectivamente; Lonbaugh se escapó y desde entonces es un prófugo. En 28 de Junio de 1897 y bajo el nombre de Frank Jones, Longbaugh en compañía de Harvy Logan [a] Curry, Tom Day y Walter Putney, tomó parte en el robo de un banco en Belle Fourche, South Dakota. Todos cayeron en manos de la policía, pero Longbaugh y Harvey Logan lograron escaparse de la cárcel de Deadwood, en 31 de Octubre del mismo año. Desde entonces Longbaugh no ha vuelto á estar preso.

LA ESPOSA DE HARRY LONGBAUGH.

NOMBRE......Sra. de Harry Longbaugh
ALIAS......Sra. de Harry A. Place; Sra. Ethel Place
NACIONALIDAD......Americana
OCUPACIÓN,......desconocida
OCUPACIÓN CRIMINAL......
EDAD......de 27 á 28 años [en 1906]......ESTATURA......5 pies 5 ó 5 pulgadas
PESO......de 110 á 115 libras..............CONSTITUCION......Regular
COLOR........Trigueña..............COLOR DEL PELO......Castaño oscuro
OBSERVACIONES........Usa peinado alto formado por un moño enroscado desde la frente.

AL IR Á PRENDER Á CUALQUIERA DE LOS INDIVIDUOS DE ESTA BANDA DE LADRONES, SE RECOMIENDA Á LOS POLICIAS QUE LO INTENTEN QUE ESTEN BIEN REFORZADOS, PERFECTAMENTE ARMADOS, QUE NO SE ARRIESGUEN, PUES DICHOS CRIMINALES RESISTEN TEMERARIAMENTE ANTES DE RENDIRSE, Y NO TITUBEAN EN MATAR SI ES NECESARIO PARA SALVARSE. SON BUENOS TIRADORES, EXPERTOS GINETES, ACOSTUMBRAN Á VIVIR EN LAS LLANURAS Y SON HÁBILES EN LA CRÍA DE GANADO.

A rare, unpublished poster written in Spanish by Frank Dimaio which he circulated in all the major South American coastal cities. These posters eventually forced Cassidy, the Sundance Kid, and Etta Place to leave their homestead and move deeper into the jungle. In the beginning it was believed that Kid Curry had accompanied the trio, but it was later established he had refused to leave the West. Curry said good-bye to Cassidy and the Sundance Kid after the Wagner, Montana, train robbery in July 1901. *The James D. Horan Civil War and Western Americana Collection*

Harvey Logan (*a*) Harvey Curry, (*a*) "Kid" Curry, (*a*) Tom Jones, (*a*) Bob Jones, se escapó el 27 de Junio de 1903 de la cárcel del Condado de Knox, Knoxville, Tenn., E. U. de A., donde estaba esperando á ser trasladado al presidio de Columbus, Ohio, para cumplir la sentencia de 20 años que se le impuso por circular billetes de bancos alterados, robados del carro del "Great Northern Express" en el ferrocarril "Great Northern," el 3 de Julio de 1901, por asaltadores de caminos de los que Logan era el jefe, y los cuales asaltaron dicho tren, contuvieron con armas de fuego á los empleados del tren, saltaron con dinamita la caja de hierro y sacaron de la misma $45,000 en billetes de banco sin firmar, que se llevaron.

SEÑAS PERSONALES.

NOMBRE..Harvey Logan

ALIAS.......Harvey Curry, "Kid" Curry, Bob Jones, Tom Jones, Bob Nevilles, Robt. Nelson, R. T. Whelan.

RESIDENCIA......Se huyó de la cárcel del Condado, Knoxville, Tenn., el sábado 27 de Junio de 1903.

LUGAR DONDE NACIO........Dodson, Mc....COLOR................................blanco

OCUPACIÓN...Vaquero, tratante

OCUPACIÓN CRIMINAL..........Asaltador de bancos y trenes, ladrón de caballos y ganado asaltador de caminos y asesino.

EDAD..38 años [en 1903.]

OJOS OSCUROS...Estatura, 5 pies 7½ pulgadas

PESO.........de 145 á 150 libras.....................CONSTITUCIÓN...............Regular

TEZ........trigueña, atezada..................NARIZ....Prominente, larga, grande y recta

COLOR DEL PELO...Negro

BARBA.........afeitada cuando se escapó, pero puede dejarse crecer una barba espesa y bigote de color algo mas claro que el pelo.

ADVERTENCIAS.—Tiene una herida de bala en el brazo derecho, entre la muñeca y el codo; habla despacio; es un poco estevado y de carácter reservado. Padece bronquitis aguda, jadea mucho; su estado físico no es del mejor; tiene dos cicatrices en la espalda que parecen proceder de una descarga con perdigones; tiene el hombro izquierdo mucho más bajo que el derecho, á causa de la herida; tiene los brazos más largos que la generalidad de las personas de su estatura; tiene los dedos bastante largos. HARVEY LOGAN también asesinó á Pike Landusky, en Landusky, Montana, el 25 de Diciembre de 1894, y tomó parte en gran número de asaltos y robos, entre ellos el robo del tren del Ferrocarril Unión del Pacífico, en Wilcox, Wyoming, el 2 de Junio de 1899, después de lo cual la fuerza civil alcanzó á Logan y su banda cerca de Casper, Wyoming, y al tratar de prender á los ladrones, el alguacil mayor, Joseph Hazen, del Condado de Converse, Wyoming fué asesinado.

HARVEY LOGAN.
Retrato tomado en 190.

GEORGE PARKER.
Primer retrato tomado el 15 de Julio de 18..

NOMBRE.................George Parker

ALIAS........"Butch" Cassidy [*a*] George Cassidy; [*a*] Ingerfield.

NACIONALIDAD.................Americano

OCUPACIÓN.............Vaquero, tratante

OCUPACIÓN CRIMINAL......Ladrón de bancos y asaltador de caminos, ladrón de ganado y caballos.

EDAD.................36 años [en 1901]

ESTATURA..........5 pies 9 pulgadas

PESO.................................165

CONSTITUCIÓN..................Regular

TEZ..............................Clara

COLOR DEL PELO..............Blondo

OJOS............................Azules

BIGOTE...........Leonado, si lo usa

OBSERVACIONES.—Tiene dos cicatrices en la nuca; cicatriz pequeña debajo del ojo izquierdo, pequeño lunar en la pantorrilla. "Butch" Cassidy es conocido como un criminal principalmente en Wyoming, Utah, Idaho, Colorado y Nevada, y ha cumplido sentencia en el presidio del Estado de Wyoming en Laramie por robo, pero fué perdonado el 19 de Enero de 1896.

GEORGE PARKER.
Último retrato tomado el 21 de Noviembre de 190.

Etta Place had left for New York City in April on the *Soldier Prince* and, according to the Houston Line, had returned to Buenos Aires on the freighter *Harorius* on August 9, 1902. Place was listed as purser and Etta Place as stewardess because the ship did not carry passengers.

I also found that the Kid and Etta Place had sailed on the coastal steamer *Chubert* from Buenos Aires to Madryn and then went into the interior on horseback. This was in April, 1902, and the rainy season started May 1.

My next step was to get posters, which I wrote in Spanish, and using the photographs New York had sent me of the trio, I distributed them up and down the coast, visiting every steamship office and freight line. Chief Beasley, meanwhile, was revealing to businessmen and travelers who would be going into the interior the real identity of the supposedly respectable Mr. and Mrs. Harry E. Place and James Ryan.

Chief Beasley, Dr. Newberry, and myself held meetings and I arranged for Chief Beasley to discuss with the Colonial Land Office the possibility of sending a letter to the Kid and Butch Cassidy, asking them to come to the city and sign some papers for the sale of the land they were homesteading.

I did this because the clerk who had helped them make out the petition in the Land Office told me they seemed very eager to have the first opportunity to buy the land. As of this time, the government considered them squatters.

I also arranged a system of ciphers with Chief Beasley to identify the outlaws in a cable to the New York office if he found they were leaving for the States: Longbaugh was lemons; Cassidy, citron; Etta Place and Longbaugh together were apricots; Etta alone was peaches; and Butch and Etta together were oranges. In other words if they sailed back to the United States as a trio, a pair, or singly, Beasley could simply cable us as though he was advising a New York concern what would be the arrival date of a cargo of fruit. The Agency's code name was Castleman, New York. Beasley also took into our confidence his assistant, Antonio Ballee, a bright young fellow and a good police officer.

I had done as much as possible. Every means of major transportation along the South American coast had been alerted to the presence of the outlaws; prominent businessmen who would be dealing with wool and beef now knew that the seemingly respectable American ranchers in the District, 16th de Octubre, were dangerous outlaws wanted for serious crimes in the United States.

I then received instructions from the home office to return. To underscore the meagre transportation facilities existing at the time, to get back to New York I was forced to first book passage on the Royal Mail Steamer, *Thames*, for Southampton, England. I left Buenos Aires on May 8, 1903, and arrived in Southampton on the 30th. I waited fifteen days before I could get passage on the American liner U.S. *New York*, which finally docked in Manhattan in the last week of June.

Now you have asked me if I believed that Cassidy, the Sundance Kid, and Etta Place had gone to South America to start a new life in a wild land. My answer is a flat No. I believe both Cassidy and the Kid had by that time reached the point of no return. Cassidy was then about thirty-six, the Sundance Kid approximately the same age. Both had served terms in prison. The Kid did seventeen months in jail at Sundance, Crook County, Wyoming, as a young horse thief and had broken out of the Deadwood Jail with Kid Curry. Cassidy spent almost two years in the Wyoming penitentiary for rustling. Sundance had taken part in a train robbery. He also was a member of the gang which held up the Belle Fourche National Bank. Then he and Butch held up the Winnemucca Bank in 1900. By the time I was searching for Longbaugh in South America the American Bankers Association and the railroads had posted a four-thousand-dollar reward for information leading to his arrest. And in 1903 that was a lot of money.

As for Butch Cassidy, bank and train robbery was a way of life for him by the time he left the States for South America. Even as a young fellow he was in with a hard-nosed gang of horse thieves that ran the herds all the way from Utah to New Mexico.

Today the outlaws of the West, like Cassidy, are viewed through the eyes of romance, but on the frontier stealing a herd of horses was like a modern gang stealing a carload of cars. A horse was an important means of a man's transportation in a wild land, and that's what Butch Cassidy was stealing before he could vote.

He was also a rustler, and in the Wild West that meant he was stealing another man's bread and butter. From a horse thief and rustler he graduated to robbing banks and trains. I've heard the old stories of how Cassidy never killed a man until he reached South America, but does that make him a better man? We must consider he was riding stirrup-to-stirrup with Harvey Logan, the most deadly killer in the West, and it took very little to make Logan go for his gun. Even in the old West the law was specific: if an express messenger was killed during the commission of a holdup, not only the man who fired the shot was responsible but also his companions who took part in the commission of that felonious robbery. There were quite a few guests of frontier necktie parties who suddenly realized that legal truth as the horse was being kicked from under them . . .

So when Cassidy reached South America he was a seasoned criminal, a horse thief, rustler, bank and train robber. It wasn't long before he would be a killer.

Etta Place? From my investigation she was a professional prostitute, working out of Fanny Porter's Sporting House in Texas, where the gang hid out and spent their money. She might have been a farm girl because later reports showed that she rode as good as Butch or the Kid, and they were experts.

After I returned to the States I kept in touch with Chief Beasley and Dr. Newberry. There is no doubt from their reports of the activities of all three that they were in South America to sit out for a time in the interior and then, when the time was ready, to make a grand tour of the South American countries and select the easiest victims for a holdup of gold trains—in those days that simply meant a few mules and the dust or money stored in a straw box guarded by a few natives —banks or company stores. The endless interior was fertile field for them—in a way they brought outlawry, Wild West-style—to the pampas of South America.

Butch Cassidy, the Sundance Kid, and Etta Place might appear very romantic half a century later, but at the time I was preparing to go after them I could only recall Dr. Newberry tapping the rough sketch he had made of their ranch outbuildings and telling me very thoughtfully that he thought they had built them as a fort.

I knew the "soldiers" of the Argentine Republic stationed at Cholilo simply meant barefoot peons or Indians. They were brave and would follow the orders of their officers to the death, but they were equipped with ancient weapons and not many bullets. I knew I would be helping to lead this ragtag army posse against a stout fortlike building . . . and in that building were two superb marksmen and a woman who could probably shoot, all equipped with the best rifles and handguns.

It looked to me at the time that there were excellent prospects I could end up wrapped in a horse blanket and buried in a jungle grave along with some Argentine foot soldiers. There was no doubt in my mind that Cassidy and Longbaugh would fight to the death rather than be captured.

And that is the way it finally happened . . .

For three years Butch Cassidy, the Sundance Kid, and Etta Place homestead-ed their fortlike ranch in District 16 of Octubre. They doubled their cattle and horse herds, increased their sheep flock, and improved the land. Their pur-suers meanwhile were curiously apathetic.

Neither the Pinkertons nor the Buenos Aires police under Chief Beasley moved against the mysterious ranch although on July 1, 1903, after a confer-ence with Dimaio, Robert Pinkerton sent a three-page letter to Beasley de-tailing the criminal background of Cassidy and the Sundance Kid and advising him that "arrangements are being made by which, if they do not return home, they may be arrested on extradition proceedings under the Treaty between the United States and the Argentine Republic."

Beasley made no effort to contact the army garrison at Cholilo. Possibly the distance, the rough land, rainy season, logistics, and the failure of his own government and the United States to act on extradition proceedings made him hesitate.

In 1906 Cassidy, the Kid, and Etta finally returned to outlawry. I believe these are the possible reasons that they abandoned a thriving ranch for the hazardous life of bank and train robbers:

They had become aware of the network of citizens and businessmen es-tablished by Dimaio which was sending information on their movements to the Buenos Aires police, and knew that it was only a matter of time before the army moved in on them.

Dimaio's "Wanted" circulars, complete with their pictures, and the reward offers had infiltrated into the interior, and the danger of bounty hunters and bushwackers had increased.

They had, as Dimaio hypothesized, completed a tour to select as prospective victims a number of loosely guarded banks, gold trains, and company stores.

Or was it, as some have said, that the wife of a nearby rancher had fallen in love with the Sundance Kid? One day, the story goes, the rancher came home unexpectedly to find the Kid and his wife in bed together. He went at the Kid with a knife, Sundance grabbed his six-shooter, which was hanging in its hol-ster at the edge of the bed, and shot the rancher in the shoulder.

"The damn fool might have killed me," the Kid complained to Cassidy.[23]

Whatever their motives, the trio rode into Villa Mercedes, in San Luis, some five hundred miles from Buenos Aires, to hold up the Bank of Nación.

The robbery took place in March 1906. Etta, acting as horse holder, was dressed in her favorite English riding breeches, a man's shirt, and a broad-brimmed sombrero under which she had tucked her long reddish-brown hair. A young Texan outlaw named Dey, on the dodge from several warrants in Texas, joined them in this robbery.

Cassidy and the Kid entered the small bank, Dey remaining on guard out-side. Cassidy vaulted the rail, waved the six-shooter inches from the nose of the startled bank manager, held out a sack, and told him to fill it with money from the vault. The bank official quickly followed orders and returned the bulging sack to Cassidy. In seconds they were pounding out of the town.[24]

The only known photograph of Butch Cassidy and the Sundance Kid in South America, taken in 1907. Cassidy is the horseman at the far left, the Kid is attending to his horse in the center. At the right is Don Carlos Mexia, son of the Mexican Minister to France and England. This photograph was given to the author in the 1950s by Percy Seibert, who provided material for the caption. *The James D. Horan Civil War and Western Americana Collection*

Rare, unpublished notes made by Frank Dimaio in South America when he was trailing Cassidy, the Sundance Kid, and Etta Place. Newberry, who Dimaio notes "will help get them," is the Buenos Aires dentist who was a neighbor of the outlaws. *The James D. Horan Civil War and Western Americana Collection*

A photograph of Cassidy taken from one of the 1907 prints. *The James D. Horan Civil War and Western Americana Collection*

Chief Beasley later described what had happened and said that the bank manager and townspeople had identified the robbers as Cassidy, the Sundance Kid, and Etta Place. There were no photographs of Dey and it would be some time before he was formally identified as the fourth member of the bandit quartet.

"These outlaws know there are not many police and there are easy hiding places in the mountains," Beasley wrote to Robert Pinkerton, "but we are asking all efforts to hunt them down."

The loot was divided at the ranch and Dey, confident in his anonymity, posed as an engineer and returned to Buenos Aires, where he checked into the Hotel Europa. There he met Dr. Carl Lovelace, from Waco, Texas, chief surgeon of the Bolivian Railway Commission. Lovelace, a former Rough Rider who had been with Teddy Roosevelt at San Juan Hill, became friendly with Dey. When Dey was leaving the hotel one of his suitcases accidentally opened and Lovelace saw that it was filled with banknotes. When he commented on Dey's apparent good fortune, the young outlaw solemnly replied:

"The Lord has treated me very generously lately."[25]

The bank robbery forced Chief Beasley to take action. Word was sent to the army commandant at Cholilo and a raid was staged on the ranch. But the solid-log main house was abandoned; Cassidy, the Kid, and Etta Place had fled.

A month later they struck again, this time robbing the Bank of Nación at Bahia Blanca, a fairly large town with a small police force. The robbery went smoothly, with Etta, "dressed like a slim young man," as Beasley reported, again acting as horse holder. The loot was twenty thousand dollars.

This time there was a chase, but Cassidy shot the lead horse of the posse to discourage pursuit.

A few weeks later they crossed the border into Bolivia, striking the bank at Eucalyptus and then riding back into the Argentine Republic to hide in Rio Gallegos, where they posed as cattle dealers from the States.

They were welcomed by the American colony, particularly by Mrs. Bishop, wife of the local bank president, who spent much time with the slender, attractive woman who had so much news of the latest New York fashions and theatre.

They stayed for a week as guests of the Bishops, riding out to inspect their herd—and to pay a visit to Bishop's bank. One morning, a few minutes after he had opened his bank, Bishop looked up into the muzzle of a six-shooter held by one of his houseguests, the smiling Jim Ryan, while another guest, Harry Place, rifle in hand, guarded the front door and the tellers. Outside Bishop could see the charming Mrs. Place, dressed in riding clothes, holding three horses.

Bishop filled the sack Cassidy held with his bank's money; as before, the outlaw trio was gone in a cloud of dust before the alarm was given.[26]

Their first train robbery took place at the Eucalyptus, Bolivia, station. Using the classic Wild West technique, the Sundance Kid and Cassidy boarded the train as it chugged out of the station. The native guards quickly dropped their guns and raised their hands to let Cassidy and the Kid scoop up the saddlebags loaded with money from a local mine. They forced the train to stop at a point where Etta and another young outlaw named McVey were holding the horses, then they disappeared into the jungle to cross the border and hide out in the Argentine.

On January 15, 1907, Robert Pinkerton received information that Cassidy, the Kid, and Etta had been located in the southwestern Argentine near Norquin, Province of Nequen, close to the Chilean border. At the request of the American Bankers Association, which his agency represented, Pinkerton had his staff prepare a new circular and photographs, which they sent to as many South American banks as possible.

Pinkerton's last paragraph in the circular read:

"When attempting to arrest either [of these fugitives] officers are warned to have sufficient assistance, be fully armed, taking no risks as they will make a determined resistance before submitting to arrest, not hesitating to kill if necessary.[27]

Then the three outlaws abruptly dropped out of sight. When they appeared again, Etta Place was missing. During the next few years Cassidy and the Sundance Kid were reported at various points in the Argentine Republic, Chile, Peru, and Bolivia.

One day Chief Beasley received the news that Cassidy and the Kid had been killed in a gunfight with a detachment of the Bolivian army at a remote Indian barrio called San Vincente . . .

What happened to Cassidy, the Kid, and Etta Place from the time they had been located near the Chilean border until the fatal gunfight at San Vincente was not known until one day in the early 1950s when I received a telephone call from a man who identified himself as Percy Seibert, an engineer who had just returned from Bolivia.

"Someone sent me a copy of your *Desperate Men*, in which you mention my name," he explained, "and I thought perhaps I could give you additional information about Butch Cassidy and the Sundance Kid to fill out the historical record."

I was startled and asked him how he could possibly know anything about two western outlaws who not only had been dead for almost half a century, but who in life had easily evaded the law in the South American countries which they had plundered.

"The explanation is very simple," he said cheerfully. "They worked for me at the Concordia Tin Mines in Bolivia, and in fact were Sunday dinner guests of myself and my wife for many years."

I met Mr. Seibert that night, the first of many more meetings. This is his story.[28]

Percy Seibert's Story of Butch Cassidy, the Sundance Kid, and Etta Place in Bolivia

I first went to Bolivia around the turn of the century to serve as the Commissary General of the Bolivian Railroad Commission for the Study of Railroads, and later became an official of the Bolivian Supply Company allied to the Concordia Tin Mines.

The building of the Bolivia Railroad was one of the most difficult engineering tasks in the world; the route had to be hacked out of a jungle, across mountains, descend into deep valleys, and span incredible rivers. The heat and the weather were indescribable: it took men of great physical strength who could endure enormous hardships to build that railroad. Men of many nationalities were drawn to the job and of course no questions were asked. They included not only adventurers but also fugitives from the law of many lands, including the American West. By 1903 there were outlaw bands in the interiors of the South American countries and before long we began to hear of western-style train and bank robberies.

By 1900 to the reading public in the States, Butch Cassidy and his Wild Bunch were as well known as Jesse James. There were always Sunday-supplement stories about them. On the trains "candy butchers" sold paperback books about outlaws along with sandwiches and coffee, and of course the *Police Gazette*, found in any barber shop, was always publishing long articles on outlaws. Most of it was trash but the kind the kids of that time would sneak out in the barn to read.

I was a good shot and a good horseman, in perfect physical condition and eager for adventure, so helping to build a railroad through the most hazardous country in the world appealed to me.

In about 1906 I was given leave to return to the States. After some months I prepared to return to Bolivia. I was in New York waiting for my steamer to sail when I decided to pay Coney Island a visit. I hadn't been out there in years and although it was late fall, the place was still colorful. After a few hours on the beach and walking up and down the boardwalk, I came upon a barker in front of one of those movie houses. They commonly called them "peep shows," trying to get people to come in to see this invention which was the talk of the day.

I bought a ticket and went in. After a while, when there were enough customers, the place darkened, a piano player struck up a chord, and the picture began. It was crude but I found this new medium tremendously exciting. The picture was a western, probably made in Fort Lee, New Jersey, something about the usual good guys and bad guys. I can't remember the actors or much of the story, but I will never forget the title: *Butch Cassidy and the Wild Bunch.*

Some weeks later, it was Christmas week I believe, I arrived in La Paz. As was his custom, Clement Rolla Glass, Superintendent of the Concordia Tin Mines where I was now employed as his assistant, closed down the mine and led all the men—Americans, Welshmen, English remittance men, Spanish, and Indians— down to the square of La Paz. Here everyone toasted each other, calling out Merry Christmas as the bells of Our Lady of Guadalupe pealed out.

Glass and my old friends at the mine gave me a wild welcome and then Clement started making the rounds with me, introducing the new men who had joined the mine since I had been away. I noticed one fellow, in his thirties, blond and stocky, who seemed to edge away every time I approached. This irritated me and finally I pushed my way through the crowd, held out my hand, and said, "I'm Percy Seibert, Mr. Glass's assistant. I don't think we met."

He hesitated a moment, then put out his hand. "I'm Jim Maxwell," he said. "Mr. Glass hired me and my partner," and he pointed to a smaller man, also with blond hair, who was in a crowd but seemed to be watching us intently.

"And what's his name?" I persisted.

"Enrique Brown," he said with a slight smile, then nodded and moved away. Not very sociable, I thought to myself.

The day after Christmas, on the way back to the mine I asked Glass about Maxwell and Brown. He was silent for a moment, then looked around and said he would talk to me later at the mine. That night he carefully closed his office door and sat down facing me across his desk.

"Perce," he said, "what I tell you now must remain confidential."

"Of course," I said, somewhat puzzled.

"About Maxwell and Brown," he continued. "Have you ever heard of Butch Cassidy and the Wild Bunch, you know, that gang of outlaws in the West?"

"Of course," I told him. "In fact, just before I left New York I saw a movie in Coney Island about him."

"Well, Maxwell is Butch Cassidy," he said, "and Brown is Harry Longbaugh, the Sundance Kid."

I **guess** I looked stunned because he packed his pipe, poured us a drink, and then told me the story.

"One day last year Cassidy or Maxwell came to the mine looking for a job. As it happened I did need a stockman, someone who knew mules. When I asked him if he knew mules he just grinned and said he knew mules as well as he knew horses. I told him I wanted somebody to go down to La Paz and buy some stock and drive them back, and offered him a hundred fifty a month and keep. He said that was fine and the next morning I gave him two hundred dollars and three hands and they left for La Paz.

"A week later they were back with a herd of fine mules. I told myself he evidently did know mules. Personally I liked the man. He didn't do much talking, seemed pleasant, and knew his job. We put him up in the bunkhouse across the valley and he seemed to be a natural leader; the other hands and the Indians took to him, and I was thinking of making him a foreman.

"Then Roy Latson appeared. He also had been out buying mules. With him was a stranger who he introduced as Enrique Brown. He was blond, like a Swedish type, with a windburned face and blue eyes. He looked a bit sullen; in fact he didn't even smile when we shook hands. Latson asked if I could use another hand, and when I said I had always room for a good man, he waved to Brown

Percy Seibert in his office on lower Broadway in New York City, March 11, 1961, after one of his many interviews with the author. *The James D. Horan Civil War and Western Americana Collection*

This is the Grand Hotel, where Cassidy and the Sundance Kid stayed when they visited La Paz between bank and mine robberies. *The James D. Horan Civil War and Western Americana Collection*

Clement Rolla Glass at the far right in front of a native hut. *The James D. Horan Civil War and Western Americana Collection*

James Patrick Ahearn, fourth from left, employee of the Concordia Tin Mines, who had a confrontation with the Sundance Kid on the Kid's first night at the Mines. *The James D. Horan Civil War and Western Americana Collection*

Clement Rolla Glass, superintendent of the Concordia Tin Mines, who hired Butch Cassidy and the Sundance Kid. Glass once warned the outlaws at gunpoint never to hold up the mine. *The James D. Horan Civil War and Western Americana Collection*

and so I hired him. Later, when Maxwell and Brown met, I had the strange feeling they knew each other. Brown was bowlegged and had the look of a cowboy. When I saw them handle horses and mules I knew they must have been cowboys somewhere in the States.

"The new mules were put in a corral when Paddy Ahern [a longtime worker at the mine] came in I had him stand night guard. On one of his tours he spotted a

Percy Seibert, an executive of the Concordia Tin Mines, who gave the author the only extant description of the last years of Butch Cassidy and the Sundance Kid in Bolivia. *The James D. Horan Civil War and Western Americana Collection*

figure rolled up in a blanket. He prodded the blanket and suddenly it whipped open and Paddy found himself looking into a six-shooter. As you know, Paddy is one of our best shots and he didn't like the idea of anyone pointing a gun at his stomach.

" 'What are you doing here?' he asked.

" 'I'm Brown, the new hand,' he was told. 'Mr. Glass hired me this afternoon.'

" 'Nobody told me about any new hands,' Paddy told him.

" 'Suppose you go and see Mr. Glass,' Brown said and rolled back in his blanket.

"Paddy was ready to explode when he woke me up but I calmed him and went back with him to formally introduce him to Brown.

"About this time I began to hear about the robberies and people coming into

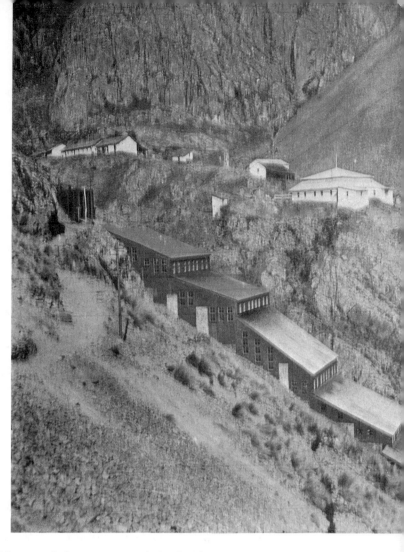

The Concordia Tin Mines, Bolivia, in 1906, when Butch Cassidy and the Sundance Kid worked there. *The James D. Horan Civil War and Western Americana Collection*

the mine had stories of the holdups and descriptions of the holdup men. At the time I didn't know their real identity.

"Suddenly it clicked with me and I knew Maxwell was Butch Cassidy and Brown was the Sundance Kid.

"Of course I had no real evidence and as far as I was concerned they were Maxwell and Brown."

Then Clement told me about the night he was awakened by Pedro, one of our older hands, who liked his "Forty Degree"—a raw grain alcohol, the favorite of the railroad hands, that had the shattering effect of someone hitting you on the head with a sledgehammer.

"I woke up with someone banging on my door," Glass told me. "When I opened it there was Pedro. He was shaking like a leaf. He kept babbling about how he had overheard Maxwell and Brown—Cassidy and the Sundance Kid—planning to rob the mine.

"When I finally calmed the old fellow down I wondered what I should do. If they really planned to rob the mine some of our people could be killed. So I made up my mind and loaded my Winchester, put a box of shells in my pocket, and walked up to the bunkhouse.

"It was dark inside but when I opened the door I could see the men in their bunks in the moonlight. I had only taken a step inside when I heard someone say:

" 'Looking for someone, Mr. Glass?'

"Then a lantern was lighted and Cassidy was holding it up and looking at me. He nodded to the Winchester.

" 'Why the hardware, Mr. Glass?'

" 'Look, I know you're Cassidy and your partner's Harry Longbaugh,' I told them.

"Cassidy just rolled and lit a cigarette and the Sundance Kid raised himself on one elbow and kept staring at me.

" 'You're right, Mr. Glass,' Cassidy said at last. 'I'm Cassidy and Brown is the Sundance Kid.'

" 'I don't care who you are,' I told him, 'but I heard you were planning to rob the mine.'

"Cassidy looked startled. 'Who told you we were going to do this?'

" 'Old Pedro. He said he heard you talking about it in Spanish.'

"Cassidy grinned. 'If we were planning to rob your mine, Mr. Glass, why would we talk in Spanish so the old man could understand? He was sitting right over there when we were talking. We knew he was listening. What we were talking about was the robbery of that train last month.'

" 'You robbed the train last time at Eucalyptus,' I said.

" 'Do you have proof, Mr. Glass?' he said. 'Did you see us do it?' He wasn't excited and spoke very calmly.

" 'I'm not a policeman,' I told them, 'what I'm concerned about is my mine. I'm responsible for the property, the money and the men who work under me.'

" 'There's a lot of men working under you who are not exactly angels,' he reminded me. 'If they were, they wouldn't be here. Hell, without them you couldn't work this place.'

"He stamped out the cigarette. 'Let's leave it like this, Mr. Glass. I'm Maxwell and the Kid is Brown. Don't worry about your mine. The people here are our friends and you've been a good boss. We don't rob people we work for. Is that a deal?'

"I told him that was fine with me and I said good night. When I left I passed the Kid, who was still in his bunk. He was leaning on one elbow but under the blanket I could see the tip of a six-shooter. I'm sure if I had made a wrong move . . .''

Butch and the Kid would disappear periodically. Word eventually would get back to the mine that a bank or a train had been robbed. It was a delicate situation; Cassidy and the Kid were, of course, prime suspects in our minds but we didn't have definite proof. By this time word had gotten out that the two Bandidos Yanqui were working at the Concordia, but the law back in La Paz didn't seem to be very anxious to do anything about them so, as Clement said many times, we were not policemen.

It must be recalled that the Bolivian interior of that time was a rugged country and, as in the American West, the law was usually what hung on a man's hip. Questions were never asked about a man's background and information was never volunteered. The men who came to build the railroad and work the mines were usually there because of the good pay, a love of adventure, to escape the law in their own country, or to leave behind a tragic episode. Some of the stories I knew were almost unbelievably melodramatic.

Somehow Cassidy took to me. Perhaps it was because I knew something of the West and the cattle business—and also I never asked questions. When Mrs. Seibert joined me, Cassidy and the Kid became our regular Sunday dinner guests.

In the white bunkhouse of the Concordia Tin Mines on the far left, Clement Rolla Glass, superintendent of the mines, confronted Cassidy and the Sundance Kid with a rifle and gained their promise never to hold up the mine's payroll. *The James D. Horan Civil War and Western Americana Collection*

Cassidy was quite popular in the countryside, particularly with the Indian children. Whenever he went to La Paz he would always come back with sticks of candy which he gave to the children. I can still see him coming up the trail to our place, followed by a pack of yelling, laughing kids, who called him Don Max.

I also realized that Cassidy was shrewdly making friends with the Indians, who would never betray him . . .

In contrast to Butch, the Sundance Kid was almost taciturn. It was only after they had had many a dinner at our place that the Kid seemed to relax. Both liked Mrs. Seibert and more than once brought her back a piece of Indian jewelry or a trinket from La Paz.

It was always accepted that Cassidy was given the seat at our table that looked over the valley and the trail that led to our house.

I found Butch an amiable man with a fatalistic philosophy: "I know how it's going to end, Perce," he said once. "I guess that's the way it's got to be."

The La Paz Stage. The owner of the line had befriended Cassidy and the Sundance Kid and out of gratitude they never attacked it. *The James D. Horan Civil War and Western Americana Collection*

We talked generally of the West and ranching, and gradually as he came to trust us; he told us about his life as an outlaw—never naming names of men who had ridden with him—and his technique, so to speak.

"I came down to South America with the idea of settling down," he said. "In the States there was nothing but jail, the noose, or being shot by a posse. I thought maybe I could change things but I guess things at this late date can't be changed."

One day when the Kid didn't come along with him for dinner, he told us about Etta Place. Privately he described her to me as "the best housekeeper in South America but she has the heart of a whore."

One day, he said, Etta had severe stomach pains. They got worse and finally the Kid took her to the nearest doctor, who diagnosed her condition as acute appendicitis. He wanted to put her in the local hospital but Etta refused. Frankly, I didn't blame her. Medical conditions were crude and unsanitary, and unless you were treated by Doctor Lovelace and his staff, who were attached to the Railway Commission in the interior, you were at the mercy of a native doctor who did everything from treating mules to pulling teeth.

Etta begged the Kid to take her back to the States; finally Cassidy and the Kid agreed that had to be done. The Sundance Kid and Etta went back to Denver, where Etta entered the hospital. The next day the operation was to be performed. That night the Kid went on a high lonesome and came back to his boardinghouse roaring drunk. He woke up with a terrible hangover and shouted for someone to bring him a cup of coffee. Of course, no one did. Then he grabbed one of his guns, which hung in a holster at the side of the bed, and fired a few rounds into the ceiling.

The Kid had forgotten he wasn't in a cow camp twenty-five years before. Denver was no longer a frontier town. The outraged landlord shouted that he was going to call the police. The Kid suddenly realized he would make a fine catch, so he threw on his clothes and ran out to hire a carriage to take him to the railroad station, where he finally got connections back to New York and a steamer to South America, where he rejoined Cassidy.

When I asked Cassidy if they had ever heard of Etta again he just shook his head.

I was always curious as to their marksmanship. Cassidy never wore a gun, although in that rough country carrying firearms was commonplace. "It makes me feel conspicuous," he told my wife. Once when I asked to see how good a shot he was, both he and the Kid came to dinner this day with their six-shooters: .45 caliber Colts.

"The long barrel can be used as a club," he explained. "If there's a hero among the passengers or train crew, it's better to hit him across the nose. A man automatically raises his hands to protect his face. It doesn't create a fuss and there's no killin'."

Butch's favorite drink was Mount Vernon. This afternoon I had a bottle and after dinner we made quite a dent in that bottle's contents. Clement Glass joined us and we decided to show how good we were with handguns and rifles.

We walked outside, Butch and the Kid each with two beer bottles. They strapped on their six-shooters and when Butch nodded they suddenly threw the bottles high in the air. As they started to curve down, first the Kid's gun leaped into his hand and the bottles vanished into splinters, then Cassidy's followed. They repeated the same trick a few times and never missed.

The gunfire echoed in the valley like a cannonade and brought out Mrs. Seibert.

"My God, boys," she said, "what on earth are you doing?"

Butch apologized. "I'm sorry, ma'am, we were just showing Perce and Mr. Glass a little western shootin'."

They refused to let her go back to the dinner dishes until they repeated the trick for her. For years my wife and I recalled that scene on that afternoon so long ago . . .

Mrs. Stella J. Seibert, who had Butch Cassidy and the Sundance Kid as Sunday dinner guests many times at the Concordia Tin Mines in Bolivia. She is holding her daughter, Jeanne A. Seibert. With them is tiny Juanita Guiba, daughter of Butch Cassidy's washerwoman. Cassidy never failed to bring back a trinket or candy from La Paz for the little girls. *The James D. Horan Civil War and Western Americana Collection*

Glass, who was an excellent rifle shot, then challenged them to a kneel-and-fire target match with Winchesters. Targets were set up and the match began. Glass outshot both Butch and the Kid and I did some fancy shooting myself that day, but no one could match their performance with a handgun.

As time went on, other outlaws came to Bolivia and the Argentine. One of the most notorious was Harry Nation, a former Texas gunfighter and train robber. Using the technique of Butch and the Kid, he and his gang held up the train again at Eucalyptus and escaped with three thousand dollars. This time no one could blame Cassidy and Longbaugh; they were working at Concordia at the time.

Another outlaw-fugitive from the States who I knew personally was Dick Clifford, one of Nation's riders. He was a big, happy-go-lucky man without a care in the world. I would meet him on the trail going to La Paz or at one of the other towns or villages. He never changed; he would have been a perfect character for Mark Twain's *Roughing It.*

One day in 1908 Clifford was staying at the Grand Hotel in La Paz when the police finally caught up with him. Before they reached the hotel an informer tipped him off. Dick had just jumped out of a bathtub and put on his underwear when the police chief—they were always polite—knocked on the door and asked to be let in.

"Just a moment," Clifford replied, then stepped out the window. He slipped on the roof's tile and slid down on his backside. The hotel was adjacent to the gardens of President Guachalla of Bolivia, who was dining with his family at the time.

Suddenly Clifford flew into sight, to land in some bushes. Although the ride down the tiles had removed some of his underwear he rose, bowed, excused himself to the startled President and his family, and walked out of the gardens as calm as if he was dressed in formal attire. Outside in the street he got a carriage or a horse and escaped while the polite police chief and his men waited in the hallway upstairs.

One day at the Concordia, Cassidy and the Kid came in to say good-bye. As Butch explained, "We're pulling out for a while." A week later they were back without any explanation and took up their jobs as though nothing had happened.

I later found out the story from Fred Brown, in charge of the Tirapati Gold Mines in Peru. Butch and the Kid had planned to rob the regular run of the Inca Gold Mine stage, which connected the mine and the Tirapati Railroad Station. The bullion that was to leave was worth a fortune.

Someone tipped off Brown and he sent the stage out with an empty box. The driver quickly obeyed when two masked men stepped out on the trail, ordered, "Throw down the box," and took off.

Fred was an old friend of mine—in fact we had worked together—and Butch jokingly hinted that perhaps I had warned Brown. But he also knew that if I had known of the robbery I would have warned Fred.

It was sort of a game we played; Cassidy and the Kid were confident that while we would never betray them, they also knew they were fair game. If the police or the army came in to take them, we would cooperate with the law; if we heard they planned to rob a bank, train, or store, we would somehow get word to the intended victim.

It was accepted that we were on one side, they were on the other . . .

During one of their long absences from the Concordia, Butch and the Kid split up, possibly because the pressure of the soldiers and police was beginning to mount. One day Butch appeared at the Penny-Duncan Mine at Huanini, 150 miles southeast of La Paz. John Bruce, an old friend of mine who had been in charge of transportation at the mine, told me the story of what happened that day.

"I'm down to my last bolivar," Butch told Bruce. "Do you have a job?"

"I'm sorry," Bruce told him, "we just laid off some help. Try us next month."

"Thanks," Butch said, "maybe I will."

As Cassidy started to turn away, Bruce called after him:

"You look like you can stand a grubstake."

Butch grinned. "Well my *petaca* [carry box] ain't filled with grub."

Bruce gestured to the mine's dining hut. "Go in there and help yourself. If anyone asks any questions tell him I sent you."

Cassidy never forgot Bruce's kindness. A few years after this incident, when he was working for me, he appeared at my place late at night and asked where Clement Glass was—he told me he couldn't find him at his office.

I explained that Glass had an asthmatic condition and at times the high altitude gave him great distress and he had to go back to La Paz for a rest and medication. Butch thanked me and left.

Clement later told me the story:

"I was in bed and there was a knock on the door late at night. When I opened it there was Butch Cassidy. He was unshaven and looked weary. I invited him in for a drink and he told me the reason for his visit. He had been informed by someone in the brush that Harry Nation and his gang were going into the Penny-Duncan Mine to kidnap old Mr. Penny and hold him for ransom. I immediately sent a rider to warn him.

"Later Penny told me that after he received my message he hired a professional gunfighter, one of those western outlaws on the dodge, and they boarded up the offices, stocked up with food and ammunition, and waited for Nation and his gang to appear. But they didn't have to; Butch and the Kid rode into Nation's camp and warned him that if any harm came to anyone at the Penny-Duncan Mine they would kill Nation."

When Butch and the Sundance Kid returned to the Concordia he gave me some business messages from Glass but he never said a word about the Penny-Duncan affair. To get to La Paz he would have had to ride for two days and two nights. The only time he touched on the incident was later that week when I heard that old man Penny was forting up at the mine waiting for some outlaws to raid the place. At the time I hadn't seen Clement Glass and didn't know the story. I was worried enough to talk to Paddy Ahern and some of the other fellows about getting up an armed group and going over and helping Bruce and the old man. But then Butch came to me and said, grinning, "I'll send Pedro over there to tell old man Penny to get rid of that tinhorn he has guarding him. Nothing is going to happen to him. You can take my word for that." He did send Pedro to the Penny-Duncan Mine and when he came back Pedro told me that Penny did dismiss the bodyguard. They never had any trouble after that. Along with the Concordia, the Penny-Duncan Mine did not have to worry about Butch or the Kid lifting its payroll.

Cassidy had a strict sense of frontier-type loyalty, in which a man never violated friendship. With the exception of a few white women like Mrs. Seibert, and some Indian women employed as servants or washerwomen, it was an all-male society in the Bolivian interior. The tightly knit group of Americans working the mines or building the railroad were bound together by the loneliness of that godforsaken place, high up in the mountains where the air was so thin we could use only a special tough breed of mule, and the only other humans were Indians. We had to rely on one another; it didn't make any difference if your neighbor was an outlaw, former western gunfighter, or fugitive from an army stockade in the States. He was all you had to share memories of the States, as a partner in chess, dominoes, or checkers, to share a drink, and to help you celebrate Christmas, New Year's, and July 4th.

An example of Butch's loyalty is what happened one day. Cassidy made a habit of dropping by my office whenever he and the Kid were ready to take off. Sometimes we had a good-bye drink—I guess we both realized we might not see each other again—or perhaps said a few words, then with a final wave they were off. I never asked him where they were going or what they had in mind but this day, on an impulse, I did ask him that.

Butch gave me a long silent stare, then said, "Well, Perce, I don't have to tell you and I don't want you telling anybody particularly, but it's going to be the Eucalyptus Station again."

I was sorry I had asked him. "Butch," I said, "people around here know we're good friends. One of these days there's going to be some talk that maybe I'm connected with the robbery. Anyway, now I'm honor bound to inform the station master. How about forgetting this one?"

He thought for a moment, then said: "Maybe you're right, Perce. I'll call off this one."

Later Nation staged another robbery at the station. Cassidy and I heard the news from one of the men who had come in from La Paz. After he rode off, Cassidy gave me a mock sad look and said:

"Friendship's certainly interfering with my business, Perce!"

As the months and the years drifted by, and the robberies of the trains, stagecoaches, and mine payrolls increased, the army began to take up the hunt for the outlaws. Some were killed, or captured and sentenced to long terms in prison. I began to see less and less of Butch and the Kid; the periods when they were not at the mine grew longer.

I also began to see a change in Cassidy: he looked older and worn; the strain was now showing. The Sundance Kid became more morose, and although we were old friends, he barely said more than the usual amenities. Their welcome was also wearing thin because the army was visiting the mines unexpectedly and hinting to the owners that it might not be wise to hire these train and bank robbers.

Also, their Robin Hood quality had been tarnished when they killed some people—one of them an innocent bank official—during a holdup. Both Clement Glass and I denounced Cassidy for the killings one night when we were sharing a glass, and Cassidy seemed surprised. "He had a gun and was about to use it," he protested. "What could we do?"

I guess this was the usual warped philosophy of the outlaw: no man has a right to protect himself or the property he is responsible for . . .

One winter Cassidy and the Kid selected the Chocaya Tin-Silver Mine for their next holdup. What took place was told to me by Mr. Roberts, general manager of the Compania Aramayo, whose payroll was stolen by Butch Cassidy and the Sundance Kid in what turned out to be their final robbery.

The payroll was for the tin mines of Aploca and was en route to Aploca from Cachisla, where the general offices were located. It was in a *petaca*, or small straw suitcase, tied on the back of a pack mule led by a *mozo*, or native guard, who was

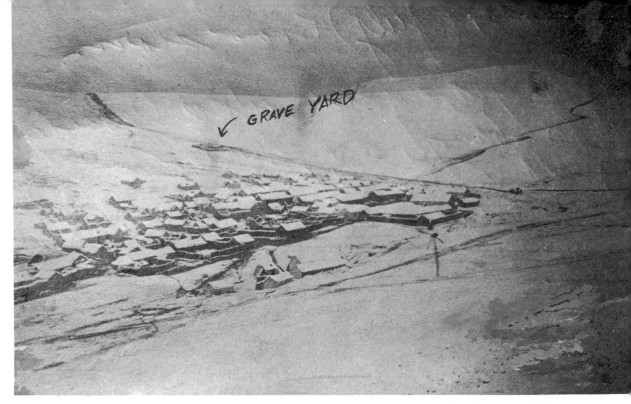

GRAVE YARD

The grim and desolate village of San Vincente, Bolivia, where Butch Cassidy and the Sundance Kid were killed. Victor J. Hampton, who took this photograph, indicated with an arrow where the outlaws are buried in the Indian graveyard. *The James D. Horan Civil War and Western Americana Collection* and *Victor J. Hampton*

This is the corral on the outskirts of San Vincente, Bolivia, where the mining company's mule, stolen by Butch Cassidy and the Sundance Kid, was kept. When the outlaws stopped at the barrio, a native recognized the animal and notified a company of Bolivian cavalrymen. *The James D. Horan Civil War and Western Americana Collection*

riding a large silver-gray mule. As I have pointed out, horses cannot live in this high altitude; a tough breed of mule is used for transportation. On the flank of this particular mule was the mine's brand.

They were heading along the trail when they were held up by Cassidy and the Sundance Kid; Cassidy also took the mozo's silver-gray mule.

The bandits then struck out for San Vincente, which is about thirty-five miles from where the robbery had taken place. This trail leads from Atocha, a small village near the Bolivian-Argentine border.

After he had been robbed, the mozo rode the remaining pack mule to Atocha where he notified the local authorities, who recruited a band of Bolivian soldiers, not more than five, who were camped nearby. At the time the Bolivian soldiers were only peons, pressed into service, many times without shoes or even bullets for their rifles. But these men were armed.

They arrived at San Vincente as dusk was falling. The village was walled, with a corral inside. The mozo and his soldiers entered by the large open wooden gate and the mozo found his mule in the corral.

Cassidy and the Kid were in an adobe hut in the opposite corner of the barrio, cooking over a small beehive baking oven. By the time the soldiers appeared they had lighted a candle.

When the Americans had entered, they had stripped the mules and placed their rifles, ammunition, and saddles against the wall, some distance from the entrance of the hut.

When the mozo found his mule he told the soldiers. One shouted to the outlaws to surrender.

The order was still echoing in the gathering darkness when one of them, believed to have been Cassidy, fired, hitting the soldier in the neck. He clutched his neck, stumbled outside the gate, and died. The others poured out after him and started to fire from the wall.

Shots were exchanged, followed by silence. The mozo and the soldiers patrolled the barrio, occasionally shouting demands to surrender, or firing, but there were no answering shots. Meanwhile a messenger had been sent to Atocha for reinforcements.

When dawn came the soldiers fired a few more rounds at the hut but there was only silence.

Then, about ten o'clock, when no reinforcements had appeared, the soldiers sent in an Indian woman carrying a baby. As the soldiers and the mozo watched, she walked across the open ground and entered the hut. In a few moments she reappeared, crying that the *bandidos Yanqui* were dead. When the soldiers and the mozo entered the hut they found Cassidy lying on the floor and the Kid squatting on his haunches on a wide adobe bench that circled the room. He had been shot through the eyes. Roberts told me that one had been critically wounded making a dash for their rifles and the other had committed suicide.

Roberts came from Atocha with the reinforcements, saw the bodies, and got

This is the walled barrio where Butch Cassidy and the Sundance Kid died after an all-night siege by a detachment of Bolivian cavalry. Victor Hampton, who took this photograph, said that the outlaws had their rifles stacked where the native is sitting at the far right. The two outlaws were cooking over a small beehive-shaped stove in the hut near the door. Their bodies were found inside, resting against the wall to the far right. The Kid had died of his wounds and Cassidy had killed himself during the night. *The James D. Horan Civil War and Western Americana Collection* and *Victor J. Hampton*

the story of what had happened from his mozo and the soldiers. The officer in charge ordered his men to bury the pair in the Indian graveyard not far from the village. This officer took Cassidy's and the Kid's rifles and side arms and a small gold watch which one of them had carried. I met this officer many times on the La Paz stage and he never tired of telling me the story and showing me the small gold watch.[29]

In the early 1950s, Victor J. Hampton, a mining engineer, also contacted me with information enabling me to complete the historical record of how Butch Cassidy and the Sundance Kid died and where they are buried.

This is his story.[30]

The Burial of Butch Cassidy and the Sundance Kid

From 1922 to 1925 I was a mining engineer at the Indian village of San Vincente, Bolivia, where I installed and operated a roasting and leaching plant for treating silver ore from the nearby mine.

The story of Butch Cassidy and the Sundance Kid was well known in that territory but it wasn't only legend; men who had known and worked with Cassidy and who had eyewitness accounts of their death were still around.

One was R. Roberts, general manager of the mine whose payroll was robbed by Cassidy and the Sundance Kid. I met Mr. Roberts in the Hotel Eden, Ouro, and he told me in detail how Butch and the Kid were killed.

After robbing the payroll they followed the trail which leads from Atocha, a small village on the Bolivian-Argentine Railroad, to San Vincente. Roberts said the soldiers arrived as darkness was closing in. The mozo, who had been the payroll's guard, went inside and found the mule. He came out and told the officer in charge of the detachment that the two Americans cooking inside the hut were surely the robbers.

Cassidy and the Kid were in the adobe hut, their rifles outside.

They were using a small beehive-type baking oven and could be seen eating in the glow of a candle. The officer led his men into the gate and shouted an order to surrender. That's when the shooting started. Roberts said they found the pair dead the next morning.

They were buried by the soldiers in the Indian graveyard. I made a trip up there and found the two graves. A German prospector is buried on one side of Cassidy. He was thawing out a package of dynamite on a stove in his house over the hill from San Vincente. As he entered the door the dynamite went off.

A Swede prospector is buried on the side of the Kid. One Sunday as he got off his mule, his gun accidentally fired, killing him. When the Indians found him, the condors had eaten all the flesh from his face and neck.

I went over Cassidy's trail from San Vincente to Atocha. Even in the 1920s it was rough. The silver mines of San Vincente have long been abandoned and the settlement has completely reverted to the Indians.

San Vincente is fifteen thousand feet above sea level in a desolate part of the Bolivian plateau. The wind blows steadily. All in all it is a miserable place to live —and just as miserable to die in . . .

THE OUTLAW
AND THE OIL FIELD

THE LAST CHAPTER OF THE WILD BUNCH ENDED ON A NOTE of incredible irony: an aging outlaw released from prison is hired as a guide for a Yale professor hunting oil fields. After a summer's makeshift course in geology over their campfire, he vanishes into the desert and discovers an oil field. Because of lack of money he is forced to abandon his claim, which is taken over by a syndicate. At the very spot where he predicted oil would be found, a well comes in. The field makes millions but he gets nothing.

The outlaw was Elza Lay and the facts for this remarkable story were given to me twenty-seven years ago by E. P. Maupin, a retired Wyoming banker who was one of Lay's four partners in the oil field.

The story began in 1914 or 1915 when Lay came to Baggs, Wyoming, with his wife, Mary, and their two children to manage his father-in-law's ranch, which ran several hundred head of cattle in the treeless, uninhabited Powder Wash area. Lay had never been interested in ranching, although in between train and bank robberies he, Cassidy, Kid Curry, Jim Lowe, and other Wild Bunch riders always managed to find work as hands on the WS Ranch near Alma, New Mexico.

Captain William French, manager of the ranch, recalled that Lay detested the grinding chores of ranching but liked breaking broncs or caring for the remuda. In his *Reminiscences of a Western Ranchman* French called Lay one

Ellsworth (Elza) Lay, also known as Bill McGinnis, the most interesting member of the Wild Bunch. He could be called the "educated" member of the gang. This photograph was taken when Lay entered the New Mexico prison to serve a life term for the killing of Sheriff Edward Farr following the Folsom, New Mexico, train robbery. *The James D. Horan Civil War and Western Americana Collection*

of the best hands he ever had. Lay left the WS after he told French that he had broken all the broncs on the ranch and was a horseman, not a cowhand. Obviously Lay had other reasons for leaving; a few days later, on July 11, 1899, the Colorado-Southern was held up at Folson, New Mexico. The robbery had been committed by Lay, Kid Curry, and Sam Ketchum. The trio was trapped in a canyon, where Lay was wounded in an exchange in which he killed Sheriff Edward Farr of Huerfano County, Colorado. Kid Curry escaped, but the wounded Lay was captured and sentenced to a life term. This was later reduced to ten years and he was released in January 1910. He married Mary Calvert and then accepted her father's offer to manage his ranch.

In Baggs, Lay, using the name "McGinnis," became friendly with a young bank cashier named E. P. Maupin, who also owned a small garage which repaired farm and ranch machinery and Henry Ford's gas buggies, occasionally seen chugging along the rutted Wyoming roads.

Lay, intellectually curious, forgot the ranch to study the repair manuals and parts of engines in the garage; under Maupin's guidance he was soon able to assist him in repairing auto engines and broken machinery.

Baggs was fifty miles from the Union Pacific and a few times a month "Mac," as Maupin called him, became his volunteer bodyguard when the cashier delivered cash and securities to the railroad. Some Baggs residents who knew Lay's background told young Maupin that he was a fool to risk the bank's money, but as the cashier would later recall:

"I felt that Lay looked upon me as a sincere friend so I often took him along as my bodyguard and he never betrayed my trust in him."

It was about 1916 when oil fever swept across the West. Despite the many exploring parties in the territory, there were only a few developed fields besides the one at Salt Creek and an older field of low-grade oil at Lander. Early that summer Professor Edward Boyle, a noted geologist from Yale University then employed for the summer by Union Pacific to find possible oil sites, called on Maupin at his bank.

"I want to do some investigating of the desert country west of here," he said, "and I need a man who knows the country and can supply horses, a light wagon, and do some cooking. Do you know anyone who can fit that bill?"

"How long will you be out there?" Maupin asked.

"The whole summer and part of the fall," Boyle replied.

Maupin suggested Lay, first telling the geologist his background but pointing out that he not only knew the country from his outlaw days but could get the horses from his father-in-law's ranch.

Boyle was intrigued by Maupin's story and asked to meet Lay. Maupin brought them together; two days later they departed for the desert country.

After two weeks Lay rode into Baggs for supplies and gave Maupin a note from Boyle asking him to order some books on geology which he wanted to give to Lay. As Boyle wrote Maupin, "Mac has become interested in the subject [Geology]."

The next time Lay came to Baggs he told Maupin that Boyle was giving him nightly lectures over their campfire about petroleum geology. By the fall, when Boyle returned to Yale, Lay was knowingly discussing anticlines, domes, synclines, drainage areas, and hydrostatic pressure until Maupin was forced to look through Lay's textbook to find out what he was talking about.

One morning Lay visited Maupin at the bank to say good-bye; he said he was going into the Powder Wash country to prospect for an oil structure. As the weeks passed, the young banker thought many times of the lonely man wandering in that vast and desolate land. Yet he knew that in a way Lay was going home: it was in this forbidden section that Lay, Butch Cassidy, Kid Curry, and all the other riders of the Wild Bunch now part of frontier history had hidden from posses and sheriffs. To Lay, the lonely campfires would be a gathering place for many memories.

One late fall night, just before midnight, there was a knock on Maupin's door. Curious as to who would visit at such a late hour, he opened the door. Lay, his face dark as an Indian's, was grinning out at him from the darkness.

In Maupin's kitchen Lay told him that he had discovered what he called a perfectly closed oil structure in the Vermillion Creek area about seventy miles southeast of Rock Springs and on the Colorado-Wyoming line. He sketched a rough map showing how Vermillion Creek cut a deep canyon which gave an open view of the dips and angles of the structure, which he estimated was about twelve miles long and six miles wide—an estimate that professionals later said was "on the nose."

Lay asked Maupin to become his partner and help finance the costs for establishing a claim under the federal Placer Mining Act.

Maupin told Lay that his job at the bank and his busy garage were taking all his time but agreed to become a partner with W. H. Coates, a retired miner, and Wif Wilson, a rancher who, like Lay, knew the desert country. A few weeks later Lay, Coates, and Wilson gathered supplies and left Baggs.

At the site they began locating oil claims. As each claim was surveyed they drilled a shallow hole, poured in water, and brought up the water—which in every case was discolored by oil. Under the Placer Mining Act this constituted a legal discovery and gave the four partners rights to the land.

As each claim was surveyed and drilled, one of the partners rode back to Baggs with the field data and Maupin filed the claim. Within a month the four had taken over the entire twelve-by-six-mile field. To keep title to the land they spent a yearly average of one hundred dollars drilling holes and building rough roads.

With the titles legally recorded, the four partners—a young banker, a former outlaw, a retired miner, and the rancher—pooled what money they had and hired a prominent geologist. Lay escorted him to the field. After several days they returned, with the geologist reporting that while Lay had found a perfect structure, getting oil out of it would be impossible because oil-producing sands were too deep. Other geologists were hired, but they also reported that there was no oil within drilling range. Then Congress revoked the Placer Mining Act and required that oil leases be obtained from the government.

Three of the partners gave up in disgust: Coates took over a mica mine in New Mexico, Lay became an oil scout for the Ohio Oil Company, and Maupin began to advance in his bank. Only Wilson, the rancher, insisted that they should negotiate the leases; he begged Lay and Maupin to form a new partnership but they refused.

Wilson later obtained new leases on the structure that Lay had discovered and went East, where he convinced a group of businessmen to join him in a wildcat attempt to drill one well regardless of what the geologists had reported.

A drill was set up on the very spot where Lay had predicted to Maupin that oil would be found. The first well came in—not at great depth—with wet gas, indicating that oil was not too far down the structure. Another brought in more and wetter gas.

The field was named Hiawatha. Pipelines were built and gas from the field went to Rock Springs, Green River, Ogden, and Salt Lake City. Oil wells were brought in and the field made millions.

Lay, the former outlaw who had learned oil geology from a Yale professor over a campfire, received nothing.

"I have a wonderful wife and children, a good job, and my health," he told Maupin with a shrug. "Who needs more than that?"

Elza Lay, who had cost Wyoming much and returned it more, died in California in 1937.

NOTES

BOOK ONE: *THE BLOOD BROTHERHOODS*

THE RENOS

1. "Great Train Robberies of the United States," by Charles Francis Bourke, *Railroadmen's Magazine*, vol. I, pp. 13-20, October 10, 1909; "The Great Train Robbery," *Chicago Sunday Tribune*, December 10, 1944, a general account of the robbery used by several contemporary historians, has minor errors, such as "Wheldon" for American Wheeler, etc. See also *The Pinkertons: The Detective Dynasty That Made History* by James D. Horan, New York, 1969, pp. 160-179, hereafter cited as *Pinkertons*; Chicago *Evening Review*, vol. VII, November 1893; *History of Jackson County and Express Robberies* by Henry Beadle, Chicago, 1876; *The Reno Boys of Seymour* (Master's thesis) by Frederick Volland; *John Reno, Life and Career* by himself, hereafter cited as *Reno*.
2. *Pinkertons*, pp. 26-29; 208-237.
3. *Reno*.
4. Reno Extradition, Records of the Department of State, Notes to Great Britain, vol. XIV, National Archives.
5. Records, Department of State, Miscellaneous Letters, September 16, 1868, National Archives.
6. *Chicago Evening Post*, February 2, 1895. See also *New Albany* (Ind.) *Independent Weekly Ledger*, December 19, 1868-January 12, 1869; *Pinkertons* and Volland. The coroner's and doctor's report on the death of John Reno can be found in the *Indianapolis Journal*, December 18, 1868.
7. *Pinkertons*, p. 778.
8. *Reno*.
9. *History of the United States*, Cincinnati, 1882, p. 556.

THE JAMES-YOUNGER GANG

1. Testimony of Charlie Ford, *Kansas City Times*, April 5, 1882, p. 1.

2. *Courier-Journal*, April 9, 1882, quoted in *The Crittenden Memoirs*, Henry Huston Critten-den, comp., New York, 1936, p. 158.

3. *The Confession of Dick Liddil*, included in *The Trial of Frank James for Murder, with Confessions of Dick Liddil and Clarence Hite, and History of the "James Gang,"* Kansas City, Missouri, 1898, p. 294. Hereafter cited as *Liddil*.

4. *Liddil*, p. 41.

5. *Kansas City Star*, October 2, 1927; *Jesse James Was His Name* by William A. Settle, Jr., Columbia, Missouri, p. 159. Hereafter cited as *Settle*.

6. *Memoirs, Reminiscences and Recollections* by John N. Edwards, privately printed, Kansas City, Mo., 1889. See also *The Man Who Made a Folk-God Out of Joe Shelby and Created a Legend for Jesse James* by Ray Lavery, *The Trail Guide*, Kansas City Westerners, vol. VI, no. 4, December 1961.

7. Missouri State Historical Society.

8. "Inside Report of 1866 Holdup," *Liberty Tribune*, February 16, 1939. The original account of the robbery "by former bushwackers" and the murder of young Wymore can be found in the *Liberty Tribune*, February 16, 1866. The bank at the time offered a reward of $2,000 and the paper suggested that the bank robbers and killers be "swung up in the most summary manner . . . desperate cases need desperate remedies. . . ." Prosecutor William Wallace identified the James and Younger gang as the Liberty Bank robbers.

9. Picked up by the *Liberty Tribune*, June 21, 1870, col. 3; Ibid., July 15, 1870, p. 1, col. 4.

10. *Kansas City Times*, October 15, 1872, p. 4, col. 4.

11. Ibid., October 20, 1872, p. 4, col. 3.

12. "HISTORY . . . A Letter from the Notorious Cole Younger," *St. Louis Republican*, November 30, 1874.

13. Summaries of Jesse's letter appeared in the *Jefferson City People's Tribune*, January 7, 1874; *Liberty Tribune*, January 9, 1874, p. 1, col. 5. The Council Bluffs robbery was not the nation's first train stickup—that was "invented" by the Reno gang.

14. *Nashville Banner*, August 4, 1875.

15. *Kansas City Times*, August 12, 1875, p. 1, col. 3.

16. Ibid., August 18, 1876, p. 1, col. 3. In the same column is a letter from Lillie Bremer, who denied statements she had made to the *Times* reporter that Charlie Pitts had told her "he knew more about the train robbers than he could learn from the newspapers." Pitts, one of Jesse's riders, was later killed in the Northfield raid.

17. *The St. Louis Dispatch*, June 9, 1874, p. 1, col. 3.

18. *Kansas City Times*, August 16, 1876, p. 1, col. 3.

19. *St. Louis Republican*, October 22, 1876.

20. "Real Facts About the Northfield, Minnesota Bank Robbery" by Thomas Coleman Younger, a chapter in *Convict Life at the Minnesota State Prison* by W. C. Heilbron, St. Paul, Minnesota, pp. 125-147, 1909.

21. *Robber and Hero* by George Huntington, Northfield, Minnesota, 1895. According to William Wallace, the Jackson County, Missouri, prosecutor, Charlie Pitts's real name was Sam Wells. Wallace claimed to have known the family. Clarence Edward Persons, a friend of Wheeler and his classmate at the University of Michigan Medical School at Ann Arbor, dug up the bodies of Stiles and Miller the night of the raid and sent them in barrels marked "fresh paint" to the school for "dissecting material." Friends of Stiles claimed his body for reburial, but Miller was reduced to a skeleton which hung for over half a century in Wheeler's Grand Forks, North Dakota, office. The late Dr. Hugh McLean, Chief Surgeon, St. Mary Hospital, Hoboken, New Jersey, told me the story. See also "Bankrobbers, Burkers, and Bodysnatchers" by William Holtz, *The Michigan Quarterly Review*, Spring 1967.

22. *Kansas City Times*, quoted in the *Richmond Democrat*, November 20, 1879.

23. *St. Louis Post-Dispatch*, November 3, 1880; *Messages and Proclamations of the Governors of the State of Missouri*, Floyd C. Shoemaker and others, editors, vol. VI, 1922-1961, p. 276.

24. *Liddil*, p. 44.

25. *Sedalia Daily Democrat*, July 19, 22, 29, 31, 1881.

26. *William H. Wallace, Speeches and Writings of William H. Wallace, with Autobiography,* Kansas City, 1914, pp. 274-283.

27. *Kansas City Evening Star*, March 31, 1881.

28. *St. Joseph Western News* (weekly), "JUDGEMENT FOR JESSE," pp. 1 and 2. See also issues of April 14, p. 2, and April 21, 1882, for excellent interviews with the Ford brothers and Jesse's widow. See also Crittenden, pp. 188-190; *St. Louis Republican*, April 4, 1882, p. 2, with six columns on Jesse's killing.

29. George Shepherd interview, *Kansas City Journal*, Tuesday, April 4, 1882.

30. Undated clipping (shortly after the killing of Jesse James) in the James D. Horan Civil War and Western Americana Collection, hereafter cited as JDHC.

31. *Kansas City Journal*, April 4-5, 1882. In a special dispatch from St. Joseph, the *Journal's* correspondent interviewed Captain Harrison Trow, a former guerilla who rode with Jesse during the Civil War, and Mattie Collins, Dick Liddil's common-law wife, who "positively identified" the body as that of Jesse James. Mrs. Liddil denounced Bob Ford as a "cowardly snot" to reporters. Trow tells how he identified Jesse in *A True Story of Chas. W. Quantrell* [sic], Vega, Texas, pp. 263-264.

32. From the newspaper accounts it appears that the Fords never stopped talking. See *Kansas City Journal*, April 4, 5, 6, 1882.

33. Crittenden, pp. 201-206. See also the *Kansas City Journal, St. Louis Globe-Democrat, Kansas City Times*, etc., for the week of the killing. All carried testimony of the inquest.

34. Crittenden, p. 188.

35. *Ralls County Herald*, April 4, 5, 6, 1882.

36. *Kansas City Daily Journal*, April 6, 1882, p. 1, col. 6.

37. *St. Louis Republican*, October 8, 1882. The correspondence between Governor Crittenden and the outlaw was released by the governor's office.

38. Crittenden, pp. 255-272. See also *Sedalia Dispatch*, October 6, 1882; *St. Louis Republican*, October 6, 1882 ("HE CAME IN").

39. Crittenden, pp. 270-271.

40. Ibid.

41. *The Missouri Republican*, October 6, 1882.

42. The Frank James trial testimony, summations by both sides, the judge's charge to the jury, and the final verdict can be found in Liddil. The book was compiled by George Miller, Jr., a cousin of William Wallace, who had use of the prosecutor's papers. The St. Joseph, Kansas City, and St. Louis newspapers covered the trial but the *St. Louis Missouri Republican*, August 21 and September 7, 1883, not only has the complete testimony but appears to be nonpartisan. See also *American State Trials*, vol. XI, pp. 661-852, St. Louis, 1914 and Settle, pp. 129-144; Wallace's reminiscences of the James-Younger gang in JDHC.

43. Liddil, pp. 34-57.

44. *St. Louis Post-Dispatch*, September 5, 6, 7, 1883. The *St. Joseph Gazette*, as a staunch Democratic organ, praised the verdict.

45. Settle, pp. 153, 154; *Sedalia Daily Democrat*, May 14, 1884.

46. *Columbia* (Missouri) *Herald*, September 24, 1897.

47. *Pinkertons*, pp. 480-484.

48. *Phrenological Reports on the Measurement of the Heads of Cole and Jim Younger* by Dr. George Morris, Minnesota State Historical Society.

49. Parole reports submitted by Thomas Coleman Younger: from the warden of the Stillwater State Prison to the author.

50. "James Younger Cannot Marry," *The Inter-Ocean*, March 14, 1902.

51. The *St. Paul Pioneer Press*, "James Younger Commits Suicide," Monday, October 20, 1902; *The Chicago Chronicle*, "Younger A Suicide," October 20, 1902; unnamed clipping, "Ends Life A Suicide," October 20, 1902; *Chicago Herald-Record*, "James Younger Dead," October 20, 1902. Curiously, the *Chronicle* was the only newspaper to identify Younger's sweetheart.

52. *Kansas City Post*, March 24, 1915.

THE DALTONS

1. James Lewis Dalton's application for an Invalid Pension, in the National Archives, describes his background and the movements of the family on the frontier. See also *Daltons Rode* by Emmett Dalton, New York, 1931, pp. 13-18. Hereafter cited as *Daltons*. Cole Younger's comments on his family's relationship to the Daltons, *Kansas City Star*, October 7, 1892. In his autobiography Dalton claimed the Youngers as cousins.

2. *Daltons*, p. 27.

3. *Marshal of the Last Frontier* by Zoe Tilghman, Western Frontiersman Series, III, Glendale, California, 1949, pp. 188-189, 205, 207, 210-211; *The Dalton Gang* by Harold Preece, New York, 1963, pp. 165-171. The files of the *Fort Smith Elevator* during this period contain many stories, some gossip, and rumors about the Daltons. A detailed account of the Red Rock robbery appeared in the *Elevator* on June 10, 1892.

4. *Daltons*, pp. 165-189.

5. *Last Raid of the Daltons, a Reliable Recital of the Battle with the Bandits at Coffeyville, Kansas, October 5, 1892,* by David Stewart Elliott [Editor, *Coffeyville Journal*], Coffeyville, Kansas, 1892. See also the editions of the *Coffeyville Journal* during that period.

The Dalton Brothers and Their Astounding Career of Crime by an Eyewitness, Chicago, 1892, is undoubtedly based on a series of interviews a writer named William Ward had with Marshal Ransom Payne. In his introduction to the 1954 reprint, Burton Roscoe insisted that Payne did not know of the Daltons before the Coffeyville Raid and that all he knew was rumor and gossip. I disagree. A great deal of what Payne told Ward consisted of eyewitness accounts.

Elliott's account of the raid is still the primary source. See also the recollections of Jack Long, an eyewitness to the raid, published in the *Coffeyville Journal*, October 5, 1949.

Other suggested reading: *Frontier Trails* by Frank M. Canton (1930); *Trigger Marshal* by Homer Croy (1952); *Old Waybills* by Alvin F. Harlow (1932); *Hell on the Border* by S. W. Harman (1898); *Oklahombres* by Everitt D. Nix (1929).

BOOK TWO: *THE OUTLAW BANDS*

JOAQUIN MURIETA

1. *San Francisco Alta*, July 27 and August 23, 1853.

2. The letters of Louise Amelia Knapp Smith Clappe, *The Pioneer Magazine* of San Francisco, 1854-1855. A preface to the first letter advised *Pioneer* readers that the letters were "written by a lady who came to California in 1849, to her sister 'in the states' as the land we left behind us, was called at the time. They are penned in that light, graceful, epistolary style, which only a lady can fall into; and as they are a transcript of the impressions which the condition of California affairs, two years ago, made on a cultivated mind, cannot fail to be of general interest."

3. *The Life and Adventures of Joaquin Murieta, the Celebrated California Bandit* by Yellow Bird [John Rollin Ridge], San Francisco, 1854.

4. The serial was published in the *California Police Gazette* in ten issues, from September 3 through November 5. The *Gazette* also put the articles together and published them in book form the same year. Both the *Gazette* series and book are exceedingly rare.

5. Beadle's Murieta books were published from 1875 to 1882. One, *Pacific Pete, the Prince of the Revolver*, by Joseph E. Badger, Jr., was serialized in the *Saturday Journal* in 1875-1876.

6. *Works of Hubert Howe Bancroft—vol. XXXIV: California Pastoral, 1769-1848*, San Francisco, 1888.

The model for the early Murieta paintings and sketches was done by Thomas Armstrong for the *Sacramento Union*, April 22, 1853.

TIBURCIO VASQUEZ

1. The facts on the early life of Vasquez came from the lengthy interview he gave to the editor of the *Los Angeles Herald*, May 16, 1874, after he was captured and lodged in the Los Angeles County jail. Hereafter cited as *Herald*.

2. *Herald.*

3. Vasquez's name appears on the register of San Quentin Penitentiary as "Basquez" (Prisoner Number 1217), and again as "Tebuzzo Baskes."

4. An excellent source material for Morse is the long feature story about him that appeared in the *New York Sun*, Sunday, September 19, 1890, p. 16, written by Charles Howard Shinn. Hereafter cited as *Sun*. Shinn also published a book on Vasquez, Murieta, and other California bandits: *Graphic Description of Pacific Coast Outlaws*, San Francisco, 1887. See also a reprint of this book by Westernlore Press, Los Angeles, 1958, with an introduction on the life of Morse by J. E. Reynolds.

   Shinn—poet, columnist, and early conservationist—organized the California State Horticultural Society in 1879. His most celebrated book, *Mining Camps*, resulted from his studies at Johns Hopkins University.

5. *New York Sun; Bad Company* by Joseph Henry Jackson, New York, 1930 (revised), 1940, pp. 310-312, hereafter cited as Jackson; *Los Angeles Daily Express*, August 27, 1873.

6. Robert Louis Stevenson, then living in Monterey, wrote *The Old Pacific Capital*, in which he offered Vasquez as an example of the clannishness of Monterey's Mexicans.

7. *New York Sun.*

8. In the *Herald* interview, Vasquez described this incident; Jackson, p. 315.

9. *Los Angeles Times*, December 29, 1889; *Los Angeles Star*, May 15, 1874, hereafter cited as *Star; Herald;* Jackson, pp. 315-317.

10. *Star.*

11. Ibid., June 12, 1874.

12. *Herald.*

13. *Star.*

SAM BASS

1. The material for this chapter was supplied by frontier newspapers during the period 1877-1878, and *Authentic History of Sam Bass and his Gang* by Thomas E. Hogg, Denton, Texas, 1878; hereafter cited as Hogg. Hogg's biography of Bass is the most authentic account of the outlaw's life. Judge Hogg not only helped chase Sam, but also obtained a great deal of information on Sam and his riders from the informer Jim Murphy, who arranged for the killing of Sam. During one chase Bass had Hogg in the sight of his six-shooter but didn't pull the trigger. *Sam Bass* by Wayne Gard, Boston, 1936, is still the most reliable modern biography of the outlaw. Judge Hogg had one advantage over Gard: he was there. Hogg's book is extremely rare. In the original, located in the Library of Congress Rare Book Room, pages 7 and 8 are missing, but from all indications this is a printer's error. All of the text is intact.

2. Hogg, p. 14.

3. Ibid., pp. 12-22.

4. Ibid., p. 30.

5. Ibid., pp. 33-38.

6. Ibid., pp. 39-44; Gard, pp. 74-84.

7. *Kansas City Times*, September 28, 1877.

8. Hogg, "Frank Jackson, his Birth, Character, Appearance, etc.," pp. 22-27.

9. Ibid., pp. 50-54.

10. *Galveston News*, February 23, 1878.

11. *Denton (Texas) Monitor*, March 8, 1878; Hogg, pp. 58-61.

12. Hogg, p. 74.

13. Quoted in Hogg, pp. 65-67.

14. Ibid., p. 67.

15. Ibid., pp. 72-73.

16. Ibid., pp. 76-77; Gard, pp. 121-123.

17. Hogg, p. 79.

18. Ibid., pp. 80-81.

19. *Denton (Texas) Monitor*, April 16, 1878.

20. Hogg, p. 90.

21. Ibid., p. 106.
22. *Denton* (Texas) *Monitor*, June 21, 1878.
23. The account of arrangements for his betrayal of Bass and the subsequent gun battle at Round Rock is taken from Jim Murphy's long and detailed statement given to Judge Hogg, which is quoted in chapters 13 and 14, pp. 112-132, of Hogg's book.
24. *Galveston News*, August 2, 1878.
25. Sam's last words, quoted in Hogg, pp. 139-141.
26. Gard, p. 225.

THE JOHNSON COUNTY WAR, THE WILD BUNCH, BUTCH CASSIDY AND THE SUNDANCE KID

1. There are many books on the Johnson County war. For years Asa Mercer's *Banditti of the Plains or the Cattlemen's Invasion of Wyoming in 1892 (Cheyenne, Wyoming 1894)* has been a good secondary source. *Malcolm Campbell, Sheriff* by Robert B. David (Casper, Wyoming, 1932) contains an excellent account of the incident. Maurice Frink's *Cow Country Cavalcade: 80 Years of the Wyoming Stock Growers Association* (Denver, Colorado, 1954) and *The War on Powder River* by Helen Huntington Smith (New York, 1966) also contain accurate accounts.
2. *The Authentic Wild West: The Gunfighters*, by James D. Horan, New York, 1976, pp. 187-220, hereafter cited as *Gunfighters*.
3. In *Butch Cassidy, My Brother* by Mrs. Lula Parker Betenson as told to Dora Flack (Utah, 1975; New York, 1976), Mrs. Betenson insists that her brother was never killed in Bolivia but "returned" to the United States in 1925, driving up to the family homestead in a "shiny new Ford."

In their book, the authors make this shocking error: they charge that in my *Desperate Men* I named Cassidy, the Sundance Kid, and Etta Place as the bandits who held up the train at Parachute, Colorado, in July 1903, after I had them sail from New York City to South America two years earlier.

On pp. 276-277 of my book I recited the story of how Kid Curry, "with a weak facsimile" of the Wild Bunch, held up the train and committed suicide when he was trapped in a canyon by a posse. The chapter ends with the disclosure of how Lowell Spence, the detective, exhumed the body and, after exhaustive legwork, finally identified the corpse as that of Kid Curry.

Nowhere in this chapter do I mention Cassidy, the Sundance Kid, or Etta Place!

In another inaccuracy the authors have "Charley Sirringo [sic]" and "Frank DiMaio [sic]" assigned as a team to go to South America and capture the outlaw trio.

As the only one who interviewed Frank Dimaio, I can assure Mrs. Betenson and her co-author that during his career as a private detective, Dimaio was exclusively assigned to his specialty—large jewel robberies and Mafia murder investigations in New Orleans and the marble fields of Pennsylvania. He was ordered to hunt for Cassidy, the Sundance Kid, and Etta Place only because he was in South America at the time on another assignment. (See Dimaio's statement to me.)

Siringo, the famous "cowboy-detective," chased the Wild Bunch, mostly Kid Curry, and later took part in investigations of frontier strikes. He and Dimaio never worked as a team; as a matter of fact, they never met and Siringo never went to South America. Dimaio did not return to pick up his investigation in the Argentine Republic, nor did the Pinkertons send anyone else down there.

In describing the "return" of her brother, Mrs. Betenson has him modestly telling the family how he gave "a little widow lady" a thousand dollars to pay off her mortgage and then how he later held up the "stuffed shirt" of a landlord who had stopped on the trail to greedily count the "little widow's" money.

Anyone mildly interested in the history of frontier outlawry can point out that this ancient tale has been used ad nauseam in accounts of Jesse James, Sam Bass, Murieta, and every other outlaw from Robin Hood to Dillinger.

Curiously, in their recital of the story told by the daughter of the owner of the hotel in Hanksville, Utah, neither Mrs. Betenson nor her co-author correct the statement "Kid Currie and Harvey Logan were two separate men." Court documents, countless newspaper articles, and the memoirs of reputable frontier lawmen make this statement ludicrous.

In recounting the story of Cassidy's "return," Mrs. Betenson has the prodigal explaining that Percy Seibert, the executive of the Concordia Tin Mines, had identified two bodies as those of Cassidy and the Sundance Kid so that the pair could return to the states and "go straight."

Seibert never identified the bodies of Cassidy and the Kid in the walled barrio of San Vincente; in fact, he never saw the dead men. A few other corrections: Cassidy never "saved" the lives of Seibert and Clement Rolla Glass; and Glass told Seibert that he had warned Cassidy and the Kid at rifle point never to touch the mine's payroll. Seibert told me many times that despite his friendship with them, Cassidy and the Kid knew that he and Glass would be on the side of the law in any confrontation.

In one of our last meetings before he died, I mentioned to Seibert the stories alleging the return of Cassidy and the Sundance Kid. His one comment: "Rubbish!"

Mrs. Betenson, by her own account, was in the cradle when Cassidy, as Robert LeRoy Parker, left home. Compassion prevents me from making any further comment about her book although I am disturbed that in their reviews, historians have overlooked these factual errors, which could have been checked by secondary sources.

4. See Dimaio's statement to me; Cassidy's description of Etta Place was made to Percy Seibert in Bolivia. See Seibert's statement to me.

5. *Desperate Men*, New York, 1962 (revised edition), p. 193, hereafter cited as *Men*; *The Outlaw Trail*, by Charles Kelly, New York, 1938, 1959, p. 3, hereafter cited as Kelly. As recently as the 1960s, Kelly wrote to me, insisting that I was wrong and Cassidy's first name was "George."

6. "End of the Wild Bunch," *San Francisco Bulletin*, August 28, 1904.

7. "Most Desperate Plot Unearthed," *Salt Lake City Herald*, September 9, 1896.

In 1958 Alice Richards McCreery, daughter of the governor and at one time his private secretary, at my request wrote down her recollections of the period:

As to the Cassidy incident. I was my father's secretary during his term. He told me of getting interested in Cassidy because his exploits showed he was an unusual man who could use his energies elsewhere. I am certain of this point. As I remember, the Governor went to Laramie on a tour of inspection and had an interview—at my father's request—with Cassidy. At this time he offered to give him a full pardon if he went straight. As I remember the story, Cassidy promised but didn't keep his promise.

I remember the attempts of the governors of the adjoining states to drive out the outlaws. One time they planned a secret meeting in Salt Lake City where they hoped to lay plans to capture some of them. The reporters got word of the plan—it was too good an item and was spread all over the Salt Lake City paper—so that the plan came to naught. My father, an old reporter himself, never could quite forgive this breach of faith.

8. "Breaking Up the Train Robbers Syndicate," *Denver Republican*, September 20, 1903; Kelly, p. 159; *Men*, pp. 210, 221-228.

9. *Illustrated Police News*, Saturday, July 1, 1899; *Men*, pp. 241-243; Kelly, pp. 239-248.

10. "Louie Logan Killed in Kansas City, Tough Here on Crooks Then," *Kansas City Post*, September 10, 1915; *Men*, pp. 259-262; *Gunfighters*, pp. 202-203.

11. The *New York Sun*, April 25, 1901; *The New York Times*, April 27, 1901; *Men*, pp. 294-295; Kelly, pp. 272-276; "A Big Detective Story of Outlaws," *Cincinnati Enquirer*, September 13, 1909.

12. *Anaconda Standard*, April 30, 1902; *Men*, pp. 272-275.

13. *Men*, pp. 240-241.

14. An original print of the famous photograph bears the name of the photographer: "John Swartz, 705 Main Street, Fort Worth, Texas."

15. Details of the visit of Cassidy, the Sundance Kid, and Etta Place to New York City and of their departure from South America come from my extended interviews with Frank Dimaio, the detective who trailed the outlaw trio in the Argentine Republic. See my Dimaio interview for his first-person story.

16. Dimaio told me that Mrs. Taylor, the woman who ran the boardinghouse, identified individual prints of the Kid and Cassidy taken from the Fort Worth group photograph, and supplied the dates when they had stayed at her place. Detectives trailed the Kid and Etta Place to Dr. Pierce's Medical Institute and then to the *Soldier Prince*, only to discover that they had already sailed. The photographs taken by DeYoung show only Etta and the Kid. Cassidy, who never objected to having his picture taken, had already returned to the West—probably in February, sometime between the picture-taking at DeYoung's studio and the departure of Etta and the Kid for South America.

17. The Sundance Kid and Harvey (Kid Curry) Logan had an affinity for photographers. While they were the most wanted men in the country, the two men, dressed as bankers took time to have their pictures taken with girls from Fanny Porter's Sporting House.

Many readers have written to me about Dr. Pierce's Medical Institute; his quack medicine bottles are now collector's items.

18. "Last of the Train Robbers" by James McParland, the detective, summed up what happened to the members of the Wild Bunch in the *Illustrated Police News*, October 17, 1903; see also the *New York Herald*, "War of Extermination Waged on Cowboy Highwaymen," December 7, 1902, and September 23, 1906.

19. Dimaio.

20. Dimaio said that in his opinion the Kid and perhaps Etta had been under treatment for venereal disease. As he pointed out, "a good number of those fellows were regular customers of frontier whorehouses. Fanny Porter's was one of the well-known places in San Antonio's Hell's Half Acre, but it was still a house of prostitution and like most of those places on the frontier, the girls were likely to be infected."

21. Dimaio.

22. I first met Frank Dimaio in the late 1940s and interviewed him at length in his hotel room in Dover, Delaware, and other places. His memory was extraordinary. Whenever he found anything that had to do with his investigation of Cassidy, the Kid, or Etta Place in South America, he would send it on to me, along with the correct spellings of South American names, towns, or villages from maps he had used.

23. Seibert told me this story but classified it as "only gossip" with no foundation in fact. But he agreed that the good-looking but surly Sundance Kid would have quickly shot the cuckolded husband if he had drawn a knife.

24. "Yankee Desperadoes Hold Up the Argentine Republic," *New York Herald*, September 23, 1906; hereafter cited as *Herald*.

25. *Men*, p. 336. See also footnote on Dr. Lovelace.

26. *Men*, p. 337.

27. Circular No. 4, issued by Pinkerton's National Detective Agency, January 15, 1907.

28. Interviews with the late Percy Seibert at my home and at his office, Chile-American Industries, 120 Broadway, New York City. The articulate Mr. Seibert supplied me with photographs, notes, and newspaper clippings.

29. Undoubtedly the watch Cassidy and the Kid had bought for Etta Place at Tiffany's when they had first arrived in New York City.

30. Interviews and letters from Victor J. Hampton. As recently as 1974, Mr. Hampton wrote to me dismissing the stories of Cassidy's having returned to the United States as myths and legends.

It is not generally known but Richard Perkins, an American outlaw who apparently had taken over after the death of Cassidy and the Sundance Kid, was arrested in Buenos Aires in September 1911 after he had appeared at a hospital seeking medical aid.

William Pinkerton claimed that his agency chased Cassidy, the Sundance Kid, and Etta Place to South America at the request of the State Department. The registers of correspondence of the Department of State (Record Group 59) in the National Archives, which include communications both sent and received between Washington and the U.S. Delegation in Argentina during the period the trio was there, do not contain any reference to Cassidy, Longbaugh, or Etta Place. There is also no mention of their robberies. Records filed at the delegation and consulate in Buenos Aires (Record Group 84) failed to produce any correspondence regarding the outlaws or the Pinkertons.

I believe that the reason the Pinkertons resumed the chase—after they had failed to notify the South Americans in time to catch the trio in Buenos Aires—was simply business. The American Bankers Association, protected by the Pinkertons, authorized the payment of expenses for Dimaio, who did what he could despite the obstacles of difficult weather, incredible distances, a primitive law enforcement, lack of transportation, and an at-times impassable jungle.

It is significant that the agency, after recalling Dimaio, did not send him back; nor did they assign any other operative to South America, although William Pinkerton did correspond with Buenos Aires Police Chief Beasley.

There is no evidence in the State Department Archives to show that it requested the aid of the Pinkertons to hunt down Cassidy, the Sundance Kid, and Etta Place, nor is there any evidence that any South American country complained to the State Department about their robberies.

The four important sources for information concerning the activities and death of Cassidy and the Kid and the return of Etta Place to the United States were Clement Rolla Glass and Percy Seibert, officials of the Concordia Tin Mines in Bolivia; Victor J. Hampton, a mining engineer who installed a roasting and leaching plant at San Vincente, where Cassidy and the Kid were killed; and Frank Dimaio, who trailed the outlaws in South America.

Glass died many years ago, but I individually interviewed Seibert, Dimaio, and Hampton a long time before Hollywood discovered Cassidy and Longbaugh. A number of writers have picked up my material—not with credit, of course. It will be amusing to see how many rewrite the Butch Cassidy-on-a-bicycle story.

During the past few years there have been vigorous claims that Cassidy did not die in Bolivia but returned to the United States. The most steadfast is that he lived and worked in the Northwest as a mechanical engineer, became manager of a company that manufactured office machines, and was a decorator of such talent that he worked on the interior of the state capitol building at St. Paul, Minnesota! The proponents of this extraordinary theory have failed to produce a satisfactory explanation of how a nineteenth-century cowboy with only, at most, an elementary-school education, whose greatest talent was stealing horses and robbing trains, could escape from a savage gunfight in an isolated Bolivian barrio, return to the States, and in his late years—Cassidy was in his thirties when he went to South America—acquire the educational background necessary for work as a mechanical engineer and suddenly bloom into an artist good enough to execute the designs for a state capitol building.

If Cassidy did return to the United States, one wonders why he remained in hiding. Obviously the nineteenth-century bank and train robbery charges would have been dropped—the witnesses were dead and no prosecutor could have or would have cared to put a living legend on trial or into prison. Like Frank James, Cassidy would have become a national tourist attraction.

He was not an introvert. He liked the adventurous role he played and enjoyed his publicity in the frontier newspapers. It was not in his character to skulk about the country like a fugitive from some heinous crime.

It is my belief, based on evidence given to me by Percy Seibert, Frank Dimaio, and Victor Hampton, that Butch Cassidy and the Sundance Kid died in the Bolivian barrio and were buried in the Indian graveyard on the edge of San Vincente.

I consider all stories of his return to be fiction.

BIBLIOGRAPHY

Books

ABBOTT, E. C., and SMITH, HELENE HUNTINGTON. *We Pointed Them North: Recollections of a Cow Puncher.* New York, 1939.

ADAMS, RAMON F. *Six-Guns and Saddle Leather.* Norman, Oklahoma, 1969.

ARNOLD, OREN. *Thunder in the Southwest: Echoes from the Wild Frontier.* Norman, Oklahoma, 1937.

ATHEARN, ROBERT G. *William Tecumseh Sherman and the Settlement of the West.* Norman, Oklahoma, 1956.

BABER, D. F. *The Longest Rope.* Caldwell, Idaho, 1940.

BAKER, PEARL. *The Wild Bunch at Robber's Roost.* Los Angeles, California, 1965.

BARNARD, EVAN G. *A Rider of the Cherokee Strip.* New York, 1936.

BENNETT, ESTELLINE. *Old Deadwood Days.* New York, 1928.

BOTKIN, B. A. (ed.) *A Treasury of Western Folklore.* New York, 1944.

BOURKE, FRANCIS. *Great American Train Robberies.* New York, 1909.

BRADLEY, T. T. *Outlaws of the Border.* Cincinnati, Ohio, 1882.

BRONAUGH, WARREN C. *The Youngers Fight for Freedom.* Columbia, Missouri, 1906.

BROWNLESS, RICHARD S. *Gray Ghosts of the Confederacy: Guerilla Warfare in the West, 1861-1865.* Baton Rouge, Louisiana, 1958.

BUEL, JAMES WILLIAM. *The Border Outlaws.* St. Louis, Missouri, 1882.

———. *The Border Bandits.* Baltimore, n.d.

———. *The James Boys.* Chicago, n.d.

———. *The Younger Brothers.* Baltimore, n.d.

BURCH, JOHN C. *Charles W. Quantrell.* Vega, Texas, 1923.

BURT, MAXWELL STRUTHERS. *Powder River: Let 'er Buck.* New York, Toronto, 1928.

CAMPBELL, MALCOLM. *Malcolm Campbell: Sheriff.* Casper, Wyoming, 1932.

CANTON, FRANK M. *Frontier Trails.* New York, 1930.

COLLIDGE, DANE. *Fighting Men of the West.* New York, 1932.

CONNELLEY, WILLIAM ELSEY. *Quantrill and the Border Wars.* Cedar Rapids, Iowa, 1909.

CRITTENDEN, HENRY HUSTON (comp.). *The Crittenden Memoirs.* New York, 1936.

CROY, HOMER. *Jesse James Was My Neighbor.* New York, 1949.

———. *He Hanged Them High.* New York, 1962.

CUMMINS, JIM. *Jim Cummins' Book.* Denver, 1903.

CUNNINGHAM, EUGENE. *Triggernometry.* New York, 1934.

DACUS, JOSEPH A. *Illustrated Lives and Adventures of Frank and Jesse James and the Younger Brothers: The Noted Western Outlaws.* St. Louis, Missouri, 1882.

DALE, EDWARD EVERITT. *Cow Country.* Norman, Oklahoma, 1942.

DALTON, EMMETT (with Jack Jungmeyer). *Last of the Daltons.* New York, 1931.

———. *When the Daltons Rode.* New York, 1931.

The Dalton Brothers and Their Astounding Career of Crime, By an Eyewitness. Chicago, 1892.

DRAGO, HARRY SINCLAIR. *Outlaws on Horseback.* New York, 1964.

DUFFUS, R. F. *The Santa Fe Trail.* New York, 1930.

EDWARDS, J. B. *Early Days in Abilene.* Abilene, Kansas, 1940.

EDWARDS, JENNIE (comp.) *John N. Edwards, Biography, Memoirs, Reminiscences and Recollections.* Kansas City, Missouri, 1889.

EDWARDS, JOHN NEWMAN. *Noted Guerillas, or the Warfare of the Border.* St. Louis, 1877.

———. *Shelby and His Men.* Cincinnati, Ohio, 1867.

———. *Shelby's Expedition to Mexico.* Kansas City, 1872.

Federal Writers' Project. *Missouri: A Guide to the "Show Me" State.* New York, 1941.

FRENCH, WILLIAM JOHN. *Some Recollections of a Western Ranchman. New Mexico, 1883-1889.* New York, 1928.

GANZHORN, JACK. *I've Killed Men.* New York, 1959.

GARD, WAYNE. *Frontier Justice.* Norman, Oklahoma, 1949.

———. *The Chisholm Trail.* New York, 1959.

———. *Sam Bass.* Boston and New York, 1936.

GARDNER, RAYMOND HATFIELD with MONROE, H. H. *The Old Wild West.* San Antonio, 1944.

GILLETT, JAMES B. *Six Years with the Texas Rangers.* New Haven, 1925.

GINTY, ELIZABETH B. *Missouri Legend.* New York, 1938.

GLASSCOCK, CARL BURGESS. *Bandits and the Southern Pacific.* New York, 1929.

"Goodbye, Jesse!" Facsimile of the Kansas City Journal. *Announcing the Death of Jesse James,* With an Introduction by Martin E. Ismert. Kansas City, Missouri, 1959.

Good Bye, Jesse James. Six of the Best News Stories from the Kansas City Journal of 1882 on the Career and Death of Jesse James. Liberty, Missouri, 1967.

GOODMAN, SGT. THOMAS M. *A Thrilling Record.* Des Moines, Iowa, 1868.

HALEY, J. EVETTS. *Charlie Goodnight: Cowman and Plainsman.* Norman, Oklahoma, 1949.

———. *Jeff Milton: Good Man with a Gun.* Norman, Oklahoma, 1948.

HARLOW, ALVIN. *Old Way Bills.* New York, 1934.

HEILBRON, W. C. *Convict Life at the Minnesota State Prison.* St. Paul, 1909.

HENDRICKS, GEORGE D. *The Bad Men of the West.* San Antonio, 1950.

History of Clay and Platte Counties, Missouri. St. Louis, 1885.

History of Daviess County, Missouri, The. Kansas City, Missouri, 1882.

HOGG, THOMAS E. *Authentic History of Sam Bass and His Gang.* Denton, Texas, 1878.

HOOLE, W. STANLEY. *The James Boys Rode South.* Tuscaloosa, Alabama, 1955.

HORAN, JAMES D. *Desperate Men.* New York, 1949 (revised), 1961, 1974.

———. *Desperate Women.* New York, 1952 (revised), 1971.

———. *The Great American West.* New York, 1959 (revised), 1962.

———. *The Pictorial History of the Wild West* (with Paul Sann). New York, 1956.

———. *The Wild Bunch.* New York, 1958, 1970.

————. *The Authentic History of the Wild West: The Gunfighters.* New York, 1976.

HOUGH, EMERSON. *The Story of the Outlaw.* New York, 1907.

HUNGERFORD, EDWARD. *Wells Fargo: Advancing the American Frontier.* New York, 1949.

JACKSON, JOSEPH HENRY. *Bad Company.* New York, 1939.

————. *Tintypes in Gold.* New York, 1939.

JAMES, MARQUIS. *They Had Their Hour.* Indianapolis, 1934.

JENNEWEIN, LEONARD J. *Black Hills Book Trails.* Mitchell, South Dakota, 1962.

KELLY, CHARLES. *The Outlaw Trail.* New York, Salt Lake City, 1939, New York, 1959.

LEFORS, JOSEPH. *Wyoming Peace Officer.* Laramie, Wyoming, 1953.

LOVE, ROBERTUS. *The Rise and Fall of Jesse James.* New York, 1926.

McCOY, JOSEPH. *Historic Sketches of the Cattle Trade of the West and Southwest.* Kansas City, Missouri, 1874.

McNEAL, THOMAS ALLEN. *When Kansas Was Young.* New York, 1922.

McNEIL, CORA. *Mizzoura.* Minneapolis, 1898.

McREYNOLDS, ROBERT. *Thirty Years on the Frontier.* Colorado Springs, 1906.

MERCER, A. S. *Banditti of the Plains.* Cheyenne, Wyoming, 1894.

MILLER, GEORGE, JR. *Missouri's Memorable Decade.* Columbia, Missouri, 1898.

MILLER, GEORGE, JR. (ed. and comp.). *The Trial of Frank James For Murder.* Columbia, Missouri, 1898.

MOKLER, JAMES ALFRED. *History of Natrona County, Wyoming, 1882-1922.* Chicago, 1923.

MONAGHAN, JAY. *Civil War on the Western Border (1854-1865).* Boston, 1955.

————. *Last of the Bad Men.* Indianapolis, 1946.

O'FLAHERTY, DANIEL. *General Jo Shelby.* Chapel Hill, North Carolina, 1954.

O'NEIL, JAMES B. *They Die But Once.* New York, 1936.

PANNELL, WALTER. *Civil War On The Range.* Los Angeles, 1943.

RAINE, WILLIAM MacLEOD. *.45 Caliber Law, The Way of Life on the Frontier.* Evanston, Illinois, 1941.

————. *Guns of the Frontier.* Boston, 1940.

————. and BARNES, WILL C. *Cattle.* New York, 1930.

————. *Famous Sheriffs and Western Outlaws.* New York, 1939.

RASCOE, BURTON. *Belle Starr.* New York, 1941.

RAYMOND, DORA NEILL. *Captain Lee Hall of Texas.* Norman, Oklahoma, 1940.

RIDGE, JOHN ROLLIN (Yellow Bird). *The Life and Adventures of Joaquin Murieta.* San Francisco, 1854.

RIDINGS, SAM P. *The Chisholm Trail.* Guthrie, Oklahoma, 1936.

RIPLEY, THOMAS. *They Died With Their Boots On.* New York, 1936.

SABIN, EDWARD L. *Wild Men of the West.* New York, 1929.

SANDOZ, MARI. *The Buffalo Hunters.* New York, 1954.

SETTLE, WILLIAM A., JR. *Jesse James Was His Name.* Columbia, Missouri, 1966.

SHIRLEY, GLENN. *Toughest of Them All.* Albuquerque, 1953.

SIRINGO, CHARLES. *A Cowboy Detective.* Chicago, 1912.

SMALL, KATHLEEN EDWARDS and SMITH, J. LARRY. *Tulare County, California* (2 vols.). Chicago, 1922.

TRENHOLM, VIRGINIA COLE. *Footprints on the Frontier.* Douglas, Wyoming, 1945.

TRIPLETT, FRANK. *The Life, Times and Treacherous Death of Jesse James.* St. Louis, 1882.

TRUMAN, BENJAMIN CUMMINGS. *Life, Adventures and Capture of Tiburcio Vasquez, The Great California Bandit and Murderer.* Los Angeles, 1874.

VESTAL, STANLEY (pseud. of Walter S. Campbell). *The Missouri.* New York, 1945.

————. *Queen of the Cowtowns: Dodge City, 1872-1880.* New York, 1952.

VOLLAND, ROBERT FREDERICK. *The Reno Gang of Seymour.* N.p., 1948.

WALLACE, WILLIAM H. *Speeches and Writings of William H. Wallace with Autobiography.* Kansas City, Missouri, 1914.

————. *Closing Speech for the State Made by William H. Wallace, Prosecuting Attorney of Jackson County, Missouri, in the Trial of Frank James for Murder. Held in Gallatin, Daviess Co., Mo., in August and September, 1884.* Kansas City, Missouri, 1884.

————. *Speeches of William H. Wallace, Democratic Nominee for Congress, Fifth Congressional District of Missouri.* Kansas City, n.d.

WARDEN, ERNEST A. *Thrilling Tales of Kansas.* Wichita, Kansas, 1932, revised edition, 1938.

WARNER, MATT, AS TOLD TO MURRAY E. KING. *The Last of the Bandit Riders.* Caldwell, Idaho, 1940.

WEBB, WALTER PRESCOTT. *The Texas Rangers: A Century of Frontier Defense.* Boston, 1935.

WELLMAN, PAUL L. *Dynasty of Outlaws.* New York, 1961.

————. *The Trampling Herd.* New York, 1939.

WILSON, ISAAC A. *Four Years in a Home-Made Hell.* Siloam Springs, Arkansas, 1894.

WILSON, NEILL COMPTON and TAYLOR, FRANK J. *Southern Pacific: The Roaring Story of a Fighting Railroad.* New York, 1952.

WOOD, M. W. (ed.) *History of Alameda County, California.* Oakland, California, 1883.

WOOLDRIDGE, MAJOR J. W. *History of Sacramento Valley California.* Chicago, 1931.

WRIGHT, AGNES SPRING. *70 Years in the Cow Country.* Laramie, Wyoming, 1942.

WRIGHT, ROBERT M. *Dodge City: The Cowboy Capitol.* Wichita, Kansas, 1913.

YOUNGER, COLE. *The Story of Cole Younger By Himself.* Chicago, 1903.

ZINK, WILBUR A. *The Roscoe Gun Battle: The Younger Brothers Vs. Pinkerton Detectives.* Appleton City, Missouri, 1967.

PERIODICALS

"Adventures of Joaquin Murieta," *California Police Gazette*, September-November 1855.

ANON. "The James Boys: Jesse and Frank." *Scholastic Magazine*, January 21, 1939.

BADGER, JOSEPH E. "Pacific Pete: The Prince of the Revolver." *Saturday Journal*, 1875-1876.

BROCK, ELMER J. "The Johnson County War and the Murder of George Wellman." *The Denver Westerners Brand Book*, March 1953.

CHAPMAN, ARTHUR. "Getting the Drop and Living." *New York Herald Tribune Magazine*, January 3, 1932.

CROY, HOMER. "Did Jesse James and Billy The Kid Meet?" *The New York Westerners Brand Book*, Spring 1954.

CURRIE, BARTON W. "American Bandits: Lone or Otherwise." *Harper's Weekly*, September 12, 1909.

CUSHMAN, GEORGE L. "Abilene, First of the Kansas Cowtowns." *Kansas State Historical Society Quarterly*, vol. LX, no. 3, August 1940.

DICK, EVERETT. "The Long Drive: The Origin of the Cow Country." *Collections of the Kansas State Historical Society*, 1926-1928, vol. XVII.

HEGERSON, LILLIAN. "History of St. Luke's Episcopal Church of Buffalo, Wyoming." Buffalo, n.d.

HENSHALL, JOHN A. "Tales of the Early California Bandits." *Overland Weekly*, second series, vol. LIII, 1909.

HOLBROOK, STEWART H. "The Bank the James Boys Didn't Rob." *American Mercury*, 1948.

HOLLANDS, JAMES WINFRED HUNT. "Buffalo Days." *The Magazine of the South*, March 1933.

HOLTZ, WILLIAM. "Bankrobbers, Burkers and Bodysnatchers: Jesse James and the Medical School." *Michigan Quarterly Review*, Spring 1967.

HORAN, JAMES D. "Robin Hood in South America: The Last Years of Butch Cassidy." *The New York Westerners Brand Book*, Spring 1954.

————. "Butch Cassidy: Robin Hood of the Pampas." Privately printed, 1954.

JONES, C. A. "The Good Bad Men." *Atlantic Monthly*, July 1934.

JORDAN, PHILIP A. "The Adair Train Robbery." *The Palimpsest*, vol. XVII, February 1936, Iowa City, Iowa.

KILPATRICK, ARTHUR ROY. "Missouri in the Early Days of the War." *Missouri Historical Review*, 1961.

LARSON, E. DIXON. "The Heritage of the American Western Holster." *American Rifleman*, April 1976.

LAVERY, RAY. "The Man Who Made a Folk-God Out of Jo Shelby and Created a Legend for Jesse James." *The Trail Guide*, December 1961.

LORD, JOHN. "Picturesque Road Agents of the Early Days." *Overland Monthly*, second series, vol. LXX, November 1917.

McPARLAND, JAMES. "Last of the Train Robbers." *Illustrated Police News*, October 17, 1903.

MICHELSON, CHARLES. "Stage Coach Robbers of the West." *Munsey's Magazine*, vol. XXV, July 1901.

NOLAN, WARREN, and WHITE, OWEN P. "The Bad Man from Missouri." *Colliers*, January 14, 1928.

RASCH, PHILIP, JR. "Did Jesse James and Billy The Kid Meet?" *The New York Westerners Brand Book*, 1954.

———. "Jesse James in New Mexico Folklore." *The New York Westerners Brand Book*, 1957.

RYDER, DAVID WARREN. "Stage Coach Days." *Sunset*, vol. LIX, September 1927, San Francisco.

SETTLE, WILLIAM A., JR. "The James Boys and Missouri Politics." *Missouri Historical Review*, vol. XXXVI, July 1942.

SHINN, CHARLES HOWARD. "Pacific Outlaws." *New York Sun*, September 19, 1890.

"Twenty Years of the English West." *The English Westerners Tally Sheet*, London, April 1974.

WALRATH, ELLEN F. "Stagecoach Holdups in the San Luis Valley." *The Colorado Magazine*, vol. XIV, January 1937, Denver.

WEAVER, BARRY ROLAND. "Jesse James in Arkansas: The War Years." *Arkansas History Quarterly*, vol. XXIII, no. 4, Winter 1964.

Westerners Brand Book: Chicago Posse, 1945-1946; 1951-1952. Contains articles on the Jameses-Youngers and the Johnson County War.

———: *Denver Posse*, edited by Harold H. Dunham. Denver, 1950, 1951. Contains an article on Cattle Kate and Jim Averill.

MANUSCRIPTS, MEMOIRS, JOURNALS, LETTERS, TAPE RECORDINGS AND OFFICIAL DOCUMENTS

Adams Express Company. Receipts, Letters. The James D. Horan Civil War and Western Americana Collection.

BLIGH, D. G. "A Biography of Yankee Bligh: The Famous Detective." The James D. Horan Civil War and Western Americana Collection.

CRITTENDEN, GOVERNOR THOMAS THEODORE. Messages and Proclamations on Outlawry in Missouri and the Breakup of the James-Younger Gang, 1883. *Messages and Proclamations of the Governors of the State of Missouri*, vol. VI, pp. 303-308; The State Historical Society of Missouri.

DACUS, JOSEPH A. Material in connection with the selling of his *Illustrated Lives and Adventures of Frank and Jesse James and the Younger Brothers, the Noted American Outlaws*. St. Louis, Missouri, 1882. The James D. Horan Civil War and Western Americana Collection.

DALTON, ADELINE LEE. Widow's Application for Pension of a Survivor of the Mexican War. National Archives.

DALTON, LEWIS. Declaration for Pension of a Mexican War Survivor. National Archives.

DIMAIO, FRANK. Recollections of Trailing Butch Cassidy, The Sundance Kid and Etta Place in South America, New York City and New York State. The James D. Horan Civil War and Western Americana Collection.

GILLIES, R. MORONI. Memories and Family Background of my cousin, Robert LeRoy Parker (Butch Cassidy). The James D. Horan Civil War and Western Americana Collection.

HAMPTON, VICTOR. The Death of Butch Cassidy and the Sundance Kid in San Vincente, Bolivia, and Their Burial in the Indian graveyard, with a Sketch and Photographs of the Barrio. The James D. Horan Civil War and Western Americana Collection.

HARRISON, PRESIDENT BENJAMIN. Letter to the War Department, April 12, 1892, Ordering the Protecting of the State of Wyoming from "Domestic Violence" During the Johnson County War (copy). The James D. Horan Civil War and Western Americana Collection.

HICKS, SAM. Reminiscences of Butch Cassidy, Elza Lay, Harvey Logan, and Bob Meeks. James D. Horan Civil War and Western Americana Collection.

"Jesse James A Suicide." Typescript and Original Copy of the *Kansas City Journal*, Saturday, May 6, 1882, p. 2, col. 4. The James D. Horan Civil War and Western Americana Collection.

HOLMES, H. A. Reminiscences of the Kilpatricks of Sheffield, Texas.

Indian-Pioneer History, Oklahoma Historical Society Interviews: Will R. Robinson on Cole Younger; Travis Carrol Ely on Belle Starr and Cole Younger; Richard Young Audd on Belle Starr as a musician; W. L. Marks, Judge Parker's Deputy U.S. Marshal, on how he arrested Belle Starr.

LAUZER, DR. E. S. Memories of Butch Cassidy and the Wild Bunch. From his grandson, Tom Kitchen and Mrs. Otto H. Bloom, County Clerk, Sublette County, Wyoming. The James D. Horan Civil War and Western Americana Collection.

MAUPIN, E. P. Memories of Elza Lay (William McGinnis) and How He Discovered the Hiawatha Oil Field. The James D. Horan Civil War and Western Americana Collection.

McCLURG, GOVERNOR JOSEPH W. Telegram to the Sheriff of Jackson County, December 24, 1869. Western Historical Manuscript Collection, State Historical Society Manuscripts, University of Missouri Library, Columbia, Missouri.

McCREERY, MRS. ALICE RICHARDS. Reminiscences of My Father, Governor W. A. Richards of Wyoming and His Offer to Butch Cassidy. The James D. Horan Civil War and Western Americana Collection.

MORRIS, GEORGE, Professor. Phrenological Analysis of Cole Younger, May 6, 1890. Phrenological Society Papers, Minnesota Historical Society.

MOYLE, S. Reminiscences of Professor Boyle. The James D. Horan Civil War and Western Americana Collection.

NIND, J. NEWTON. An Account of the Hunt for Jesse and Frank James and the Youngers Following the Northfield Raid by a Newspaperman Who Was a Member of the Posse. June 30, 1905. The James D. Horan Civil War and Western Americana Collection.

Outlaw Articles in Daily and Weekly Newspapers, 1868-1909. The James D. Horan Civil War and Western Americana Collection.

PUNTENEY, WALTER. Memories of Walter Punteney and His Last Will and Testament. From Mrs. Otto H. Bloom, County Clerk, Sublette County, Wyoming. The James D. Horan Civil War and Western Americana Collection.

———. Letters to the Author. The James D. Horan Civil War and Western Americana Collection.

RAWLINSON, J. L. Reminiscences of Butch Cassidy in Bolivia, the Robbery of the Eucalyptus, Bolivia, train and the Bolivian Army vs. Cassidy and the Sundance Kid. James D. Horan Civil War and Western Americana Collection.

The Reno Family and the Seymour Tragedy: The Only True History of the Affair. N.d., n.a.p. The Indiana State Library.

SEIBERT, PERCY A. Memories of Butch Cassidy, The Sundance Kid and Etta Place in Bolivia. The James D. Horan Civil War and Western Americana Collection.

SIRINGO, CHARLES. Letters on Outlaws and Gunfighters. The James D. Horan Civil War and Western Americana Collection.

STARR, BELLE. The Death and Burial of Belle Starr, February, 1889. Typescript. The James D. Horan Civil War and Western Americana Collection.

STEVENS, WALTER B. Telegram from John Newman Edwards. Western Historical Manuscript Collection, State Historical Society Manuscripts, University of Missouri, Columbia, Missouri.

TILGHMAN, ZOE. Letters and Interviews on the Life of Her Husband, William Tilghman. The James D. Horan Civil War and Western Americana Collection.

VASQUEZ, TIBURCIO. An autobiography, May 1874. The James D. Horan Civil War and Western Americana Collection.

WALLACE, WILLIAM H. "He was Not With Frank James." 1901. The James D. Horan Civil War and Western Americana Collection.

WOODSON, GOVERNOR SILAS. Papers State Historical Society of Missouri, Columbia, Missouri.

YOUNGER, COLE. Monthly reports to Henry Wolfer, Warden of the Minnesota State Prison, Stillwater. From the Archives of the Office of the Warden.